Java™ Data Objects

tape

Related titles from O'Reilly

Ant: The Definitive Guide

Building Java™ Enterprise Applications

Database Programming with JDBC and Java™

Developing JavaBeans™

Enterprise JavaBeans™

J2ME in a Nutshell

Java™ 2D Graphics

Java™ and SOAP

Java™ & XML

Java™ and XML Data Binding

Java™ and XSLT

Java™ Cookbook

Java™ Cryptography

Java™ Data Objects

Java™ Distributed Computing

Java™ Enterprise in a Nutshell

Java™ Examples in a Nutshell

Java™ Foundation Classes in a Nutshell

Java™ I/O

Java™ in a Nutshell

Java™ Internationalization

Java™ Message Service

Java™ Network Programming

Java™ NIO

Java™ Performance Tuning

Java™ Programming with Oracle SQLJ

Java™ Security

JavaServer™ Pages

Java™ Servlet Programming

Java™ Swing

Java™ Threads

Java™ Web Services

JXTA in a Nutshell

Learning Java™

Mac OS X for Java™ Geeks

NetBeans: The Definitive Guide

Programming Jakarta Struts

Java™ Data Objects

David Jordan and Craig Russell

O'REILLY®

Beijing · Cambridge · Farnham · Köln · Paris · Sebastopol · Taipei · Tokyo

Java™ Data Objects
by David Jordan and Craig Russell

Published by O'Reilly & Associates, Inc., 1005 Gravenstein Highway North, Sebastopol, CA 95472.

O'Reilly & Associates books may be purchased for educational, business, or sales promotional use. Online editions are also available for most titles (*safari.oreilly.com*). For more information, contact our corporate/institutional sales department: (800) 998-9938 or *corporate@oreilly.com*.

Editor:	Mike Loukides
Production Editor:	Brian Sawyer
Cover Designer:	Hanna Dyer
Interior Designer:	David Futato

Printing History:

April 2003:	First Edition.

ISBN: 0-596-00276-9
[M]   [7/03]

To my wife Tina,
whose emotional and financial support
made this book possible;
and to Jennifer and Jeremy, who now think that
their daddy has become addicted to his computer.

—David Jordan

To Kathy, Chris, Ali, and Juliana.

—Craig Russell

Table of Contents

Foreword .... **xv**

Preface .... **xvii**

1. An Initial Tour **1**

Defining a Persistent Object Model   2

   The Classes to Persist   3

   Declaring Classes to Be Persistent   7

Project Build Environment   8

   Jars Needed to Use the JDO Reference Implementation 9

   Project Directory Structure   10

   Enhancing Classes for Persistence   10

Establish a Datastore Connection and Transaction   11

   Acquiring a PersistenceManager   11

   Creating a FOStore Datastore   12

Operations on Instances   14

   Making Instances Persistent   15

   Accessing Instances   18

   Modifying an Instance   22

   Deleting Instances   26

Summary   27

2. An Overview of JDO Interfaces **28**

The javax.jdo Package   28

   JDO Exception Classes   31

The javax.jdo.spi Package   34

Optional Features   35

    Identity Options   36

    Optional Collections   36

    Transaction-Related Optional Features   37

3. JDO Architectures **38**

Architecture Within Application JVM   40

    Single PersistenceManager   40

    Multiple PersistenceManagers Accessing the Same Datastore   41

    Multiple PersistenceManagers Accessing Different Datastores   43

    Shared Implementation Cache   44

Datastore Access   46

    Direct Access of Filesystem or Local Datastore   46

    Remote Access of a JDO Server   46

    Remote Access of a SQL Datastore   46

System Architectures with a JDO Application   48

    JDO Rich Client with Local Datastore   48

    JDO Applications in a Web Server   48

    JDO Applications as Web Services   48

    Rich Client Connecting to Application Server with EJB Components   49

    Web Server with EJB Server   50

    EJB Session Beans Using Session Bean Façades   50

    JDO Providing Container-Managed Persistence   51

4. Defining Persistent Classes **52**

Kinds of Classes and Instances   52

    Kinds of Classes   53

    Kinds of Instances   53

Java Classes and Metadata   54

    JDO Metadata   55

    Inheritance   58

    The Media Mania Object Model   60

Fields   63

    Supported Types   64

    Persistence of Fields   66

    Complete Metadata for the Media Mania Model   68

5. Datastore Mappings **70**

Mapping Approaches   71

Relational Modeling Constructs   72

    SQL 99   73

Modeling Constructs in Java and Relational Models   74

Mapping Classes to Tables   75

Mapping a Single-Valued Field to a Column   76

    Name-Mapping   76

    Type-Mapping   77

    Indexes   78

Identity   78

Inheritance   80

References   82

Collections and Relationships   83

    Using a Foreign Key   83

    Using a Join Table   89

    One-to-One Relationships   90

    Representing Lists and Maps   92

6. Class Enhancement **94**

Enhancement Approaches   95

    Reference Enhancer   96

    Vendor-Specific Enhancement   96

Binary Compatibility   97

Enhancement Effects on Your Code   98

Changes Made by the Enhancer   98

    Metadata   99

    Instance-Level Data   100

    Field Mediation   101

7. Establishing a JDO Runtime Environment **104**

Configuring a PersistenceManagerFactory   105

    Connection Properties   108

    Optional Feature Properties   110

    Flags   111

    Flags Settings in Multiple Interfaces   111

    Determining the Optional Features and Default Flag Settings   112

Vendor-Specific Properties 115
Nonconfigurable Properties 115
Acquiring a PersistenceManager 115
User Object 116
Closing a PersistenceManager 116
Closing a PersistenceManagerFactory 117
Transactions 117
Properties of Transactions 118
Transactions and Locking in the Datastore 118
Types of Transactions in JDO 121
Acquiring a Transaction 121
Setting the Transaction Type 122
Transaction Demarcation 122
Restoring Values on Rollback 125
Determining Whether a Transaction Is Active 126
Multiple PersistenceManagers 126
Multithreading 126

8. **Instance Management** **128**
Persistence of Instances 129
Explicit Persistence 129
Persistence-by-Reachability 131
Extent Access 136
Accessing an Extent 137
Extent Iteration 137
Ignoring the Cache 139
Accessing and Updating Instances 139
Explicit Marking of Modified Instances 141
Deleting Instances 142
Delete Propagation 143

9. **The JDO Query Language** **145**
Query Components 146
Creating and Initializing a Query 149
Changes in the Cache 152
Query Namespaces 153
Type Names 153
Field, Parameter, and Variable Names 154

Keywords 154

Literals 155

Query Execution 155

Parameter Declarations 155

Executing a Query 156

Compiling a Query 159

The Query Filter 160

General Characteristics of Expressions 161

Query Operators 161

References 166

Collections 168

Ordering Query Results 171

Closing a Query 173

10. Identity **174**

Overview 175

JDO Identity Types 175

Metadata 176

Identity Class 177

Datastore Identity 178

Application Identity 179

Primary-Key Fields 179

Persistent Class equals() and hashCode() Methods 180

The Application-Identity Class 180

A Single-Field Primary Key 181

A Compound Primary Key 184

A Compound Primary Key That Contains a Foreign Key 187

Application Identity in an Inheritance Hierarchy 190

Nondurable Identity 195

Identity Methods 196

Get the Identity Class 197

Get the Identity of an Instance 198

Getting an Instance via Its Identity 200

Changing the Application Identity of an Instance 202

Get the Current Application Identity of an Instance 202

The String Representation of Identity 203

Advanced Topics   203
    Choosing an Identity Type   204
    Using Identity Versus a Query   204
    Identity Across PersistenceManagers   204

11. Lifecycle States and Transitions **206**
Lifecycle States   206
    Transient   207
    Persistent-New   207
    Hollow   208
    Persistent-Clean   210
    Persistent-Dirty   210
    Persistent-Deleted   210
    Persistent-New-Deleted   210
State Interrogation   211
State Transitions   212
    State Transitions During a Datastore Transaction   212
    State Transitions When a Transaction Completes   213
    States Between Transactions   214

12. Field Management **215**
Transactional Fields   215
null Values   215
Retrieval of Fields   216
    Default Fetch Group   216
    Retrieving All Fields   217
    The Management of Fields   219
Serialization   219
Managing Fields During Lifecycle Events   220
First- and Second-Class Objects   221
    Specifying a Second-Class Object   224
    Embedding Collection Elements   225
    Persistent Classes as Second-Class Objects   226
    Sharing of Instances   226

13. Cache Management **228**

Explicit Management of Instances in the Cache   228

    Refreshing Instances   229

    Evicting Instances   229

Cloning   230

Transient-Transactional Instances   231

    Transient-Transactional Lifecycle States   231

    State Interrogation   232

    State Transitions   232

Making a Persistent Instance Transient   233

14. Nontransactional Access **235**

Nontransactional Features   235

Reading Outside a Transaction   238

Persistent-Nontransactional State   239

Retaining Values at Transaction Commit   241

Restoring Values at Transaction Rollback   242

    Before Image   243

    Restoring Persistent Instances   244

    Restoring Persistent-New Instances   244

Modifying Persistent Instances Outside a Transaction   245

    Hot Cache Example   246

15. Optimistic Transactions **251**

Verification at Commit   252

    Recovery from a Failed Transaction   253

    Setting Optimistic Transaction Behavior   254

    Optimistic Example   254

Optimistic Transaction State Transitions   256

Deleting Instances   257

Making Instances Transactional   257

Modifying Instances   257

Commit   258

Rollback   258

16. The Web-Server Environment **259**

Web Servers 259

    Accessing the PersistenceManagerFactory 261

    Servicing Requests 263

    PersistenceManager per Request 264

    PersistenceManager per Application 264

    PersistenceManager per Transactional Request 265

    PersistenceManager per Session 265

    Transactions 265

    JavaServer Pages 266

Struts with JDO 267

17. J2EE Application Servers **272**

Enterprise JavaBeans Architecture 273

Stateless Session Beans 274

    Configuring the PersistenceManagerFactory 275

    Stateless Session Beans with Container-Managed Transactions 278

    Stateful Session Beans with Container-Managed Transactions 280

Bean-Managed Transactions 281

    javax.transaction.UserTransaction 282

    javax.jdo.Transaction 282

    Stateless Session Beans with Bean-Managed Transactions 283

    Stateful Session Beans with Bean-Managed Transactions 283

Message-Driven Beans 283

Persistent Entities and JDO 284

    Local Persistent Storage 284

    Remote Persistent Storage 286

A. Lifecycle States and Transitions **293**

B. JDO Metadata DTD **296**

C. JDO Interfaces and Exception Classes **298**

D. JDO Query Language BNF **308**

E. Source Code for Examples **313**

Index **345**

Foreword

Java Data Objects (JDO) is an important innovation for the Java platform. At a time when developers were using JDBC almost exclusively for database access, and expert groups from major enterprise vendors were devising the much-touted Enterprise Java Beans APIs for entity beans and container-managed persistence, Craig Russell and David Jordan had the courage to take a different course. With a handful of others, they looked for a simpler way to provide persistence in the Java platform, something that would be both natural and convenient for programmers. This book describes the result of their work: JDO.

The key, unique idea behind JDO is to provide database persistence in Java with a minimum of extra stuff for the programmer to do. The programmer doesn't need to learn SQL, doesn't need to tediously copy data into and out of their Java objects using JDBC calls, and can use Java classes, fields, and references in a way that is natural to them, without lots of extra method calls and coding that is extraneous to the programmer's focus and intent. Even queries can be written using Java predicates instead of SQL. In other words, the programmer just writes Java; the persistence part is automatic.

In addition to this transparent persistence, code written to JDO benefits from binary compatibility across implementations on different datastores. JDO can be used with an object/relational mapping, in which JDBC calls are generated automatically to map the data between Java objects and existing relational databases. Alternatively, the JDO objects can be stored directly in file pages, providing the functionality and performance of an object-oriented database.

The hard work on JDO paid off: the idea of transparent persistence has proven quite popular. JDO has its own community web site, *JDOCentral.com*, and on enterprise Java discussion sites such as *TheServerSide.com*, developers praise the simplicity and utility of JDO. Many developers use JDO as a replacement for entity beans, by using data objects from within session beans. Others use JDO as a convenient high-level replacement for JDBC calls in JSP pages or other Java code. JDO has come a long way from the JDBC interface I defined in 1995 with Graham Hamilton, and JDO is quite valuable in conjunction with J2EE.

I can't think of two individuals better qualified to write a book about JDO. Craig is the specification lead for the JDO expert group, and Dave was one of the most active members of that group. But their qualifications go far beyond that, and JDO was well designed as a result of those qualifications. Both have over a decade of experience with issues in programming language persistence, including subtle transaction semantics, different persistence models, relationships between objects, caching performance, interactions between transient and persistent objects, and programming convenience in practice. Both had extensive experience with C++ persistence before they applied their experience to Java. Both were key members of the Object Data Management Group (*http://www.odmg.org*) for years. And, most importantly, both were developers who appreciated and needed the functionality that JDO provides.

Craig and Dave have put together a thorough, readable, and useful book. I hope you enjoy it as much as I did.

—Rick Cattell, Deputy Software CTO
Sun Microsystems, February 16, 2003

Preface

JDO provides transparent persistence of your Java object models in transactional datastores. It allows you to define your object model using all the capabilities provided in Java and it handles the mapping of that data to a variety of underlying datastores. You do not need to learn and understand a different data-modeling language like SQL. You will discover that JDO is very easy to use. Many development organizations are discovering the significant development productivity advantages that can be realized by using JDO.

Who Should Read This Book?

If you are a Java programmer who writes software that needs to store data beyond the duration of a single Java Virtual Machine (JVM) context, then you should read this book. We assume that you already know Java. But you don't need to have a lot of knowledge of databases, because JDO insulates you from needing to know much about them.

Many Java developers have been using Java Database Connectivity (JDBC) to store their data in a database. JDBC requires that you learn SQL. When you interact with a database via JDBC, you must view your information model from the perspective of the relational data model, which is very different from Java. Many developers never attain the advantages of object-oriented programming because they never define an object model for their persistent data. Most of the application software becomes very procedural-like code that manages data in the tables of the relational data model.

With JDO, Java becomes your data model and you only need to deal with instances of your classes when interacting with the database. Having just the single data model of Java as the basis of your data management simplifies your development task considerably.

Organization

This book has 17 chapters and 5 appendixes. The first three chapters provide a good overview, showing a complete example, a high-level overview of the JDO interfaces, and a discussion of the architectures in which JDO can be used. Chapters 3 through 6 deal with object modeling, schema design, and aspects of the JDO software-development process. Chapter 7 covers aspects of establishing a JDO runtime environment, which includes connecting to a datastore and issuing transactions. The remaining chapters cover aspects of using JDO to store, access, and query instances in the datastore. We start by presenting the basic concepts and gradually move to more advanced topics, including features that are optional in JDO implementations. We complete the book by discussing how you can integrate your applications into application-server and J2EE environments.

The following list provides a brief description of each chapter and appendix:

Chapter 1, *An Initial Tour*
> Provides an introductory overview of JDO by walking through a small application that illustrates many of JDO's capabilities.

Chapter 2, *An Overview of JDO Interfaces*
> Provides a high-level introduction to all of JDO's interfaces. Details of these interfaces are covered in the rest of the book. We also discuss class enhancement and the optional features in JDO.

Chapter 3, *JDO Architectures*
> Provides a description of the architectural components within a single JDO application and also describes the various system architectures in which JDO implementations have been deployed.

Chapter 4, *Defining Persistent Classes*
> JDO maps your object models into a database. This chapter covers the Java object-modeling capabilities supported by JDO.

Chapter 5, *Datastore Mappings*
> Explains approaches used for mapping your Java object models to the modeling components of the underlying datastore.

Chapter 6, *Class Enhancement*
> Covers the process and effects of enhancing your classes.

Chapter 7, *Establishing a JDO Runtime Environment*
> Explains how to establish a connection with a datastore and establish a transaction context in which to access objects in the database.

Chapter 8, *Instance Management*
> Covers all aspects of the CRUD operations of using a database: Create, Read, Update, and Delete. We show how to make objects persistent, accessing them from the database via extents and navigation, and how to modify and delete them.

Chapter 9, *The JDO Query Language*

JDO includes its own query language, which is based largely on Java, using its operators and syntax to access objects using the data model defined by your classes.

Chapter 10, *Identity*

Identifies the various approaches for uniquely identifying an object in the database.

Chapter 11, *Lifecycle States and Transitions*

Covers the lifecycle states used by a JDO implementation to manage objects in memory, describing the state transitions that occur as your application and the JDO implemenation perform operations on the objects.

Chapter 12, *Field Management*

Describes transactional fields, null values in fields, special facilities that control the access of fields, and mechanisms for you to manage fields during certain lifecycle events. The chapter concludes with a discussion of first- and second-class objects.

Chapter 13, *Cache Management*

Covers advanced topics related to managing instances in the cache, including making persistent instances transient, making transient instances transactional, cloning instances, and refreshing and evicting instances in the cache.

Chapter 14, *Nontransactional Access*

Covers techniques for accessing instances outside of a transaction.

Chapter 15, *Optimistic Transactions*

Covers all aspects of optimistic transactions in JDO.

Chapter 16, *The Web-Server Environment*

Explains how to use JDO in an application-server environment.

Chapter 17, *J2EE Application Servers*

Explains the use of JDO in an Enterprise Java Beans environment, using JDO as the persistence service for session and entity beans, using either bean-managed persistence (BMP) or container-managed persistence (CMP).

Appendix A, *Lifecycle States and Transitions*

Provides a table containing all the lifecycle states and all transitions that occur for any operation that changes the state of an instance.

Appendix B, *JDO Metadata DTD*

Provides the XML Document Type Descriptor (DTD) for JDO metadata.

Appendix C, *JDO Interfaces and Exception Classes*

Provides the signature for all the methods in each JDO interface.

Appendix D, *JDO Query Language BNF*

Provides the Backus-Naur Form (BNF) for the JDO Query Language.

Appendix E, *Source Code for Examples*

Provides complete source code for the major classes used in the examples throughout the book.

Software and Versions

This book is based on JDO release 1.0.1.

Conventions

The following typographical conventions are used in this book:

Italic
> Used for filenames and pathnames, hostnames, domain names, URLs, and email addresses. *Italic* is also used for new terms where they are defined.

`Constant width`
> Used for code examples and fragments, XML elements and tags, and SQL commands, table names, and column names. `Constant width` is also used for class, variable, and method names and for Java keywords used within the text.

`Constant width bold`
> Used for emphasis in some code examples.

`Constant width italic`
> Used to indicate text that is replaceable. For example, in *`BeanName`*`PK`, you would replace *`BeanName`* with a specific bean name.

Comments and Questions

Please address comments and questions concerning this book to the publisher:

> O'Reilly & Associates, Inc.
> 1005 Gravenstein Highway North
> Sebastopol, CA 95472
> (800) 998-9938 (in the United States or Canada)
> (707) 829-0515 (international/local)
> (707) 829-0104 (fax)

There is a web page for this book, which lists errata, examples, or any additional information. You can access this page at:

> *http://www.oreilly.com/catalog/jvadtaobj*

To comment or ask technical questions about this book, send email to:

> *bookquestions@oreilly.com*

For more information about books, conferences, Resource Centers, and the O'Reilly Network, see the O'Reilly web site at:

> *http://www.oreilly.com*

Acknowledgements

We would like to thank our technical reviewers, who provided very valuable input. They include S. Rajesh Babu (ObjectFrontier), Michael Bouschen (Tech@Spree), Ron Hitchens (Ronsoft Technologies), Dennis Leinbaugh, Patrick Linskey (SolarMetric), Marc Prud'hommeaux (SolarMetric), Eric Samson (LIBeLIS), David Tinker (Hemisphere Technologies), Mike Warren (Chemical Abstract Service), and Abe White (SolarMetric). We also appreciate the valuable feedback from Linda DeMichiel, Sun Microsystem's EJB specification lead. The feedback and suggestions from these technical reviewers was invaluable.

We especially acknowledge the support and guidance of our editor, Michael Loukides. We would also like to thank some of the other staff at O'Reilly, including David Futato, Robert Romano, Brian Sawyer, and Mike Sierra.

CHAPTER 1

An Initial Tour

Java is a language that defines a runtime environment in which user-defined classes execute. Instances of these user-defined classes may represent real-world data that is stored in a database, filesystem, or mainframe transaction processing system. Additionally, small-footprint environments often require a means of managing persistent data in local storage.

Because data-access techniques are different for each type of data source, accessing the data presents a challenge to application developers, who need to use a different application programming interface (API) for each type of data source. This means that you need to know at least two languages to develop business logic for these data sources: the Java programming language and the specialized data-access language required by the data source. The data-access language is likely to be different for each data source, driving up the costs to learn and use each data source.

Prior to the release of Java Data Objects (JDO), three standards existed for storing Java data: serialization, Java DataBase Connectivity (JDBC), and Enterprise Java-Beans (EJB) Container Managed Persistence (CMP). Serialization is used to write the state of an object, and the graph of objects it references, to an output stream. It preserves the relationships of Java objects such that the complete graph can be reconstructed at a later point in time. But serialization does not support transactions, queries, or the sharing of data among multiple users. It allows access only at the granularity of the original serialization and becomes cumbersome when the application needs to manage multiple serializations. Serialization is only used for persistence in the simplest of applications or in embedded environments that cannot support a database effectively.

JDBC requires you to manage the values of fields explicitly and map them into relational database tables. The developer is forced to deal with two very different data-model, language, and data-access paradigms: Java and SQL's relational data model. The development effort to implement your own mapping between the relational data model and your Java object model is so great that most developers never define an object model for their data; they simply write procedural Java code to manipulate the tables of the underlying relational database. The end result is that they are not benefiting from the advantages of object-oriented development.

The EJB component architecture is designed to support distributed object computing. It also includes support for persistence through Container Managed Persistence (CMP). Largely due to their distributed capabilities, EJB applications are more complex and have more overhead than JDO. However, JDO has been designed so that implementations can provide persistence support in an EJB environment by integrating with EJB containers. If your application needs object persistence, but does not need distributed object capabilities, you can use JDO instead of EJB components. The most popular use of JDO in an EJB environment is to have EJB session beans directly manage JDO objects, avoiding the use of Entity Beans. EJB components must be run in a managed, application-server environment. But JDO applications can be run in either managed or nonmanaged environments, providing you with the flexibility to choose the most appropriate environment to run your application.

You can develop applications more productively if you can focus on designing Java object models and using JDO to store instances of your classes directly. You need to deal with only a single information model. JDBC requires you to understand the relational model and the SQL language. When using EJB CMP, you are also forced to learn and deal with many other aspects of its architecture. It also has modeling limitations not present in JDO.

JDO specifies the contracts between your persistent classes and the JDO runtime environment. JDO is engineered to support a wide variety of data sources, including sources that are not commonly considered databases. We therefore use the term *datastore* to refer to any underlying data source that you access with JDO.

This chapter explores some of JDO's basic capabilities, by examining a small application developed by a fictitious company called Media Mania, Inc. They rent and sell various forms of entertainment media in stores located throughout the United States. Their stores have kiosks that provide information about movies and the actors in those movies. This information is made available to the customers and store staff to help select merchandise that will be of interest to the customers.

Defining a Persistent Object Model

Figure 1-1 is a Unified Modeling Language (UML) diagram of the classes and interrelationships in the Media Mania object model. A Movie instance represents a particular movie. Each actor who has played a role in at least one movie is represented by an instance of Actor. The Role class represents the specific roles an actor has played in a movie and thus represents a relationship between Movie and Actor that includes an attribute (the name of the role). Each movie has one or more roles. An actor may have played a role in more than one movie or may have played multiple roles in a single movie.

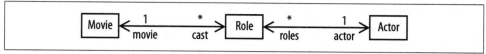

Figure 1-1. UML diagram of the Media Mania object model

We will place these persistent classes and the application programs used to manage their instances in the Java com.mediamania.prototype package.

The Classes to Persist

We will make the Movie, Actor, and Role classes persistent, so their instances can be stored in a datastore. First we will examine the complete source code for each of these classes. An import statement is included for each class, so it is clear which package contains each class used in the example.

Example 1-1 provides the source code for the Movie class. JDO is defined in the javax.jdo package. Notice that the class does not require you to import any JDO-specific classes. Java references and collections defined in the java.util package are used to represent the relationships between our classes, which is the standard practice used by most Java applications.

The fields of the Movie class use standard Java types such as String, Date, and int. You can declare fields to be private; it is not necessary to define a public get and set method for each field. The Movie class includes some methods to get and set the private fields in the class, though those methods are used by other parts of the application and are not required by JDO. You can use encapsulation, providing only the methods that support the abstraction being modeled. The class also has static fields; these are not stored in the datastore.

The genres field is a String that contains the genres of the movie (action, romance, mystery, etc.). A Set interface is used to reference a set of Role instances, representing the movie's cast. The addRole( ) method adds elements to the cast collection, and getCast( ) returns an unmodifiable Set containing the elements of the cast collection. These methods are not a JDO requirement, but they are implemented as convenience methods for the application. The parseReleaseDate( ) and formatReleaseDate( ) methods are used to standardize the format of the movie's release date. To keep the code simple, a null is returned if the parseReleaseDate( ) parameter is in the wrong format.

Example 1-1. Movie.java

```
package com.mediamania.prototype;

import java.util.Set;
import java.util.HashSet;
import java.util.Collections;
import java.util.Date;
import java.util.Calendar;
```

Example 1-1. Movie.java (continued)

```java
import java.text.SimpleDateFormat;
import java.text.ParsePosition;

public class Movie {
    private static SimpleDateFormat yearFmt = new SimpleDateFormat("yyyy");
    public  static final String[] MPAAratings =
                            { "G", "PG", "PG-13", "R", "NC-17", "NR" };
    private String      title;
    private Date        releaseDate;
    private int         runningTime;
    private String      rating;
    private String      webSite;
    private String      genres;
    private Set         cast;      // element type: Role

    private Movie( )
    { }

    public Movie(String title, Date release, int duration, String rating,
                 String genres) {
        this.title = title;
        releaseDate = release;
        runningTime = duration;
        this.rating = rating;
        this.genres = genres;
        cast = new HashSet( );
    }
    public String getTitle( ) {
        return title;
    }
    public Date getReleaseDate( ) {
        return releaseDate;
    }
    public String getRating( ) {
        return rating;
    }
    public int getRunningTime( ) {
        return runningTime;
    }
    public void setWebSite(String site) {
        webSite = site;
    }
    public String getWebSite( ) {
        return webSite;
    }
    public String getGenres( ) {
        return genres;
    }
    public void addRole(Role role) {
        cast.add(role);
    }
    public Set getCast( ) {
        return Collections.unmodifiableSet(cast);
    }
```

Example 1-1. Movie.java (continued)

```java
    public static Date parseReleaseDate(String val) {
        Date date = null;
        try {
            date = yearFmt.parse(val);
        } catch (java.text.ParseException exc) { }
        return date;
    }
    public String formatReleaseDate() {
        return yearFmt.format(releaseDate);
    }
}
```

JDO imposes one requirement to make a class persistent: a no-arg constructor. If you do not define any constructors in your class, the compiler generates a no-arg constructor. However, this constructor is not generated if you define any constructors with arguments; in this case, you need to provide a no-arg constructor. You can declare it to be private if you do not want your application code to use it. Some JDO implementations can generate one for you, but this is an implementation-specific, nonportable feature.

Example 1-2 provides the source for the Actor class. For our purposes, all actors have a unique name that identifies them. It can be a stage name that is distinct and different from the given name. Therefore, we represent the actor's name by a single String. Each actor has played one or more roles, and the roles member models the Actor's side of the relationship between Actor and Role. The comment on line ❶ is used merely for documentation; it does not serve any functional purpose in JDO. The addRole( ) and removeRole( ) methods in lines ❷ and ❸ are provided so that the application can maintain the relationship from an Actor instance and its associated Role instances.

Example 1-2. Actor.java

```java
package com.mediamania.prototype;

import java.util.Set;
import java.util.HashSet;
import java.util.Collections;

public class Actor {
    private String  name;
    private Set     roles; // element type: Role

    private Actor()
    { }
    public Actor(String name) {
        this.name = name;
        roles = new HashSet();
    }
    public String getName() {
        return name;
    }
```

❶ appears at the line `private Set     roles; // element type: Role`

Example 1-2. Actor.java (continued)

```
❷      public void addRole(Role role) {
            roles.add(role);
        }
❸      public void removeRole(Role role) {
            roles.remove(role);
        }
        public Set getRoles( ) {
            return Collections.unmodifiableSet(roles);
        }
}
```

Finally, Example 1-3 provides the source for the Role class. This class models the relationship between a Movie and Actor and includes the specific name of the role played by the actor in the movie. The Role constructor initializes the references to Movie and Actor, and it also updates the other ends of its relationship by calling addRole( ), which we defined in the Movie and Actor classes.

Example 1-3. Role.java

```
package com.mediamania.prototype;

public class Role {
    private String   name;
    private Actor    actor;
    private Movie    movie;

    private Role( )
    { }
    public Role(String name, Actor actor, Movie movie) {
        this.name = name;
        this.actor = actor;
        this.movie = movie;
        actor.addRole(this);
        movie.addRole(this);
    }
    public String getName( ) {
        return name;
    }
    public Actor getActor( ) {
        return actor;
    }
    public Movie getMovie( ) {
        return movie;
    }
}
```

We have now examined the complete source code for each class that will have instances in the datastore. These classes did not need to import and use any JDO-specific types. Furthermore, except for providing a no-arg constructor, no data or methods needed to be defined to make these classes persistent. The software used to access and modify fields and define and manage relationships among instances corresponds to the standard practice used in most Java applications.

Declaring Classes to Be Persistent

It is necessary to identify which classes should be persistent and specify any persistence-related information that is not expressible in Java. JDO uses a metadata file in XML format to specify this information.

You can define metadata on a class or package basis, in one or more XML files. The name of the metadata file for a single class is the name of the class, followed by a *.jdo* suffix. So, a metadata file for the Movie class would be named *Movie.jdo* and placed in the same directory as the *Movie.class* file. A metadata file for a Java package is contained in a file named *package.jdo*. A metadata file for a Java package can contain metadata for multiple classes and multiple subpackages. Example 1-4 provides the metadata for the Media Mania object model. The metadata is specified for the package and contained in a file named *com/mediamania/prototype/package.jdo*.

Example 1-4. JDO metadata in the file prototype/package.jdo

```
    <?xml version="1.0" encoding="UTF-8" ?>
❶  <!DOCTYPE jdo PUBLIC
        "-//Sun Microsystems, Inc.//DTD Java Data Objects Metadata 1.0//EN"
        "http://java.sun.com/dtd/jdo_1_0.dtd">
    <jdo>
❷      <package name="com.mediamania.prototype" >
❸          <class name="Movie" >
❹              <field name="cast" >
❺                  <collection element-type="Role"/>
                </field>
            </class>
❻          <class name="Role" />
            <class name="Actor" >
                <field name="roles" >
                    <collection element-type="Role"/>
                </field>
            </class>
        </package>
    </jdo>
```

The *jdo_1_0.dtd* file specified on line ❶ provides a description of the XML elements that can be used in a JDO metadata file. This document type definition (DTD) is standardized in JDO and should be provided with a JDO implementation. It is also available for download at *http://java.sun.com/dtd*. You can also alter the DOCTYPE to refer to a local copy in your filesystem.

The metadata file can contain persistence information for one or more packages that have persistent classes. Each package is defined with a package element, which includes the name of the Java package. Line ❷ provides a package element for our com.mediamania.prototype package. Within the package element are nested class elements that identify a persistent class of the package (e.g., line ❸ has the class element for the Movie class). The file can contain multiple package elements listed serially; they are not nested.

If information must be specified for a particular field of a class, a field element is nested within the class element, as shown on line ❹. For example, you could declare the element type for each collection in the model. This is not required, but it can result in a more efficient mapping. The Movie class has a collection named cast, and the Actor class has a collection named roles; both contain Role references. Line ❺ specifies the element type for cast. In many cases, a default value for an attribute is assumed in the metadata that provides the most commonly needed value.

All of the fields that can be persistent are made persistent by default. Static and final fields cannot be made persistent. A field declared in Java to be transient is not persistent by default, but such a field can be declared as persistent in the metadata file. Chapter 4 describes this capability.

Chapters 4, 10, 12, and 13 cover other characteristics you can specify for classes and fields. For a simple class like Role, which does not have any collections, you can just list the class in the metadata as shown on line ❻, if no other metadata attributes are necessary.

Project Build Environment

In this section, we examine a development environment to compile and run our JDO application. This includes the project directory structure, the jar files necessary to build applications, and the syntax for enhancing persistent classes. We describe class enhancement later in this section. The environment setup partly depends on which JDO implementation you use. Your specific project's development environment and directory structure may differ.

You can use either the Sun JDO reference implementation or another implementation of your choosing. The examples in this book use the JDO reference implementation. You can download the JDO reference implementation by visiting *http://www.jcp.org* and selecting JSR-12. Once you have installed a JDO implementation, you will need to establish a project directory structure and define a classpath that includes all the directories and jar files necessary to build and run your application.

JDO introduces a new step in your build process, called *class enhancement*. Each persistent class must be enhanced so that it can be used in a JDO runtime environment. Your persistent classes are compiled using a Java compiler that produces a class file. An enhancer program reads these class files and JDO metadata and creates new class files that have been enhanced to operate in a JDO environment. Your JDO application should load these enhanced class files. The JDO reference implementation includes an enhancer called the *reference enhancer*.

Jars Needed to Use the JDO Reference Implementation

When using the JDO reference implementation, you should include the following jar files in your classpath during development. At runtime, all of these jar files should be in your classpath.

jdo.jar

> The standard interfaces and classes defined in the JDO specification.

jdori.jar

> Sun's reference implementation of the JDO specification.

btree.jar

> Software used by the JDO reference implementation to manage the storage of data in a file. The reference implementation uses a file for the storage of persistent instances.

jta.jar

> The Java Transaction API. The Synchronization interface defined in package javax.transaction is used in the JDO interface and contained in this jar file. Other facilities defined in this file are likely to be useful to a JDO implementation. You can download this jar from *http://java.sun.com/products/jta/index.html*.

antlr.jar

> Parsing technology used in the implementation of the JDO query language. The reference implementation uses Version 2.7.0 of Antlr. You can download it from *http://www.antlr.org*.

xerces.jar

> The reference implementation uses Xerces-J Release 1.4.3 to parse XML. It can be downloaded from *http://xml.apache.org/xerces-j/*.

The first three jar files are included with the JDO reference implementation; the last three can be downloaded from the specified web sites.

The reference implementation includes an additional jar, *jdori-enhancer.jar*, that contains the reference enhancer implementation. The classes in *jdori-enhancer.jar* are also in *jdori.jar*. In most cases, you will use *jdori.jar* in both your development and runtime environment, and not need *jdori-enhancer.jar*. The *jdori-enhancer.jar* is packaged separately so that you can enhance your classes using the reference enhancer independent of a particular JDO implementation. Some implementations, besides the reference implementation, may distribute this jar for use with their implementation.

If you use a different JDO implementation, its documentation should provide you with a list of all the necessary jars. An implementation usually places all the necessary jars in a particular directory in their installation. The *jdo.jar* file containing the interfaces defined in JDO should be used with all implementations. This jar file is usually included with a vendor's implementation. JDOcentral.com (*http://www.jdocentral.com*) provides numerous JDO resources, including free trial downloads of many commercial JDO implementations.

Project Directory Structure

You should use the following directory structure for the Media Mania application development environment. The project must have a *root* directory placed somewhere in the filesystem. The following directories reside beneath the project's *root* directory:

src

> This directory contains all of the application's source code. Under *src*, there is a subdirectory hierarchy of *com/mediamania/prototype* (corresponding to the Java com.mediamania.prototype package). This is where the *Movie.java*, *Actor.java*, and *Role.java* source files reside.

classes

> When the Java source files are compiled, their class files are placed in this directory.

enhanced

> This is the directory that contains the enhanced class files (produced by the enhancer).

database

> This directory contains the files used by the reference implementation to store our persistent data.

Though this particular directory structure is not a requirement of JDO or the reference implementation, you need to understand it to follow our description of the Media Mania application.

When you execute your JDO application, the Java runtime must load the enhanced version of the class files, which are located in our *enhanced* directory. Therefore, the *enhanced* directory should be listed prior to the *classes* directory in your classpath. As an alternative approach, you can also enhance in-place, replacing your unenhanced class file with their enhanced form.

Enhancing Classes for Persistence

A class must be enhanced before its instances can be managed in a JDO environment. A JDO enhancer adds data and methods to your classes that enable their instances to be managed by a JDO implementation. An enhancer reads a class file produced by the Java compiler and, using the JDO metadata, produces a new, enhanced class file that includes the necessary functionality. JDO has standardized the modifications made by enhancers so that enhanced class files are binary-compatible and can be used with any JDO implementation. These enhanced files are also independent of any specific datastore.

As mentioned previously, the enhancer provided with Sun's JDO reference implementation is called the *reference enhancer*. A JDO vendor may provide its own enhancer; the command-line syntax necessary to execute an enhancer may differ from the syntax shown here. Each implementation should provide you with documentation explaining how to enhance your classes for use with their implementation.

Example 1-5 provides the reference enhancer command for enhancing the persistent classes in our Media Mania application. The -d argument specifies the *root* directory in which to place the enhanced class files; we have specified our *enhanced* directory. The enhancer is given a list of JDO metadata files and a set of class files to enhance. The directory separator and line-continuation symbols may vary, depending on your operating system and build environment.

Example 1-5. Enhancing the persistent classes

```
java com.sun.jdori.enhancer.Main -d enhanced  \
    classes/com/mediamania/prototype/package.jdo  \
    classes/com/mediamania/prototype/Movie.class  \
    classes/com/mediamania/prototype/Actor.class  \
    classes/com/mediamania/prototype/Role.class
```

Though it is convenient to place the metadata files in the directory with the source code, the JDO specification recommends that the metadata files be available via resources loaded by the same class loader as the class files. The metadata is needed at both build and runtime. So, we have placed the *package.jdo* metadata file under the *classes* directory hierarchy in the directory for the prototype package.

The class files for all persistent classes in our object model are listed together in Example 1-5, but you can also enhance each class individually. When this command executes, it places new, enhanced class files in the *enhanced* directory.

Establish a Datastore Connection and Transaction

Now that our classes have been enhanced, their instances can be stored in a datastore. We now examine how an application establishes a connection with a datastore and executes operations within a transaction. We begin to write software that makes direct use of the JDO interfaces. All JDO interfaces used by an application are defined in the javax.jdo package.

JDO has an interface called PersistenceManager that has a connection with a datastore. A PersistenceManager has an associated instance of the JDO Transaction interface used to control the start and completion of a transaction. The Transaction instance is acquired by calling currentTransaction() on the PersistenceManager instance.

Acquiring a PersistenceManager

A PersistenceManagerFactory is used to configure and acquire a PersistenceManager. Methods in the PersistenceManagerFactory are used to set properties that control the behavior of the PersistenceManager instances acquired from the factory. Therefore, the first step performed by a JDO application is the acquisition of a PersistenceManagerFactory instance. To get this instance, call the following static method of the JDOHelper class:

```
static PersistenceManagerFactory getPersistenceManagerFactory(Properties props);
```

The Properties instance can be populated programmatically or by loading property values from a property file. Example 1-6 lists the contents of the property file we will use in our Media Mania application. The PersistenceManagerFactoryClass property on line ❶ specifies which JDO implementation we are using by providing the name of the implementation's class that implements the PersistenceManagerFactory interface. In this case, we specify the class defined in Sun's JDO reference implementation. Other properties listed in Example 1-6 include the connection URL used to connect to a particular datastore and a username and password, which may be necessary to establish a connection to the datastore

Example 1-6. Contents of jdo.properties

```
❶  javax.jdo.PersistenceManagerFactoryClass=com.sun.jdori.fostore.FOStorePMF
   javax.jdo.option.ConnectionURL=fostore:database/fostoredb
   javax.jdo.option.ConnectionUserName=dave
   javax.jdo.option.ConnectionPassword=jdo4me
   javax.jdo.option.Optimistic=false
```

The format of the connection URL depends on the particular datastore being accessed. The JDO reference implementation has its own storage facility called File Object Store (FOStore). The ConnectionURL property in Example 1-6 specifies that the datastore is located in the *database* directory, which is located in our project's *root* directory. In this case, we have provided a relative path; it is also possible to provide an absolute path to the datastore. The URL specifies that the FOStore datastore files will have a name prefix of *fostoredb*.

If you are using a different implementation, you will need to provide different values for these properties. You may also need to provide values for additional properties. Check with your implementation's documentation to determine the properties that are necessary.

Creating a FOStore Datastore

To use FOStore we must first create a datastore. The program in Example 1-7 creates a datastore using the *jdo.properties* file; all applications use this property file. Line ❶ loads the properties from *jdo.properties* into a Properties instance. The program adds the com.sun.jdori.option.ConnectionCreate property on line ❷ to indicate that the datastore should be created. Setting it to true instructs the implementation to create the datastore. We then call getPersistenceManagerFactory( ) on line ❸ to acquire the PersistenceManagerFactory. Line ❹ creates a PersistenceManager.

To complete the creation of the datastore, we must also begin and commit a transaction. The PersistenceManager method currentTransaction( ) is called on line ❺ to access the Transaction instance associated with the PersistenceManager. The Transaction methods begin( ) and commit( ) are called on lines ❻ and ❼ to start and commit a transaction. When you execute this application, a FOStore datastore is created in the *database* directory. Two files are created: *fostore.btd* and *fostore.btx*.

Example 1-7. Creating a FOStore datastore

```
package com.mediamania;

import java.io.FileInputStream;
import java.io.InputStream;
import java.util.Properties;
import javax.jdo.JDOHelper;
import javax.jdo.PersistenceManagerFactory;
import javax.jdo.PersistenceManager;
import javax.jdo.Transaction;

public class CreateDatabase {
    public static void main(String[] args) {
        create( );
    }
    public static void create( ) {
        try {
            InputStream propertyStream = new FileInputStream("jdo.properties");
            Properties jdoproperties = new Properties( );
            jdoproperties.load(propertyStream);
            jdoproperties.put("com.sun.jdori.option.ConnectionCreate", "true");
            PersistenceManagerFactory pmf =
                        JDOHelper.getPersistenceManagerFactory(jdoproperties);
            PersistenceManager pm = pmf.getPersistenceManager( );
            Transaction tx = pm.currentTransaction( );
            tx.begin( );
            tx.commit( );
        } catch (Exception e) {
            System.err.println("Exception creating the database");
            e.printStackTrace( );
            System.exit(-1);
        }
    }
}
```

The JDO reference implementation provides this programmatic means to create a database. Most databases provide a utility separate from JDO for creating a database. JDO does not define a standard, vendor-independent interface for creating a database. Creation of a datastore is always datastore-specific. This program illustrates how it is done using the FOStore datastore.

In addition, when you are using JDO with a relational database, there is often an additional step of creating or mapping to an existing relational schema. The procedure to follow for establishing a schema that corresponds with your JDO object model is implementation-specific. You should examine the documentation of the implementation you are using to determine the necessary steps.

Operations on Instances

Now we have a datastore in which we can store instances of our classes. Each application needs to acquire a PersistenceManager to access and update the datastore. Example 1-8 provides the source for the MediaManiaApp class, which serves as the base class for each application in this book. Each application is a concrete subclass of MediaManiaApp that implements its application logic in the execute( ) method.

MediaManiaApp has a constructor that loads the properties from *jdo.properties* (line ❶). After loading properties from the file, it calls getPropertyOverrides( ) and merges the returned properties into jdoproperties. An application subclass can redefine getPropertyOverrides( ) to provide any additional properties or change properties that are set in the *jdo.properties* file. The constructor gets a PersistenceManagerFactory (line ❷) and then acquires a PersistenceManager (line ❸). We also provide the getPersistenceManager( ) method to access the PersistenceManager from outside the MediaManiaApp class. The Transaction associated with the PersistenceManager is acquired on line ❹.

The application subclasses make a call to executeTransaction( ), defined in the MediaManiaApp class. This method begins a transaction on line ❺. It then calls execute( ) on line ❻, which will execute the subclass-specific functionality.

We chose this particular design for application classes to simplify and reduce the amount of redundant code in the examples for establishing an environment to run. This is not required in JDO; you can choose an approach that is best suited for your application environment.

After the return from the execute( ) method (implemented by a subclass), an attempt is made to commit the transaction (line ❼). If any exceptions are thrown, the transaction is rolled back and the exception is printed to the error stream.

Example 1-8. MediaManiaApp base class

```
package com.mediamania;

import java.io.FileInputStream;
import java.io.InputStream;
import java.util.Properties;
import java.util.Map;
import java.util.HashMap;
import javax.jdo.JDOHelper;
import javax.jdo.PersistenceManagerFactory;
import javax.jdo.PersistenceManager;
import javax.jdo.Transaction;
```

Example 1-8. MediaManiaApp base class (continued)

```
public abstract class MediaManiaApp {
    protected PersistenceManagerFactory pmf;
    protected PersistenceManager        pm;
    protected Transaction               tx;

    public abstract void execute();  // defined in concrete application subclasses

    protected static Map getPropertyOverrides() {
        return new HashMap();
    }
    public MediaManiaApp() {
        try {
            InputStream propertyStream = new FileInputStream("jdo.properties");
            Properties jdoproperties = new Properties();
❶           jdoproperties.load(propertyStream);
            jdoproperties.putAll(getPropertyOverrides());
❷           pmf = JDOHelper.getPersistenceManagerFactory(jdoproperties);
❸           pm = pmf.getPersistenceManager();
❹           tx = pm.currentTransaction();
        } catch (Exception e) {
            e.printStackTrace(System.err);
            System.exit(-1);
        }
    }
    public PersistenceManager getPersistenceManager() {
        return pm;
    }
    public void executeTransaction() {
        try {
❺           tx.begin();
❻           execute();
❼           tx.commit();
        } catch (Throwable exception) {
            exception.printStackTrace(System.err);
            if (tx.isActive()) tx.rollback();
        }
    }
}
```

Making Instances Persistent

Let's examine a simple application, called `CreateMovie`, that makes a single `Movie` instance persistent, as shown in Example 1-9. The functionality of the application is placed in `execute()`. After constructing an instance of `CreateMovie`, we call `executeTransaction()`, which is defined in the `MediaManiaApp` base class. It makes a call to `execute()`, which will be the method defined in this class. The `execute()` method instantiates a single `Movie` instance on line ❺. Calling the `PersistenceManager` method `makePersistent()` on line ❻ makes the `Movie` instance persistent. If the transaction commits successfully in `executeTransaction()`, the `Movie` instance will be stored in the datastore.

Example 1-9. Creating a Movie instance and making it persistent

```java
package com.mediamania.prototype;

import java.util.Calendar;
import java.util.Date;
import com.mediamania.MediaManiaApp;

public class CreateMovie extends MediaManiaApp {
    public static void main(String[] args) {
        CreateMovie createMovie = new CreateMovie();
        createMovie.executeTransaction();
    }
    public void execute() {
        Calendar cal = Calendar.getInstance();
        cal.clear();
        cal.set(Calendar.YEAR, 1997);
        Date date = cal.getTime();
        Movie movie = new Movie("Titanic", date, 194, "PG-13", "historical, drama");
        pm.makePersistent(movie);
    }
}
```

❺
❻

Now let's examine a larger application. LoadMovies, shown in Example 1-10, reads a file containing movie data and creates multiple instances of Movie. The name of the file is passed to the application as an argument, and the LoadMovies constructor initializes a BufferedReader to read the data. The execute() method reads one line at a time from the file and calls parseMovieData(), which parses the line of input data, creates a Movie instance on line ❶, and makes it persistent on line ❷. When the transaction commits in executeTransaction(), all of the newly created Movie instances will be stored in the datastore.

Example 1-10. LoadMovies

```java
package com.mediamania.prototype;

import java.io.FileReader;
import java.io.BufferedReader;
import java.util.Calendar;
import java.util.Date;
import java.util.StringTokenizer;
import javax.jdo.PersistenceManager;
import com.mediamania.MediaManiaApp;

public class LoadMovies extends MediaManiaApp {
    private BufferedReader  reader;

    public static void main(String[] args) {
        LoadMovies loadMovies = new LoadMovies(args[0]);
        loadMovies.executeTransaction();
    }
```

Example 1-10. LoadMovies (continued)

```
public LoadMovies(String filename) {
    try {
        FileReader fr = new FileReader(filename);
        reader = new BufferedReader(fr);
    } catch (Exception e) {
        System.err.print("Unable to open input file ");
        System.err.println(filename);
        e.printStackTrace( );
        System.exit(-1);
    }
}
public void execute( ) {
    try {
        while ( reader.ready( ) ) {
            String line = reader.readLine( );
            parseMovieData(line);
        }
    } catch (java.io.IOException e) {
        System.err.println("Exception reading input file");
        e.printStackTrace(System.err);
    }
}
public void parseMovieData(String line) {
    StringTokenizer tokenizer = new StringTokenizer(line, ";");
    String title = tokenizer.nextToken( );
    String dateStr = tokenizer.nextToken( );
    Date releaseDate = Movie.parseReleaseDate(dateStr);
    int runningTime = 0;
    try {
        runningTime = Integer.parseInt(tokenizer.nextToken( ));
    } catch (java.lang.NumberFormatException e) {
        System.err.print("Exception parsing running time for ");
        System.err.println(title);
    }
    String rating = tokenizer.nextToken( );
    String genres = tokenizer.nextToken( );
    Movie movie = new Movie(title, releaseDate, runningTime, rating, genres);
    pm.makePersistent(movie);
}
}
```

❶
❷

The movie data is in a file with the following format:

```
movie title;release date;running time;movie rating;genre1,genre2,genre3
```

The format to use for release dates is maintained in the Movie class, so parseReleaseDate( ) is called to create a Date instance from the input data. A movie is described by one or more genres, which are listed at the end of the line of data.

Accessing Instances

Now let's access the Movie instances in the datastore to verify that they were stored successfully. There are several ways to access instances in JDO:

- Iterate an extent
- Navigate the object model
- Execute a query

An *extent* is a facility used to access all the instances of a particular class or the class and all its subclasses. If the application wants to access only a subset of the instances, a query can be executed with a filter that constrains the instances returned to those that satisfy a Boolean predicate. Once the application has accessed an instance from the datastore, it can navigate to related instances in the datastore by traversing through references and iterating collections in the object model. Instances that are not yet in memory are read from the datastore on demand. These facilities for accessing instances are often used in combination, and JDO ensures that each persistent instance is represented in the application memory only once per PersistenceManager. Each PersistenceManager manages a single transaction context.

Iterating an extent

JDO provides the Extent interface for accessing the extent of a class. The extent allows access to all of the instances of a class, but using an extent does not imply that all the instances are in memory. The PrintMovies application, provided in Example 1-11, uses the Movie extent.

Example 1-11. Iterating the Movie extent

```
package com.mediamania.prototype;

import java.util.Iterator;
import java.util.Set;
import javax.jdo.PersistenceManager;
import javax.jdo.Extent;
import com.mediamania.MediaManiaApp;

public class PrintMovies extends MediaManiaApp {

    public static void main(String[] args) {
        PrintMovies movies = new PrintMovies();
        movies.executeTransaction();
    }

    public void execute() {
        Extent extent = pm.getExtent(Movie.class, true);
        Iterator iter = extent.iterator();
        while (iter.hasNext()) {
            Movie movie = (Movie) iter.next();
            System.out.print(movie.getTitle());          System.out.print(";");
            System.out.print(movie.getRating());         System.out.print(";");
```

❶
❷

❸

Example 1-11. Iterating the Movie extent (continued)

```
              System.out.print(movie.formatReleaseDate() );    System.out.print(";");
              System.out.print(movie.getRunningTime());        System.out.print(";");
❹            System.out.println(movie.getGenres());

❺            Set cast = movie.getCast();
              Iterator castIterator = cast.iterator();
              while (castIterator.hasNext()) {
❻                Role role = (Role) castIterator.next();
                  System.out.print("\t");
                  System.out.print(role.getName());
                  System.out.print(", ");
❼                System.out.println(role.getActor().getName());
              }
          }
❽        extent.close(iter);
      }
  }
```

On line ❶ we acquire an Extent for the Movie class from the PersistenceManager. The second parameter indicates whether to include instances of Movie subclasses. A value of false causes only Movie instances to be returned, even if there are instances of subclasses. Though we don't currently have any classes that extend the Movie class, providing a value of true will return instances of any such classes that we may define in the future. The Extent interface has the iterator() method, which we call on line ❷ to acquire an Iterator that will access each element of the extent. Line ❸ uses the Iterator to access Movie instances. The application can then perform operations on the Movie instance to acquire data about the movie to print. For example, on line ❹ we call getGenres() to get the genres associated with the movie. On line ❺ we acquire the set of Roles. We acquire a reference to a Role on line ❻ and then print the role's name. On line ❼ we navigate to the Actor for that role by calling getActor(), which we defined in the Role class. We then print the actor's name.

Once the application has completed iteration through the extent, line ❽ closes the Iterator to relinquish any resources required to perform the extent iteration. Multiple Iterator instances can be used concurrently on an Extent. This method closes a specific Iterator; closeAll() closes all the Iterator instances associated with an Extent.

Navigating the object model

Example 1-11 demonstrates iteration of the Movie extent. But on line ❻ we also navigate to a set of related Role instances by iterating a collection in our object model. On line ❼ we use the Role instance to navigate through a reference to the related Actor instance. Line ❺ and ❼ demonstrate, respectively, traversal of *to-many* and *to-one* relationships. A relationship from one class to another has a cardinality that indicates whether there are one or multiple associated instances. A *reference* is used for a cardinality of one, and a *collection* is used when there can be more than one instance.

The syntax needed to access these related instances corresponds to the standard practice of navigating instances in memory. The application does not need to make any direct calls to JDO interfaces between lines ❸ and ❼. It simply traverses among objects in memory. The related instances are not read from the datastore and instantiated in memory until they are accessed directly by the application. Access to the datastore is transparent; instances are brought into memory on demand. Some implementations provide facilities separate from the Java interface that allow you to influence the implementation's access and caching algorithms. Your Java application is insulated from these optimizations, but it can take advantage of them to affect its overall performance.

The access of related persistent instances in a JDO environment is identical to the access of transient instances in a non-JDO environment, so you can write your software in a manner that is independent of its use in a JDO environment. Existing software written without any knowledge of JDO or any other persistence concerns is able to navigate objects in the datastore through JDO. This capability yields dramatic increases in development productivity and allows existing software to be incorporated into a JDO environment quickly and easily.

Executing a query

It is also possible to perform a query on an Extent. The JDO Query interface is used to select a subset of the instances that meet certain criteria. The remaining examples in this chapter need to access a specific Actor or Movie based on a unique name. These methods, shown in Example 1-12, are virtually identical; getActor( ) performs a query to get an Actor based on a name, and getMovie( ) performs a query to get a Movie based on a name.

Example 1-12. Query methods in the PrototypeQueries class

```
package com.mediamania.prototype;

import java.util.Collection;
import java.util.Iterator;
import javax.jdo.PersistenceManager;
import javax.jdo.Extent;
import javax.jdo.Query;

public class PrototypeQueries {
    public static Actor getActor(PersistenceManager pm, String actorName)
    {
        Extent actorExtent = pm.getExtent(Actor.class, true);
        Query query = pm.newQuery(actorExtent, "name == actorName");
        query.declareParameters("String actorName");
        Collection result = (Collection) query.execute(actorName);
        Iterator iter = result.iterator( );
        Actor actor = null;
        if (iter.hasNext()) actor = (Actor)iter.next( );
        query.close(result);
```

The circled numbers ❶ ❷ ❸ ❹ ❺ ❻ appear in the left margin beside the corresponding lines of code.

Example 1-12. Query methods in the PrototypeQueries class (continued)

```
        return actor;
    }
    public static Movie getMovie(PersistenceManager pm, String movieTitle)
    {
        Extent movieExtent = pm.getExtent(Movie.class, true);
        Query query = pm.newQuery(movieExtent, "title == movieTitle");
        query.declareParameters("String movieTitle");
        Collection result = (Collection) query.execute(movieTitle);
        Iterator iter = result.iterator();
        Movie movie = null;
        if (iter.hasNext()) movie = (Movie)iter.next();
        query.close(result);
        return movie;
    }
}
```

Let's examine getActor( ). On line ❶ we get a reference to the Actor extent. Line ❷ creates an instance of Query using the newQuery( ) method defined in the PersistenceManager interface. The query is initialized with the extent and a query filter to apply to the extent.

The name identifier in the filter is the name field in the Actor class. The namespace used to determine how to interpret the identifier is based on the class of the Extent used to initialize the Query instance. The filter expression requires that an Actor's name field is equal to actorName. In the filter we can use the == operator directly to compare two Strings, instead of using the Java syntax (name.equals(actorName)).

The actorName identifier is a *query parameter*, which is declared on line ❸. A query parameter lets you provide a value to be used when the query is executed. We have chosen to use the same name, actorName, for the method parameter and query parameter. This practice is not required, and there is no direct association between the names of our Java method parameters and our query parameters. The query is executed on line ❹, passing getActor( )'s actorName parameter as the value to use for the actorName query parameter.

The result type of Query.execute( ) is declared as Object. In JDO 1.0.1, the returned instance is always a Collection, so we cast the query result to a Collection. It is declared in JDO 1.0.1 to return Object, to allow for a future extension of returning a value other than a Collection. Our method then acquires an Iterator and, on line ❺, attempts to access an element. We assume here that there can only be a single Actor instance with a given name. Before returning the result, line ❻ closes the query result to relinquish any associated resources. If the method finds an Actor instance with the given name, the instance is returned. Otherwise, if the query result has no elements, a null is returned.

Modifying an Instance

Now let's examine two applications that modify instances in the datastore. Once an application has accessed an instance from the datastore in a transaction, it can modify one or more fields of the instance. When the transaction commits, all modifications that have been made to instances are propagated to the datastore automatically.

The UpdateWebSite application provided in Example 1-13 is used to set the web site associated with a movie. It takes two arguments: the first is the movie's title, and the second is the movie's web site URL. After initializing the application instance, executeTransaction( ) is called, which calls the execute( ) method defined in this class.

Line ❶ calls getMovie( ) (defined in Example 1-12) to retrieve the Movie with the given title. If getMovie( ) returns null, the application reports that it could not find a Movie with the given title and returns. Otherwise, on line ❷ we call setWebSite( ) (defined for the Movie class in Example 1-1), which sets the webSite field of Movie to the parameter value. When executeTransaction( ) commits the transaction, the modification to the Movie instance is propagated to the datastore automatically.

Example 1-13. Modifying an attribute

```
package com.mediamania.prototype;

import com.mediamania.MediaManiaApp;

public class UpdateWebSite extends MediaManiaApp {
    private String  movieTitle;
    private String  newWebSite;

    public static void main (String[] args) {
        String title = args[0];
        String website = args[1];
        UpdateWebSite update = new UpdateWebSite(title, website);
        update.executeTransaction( );
    }
    public UpdateWebSite(String title, String site) {
        movieTitle = title;
        newWebSite = site;
    }
    public void execute( ) {
        Movie movie = PrototypeQueries.getMovie(pm, movieTitle);
        if (movie == null) {
            System.err.print("Could not access movie with title of ");
            System.err.println(movieTitle);
            return;
        }
        movie.setWebSite(newWebSite);
    }
}
```

As you can see in Example 1-13, the application does not need to make any direct JDO interface calls to modify the Movie field. This application accesses an instance and calls a method to modify the web site field. The method modifies the field using standard Java syntax. No additional programming is necessary prior to commit in order to propagate the data to the datastore. The JDO environment propagates the modifications automatically. This application performs an operation on persistent instances, yet it does not directly import or use any JDO interfaces.

Now let's examine a larger application, called LoadRoles, that exhibits several JDO capabilities. LoadRoles, shown in Example 1-14, is responsible for loading information about the movie roles and the actors who play them. LoadRoles is passed a single argument that specifies the name of a file to read, and the constructor initializes a BufferedReader to read the file. It reads the text file, which contains one role per line, in the following format:

```
movie title;actor's name;role name
```

Usually, all the roles associated with a particular movie are grouped together in this file; LoadRoles performs a small optimization to determine whether the role information being processed is for the same movie as the previous role entry in the file.

Example 1-14. Instance modification and persistence-by-reachability

```
package com.mediamania.prototype;

import java.io.FileReader;
import java.io.BufferedReader;
import java.util.StringTokenizer;
import com.mediamania.MediaManiaApp;

public class LoadRoles extends MediaManiaApp {
    private BufferedReader  reader;

    public static void main(String[] args) {
        LoadRoles loadRoles = new LoadRoles(args[0]);
        loadRoles.executeTransaction( );
    }
    public LoadRoles(String filename) {
        try {
            FileReader fr = new FileReader(filename);
            reader = new BufferedReader(fr);
        } catch(java.io.IOException e){
            System.err.print("Unable to open input file ");
            System.err.println(filename);
            System.exit(-1);
        }
    }
    public void execute( ) {
        String lastTitle = "";
        Movie movie = null;
        try {
```

Example 1-14. Instance modification and persistence-by-reachability (continued)

```
          while (reader.ready( )) {
              String line = reader.readLine( );
              StringTokenizer tokenizer = new StringTokenizer(line, ";");
              String title    = tokenizer.nextToken( );
              String actorName = tokenizer.nextToken( );
              String roleName  = tokenizer.nextToken( );
              if (!title.equals(lastTitle)) {
❶                movie = PrototypeQueries.getMovie(pm, title);
                  if (movie == null) {
                      System.err.print("Movie title not found: ");
                      System.err.println(title);
                      continue;
                  }
                  lastTitle = title;
              }
❷            Actor actor = PrototypeQueries.getActor(pm, actorName);
              if (actor == null) {
❸                actor = new Actor(actorName);
❹                pm.makePersistent(actor);
              }
❺            Role role = new Role(roleName, actor, movie);
          }
      } catch (java.io.IOException e) {
          System.err.println("Exception reading input file");
          System.err.println(e);
          return;
      }
  }
}
```

The execute( ) method reads each entry in the file. First, it checks to see whether the new entry's movie title is the same as the previous entry. If it is not, line ❶ calls getMovie( ) to access the Movie with the new title. If a Movie with that title does not exist in the datastore, the application prints an error message and skips over the entry. On line ❷ we attempt to access an Actor instance with the specified name. If no Actor in the datastore has this name, a new Actor is created and given this name on line ❸, and made persistent on line ❹.

Up to this point in the application, we have just been reading the input file and looking up instances in the datastore that have been referenced by a name in the file. We perform the real task of the application on line ❺, where we create a new Role instance. The Role constructor was defined in Example 1-3; it is repeated here so that we can examine it in more detail:

```
      public Role(String name, Actor actor, Movie movie) {
❶        this.name = name;
❷        this.actor = actor;
❸        this.movie = movie;
❹        actor.addRole(this);
❺        movie.addRole(this);
      }
```

Line ❶ initializes the name of the Role. Line ❷ establishes a reference to the associated Actor, and line ❸ establishes a reference to the associated Movie instance. The relationships between Actor and Role and between Movie and Role are bidirectional, so it is also necessary to update the other side of each relationship. On line ❹ we call addRole( ) on actor, which adds this Role to the roles collection in the Actor class. Similarly, line ❺ calls addRole( ) on movie to add this Role to the cast collection field in the Movie class. Adding the Role as an element in Actor.roles and Movie.cast causes a modification to the instances referenced by actor and movie.

The Role constructor demonstrates that you can establish a relationship to an instance simply by initializing a reference to it, and you can establish a relationship with more than one instance by adding references to a collection. This process is how relationships are represented in Java and is supported directly by JDO. When the transaction commits, the relationships established in memory are preserved in the datastore.

Upon return from the Role constructor, load( ) processes the next entry in the file. The while loop terminates once we have exhausted the contents of the file.

You may have noticed that we never called makePersistent( ) on the Role instances we created. Still, at commit, the Role instances are stored in the datastore because JDO supports *persistence-by-reachability*. Persistence-by-reachability causes any transient (nonpersistent) instance of a persistent class to become persistent at commit if it is reachable (directly or indirectly) by a persistent instance. Instances are reachable through either a reference or collection of references. The set of all instances reachable from a given instance is an object graph that is called the instance's *complete closure* of related instances. The reachability algorithm is applied to all persistent instances transitively through all their references to instances in memory, causing the complete closure to become persistent.

Removing all references to a persistent instance does not automatically delete the instance. You need to delete instances explicitly, which we cover in the next section. If you establish a reference from a persistent instance to a transient instance during a transaction, but you change this reference and no persistent instances reference the transient instance at commit, it remains transient.

Persistence-by-reachability lets you write a lot of your software without having any explicit calls to JDO interfaces to store instances. Much of your software can focus on establishing relationships among the instances in memory, and the JDO implementation takes care of storing any new instances and relationships you establish among the instances in memory. Your applications can construct fairly complex object graphs in memory and make them persistent simply by establishing a reference to the graph from a persistent instance.

Deleting Instances

Now let's examine an application that deletes some instances from the datastore. In Example 1-15, the DeleteMovie application is used to delete a Movie instance. The title of the movie to delete is provided as the argument to the program. Line ❶ attempts to access the Movie instance. If no movie with the title exists, the application reports an error and returns. On line ❻ we call deletePersistent( ) to delete the Movie instance itself.

Example 1-15. Deleting a Movie from the datastore

```
package com.mediamania.prototype;

import java.util.Collection;
import java.util.Set;
import java.util.Iterator;
import javax.jdo.PersistenceManager;
import com.mediamania.MediaManiaApp;

public class DeleteMovie extends MediaManiaApp {
    private String  movieTitle;

    public static void main(String[] args) {
        String title = args[0];
        DeleteMovie deleteMovie = new DeleteMovie(title);
        deleteMovie.executeTransaction( );
    }
    public DeleteMovie(String title) {
        movieTitle = title;
    }
    public void execute( ) {
        Movie movie = PrototypeQueries.getMovie(pm, movieTitle);
        if (movie == null) {
            System.err.print("Could not access movie with title of ");
            System.err.println(movieTitle);
            return;
        }
        Set cast = movie.getCast( );
        Iterator iter = cast.iterator( );
        while (iter.hasNext( )) {
            Role role = (Role) iter.next( );
            Actor actor = role.getActor( );
            actor.removeRole(role);
        }
        pm.deletePersistentAll(cast);
        pm.deletePersistent(movie);
    }
}
```

❶ (line: `Movie movie = PrototypeQueries.getMovie(pm, movieTitle);`)
❷ (line: `Set cast = movie.getCast( );`)
❸ (line: `Actor actor = role.getActor( );`)
❹ (line: `actor.removeRole(role);`)
❺ (line: `pm.deletePersistentAll(cast);`)
❻ (line: `pm.deletePersistent(movie);`)

But it is also necessary to delete the Role instances associated with the Movie. In addition, since an Actor includes a reference to the Role instance, it is necessary to remove this reference. On line ❷ we access the set of Role instances associated with the

Movie. We then iterate through each Role and access the associated Actor on line ❸. Since we will be deleting the Role instance, on line ❹ we remove the actor's reference to the Role. On line ❺ we make a call to deletePersistentAll( ) to delete all the Role instances in the movie's cast. When we commit the transaction, the Movie instance and associated Role instances are deleted from the datastore, and the Actor instances associated with the Movie are updated so that they no longer reference the deleted Role instances.

You must call these deletePersistent( ) methods explicitly to delete instances from the datastore. They are not the inverse of makePersistent( ), which uses the persistence-by-reachability algorithm. Furthermore, there is no JDO datastore equivalent to Java's garbage collection, which deletes instances automatically once they are no longer referenced by any instances in the datastore. Implementing the equivalent of a persistent garbage collector is a very complex undertaking, and such systems often have poor performance.

Summary

As you can see, a large portion of an application can be written in a completely JDO-independent manner using conventional Java modeling, syntax, and programming techniques. You can define your application's persistent information model solely in terms of a Java object model. Once you access instances from the datastore via an extent or query, your software looks no different from any other Java software that accesses instances in memory. You do not need to learn any other data model or access language like SQL. You do not need to figure out how to provide a mapping of your data between a database representation and an in-memory object representation. You can fully exploit the object-oriented capabilities of Java without any limitation. This includes use of inheritance and polymorphism, which are not possible using technologies like JDBC and the Enterprise JavaBeans (EJB) architecture. In addition, you can develop an application using an object model with much less software than when using competitive architectures. Plain, ordinary Java objects can be stored in a datastore and accessed in a transparent manner. JDO provides a very easy-to-learn and productive environment to build Java applications that manage persistent data.

CHAPTER 2

An Overview of JDO Interfaces

JDO's interfaces are defined in two packages: javax.jdo and javax.jdo.spi. You use the interfaces defined in the javax.jdo package to write your applications. This chapter introduces and describes each of these interfaces at a high level. Each method defined in these interfaces is covered thoroughly in this book. You can use the index to find information on a particular method.

The javax.jdo.spi package contains interfaces that JDO implementations use (spi stands for *service provider interface*). It is a common practice to have such a package that defines interfaces for use by the implementation of a Java API, distinct from the package that contains the interfaces for use of the API. You should not directly use any of the interfaces defined in javax.jdo.spi. We provide brief coverage of a few of the javax.jdo.spi interfaces that are directly involved in the management of persistent class instances. If you are interested in a thorough understanding of the interfaces in javax.jdo.spi, we encourage you to read the JDO specification.

We conclude this chapter by enumerating the optional features in JDO.

The javax.jdo Package

The javax.jdo package contains all the interfaces you should use:

- PersistenceManager
- PersistenceManagerFactory
- Transaction
- Extent
- Query
- InstanceCallbacks

It also contains the JDOHelper class and a set of exception classes.

This is the complete set of JDO application interfaces! JDO has a relatively small API, allowing you to learn it quickly and become productive applying it. JDO uses your Java classes as the data model for representing and managing data, which is major contributing factor in its simplicity and ease of use.

Every method in each of these interfaces is described somewhere in this book. We introduce basic JDO concepts first and gradually progress to more advanced topics. Semantically related methods are often covered in the same section, but coverage of the methods for a particular interface is usually dispersed throughout the text. Appendix C provides the signature for every method in each interface. The index provides a reference to each place in the book where a method is covered. Here's a brief description of each interface in the package:

PersistenceManager

> PersistenceManager is your primary interface when using JDO. It provides methods to create query and transaction objects, and it manages the lifecycle of persistent instances. Each chapter introduces a few PersistenceManager methods. The interface is used for the basic and advanced features in JDO.

PersistenceManagerFactory

> The PersistenceManagerFactory is responsible for configuring and creating PersistenceManager instances. It represents the particular JDO implementation you are using; it has methods to determine the properties and optional features the implemention supports. PersistenceManagerFactory also provides methods to control property values used to establish a datastore connection and affect the configuration of the runtime environment in which the PersistenceManager instances run; these methods are covered in Chapter 7.

JDOHelper

> JDOHelper is a class that provides several static utility methods. As shown in Chapter 1, it is used to construct a PersistenceManagerFactory instance from a Properties object. It also provides methods to interrogate the lifecycle state of instances (covered in Chapter 11).

Transaction

> The Transaction interface provides methods to manage the demarcation (begin and commit/rollback) of transactions. Chapter 7 covers these methods in detail. Each PersistenceManager instance has one associated Transaction instance, accessible via currentTransaction(). Transaction also has methods for controlling the values of transaction options.

Extent

> The Extent interface is used to access all the instances of a class (and, potentially, its subclasses). You acquire an Extent by calling the getExtent() method of a PersistenceManager. You can either iterate over the Extent or use it to perform a query. Chapter 8 covers the Extent interface in detail.

Query

You use the Query interface to perform queries. A Query instance has several components, and the interface provides methods to specify a value for each of them. The query evaluates a filter expressed in the JDO Query Language (JDOQL). Chapter 9 covers the Query interface in detail.

InstanceCallbacks

The InstanceCallbacks interface provides a means for you to specify some behavior to perform when specific lifecycle events occur in an instance of a persistent class. The interface defines methods that are called on an instance when it undergoes a lifecycle change. A persistent class must implement the InstanceCallbacks interface for these methods to be called. Chapters 12 and 13 cover this interface and its callback methods.

Figure 2-1 illustrates the relationships among the JDO interfaces and shows the method used to create or navigate to the related instance.

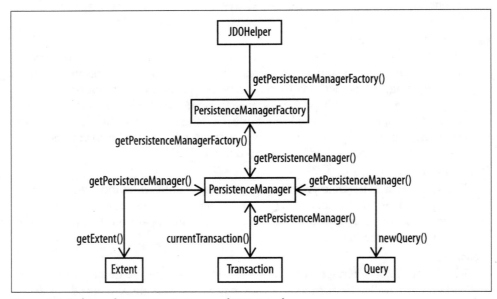

Figure 2-1. Relationships among instances of JDO interfaces

Some methods in the JDO interfaces are used to perform advanced operations. Some applications may use advanced JDO features, but a large percentage of the software in such applications will use only a small subset of JDO's methods. The following list of core JDO interfaces provide the majority, and, in many cases, all of the functionality necessary to use JDO:

- PersistenceManagerFactory properties
  - javax.jdo.PersistenceManagerFactoryClass
  - javax.jdo.option.ConnectionURL

- — `javax.jdo.option.ConnectionUserName`
- — `javax.jdo.option.ConnectionPassword`
- `JDOHelper`
  - — `getPersistenceManagerFactory(Properties)`
- `PersistenceManagerFactory`
  - — `getPersistenceManager()`
- `PersistenceManager`
  - — `makePersistent(Object)`
  - — `deletePersistent(Object)`
  - — `close()`
  - — `newQuery(Class, String)`
  - — `currentTransaction()`
- `Transaction`
  - — `begin()`
  - — `commit()`
  - — `rollback()`
- `Query`
  - — `declareParameters(String)`
  - — `execute()`

We demonstrated the use of most of these methods in Chapter 1. The fact that this list of interfaces is so small is a major reason JDO is so easy to use.

Your persistent classes can have fields of the following standard Java types: `byte`, `short`, `char`, `int`, `long`, `float`, `double`, `Byte`, `Short`, `Character`, `Integer`, `Long`, `Float`, `Double`, `BigInteger`, `BigDecimal`, `String`, `Date`, `Set`, and `HashSet`. Your persistent classes can contain references to both persistent and transient classes. You can also define inheritance hierarchies and have references that refer to instances of subclasses. JDO directly supports the persistence of your Java object models, without requiring you to learn and use any new datatypes.

JDO Exception Classes

There are many opportunities for a component to fail that are not under the application's control. A JDO implementation is often built as a layer on an underlying datastore interface, which itself might use a layered protocol to another tier in a system's architecture. The source of an error may be caused by the application, the JDO implementation, or the underlying datastore on one or several tiers in an architecture.

JDO's exception philosophy is to treat all exceptions as runtime exceptions. This preserves the transparency of JDO's interface as much as possible, allowing you to choose which specific exceptions to catch based upon your application requirements.

JDO exceptions fall into several broad categories, each of which is treated separately:

- Program errors that can be corrected and retried
- Program errors that cannot be corrected, because the state of underlying components has been changed and cannot be undone
- Logic errors internal to the JDO implementation, which should be reported to the vendor's technical support
- Errors in the underlying datastore that can be corrected and retried
- Errors in the underlying datastore that cannot be corrected, due to a failure of the datastore or the communication path to the datastore

JDO uses several interfaces external to the JDO API itself (e.g., the Collection interfaces). An exception that results from using one of these interfaces is used directly, without modification. If an exception occurs in the underlying datastore, the exception is wrapped inside a JDO exception. If your application causes a JDO exception, the exception contains the reason it was thrown.

Figure 2-2 illustrates the JDO exception inheritance hierarchy. The base exception class is called JDOException, and it extends RuntimeException. The classes that extend JDOException divide exceptions into those that are fatal and those that can be retried. The hierarchy is then extended based on the original source of the error. JDO exceptions are serializable.

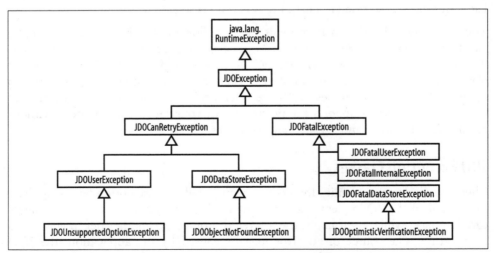

Figure 2-2. JDOException inheritance hierarchy

This chapter provides complete coverage of the exception classes in the book. Let's examine each exception class:

JDOException

> JDOException is the base class for all JDO exceptions. Since it is a subclass of RuntimeException, JDO exceptions do not need to be declared or caught. The class includes a toString( ) method that returns a value indicating the nature of the exception. If the PersistenceManager is internationalized, the descriptive string is also internationalized.
>
> If an exception is relative to a specific instance of one of your classes, you can call getFailedObject( ) to retrieve the instance. If the exception is caused by multiple instances, then each instance is wrapped in its own exception instance, and all of these exceptions are nested inside an exception that is thrown to the application. Such nested exceptions can occur as a result of multiple underlying exceptions or from an exception that involves multiple instances. You may have called a method that accepts a collection of instances, and multiple instances in the collection failed the operation. Or you may have called commit( ) in Transaction, which can fail on instances accessed during the transaction. In these cases, you can call getNestedExceptions( ) on the thrown exception to retrieve the array of nested exceptions. Each nested exception may have its own failed instance, returned by getFailedObject( ).
>
> JDOException contains all of the functionality needed to access information about the exception. Its subclasses do not add any additional functionality to access information; they are used strictly to categorize the type of exception and provide a means for the application to catch and respond to an exception differently, based on its type and associated category.

JDOCanRetryException

> This is the base class for exceptions that can be retried.

JDODataStoreException

> This is the base class for datastore exceptions that can be retried.

JDOUserException

> This is the base class for exceptions caused by your application that can be retried.

JDOUnsupportedOptionException

> This exception is thrown if you attempt to use an optional JDO feature that the implementation does not support.

JDOObjectNotFoundException

> This exception occurs if an attempt is made to fetch an object that does not exist in the datastore.

JDOFatalException

This is the base class for exceptions that are fatal and cannot be retried. Usually, when this exception is thrown, the transaction has been rolled back and should be abandoned.

JDOFatalInternalException

This is the base class for all failures within the JDO implementation itself. There is no action that can be taken to recover from this exception. You should report this exception to the JDO vendor for corrective action.

JDOFatalUserException

This is the base class for exceptions caused by your application that cannot be retried.

JDOFatalDataStoreException

This is the base class for fatal datastore exceptions. When this exception is thrown, the transaction has been rolled back. The cause of the exception may be a connection timeout, an unrecoverable media error, an unrecoverable concurrency conflict, or some other cause outside of the application's control.

JDOOptimisticVerificationException

A verification step (which is described in Chapter 15) is performed on all instances that are new, modified, or deleted when you make a call to commit an optimistic transaction. If any instances fail this verification step, a JDOOptimisticVerificationException is thrown. It contains an array of nested exceptions; each nested exception contains an instance that failed verification. More details on optimistic transactions and the verification step can be found in Chapter 15.

The javax.jdo.spi Package

The javax.jdo.spi package defines interfaces used by JDO implementations. Your application should not use the interfaces in this package. However, a few interfaces in this package are useful for you to be aware of, as they are directly responsible for managing the state of persistent instances.

PersistenceCapable

The PersistenceCapable interface allows an implementation to manage the values of fields and the lifecycle state of persistent instances. Every instance managed by a PersistenceManager needs to be of a class that implements PersistenceCapable. When you enhance a persistent class, code is added to the class to implement the PersistenceCapable interface.

You should not directly use the PersistenceCapable methods added by the enhancer. Some of its methods provide information useful to your application; these methods are made accessible to you through the JDOHelper and PersistenceManager interfaces.

StateManager

Every persistent and transactional instance has a reference to a StateManager instance. (Chapter 13 covers transactional instances.) A StateManager interfaces with the PersistenceManager and is responsible for managing the values of fields and state transitions of an instance. (Chapter 11 covers state transitions.)

JDOPermission

The JDOPermission class is used to grant the JDO implementation permission to perform privileged operations if you have a Java security manager in your Java runtime environment. JDOPermission extends java.security.BasicPermission. The following permissions are defined:

setStateManager

This permission allows a StateManager instance to manage an instance of PersistenceCapable, allowing it to access and modify any of the fields in the class that are defined as persistent or transactional. (Chapter 12 covers transactional fields.)

getMetadata

This permission allows a StateManager instance to access the metadata of any registered persistent class.

closePersistenceManagerFactory

This permission must be granted to close a PersistenceManagerFactory.

Use of the JDOPermission class allows the security manager to restrict potentially malicious classes from accessing information contained in instances of persistent classes.

Assume that you have placed the jar files for the JDO implementation you are using in the /home/jdoImpl directory. The following sample policy-file entry grants any jars or class files in that directory permission to get metadata and manage the state of persistent instances:

```
grant codeBase "file:/home/jdoImpl/" {
    permission javax.jdo.spi.JDOPermission "getMetadata";
    permission javax.jdo.spi.JDOPermission "setStateManager";
};
```

Optional Features

JDO defines some features that are optional; JDO-compliant implementations are not required to implement them. Each optional feature is identified by a unique name, which includes a javax.jdo.option prefix. You can call the supportedOptions( ) method, defined in PersistenceManagerFactory, to determine which options an implementation supports; it returns a Collection of Strings that contain an option string. Chapter 7 presents an example using this method. Here we enumerate all the optional features and their names.

The optional features can be grouped into the following categories:

- Identity options
- Optional collections
- Transaction-related optional features

Identity Options

Each instance managed in a JDO environment must have a unique identifier. The following options are associated with identity:

- `javax.jdo.option.ApplicationIdentity`
- `javax.jdo.option.DatastoreIdentity`
- `javax.jdo.option.NonDurableIdentity`
- `javax.jdo.option.ChangeApplicationIdentity`

The first three options represent different kinds of identity. The fourth option indicates whether you can change the value of the fields that represent the application identity of an instance.

Support for each form of identity is optional. However, an implementation must support either datastore or application identity, and may support both. In Chapter 1 we used datastore identity, which is supported by all of the current JDO implementations. Until we cover identity in depth in Chapter 10, all of our examples will use datastore identity.

Optional Collections

All JDO implementations support the Collection and Set collection interfaces and the HashSet collection class defined in the java.util package. Other collections are optional in JDO, though current implementations support most of them. The following collection options are associated with a corresponding collection interface or class in the java.util package:

- `javax.jdo.option.ArrayList`
- `javax.jdo.option.HashMap`
- `javax.jdo.option.Hashtable`
- `javax.jdo.option.LinkedList`
- `javax.jdo.option.TreeMap`
- `javax.jdo.option.TreeSet`
- `javax.jdo.option.Vector`
- `javax.jdo.option.Map`

- `javax.jdo.option.List`
- `javax.jdo.option.Array`
- `javax.jdo.option.NullCollection`

Chapter 4 discusses optional collections in more detail. The `Array` option indicates whether Java's built-in arrays are supported. The `NullCollection` option indicates whether you can have a `null` value for a reference to a collection.

Transaction-Related Optional Features

The following options deal with transactions and special handling of instances relative to transactions:

- `javax.jdo.option.NontransactionalRead`
- `javax.jdo.option.NontransactionalWrite`
- `javax.jdo.option.RetainValues`
- `javax.jdo.option.TransientTransactional`
- `javax.jdo.option.Optimistic`

Some implementations allow you to read or modify an instance in memory outside of a transaction; this capability is indicated by the `NontransactionalRead` and `NontransactionalWrite` options. Some allow the instances you access during a transaction to be retained and made available after the transaction commits; this capability is determined by the `RetainValues` option. Chapter 14 covers nontransactional access and retaining of instances after commit. Some implementations let you have instances that are transient yet also support transactional semantics; these are called *transient transactional instances*, and they are covered in Chapter 13. The `Optimistic` option indicates whether optimistic transactions are supported; these transactions are covered in Chapter 15.

CHAPTER 3

JDO Architectures

One of JDO's primary objectives is to provide you with a transparent, Java-centric view of persistent information stored in a wide variety of datastores. You can use the Java programming model to represent the data in your application domain and transparently retrieve and store this data from various systems, without needing to learn a new data-access language for each type of datastore. The JDO implementation provides the necessary mapping from your Java objects to the special datatypes and relationships of the underlying datastore. Chapter 4 discusses Java modeling capabilities you can use in your applications. This chapter provides a high-level overview of the architectural aspects of JDO, as well as examples of environments in which JDO can be used. We cannot enumerate all such environments in this book, because JDO is capable of running in a wide variety of architectures.

A JDO implementation is a collection of classes that implement the interfaces defined in the JDO specification. The implementation may be provided by an Enterprise Information System (EIS) vendor or a third-party vendor; in this context, we refer to both as *JDO vendors*. A JDO implementation provided by an EIS vendor will most likely be optimized for the specific EIS.

The JDO architecture simplifies the development of scalable, secure, and transactional JDO implementations that support the JDO interface. You can access a wide variety of storage solutions that have radically different architectures and data models, but you can use a single, consistent, Java-centric view of the information from all the datastores.

The JDO architecture can be used to access and manage data contained in local storage systems and heterogeneous EISs, such as enterprise resource planning (ERP) systems, mainframe transaction processing systems, and database systems. JDO was designed to be suitable for a wide range of uses, from embedded small-footprint systems to large-scale enterprise application servers. A JDO implementation may provide an object-relational mapping tool that supports a broad array of relational databases. JDO vendors can build implementations directly on the filesystem or as a layer on top of a protocol stack with multiple components.

JDO has been designed to work in three primary environments:

Nonmanaged, single transaction

Involves a single transaction and a single JDO implementation, where compactness is the primary concern. *Nonmanaged* refers to the lack of distribution and security within the JVM. The security of the datastore is implemented by name/password controls.

Nonmanaged, multiple transactions

Identical to the first, except that the application uses extended features, such as concurrent transactions.

Managed

Uses the full range of capabilities of an application server, including distributed components and coordinated transactions. Security policies are applied to components based on user roles and security domains.

You can focus on developing your application's business and presentation logic without having to get involved in the issues related to connecting to a specific EIS. The JDO implementation hides the EIS-specific issues, such as datatype mapping, relationship mapping, and the retrieval and storage of data. Your application sees only a Java view of the data, organized as classes using native Java constructs. EIS-specific issues are important only during deployment of your application.

In a nonmanaged environment, you do not rely on the managed services of security, transaction, and connection management offered by a middle-tier application server. Chapters 1 through 15 cover the uses of JDO in a nonmanaged environment, most of which also apply to a managed environment.

When JDO is deployed in a managed environment, it uses the J2EE Java Connector Architecture, which defines a set of portable, scalable, secure, and transactional mechanisms for integrating an EIS with an application server. These mechanisms focus on important aspects of integration with heterogeneous systems: instance management, connection management, and transaction management. The Java Connector Architecture enables a standard JDO implementation to be pluggable across application servers from multiple vendors.

Managed environments also provide transparency for application components' use of system-level mechanisms—distributed transactions, security, and connection management—by hiding the contracts between JDO implementation and the application server. Chapter 16 covers the use of JDO in the web server environment. Chapter 17 explains how to use JDO to provide persistence services in a J2EE application-server environment, which supports the Enterprise JavaBeans (EJB) architecture.

Multiple JDO implementations—possibly multiple implementations per type of EIS or local storage—can be plugged into an application server concurrently, or they can be used directly in a two-tier or embedded architecture. JDO also allows a persistent class to be used concurrently with multiple JDO implementations in the same Java

Virtual Machine (JVM) or application-server environment. This enables application components—deployed on a middle-tier application server or client-tier—to access the underlying datastores using the same consistent, Java-centric view of data.

The persistent classes that you define can migrate easily from one environment to another. This also allows you to debug persistent classes and parts of your application code in a simple one- or two-tier environment and deploy them in another tier of the system architecture.

Architecture Within Application JVM

JDO supports a variety of architectures within the application's JVM context. Your application can have one or multiple PersistenceManagers accessing the same or different datastores concurrently. Each PersistenceManager has its own persistent instance *cache* and its own associated Transaction instance, which manages a distinct transactional context. A JDO implementation may also maintain a shared cache of instances (not visible to applications) to optimize the application's access of data in the datastore.

Single PersistenceManager

The simplest JDO application architecture has a single PersistenceManager, as illustrated in Figure 3-1. A PersistenceManager is the primary interface used by the application to access persistent services. It is an interface that is implemented by an instance of the JDO implementation. The persistent instances are managed in a *cache*, where they are used directly by the application. The JDO implementation manages the persistent instances both by using application control (e.g., using PersistenceManager and Query methods), and transparently (when the application accesses a field that is not loaded). The cache contains other *artifacts*, used to track the identity and state of the instances, but these artifacts are not visible to the application. Whenever we mention the *cache*, we are referring to the cache of persistent instances.

The application cache is not a specific region of memory, as Figure 3-1 might imply; it is simply part of the JVM's object heap. Each persistent class has a field, named jdoStateManager, added by the enhancer to reference a StateManager. The StateManager manages the field values and lifecycle state of the instance, and has a reference to its associated PersistenceManager. A PersistenceManager may use one or more StateManagers; this detail is implementation-specific. The jdoStateManager field for any instance being managed (either a persistent or transient transactional instance) is set to reference a StateManager; otherwise, the jdoStateManager field is null.

A persistent instance in the cache can directly reference other persistent instances in the same cache. You can navigate from one instance to another using standard Java

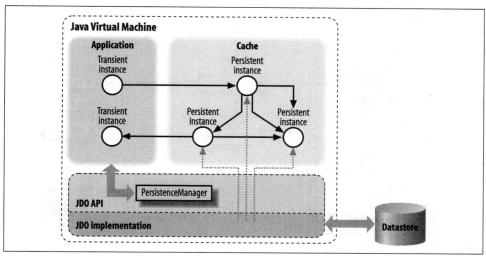

Figure 3-1. Application using a single PersistenceManager to access a datastore

syntax. Instances of transient classes (for example, your application class) can also reference these persistent instances. A persistent instance in the cache can also reference transient instances of both persistent and transient classes. The persistent classes themselves are responsible for managing references to transient instances; the JDO implementation does not manage these references.

Figure 3-2 shows the relationships between the persistent instances, the StateManager, and the PersistenceManager. Each persistent instance contains a reference to a StateManager, which can manage one or more persistent instances. Each StateManager contains a reference to its PersistenceManager, which can manage one or more StateManagers. Each PersistenceManager contains a reference to its PersistenceManagerFactory, which can manage one or more PersistenceManagers. Each PersistenceManager can manage one transaction serially, and contains a reference to its Transaction instance. The PersistenceManager uses a StoreManager to interact with the datastore; this relationship is not defined by the JDO specification.

Multiple PersistenceManagers Accessing the Same Datastore

You can instantiate multiple PersistenceManagers in your application from the same or different PersistenceManagerFactorys. Figure 3-3 illustrates an application with two PersistenceManagers from the same PersistenceManagerFactory.

Each PersistenceManager manages its own transaction context and application cache. In this particular example, both PersistenceManagers access the same datastore and are from the same JDO implementation. This is the typical architecture for managed environments where different instances of the same component access the same datastore via different PersistenceManagers.

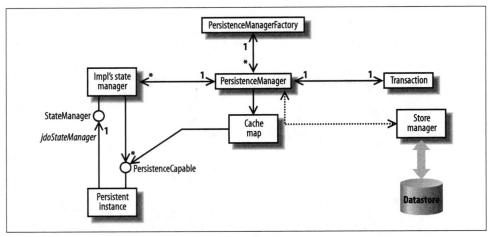

Figure 3-2. UML diagram of persistent instance cache

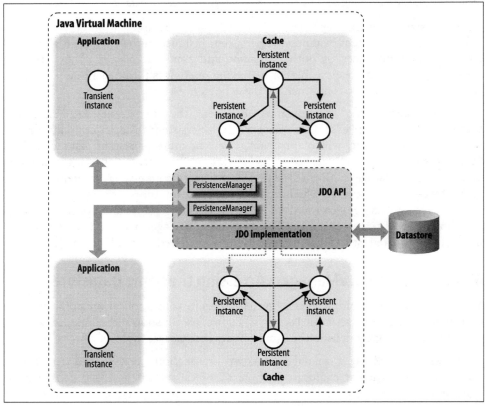

Figure 3-3. Application with multiple PersistenceManagers

Both `PersistenceManagers` may have the same datastore instance in their caches, represented by different persistent instances. This architecture provides for transactional isolation of changes made to the same datastore instance by different transactions.

Multiple PersistenceManagers Accessing Different Datastores

Figure 3-4 illustrates `PersistenceManagers` accessing different datastores. These `PersistenceManagers` could be from the same or different implementations. For example, one datastore may be a relational database and the other an object database. Due to JDO's binary-compatibility contract (covered in Chapter 6), `PersistenceManagers` from different implementations can manage different instances of the same persistent classes. JDO is the first database-interface technology to offer this high level of portability across database architectures.

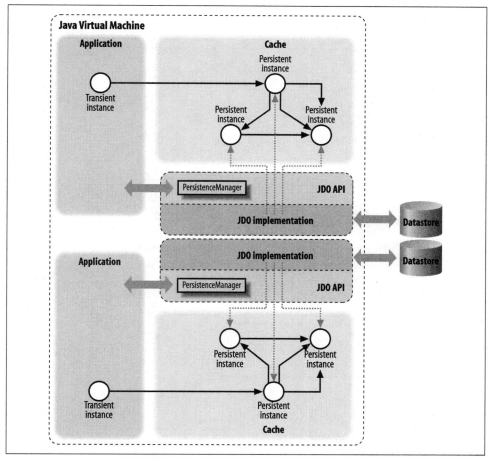

Figure 3-4. Application with multiple JDO implementations

Shared Implementation Cache

In addition to the application cache, some JDO implementations also maintain their own persistent instance cache that sits between the application cache and the datastore. Your application does not have access to this implementation cache. Its role is to cache the state of objects from the datastore in memory, so they can be provided to the application without requiring access to the datastore. Use of caches can result in significant performance improvements. A shared implementation cache is most useful when you use nontransactional access, covered in Chapter 14, or optimistic transactions, covered in Chapter 15. When you use datastore transactions, the shared cache is usually bypassed.

Shared implementation cache within a single JVM

Figure 3-5 illustrates a shared implementation cache that is managed within a single JVM. It allows each of the PersistenceManagers to quickly access the state of objects that have been accessed from the same datastore.

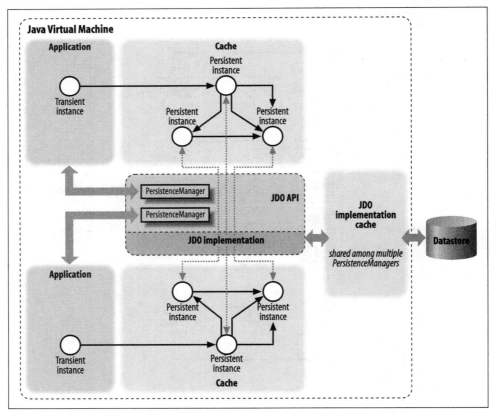

Figure 3-5. Implementation of a shared cache for transactions accessing the same datastore

For example, if one PersistenceManager accesses a particular instance, the implementation needs to read the instance from the datastore. But if the other PersistenceManager then accesses the same instance, the implementation can use the data in the shared implementation cache and avoid having to access the datastore.

Shared implementation cache distributed among JVMs

Several JDO implementations provide a distributed cache architecture, which allows them to migrate the state of objects between JVMs. Figure 3-6 illustrates this architecture.

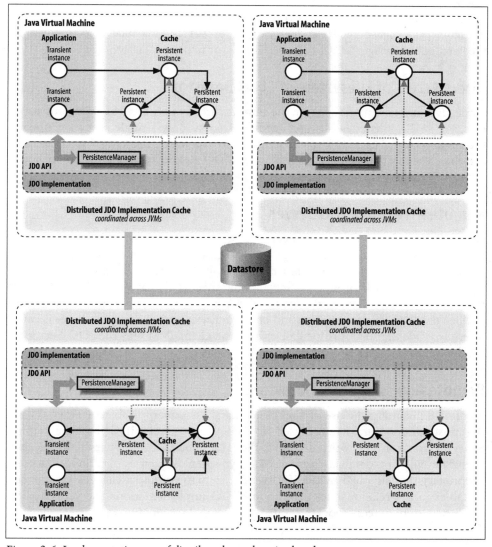

Figure 3-6. Implementation use of distributed, synchronized caches

Again, the goal with these implementations is to avoid a datastore access whenever possible. For some systems where multiple applications may access the same objects, these implementations demonstrate substantial performance improvements.

Datastore Access

We have explored the architecture in the application's JVM and discussed the application cache and implementation cache. Now let's examine the architectures of JDO implementations. We'll discuss each type of datastore separately.

These architectures don't affect your application's programming model, but they affect the configuration of the environment in which your application executes. In particular, the ConnectionURL property of the Properties instance used to construct the PersistenceManagerFactory refers to a local or remote datastore.

Direct Access of Filesystem or Local Datastore

Some JDO implementations store the objects directly in a local filesystem or datastore. Figure 3-1 illustrates this architecture. There is only a single process context in this architecture. The JDO implementation uses the Java I/O classes directly to manage the storage of the objects in a file. The JDO Reference Implementation implements this architecture, as do some object databases.

Remote Access of a JDO Server

Some JDO implementations connect to a separate server that manages the datastore, as illustrated in Figure 3-7. The JDO Reference Implementation implements this architecture, as do most object databases. In this particular example, the JDO implementation itself provides a server built specifically for object storage, which then manages the filesystem directly. The component that executes in the same JVM as the JDO implementation and communicates with the remote server is called a *resource adapter*. The protocols between the client JVM and the JDO Server are vendor-specific.

Remote Access of a SQL Datastore

Figure 3-8 illustrates the use of a relational database server for object storage. This is the most common architecture used by current commercial JDO implementations. Since the application is written in Java, the JDO implementation uses JDBC to communicate with the database server. When you deploy your application, you use a proprietary tool supplied by the JDO vendor to map your application's Java objects to tables in the relational database. Some JDO implementations use your application's persistent object model to create the *relational schema* for you.

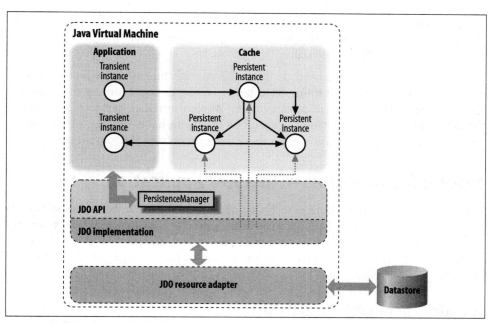

Figure 3-7. Client access of a JDO server

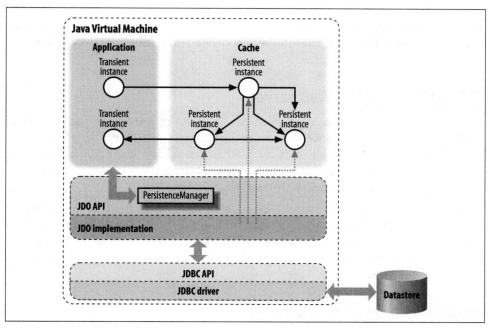

Figure 3-8. Client access of a SQL datastore

The relational vendor or a third party provides a JDBC driver to communicate with the database, using protocols specific to the database. The JDBC driver is the resource adapter in this architecture.

Since the JDBC interface is well defined, this architecture offers a high degree of portability. JDO implementations have been written to use a variety of datastores that provide a JDBC driver implementation. While the JDBC interface is standard, the SQL data manipulation language, used by the relational databases, varies considerably; the JDO implementation hides these differences from JDO applications.

System Architectures with a JDO Application

Now we'll examine where JDO objects and application logic can be placed relative to an application's overall system architecture, including both managed and nonmanaged environments. In the remaining examples in this chapter, we don't show the details of how the JDO implementation manages the storage for the persistent instances.

JDO Rich Client with Local Datastore

The simplest form of system architecture is a one- or two-tier application that may be executed from the command line, from a shell script, or via a graphical user interface. We refer to the application as a *rich client* to distinguish it from a browser that simply displays HTML and executes applets. The application uses local filesystem and JDO persistent services directly.

JDO Applications in a Web Server

Figure 3-9 illustrates how an application can use JDO to provide persistent services to the implementation of a web servlet or JavaServer Pages (JSP). When using JSP pages, the application typically will use JDO in one of two ways: by calling JDO's APIs directly in Java, or using a JSP tag library to abstract the JDO API (similar to the way the JSP Standard Tag Library abstracts the JDBC API).

With this architecture, the servlet/JSP page gets data from the browser in the form of strings from an HTTP doGet( ) or doPost( ) request and uses JDO to implement the request. Your application may use the *Struts* framework to implement the servlets and JSP pages in this architecture. We will discuss the web-server access patterns in detail in Chapter 16.

JDO Applications as Web Services

Figure 3-9 also illustrates the use of JDO as the persistence implementation for a web server implementation of a web services endpoint. The web server may register the service using UDDI and a registry service, and clients may find the service via the same registry.

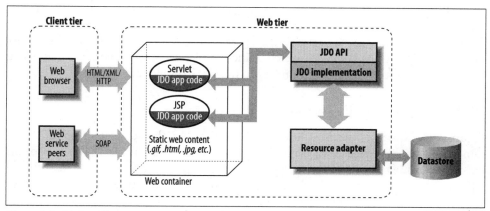

Figure 3-9. JDO application running in a web server

A web server implementation uses a servlet to implement the service endpoint. The servlet can use the JDO API for the persistent service, exactly as it does for servicing HTTP requests. The primary difference between SOAP and standard HTTP is that with SOAP requests, the message data in the HTTP message is formatted as SOAP XML instead of get/post data.

Rich Client Connecting to Application Server with EJB Components

Figure 3-10 illustrates a rich client connecting directly to an application server using EJB beans. This architecture typically is implemented behind the firewall of a company, as it directly exposes enterprise services to clients. The clients use the JNDI services of the J2EE client container to look up services by name (including EJB beans) and to connect to the server via RMI/IIOP or a proprietary protocol. Alternatively, a client may use SOAP protocols to access the middle-tier server.

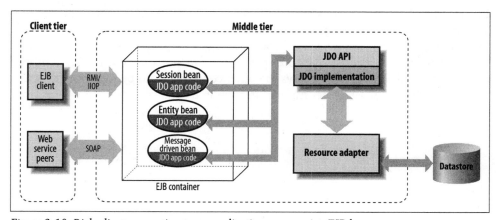

Figure 3-10. Rich-client connection to an application server using EJB beans

The EJB components inside the EJB container use other EJB components to implement their services. They use a combination of JDBC and JDO to access persistent services. Session beans and message-driven beans use JDO and JDBC directly. Entity beans use JDO transparently (the container implements CMP entity beans using JDO but does not expose JDO as an API to the CMP developer).

Web Server with EJB Server

Figure 3-11 illustrates servlets and JSP pages that use the services of an EJB container to implement the business logic of an enterprise application. The EJB beans executing inside the EJB container use JDO as their persistence service. The web and EJB containers often reside in the same JVM in this architecture, even though they represent different tiers of the architecture.

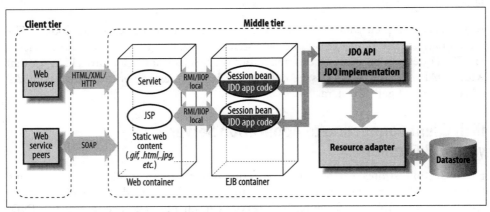

Figure 3-11. Servlets and JSP pages access services of the EJB container

EJB Session Beans Using Session Bean Façades

Figure 3-12 illustrates the session bean delegating parts of the business logic to session bean façades that use JDO as their implementation. This architecture allows location transparency among the components. For example, if the session bean that interacts directly with clients delegates part of the functionality to other session-bean components, this architecture allows the other components to be located in different machines. Chapter 17 describes this architecture in detail.

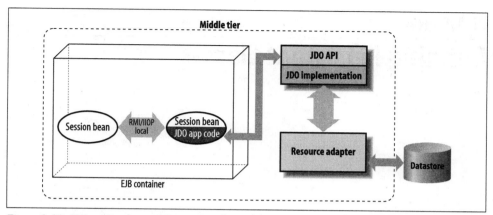

Figure 3-12. EJB session beans using session bean delegates

JDO Providing Container-Managed Persistence

As a side note, an EJB server may implement J2EE container-managed persistence (CMP) entity beans using JDO as the persistence layer. The J2EE components and the users of these components are unaware that JDO is used for the implementation of the persistence service.

CHAPTER 4
Defining Persistent Classes

A Java program consists of many different kinds of classes, including:

- Classes that model business objects
- Classes that serve as user interface objects
- Classes that provide various kinds of glue between different parts of the application
- System classes of various sorts

JDO focuses on the classes whose data has a corresponding representation in the underlying datastore: classes that represent business objects or classes that represent application-specific data that must remain persistent between application invocations.

These classes may represent data that comes from a single entity in the datastore, or they may represent data from several entities; JDO doesn't place any limitations on where the data comes from. For example, the data may come from:

- A single object in an object-oriented database
- A single row of a relational database
- The result of a relational database query, consisting of several rows
- The merging of several tables in a relational database
- The execution of a method from a data retrieval API that accesses an Enterprise Resource Planning (ERP) system

A JDO implementation maps data from its representation in the datastore to its representation in memory as a Java object, and vice versa. The mapping is based on metadata, which must be available both when the Java class is enhanced and at runtime. JDO does not standardize the mapping to a specific datastore.

Kinds of Classes and Instances

First, we must define some terms and provide some distinctions that are essential for understanding JDO. The term "object" often refers to either a class or an instance of a class, which can be confusing sometimes. Therefore, we will use the terms "instance" and "class" instead of "object," because it will be essential for you to understand which we are discussing.

Kinds of Classes

When using JDO, every class falls into one of the following two categories:

Persistent class
> A persistent class can have its instances stored in the datastore. To be persistent, a class must be specified in a metadata file and enhanced. The JDO specification refers to these as *persistence-capable* classes.

Transient class
> A transient class cannot have its instances stored in the datastore. Transient classes are not listed in a metadata file.

Furthermore, classes can be distinguished by their use of the JDO API:

JDO-aware class
> A JDO-aware class makes direct use of the JDO API. For example, it can perform a JDO query to retrieve instances from the datastore, or make specific instances persistent.

JDO-transparent class
> A JDO-transparent class does not make direct use of the JDO API.

Whether a class is JDO-aware or JDO-transparent is unrelated to whether it is persistent. For example, the persistent classes Movie, Actor, and Role that we introduced in Chapter 1 are JDO-transparent, because they never made an explicit call to the JDO API. On the other hand, the MediaManiaApp class is JDO-aware, because it uses the JDO API directly: it creates a PersistenceManager and uses it to execute transactions. MediaManiaApp is not persistent.

Kinds of Instances

JDO supports several kinds of instances. The names we introduce in this section are used throughout the book to refer to these different kinds of instances. In particular, we use specific terminology to differentiate a transient instance of a transient class from a transient instance of a persistent class. All JDO implementations support the first three kinds of instances listed here; the last two are optional:

Instance of a transient class
> All instances of a transient class are transient. For the most part, however, we focus on instances of persistent classes.

Transient instance
> A transient instance is an instance of a persistent class that is not associated with the datastore. It is simply an instance you create in your application that is never made persistent and is used independent of the datastore.

Persistent instance

A persistent instance is an instance of a persistent class whose behavior is linked to a transactional datastore. Its fields are watched by the JDO implementation and saved to or restored from the datastore, as appropriate. The datastore manages the state of its persistent fields and information identifying its class.

Transient transactional instance

A transient transactional instance is transient and is not represented in the datastore. But it is transactional, and its state is rolled back if a transactional rollback occurs. For JDO to manage a transient transactional instance, you need to enhance its class. Transient transactional instances are covered in Chapter 13.

Persistent nontransactional instance

A persistent-nontransactional instance is persistent, but it is not managed as part of a transaction. Persistent nontransactional instances are discussed in Chapter 14.

Table 4-1 illustrates these different kinds of instances, based on their persistence and transactional behavior.

Table 4-1. Kinds of instances

Behavior	Instance of a transient class	Transient instance	Persistent instance
Transactional		Transient transactional instance	Persistent instance
Nontransactional	Instance of a transient class	Transient instance	Persistent nontransactional instance

Java Classes and Metadata

You can make most of your classes persistent in a JDO environment. JDO has the ability to make *plain ordinary Java objects* (POJOs) persistent. This includes classes that represent the entities in your application domain, utility classes that model other data, and abstractions you need to support your application's functionality. Your classes can also use all of Java's class and field modifiers, including: private, public, protected, static, transient, abstract, final, synchronized, and volatile. In some cases, as we will explore later in this chapter, some of these modifiers cannot be used with persistent fields.

The persistent state of a persistent class is represented entirely by the values of its Java fields. If you have a class that has some state that needs to be preserved and it depends on inaccessible or remote objects (e.g., it extends java.net.SocketImpl or uses Java Native Interface (JNI)), you cannot make the class persistent. You also cannot have a persistent nonstatic inner class, because the state of the inner class instance depends on the state of its enclosing instance.

With a few exceptions, system-defined classes (those defined in java.lang, java.io, java.net, etc.) cannot be persistent. They are also not allowed to be the type of a persistent field. This includes classes such as System, Thread, Socket, and File. We list the system classes that are supported in Table 4-2 later in this chapter. You may be using an implementation that supports additional system-defined classes, especially those for modeling state information. Relying on support for these additional types will make your software dependent on that implementation.

As discussed in Chapter 1, each persistent class needs to have a no-arg constructor. If your class does not define any constructors, the Java compiler generates a no-arg constructor automatically (called the *default constructor*). But if you do define one or more constructors with arguments in a persistent class, then you must also define a no-arg constructor manually.

When your application first accesses a persistent instance, the JDO implementation needs to construct an instance, so it calls the no-arg constructor. The availability of a no-arg constructor is the only requirement JDO imposes on your persistent classes. Some JDO enhancers can generate this no-arg constructor for you if it does not already exist, but they are not required to do so.

You may not want other classes in your application calling the no-arg constructor. If this is the case, you can declare it to be private. Or, if the class will have subclasses, declare it to be protected so that the subclass constructors can call it.

JDO Metadata

Every class that you want to be persistent must be declared in a JDO metadata file. This file cannot include any system classes. Any class that is not declared in a metadata file is a transient class, except for the system classes that all implementations support. You typically place additional persistence-related information that is not expressable in Java in the metadata file. This metadata is used when a class is enhanced and also at runtime.

JDO metadata is stored in XML format. An XML Document Type Definition (DTD) defines the elements in a JDO metadata file. The JDO DTD is provided in Appendix B. It should be identical across all implementations.

Metadata filenames

You can place the metadata for your application's classes in one or more XML files. A few rules exist for the naming and directory placement of metadata files to assure portability among implementations. For portability, metadata files should be available via resources loaded by the same class loader as the persistent classes.

If you have a metadata file that contains information for a package or multiple packages, then the name of the XML file should be *package.jdo*. (Here we literally mean the word "package," not the name of an actual Java package.) The *package.jdo* file can be placed in one of the following directories:

META-INF
> In this case, *package.jdo* can contain metadata for any class in your application.

WEB-INF
> Files like *package.jdo* should be placed in this directory when deploying a JDO application in a web container.

(no directory)
> The *package.jdo* file is not in any subdirectory of the classpath.

<package>
> The *package.jdo* file is placed in the subdirectory that corresponds to the package defined in the metadata. Thus, if *package.jdo* contains the metadata for the com.mediamania.content package, it would placed in the *com/mediamania/content* directory.

If you have a metadata file that only contains information for a single class named *classname*, then its filename should be *classname.jdo* and it should reside in the same directory as the class file, based on the package of the class.

When the JDO implementation needs metadata for a class and the metadata has not been loaded yet, the metadata is searched in the following order:

1. *META-INF/package.jdo*
2. *WEB-INF/package.jdo*
3. *package.jdo*
4. *<package>/package.jdo*
5. *<package>/<class>.jdo*

where *<package>* represents the directory corresponding to the package of the class and *<class>* represents the name of the class.

A search for the metadata for the Customer class in the com.mediamania.store package is performed in the following order:

1. *META-INF/package.jdo*
2. *WEB-INF/package.jdo*
3. *package.jdo*
4. *com/package.jdo*
5. *com/mediamania/package.jdo*
6. *com/mediamania/store/package.jdo*
7. *com/mediamania/store/Customer.jdo*

If no metadata is found for the Customer class in any of these locations, it is considered a transient class.

Once the metadata for a class has been loaded, it is not replaced. Metadata contained in a file higher in the search order is used instead of metadata lower in the search order. This search order is optimized so that implementations can cache metadata as soon as it is encountered, reducing the number of file accesses that are needed to load the metadata.

Metadata that is not in its natural location may override metadata that is in its natural location. For example, when the JDO implementation searches for the metadata for com.mediamania.content.Movie, it may find the metadata for the com.mediamania. store.Rental class in the *com/mediamania/package.jdo* file. In this case, a subsequent search for the metadata for com.mediamania.store.Rental will use the metadata that has already been cached, instead of looking in *com/mediamania/store/package.jdo* or *com/mediamania/store/Rental.jdo*.

These rules for the name and location of the metadata files apply both during enhancement and at runtime. From now on, the term "metadata" refers to the aggregate of all the JDO metadata for all packages and classes, regardless of their physical packaging in multiple files and directory placement.

jdo, package, and class metadata elements

The jdo element is the highest-level XML element in the metadata hierarchy. It does not have any attributes of its own. It contains one or more nested package elements. A package element is used to represent a specific Java package. It has a single required attribute, called name, that contains the completely qualified name of the Java package.

Within a package element, you can nest one or more class elements. A class element identifies a specific Java class in the enclosing package as persistent. The class element's only required attribute is name, which is given the name of the class. You should only list classes in the metadata that you want to be persistent.

The class element has the following additional optional attributes:

- identity-type
- objectid-class
- requires-extent
- persistence-capable-superclass

The identity-type attribute indicates which type of identity should be used with the class. It defaults to datastore identity, which does not require any additional effort from you. The objectid-class attribute identifies a class defined by the application to serve as the application identity of the class. Chapter 10 covers the various forms of identity in detail; until then, we will use datastore identity in all of our examples. The requires-extent attribute indicates whether an extent is maintained for the class. Extents are covered in Chapter 8. The `persistence-capable-superclass` attribute identifies the closest superclass in the inheritance hierarchy that is persistent, if there is one.

Vendor extensions

The extension element specifies vendor-specific metadata extensions in a uniform manner. All JDO metadata elements can have nested extension elements. The required vendor-name attribute associates the extension with a specific vendor. Each vendor uses a unique name to identify metadata extensions for their implementation. The vendor name "JDORI" is reserved for use with the JDO reference implementation. A JDO implementation ignores any extension elements that have a vendor-name value that does not correspond to their implementation. The extension element also has optional key and value attributes. A key may or may not have an associated value. The vendor chooses values for these attributes that they recognize and interpret. Consult your documentation to see what metadata extensions are provided.

Nesting of metadata elements

The following illustrates the hierarchical nesting of metadata elements:

```
jdo
    package
        class
            field
                collection
                    extension
                extension
            field
                map
                    extension
            field
                array
                    extension
            extension
        extension
    extension
    extension
```

One or more extension elements can be nested within each of these elements (including extension itself) to provide vendor-specific information. The field metadata elements (field, collection, map, and array) are covered later in this chapter.

Inheritance

Each class in an inheritance hierarchy can be transient or persistent, independent of the persistence of other classes in the hierarchy. Thus, a class can be persistent, even if its superclass is not. This allows you have a persistent class that extends a transient class that was not designed to be persistent. Likewise, a subclass of a persistent class may be transient or persistent.

If a persistent class has one or more persistent superclasses, the class element's persistence-capable-superclass attribute must identify the most immediate persistent superclass. If the superclass is in a different package, it must be specified with its fully qualified name. If the superclass is in the same package, you can omit the package qualifier. You may wonder why you need to specify this in the metadata. After all, the Java class declarations specify the branch of superclasses from a class up to Object in an inheritance hierarchy, and your metadata identifies which of these classes are persistent. But the metadata for a superclass may be specified in a different metadata file. JDO is designed such that the enhancer can enhance a class in a stateless fashion, independent from other classes. The order in which classes are enhanced is irrelevant, and a class can be enhanced without the presence of any other classes. This greatly supports the simplicity of enhancer design, ease of use, integration with classloaders, and—last, but not least—easy reproducability of errors.

To illustrate these concepts, the UML diagram in Figure 4-1 describes two inheritance hierarchies. We use the stereotyping facility in UML to indicate whether a class is persistent or transient. In practice, you are not likely to have an inheritance hierarchy with such a complicated mix of persistent and transient classes. In many cases, the classes in an inheritance hierarchy are either all transient or all persistent. But JDO provides you with the flexibility to choose whether each class in an inheritance hierarchy is transient or persistent, as we have demonstrated here.

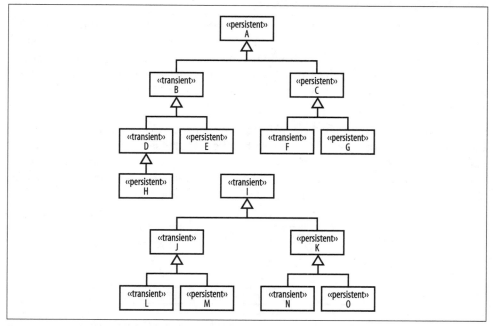

Figure 4-1. Persistence within an inheritance hierarchy

The following metadata identifies the persistent superclass for each persistent class shown in Figure 4-1. This metadata is placed in the *com/mediamania/inheritexample/ package.jdo* file.

```xml
<?xml version="1.0" encoding="UTF-8" ?>
<!DOCTYPE jdo PUBLIC
    "-//Sun Microsystems, Inc.//DTD Java Data Objects Metadata 1.0//EN"
    "http://java.sun.com/dtd/jdo_1_0.dtd">
<jdo>
    <package name="com.mediamania.inheritexample" >
        <class name="A" />
        <class name="C"
                persistence-capable-superclass="A"/>
        <class name="E"
                persistence-capable-superclass="A"/>
        <class name="G"
                persistence-capable-superclass="C"/>
        <class name="H"
                persistence-capable-superclass="A"/>
        <class name="K" />
        <class name="M" />
        <class name="O"
                persistence-capable-superclass="K"/>
    </package>
</jdo>
```

The Media Mania Object Model

Let's examine the object model we use in most of the examples throughout this book. Media Mania, Inc. provides a system in their stores that contains information about the various forms of media that customers can rent or purchase. In Chapter 1 we created a prototype application contained in com.mediamania.prototype. Now, we replace this prototype with two new packages: com.mediamania.content and com.mediamania.store.

The com.mediamania.content Java package contains classes that represent generic media content information. The content handled by the stores includes movies and games. The Movie and Game classes extend an abstract base class called MediaContent. The Studio class contains information about the studio that produced the game or movie. Figure 4-2 illustrates the relationships among these classes.

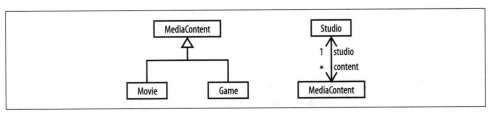

Figure 4-2. Studio and MediaContent classes in com.mediamania.content package

Each person involved in a movie, as either the director or an actor, is represented by an instance of `MediaPerson`. Figure 4-3 illustrates the relationships among `Movie` and `MediaPerson` instances.

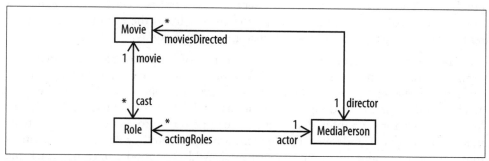

Figure 4-3. Movie, Role, and MediaPerson classes in com.mediamania.content package

A `Movie` instance has one or more `Role` instances representing the cast of the movie. It also has a reference to the `MediaPerson` for the director of the movie. We assume a movie has a single director (though in real life this is not always the case). The `Role` class references its `Movie` and a `MediaPerson` who served as the actor for the particular role. Given a specific `MediaPerson` instance, it is possible to access all the movies they directed and all the roles they have played in a movie. This model also allows for an actor who has played multiple roles in the same movie.

In addition to the media content information, each store tracks the rental and purchase activities of its customers. The `com.mediamania.store` package contains the classes representing store-specific information. Figure 4-4 illustrates the relationships among these classes.

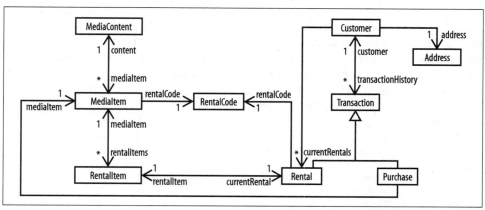

Figure 4-4. Classes in the com.mediamania.store package (except MediaContent in the content package)

Each customer that has rented or purchased some media content at the store is represented by an instance of the Customer class. An Address instance contains address information for the customer. The store tracks two kinds of transactions: rentals and purchases. These are represented by Rental and Purchase classes that extend a Transaction base class. The store tracks the current items the customer has out for rent and also keeps a history of all the customer's transactions.

A MediaItem instance represents a particular format of a given MediaContent item. For example, a Movie can exist in VHS and DVD formats and a Game may be supported in formats for the Playstation, Playstation 2, Xbox, and Nintendo GameCube. The stock of media items is designated as items to be sold or rented. A RentalItem instance exists for each individual item that can be rented to a customer. The items in stock that are currently available for rent are represented by RentalItem instances that have a null value for their currentRental field. The model does not track the individual items that are sold, but the MediaItem class tracks how many items for purchase are in stock and how many have been sold year-to-date. Each Purchase instance contains a reference to the specific MediaItem that the customer bought.

The store has different rental policies and prices, based on the popularity of an item and how recently it became available. A RentalCode instance maintains information about a particular rental policy. Each MediaItem instance is associated with a particular RentalCode, which may change over time.

A Rental instance represents a customer's rental of a particular media item; it references the specific RentalItem rented. This is necessary so the store can track which item has been rented and update the customer account when it is returned, taking into account any late fees that may be due. The RentalCode associated with the MediaItem at the time of rental is associated with the Rental instance. This is necessary because the RentalCode for a MediaItem will change occasionally.

Appendix E provides all the classes for the model. The following metadata specifies the packages and persistent classes for the object model. Since it contains metadata information for the com.mediamania.content and com.mediamania.store packages, we place the metadata in a file named *com/mediamania/package.jdo*, based on their common base package name.

```
<?xml version="1.0" encoding="UTF-8" ?>
<!DOCTYPE jdo PUBLIC
    "-//Sun Microsystems, Inc.//DTD Java Data Objects Metadata 1.0//EN"
    "http://java.sun.com/dtd/jdo_1_0.dtd">
<jdo>
    <package name="com.mediamania.content" >
        <class name="Studio" >
        </class>
        <class name="MediaContent" />
        <class name="Movie"
          persistence-capable-superclass="MediaContent">
        </class>
```

```
            <class name="MediaPerson" >
            </class>
            <class name="Game" />
            <class name="Role" />
        </package>
        <package name="com.mediamania.store" >
            <class name="MediaItem" >
            </class>
            <class name="RentalItem"/>
            <class name="Customer" >
            </class>
            <class name="Address" />
            <class name="Transaction" />
            <class name="Purchase"
               persistence-capable-superclass="Transaction"/>
            <class name="Rental"
               persistence-capable-superclass="Transaction"/>
            <class name="RentalCode" />
        </package>
    </jdo>
```

The metadata lists each persistent class in the content and store packages. If an inheritance relationship exists, the metadata specifies the persistent superclass. Later in this chapter, we will add more information that provides information about the fields and relationships.

Fields

Fields contain the state of an instance. JDO provides for the access, management, and storage of an instance's fields in a datastore. All of Java's field type categories are supported: primitive types, reference types, and interface types. JDO also supports all of Java's field modifiers, including private, public, protected, static, transient, final, and volatile. But static and final fields cannot be persistent, as we will discuss later in this chapter.

As we explained earlier, you can have both transient and persistent instances of a persistent class. The individual fields of a persistent class can also be transient or persistent for all of the class's persistent instances. A field's type and modifiers determine whether it is persistent or transient, by default. You can override the default persistence of a field in the metadata. We cover transient fields later in this chapter.

You can specify persistence-related information about a field by using the field metadata element. Its required name attribute should have the name of the field in the Java class declaration. It has attributes to control the field's persistence and the type of its elements if it is a collection. We cover these attributes later in this chapter. If the class uses application identity, one or more fields need to indicate they are a primary-key field; Chapter 10 covers this in detail. Chapter 12 addresses advanced field-management facilities enabled by the remaining field element attributes.

You do not need to provide metadata for every field in a class. Default values are assumed for any fields that lack metadata declarations. These default values usually provide the behavior that you need. So, in many circumstances, you do not need to provide field metadata.

Supported Types

You cannot make many system-defined classes persistent, nor can you have a field of a system-defined class. Table 4-2 lists the system-defined types in the Java language environment that JDO implementations do support.

Table 4-2 . Supported field types

Primitives	java.lang	java.util	java.math
boolean	Boolean	Locale	BigInteger
byte	Byte	Date	BigDecimal
short	Short	HashSet	
char	Character	Collection	
int	Integer	Set	
long	Long		
float	Float		
double	Double		
	String		
	Number		
	Object		

You can declare a field to refer to a persistent class instance. In addition, you can use Java's polymorphism to declare a field that refers to a base class and have it reference a subclass instance. You should be accustomed to using polymorphic references in your object models. Object databases have supported them for many years, but this modeling capability has not been available in relational database schemas and interfaces. The JDO implementation is responsible for implementing such polymorphic references on top of the underlying datastore, including a relational datastore. If a field is declared to be a reference to a transient class, and you assign a reference to an instance of a subclass that is persistent, the instance is not stored, because the field's declared type is not persistent.

You can use fields of Object and interface types. You can assign a reference to an instance of any class to an Object field, and an instance of any class implementing an interface can be assigned to an interface. You can also use interface inheritance in your model. Interface fields are transient by default, so you need to declare the field persistent explicitly in your metadata. We recommend you assign only instances of types supported by JDO to Object and interface fields. If an implementation restricts the type of instance that can be assigned to such a field, it will throw a ClassCastException when an incorrect assignment is made.

Collections

You can use a collection to represent multiple values of a given type or to represent *to-many relationships* among classes in an object model. Table 4-3 lists the `Collection` and `Set` collection interfaces and the `HashSet` collection class from the `java.util` package that are available in all JDO implementations. Additional collection classes that are optional in JDO are listed with their associated option property name. If an implementation supports the collection, it will return the collection's associated property string when you call `PersistenceManagerFactory.supportedOptions()`.

Table 4-3. Collection interfaces and classes

Interface in the java.util package	Class implementing the interface in the java.util package	JDO option property
Collection		portable (all implementations)
Set		portable (all implementations)
	HashSet	portable (all implementations)
	Hashtable	javax.jdo.option.Hashtable
	TreeSet	javax.jdo.option.TreeSet
List		javax.jdo.option.List
	ArrayList	javax.jdo.option.ArrayList
	LinkedList	javax.jdo.option.LinkedList
	Vector	javax.jdo.option.Vector
Map		javax.jdo.option.Map
	HashMap	javax.jdo.option.HashMap
	TreeMap	javax.jdo.option.TreeMap

You use a `collection` element to specify a collection's characteristics in the metadata. By default, collection-typed fields are persistent with an `Object` element type. You use the `collection` element's `element-type` attribute to specify the collection's element type. Specifying the element type is not required, but we recommend you specify it. The type name you specify uses Java's rules for naming: if no package is provided in the name, the package is assumed to be the same package as the enclosing persistent class in the metadata. Inner classes are identified with the $ marker. At some point, the Java language may allow you to specify a collection's element type directly when you declare the collection in your Java code, in which case this metadata will no longer be necessary.

A `Map` maintains a set of key-value pairs; both the key and value have a type. You use a `map` element to specify the characteristics of map's keys and values in the metadata. By default, map-typed fields are persistent and their key and value types are `Object`. You can use the `map` element's `key-type` and `value-type` attributes to specify a more specific type. As with collections, Java's rules for naming apply if the package is not provided, and inner classes can be identified with the $ marker.

We encourage you to specify the types of collection elements and the keys and values of Maps. Some implementations use a far less efficient means of accessing the elements if you do not specify the type.

Arrays

Array fields are optional in JDO. The JDO javax.jdo.option.Array option property indicates whether an implementation supports them. You should not share a specific array among several persistent instances. The JDO specification does not state whether multidimensional arrays are supported. Support for multidimensional arrays varies among implementations.

Persistence of Fields

A field's type and modifiers in a Java class declaration determine whether it is persistent by default. You can also override the default persistence of a field by declaring it as persistent or transient in the metadata.

Some fields cannot be persistent. A field declared in Java to be static or final is always transient. A static field has only one value; the field is associated with the class itself and shared by all instances. A final field has one value per instance. But a final field is initialized once by the constructor and its value can never be changed once the instance is constructed. Each constructor may initialize a final field differently. JDO implementations call the no-arg constructor to create an instance you access from the datastore. The field values from the datastore are set after the no-arg constructor is called. Thus, it is not possible for the JDO implementation to manage a final field's persistent state in memory.

Fields of the following types are persistent by default:

- Any type identified in Table 4-2 or Table 4-3 (except for Object)
- References to instances of persistent classes

Fields of the following types are transient by default:

- References to transient application classes
- References to system classes defined in JDK packages (unless supported in JDO)
- Interface references
- Object references

Though interface and Object references are transient by default, you can still declare them to be persistent in the metadata.

Controlling field persistence with metadata

Java's transient modifier is used to specify whether a field and the object graph it may reference should be serialized. By default, a field declared transient in a Java class declaration is transient from a JDO perspective, but you can override this in the metadata. You can use the `field` element's `persistence-modifier` attribute to specify whether a field is persistent, by giving it one of the following values:

`"persistent"`
> The field is persistent.

`"none"`
> The field is transient.

`"transactional"`
> The field is a transactional field, which is a transient field that has transactional behavior. Chapter 12 covers transactional fields.

So, a transient field in Java (specified via the `transient` modifier in the Java class declaration) is distinct from a transient field in JDO. If you declare a field in a Java class declaration with the `transient` modifier, it can be transient or persistent in JDO; and if a field does not have the Java `transient` modifier, it can also be transient or persistent, depending on the field's `persistence-modifier` attribute. If you do not specify the `persistence-modifier` attribute in the metadata, its default value is based on the field's type and modifiers, as defined in the Java class declaration.

There is no restriction on the type of a transient field. Transient fields are managed entirely by the application, not by the JDO implementation. A JDO implementation calls the no-arg constructor to instantiate an instance when the application accesses it from the datastore. You can define the default constructor to initialize transient and final fields. The `InstanceCallbacks` interface can also be used to manage the state of transient fields; this is covered in Chapter 12.

Persistent and transactional fields are also referred to as *managed fields*, since the JDO implementation manages their state. Figure 4-5 illustrates which kinds of fields are managed and which are transient.

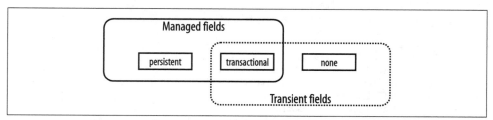

Figure 4-5. Managed and transient fields

Inherited fields

A class's metadata cannot specify characteristics for any field it inherits from a superclass, so a subclass cannot alter the persistence of an inherited field. Therefore, a field identified as persistent by the class's metadata is persistent in all subclasses; if it is transactional, it is transactional in all subclasses, and if it is transient, it is transient in all subclasses.

Consider class E, contained in the inheritance hierarchy depicted in Figure 4-1. E is a persistent class that extends the transient class B. B extends the persistent class A. For any instance of B, E, or any class extending E, the fields of B are transient, and you cannot make them persistent in the metadata unless you make B a persistent class.

Of course, you can declare a class with a field that has the same name as a field in a superclass. Even though the field name is the same, these are two different fields. Therefore, you can have different values for their persistence-modifier attribute.

Complete Metadata for the Media Mania Model

Now we can present the complete metadata for our Media Mania model, including the additional metadata we have covered:

```xml
<?xml version="1.0" encoding="UTF-8" ?>
<!DOCTYPE jdo PUBLIC
    "-//Sun Microsystems, Inc.//DTD Java Data Objects Metadata 1.0//EN"
    "http://java.sun.com/dtd/jdo_1_0.dtd">
<jdo>
    <package name="com.mediamania.content" >
        <class name="Studio" >
            <field name="content" >
                <collection element-type="MediaContent"/>
            </field>
        </class>
        <class name="MediaContent" >
            <field name="mediaItems" >
                <collection element-type="com.mediamania.store.MediaItems"/>
            </field>
        </class>
        <class name="Movie"
          persistence-capable-superclass="MediaContent">
            <field name="cast" >
                <collection element-type="Role"/>
            </field>
        </class>
        <class name="MediaPerson" >
            <field name="actingRoles" >
                <collection element-type="Role"/>
            </field>
            <field name="moviesDirected" >
                <collection element-type="Movie"/>
            </field>
        </class>
        <class name="Game"
          persistence-capable-superclass="MediaContent" />
        <class name="Role" />
    </package>
    <package name="com.mediamania.store" >
        <class name="MediaItem" >
```

```
                    <field name="rentalItems">
                        <collection element-type="RentalItem"/>
                    </field>
                </class>
                <class name="RentalItem"/>
                <class name="Customer" >
                    <field name="currentRentals">
                        <collection element-type="Rental"/>
                    </field>
                    <field name="transactionHistory">
                        <collection element-type="Transaction"/>
                    </field>
                </class>
                <class name="Address" />
                <class name="Transaction" />
                <class name="Purchase"
                  persistence-capable-superclass="Transaction"/>
                <class name="Rental"
                  persistence-capable-superclass="Transaction"/>
                <class name="RentalCode" />
            </package>
        </jdo>
```

We specified each collection's element type in the model. The mediaItems field in MediaContent is the only collection whose element type is a class in a different package, so we specified the full package name.

CHAPTER 5
Datastore Mappings

JDO supports the storage of your object model in a variety of datastore architectures. The primary datastore architectures envisioned for use with JDO are:

Relational database

> Organized as a set of tables, each containing a set of rows and columns. A column can store values of a particular atomic type. Each table cell in a particular row and column stores a value of the column's type. The value stored can be a null value. Instances are identified uniquely by the value of *primary-key columns*. Relationships are defined, and may be enforced, by annotating specific columns as foreign keys that reference columns in a table.

Pure object database

> An extension of the JVM object model. Domain objects are stored with their primitive fields, just as instances are stored in the JVM. Instances are identified by a system-generated unique identifier. References are stored as objects, including instances of system-defined classes. Unreferenced instances are garbage collected. An extent is not an intrinsic construct in a pure object database; it is implemented as a class containing a set of objects. In this model, any reference type can be shared among multiple objects, and changes made to the instance of the reference type are visible to all objects that reference it.

Hybrid object database

> Organized as a set of class extents, each containing a set of instances in which primitive and complex fields are stored. Domain objects are stored with their primitive fields; some complex field types (e.g., collections of primitive types and reference types) are also stored with the domain object. Instances are identified by a system-generated unique identifier. Unreferenced instances must be deleted explicitly.

Application Programming Interface (API)

> Defined by an API to an abstract domain model. The API defines methods to create, read, update, and delete abstract domain instances. The underlying datastore implementation is completely hidden by the API. Many complex system products use this type of architecture.

The JDO 1.0.1 Specification does not specify a standard for mapping to specific datastores. JDO implementations support one or more datastores and often provide a means for you to direct the mapping process by specifying additional, vendor-specific metadata. These mapping directives can be placed in the JDO metadata files or in an implementation-specific location. Some vendors allow you to specify the mapping via a graphical environment that depicts the Java and datastore models, allowing you to associate items in the two models to define a mapping. Regardless of where this vendor-specific mapping information is placed, it does not affect your Java source code.

Current JDO implementations provide support for relational databases, as well as pure and hybrid object databases. As JDO implementations become available for other database architectures, other mapping facilities will likely be considered. For example, there are databases based on the XML data model. Mappings might soon be defined between the XML database and a set of Java classes. Such an interface would likely be based on the Java Architecture for XML Binding (JAXB) standard.

SQL is the dominant relational language in use. Today, most Java applications access a relational database through Java Database Connectivity (JDBC), which provides an interface for Java applications to issue SQL commands to a relational database. Since a relational database uses the relational data model, which is different from Java's object model, a mapping is required between the modeling constructs of Java and the relational database.

Since relational databases are prevalent, and because most people are familiar with the relational data model, we will focus on the mapping strategies and approaches employed when JDO is used with a relational database. However, much of the discussion is fairly generic and can apply to other database architectures.

Mapping Approaches

Several approaches can be used to establish a mapping between your persistent Java classes and a relational schema:

Generate a relational schema from your persistent Java classes
> If you are developing a new application in Java and you do not have an existing relational database schema, you can let the JDO implementation generate a relational schema from your object model. This approach is commonly called *forward engineering* the model. This approach yields a high level of development productivity because all of the schema design and mapping work is done automatically by the JDO implementation. The JDO specification does not require support for the automatic generation of a schema. Some implementations do not support this approach and require you to define the mapping to an existing schema. Many of the implementations that do support schema generation let you specify some metadata to help direct the algorithms generating the schema.

Generate your persistent Java classes from a relational schema

In many cases, you may already be using a relational database schema and you would like to write a new application with an object view of the data. In this scenario, many implementations provide tools you can use that analyze your relational schema and generate a Java object model for you. This approach lets you develop an object-oriented Java application quickly. It is commonly called *reverse-engineering* the model.

Define a mapping between Java classes and a relational schema

You may have an existing relational schema and a separately designed object model and you would like to define a mapping between the two. In this case, you can use metadata directives to define how a class and its fields should be mapped to the underlying datastore. This approach is commonly called a *bridge mapping* between the two models.

If you are using JDO with a relational database, JDO does not preclude you from having some applications access the datastore with JDBC and others access it with JDO. This capability allows you to migrate to JDO gradually from a suite of JDBC-based applications. If you have an existing relational schema, you will likely use reverse-engineering or a bridge mapping. If you access the relational database with JDO and JDBC, it becomes more important to understand how the object model is mapped to the relational schema and follow any rules the implementation may have about accessing the additional columns and tables it requires.

Once you have developed a JDO application with an object model and associated datastore, the object model and the datastore schema will likely evolve as the needs of your application evolve. The JDO metadata can be used to deal with this evolution of the two data models. JDO does not define any specific support for datastore-schema evolution, object-model evolution, or the associated aspects of evolving the two distinct data models. Support for these is implementation-specific.

Relational Modeling Constructs

Before we discuss the mapping between Java classes and a relational schema, we will first provide a brief summary of the modeling constructs found in relational schemas. This is not meant to cover all aspects of a relational schema; it will simply define the terms we use in this chapter.

A relational schema is organized as a set of *tables*. A table is usually defined for each entity in the application domain you are modeling. When you design an object model, an entity is represented by a class. Each table consists of rows and columns. A *row* contains the data for a specific instance of an entity being modeled. A *column* contains the values for one of the attributes of the entity. A table *cell* is the intersection of a particular row and column in the table, and it contains the value of an attribute for a specific entity instance.

The type of a column is the same for all rows of a table. Relational databases do not support Java's capability for a field to reference one of many different types. ANSI SQL 92 defines a standard set of supported column datatypes. Relational database products support these standard datatypes and usually support their own additional, proprietary datatypes. One issue developers often contend with is the use of a datatype that is specific to one database product but not supported by another. JDO helps insulate your applications from these datatype differences, since you only deal with Java types, which are then mapped to the various underlying datastore types.

Often, one or more columns are defined as the table's *primary key* to identify a row uniquely. A table can have only one primary-key constraint. The primary-key constraint requires that the columns have a unique value for each row, and the primary-key columns cannot contain a null value.

One or more columns in a table may be defined as a *foreign-key* constraint, which is used to enforce *referential integrity* in the datastore. A row's foreign-key columns contain the same values as columns in a specific row of the referenced table.

A relationship between the rows of tables can be coerced by specifying a *join condition*, which is an expression that uses the columns of the tables being joined. Primary-key and foreign-key constraints can be used to define relationships between tables, and, they can be used as the basis of a join. To establish a relationship between table A and B, where table B has a foreign key referencing table A, a join condition requires that the foreign key in B is equal to the primary key in A. This is the primary means of expressing a relationship between rows, so relational databases have optimized their performance of these join conditions using indexes. But it is not necessary to use columns in primary- and foreign-key constraints to perform a join; any columns in the tables may be used to establish an association among tables.

A table may have one or more *indexes*, associated with one or more columns. Indexes are used to optimize the performance of access to rows with specific values or a range of values for one or more columns. Indexes help optimize the performance of join operations.

SQL 99

The SQL 99 specification includes some support for defining object constructs in SQL. It has introduced the notion of *table inheritance*: a table can have subtables. In addition, a column can contain structured datatypes, such as arrays and User-Defined Types (UDTs). You can also define inheritance hierarchies of UDTs.

At this time, the level of support for SQL 99 varies considerably among relational databases. Some databases do not support any of the constructs defined in SQL 99. Others have implemented only a subset of its facilities, sometimes with nonstandard syntax.

Many applications do not use the object capabilities found in those databases that do support them. Many developers defining objects in languages like Java prefer to specify their object model once in Java and then use an interface like JDO to map their Java modeling constructs to the underlying datastore. As the relational database vendors broaden their support for SQL 99 object constructs, JDO implementations will be able to map the Java models onto the SQL 99 constructs, based on customer demand. The examples in this book do not assume the availability of SQL 99 facilities.

Modeling Constructs in Java and Relational Models

The Java object model and the relational data model are two separate and distinct data models with separate type systems and approaches for representing data and expression computations. Table 5-1 summarizes the typical data-specific mappings that are specified between an object model and a relational schema.

Table 5-1. Mapping between object models and relational schemas

Java modeling construct	Relational modeling construct
Class	Table
Field	Column
Instance	Row
Identity	Primary key
Reference	Foreign key
Interface	No relational equivalent
Collection	No relational equivalent
Class inheritance	One or multiple tables

Collections in JDO can be represented only as memory instances, with no direct representation as a collection in the datastore. They are instantiated on demand and discarded when they are no longer needed. There are exceptions to these general rules, and some implementations support more advanced mappings. This chapter examines several ways of representing a Java collection in a relational datastore.

If you start with a set of Java classes and let the JDO implementation generate a relational schema for them, it will choose an appropriate relational representation of your Java model and define the mapping between your classes and the relational tables. The implementation will make a number of relational schema design decisions, including choosing names for tables and columns, column types for your Java fields, and how collections and relationships in your model are represented. It may provide graphical tools or metadata extensions that you can use to help direct its schema generation and relational mapping process.

It is beneficial to understand the various mapping decisions that are made. This will allow you to assess the flexibility that various JDO implementations offer and determine which ones will integrate more easily into your current environment. We don't describe specific vendor capabilities in this book, because more JDO implementations are becoming available and each vendor's capabilities are also broadening. Vendor-specific descriptions would soon be out-of-date.

The following sections describe the various relational mapping situations and how implementations typically address them.

Mapping Classes to Tables

If your object model does not use inheritance, you usually have a separate relational table for each class. We cover the mapping of classes in an inheritance hierarchy later in this chapter. To establish a mapping from a Java class to a specific table, in most JDO implementations you specify the mapping in your JDO metadata with an extension element nested within the class element. For example, the following example illustrates the metadata necessary to map the MediaItem class to a table called Items:

```
<class name="MediaItem" >
    <field name="rentalItems">
        <collection element-type="RentalItem"/>
    </field>
    <extension vendor-name="vendorX" key="table" value="Items" />
    <extension vendor-name="vendorY" key="sqlname" value="Items" />
</class>
```

You identify the implementation you are using in the vendor-name attribute. As we mentioned previously, the datastore mappings in JDO 1.0.1 are implementation-specific. This may be standardized in JDO 2.0. Each JDO vendor provides documentation explaining which value to use for the vendor-name attribute and which values are supported for the key attribute.

In the previous code, we provided the metadata for two vendors, identified as vendorX and vendorY. An implementation will use only metadata extensions that it recognizes. This allows you to place the metadata for multiple vendors in the same JDO metadata file. vendorX uses a value of "table" for the key attribute to indicate which relational table the MediaItem class should be mapped to, and vendorY uses the value "sqlname". You should check the implementation's documentation to see which values they require. We provide the name of the table (Items) in the relational schema in the value attribute. If you were to port your application to another JDO implementation, you would need to add an extension element that has values in the vendor-name and key attributes that are appropriate for that implementation. However, your Java class would not have to change.

If you don't specify a table for a class, most implementations assume that you would like them to generate the table name for you. You may or may not like the name that they use. If you are just prototyping your application and do not have an existing schema to map to, it can be more productive to just let the implementation generate any name. Once you move beyond the prototype stage of your project, you can always add this metadata to specify a specific name for the table.

You may wish to partition the fields of your class across multiple tables. Not all relational JDO implementations support this capability. To partition the fields of a class among several tables, you need to specify which table (and column) each field should be mapped to. An extension that is similar, or identical, to the one provided earlier would be placed in the field element instead of the class element.

If you use optimistic transactions, the JDO implementation requires either a version-number column or a list of columns whose values are used to detect concurrency violations. These track whether another transaction has performed a concurrent update on an instance. Another approach is to have a timestamp field that is updated whenever a row changes. Chapter 15 covers optimistic transactions and how they are implemented. Most implementations allow you to specify the name of the version column. If you don't specify the column name, the implementation uses a default column name.

Mapping a Single-Valued Field to a Column

A primitive or single-valued Java field usually is mapped to a single column of a table. Some implementations allow a field to be mapped to multiple columns, but such a feature is not supported by most implementations or needed in most applications. When mapping a Java field to a relational column, you need to consider the name and the type to be used for the associated column. The types are always different, since Java and SQL have their own distinct type systems. The name of the field and column can be either the same or different.

Name-Mapping

When you're mapping a field in Java to a relational column, you can use different names. In some cases, you may have to use a different name, because some names in Java may not be allowable as a column name in the relational database. In Java, class and field names are case-sensitive Unicode characters. Some relational databases and JDBC drivers may have restrictions on the names that are used (e.g., the table and column names must be US ASCII, names are case-insensitive, or names must be uppercase). Using a field or class name that is a keyword in SQL or the relational database also necessitates a mapping to a different name in the datastore.

You may wish to map the firstName field of the Customer class to a column named fname:

```
<class name="Customer" >
  <field name="firstName" >
    <extension vendor-name="vendorX" key="column" value="fname"/>
    <extension vendor-name="vendorY" key="sqlname" value="fname"/>
  </field>
</class>
```

If the firstName field does not already have a field element, you need to add one to specify the column name in a nested extension element. In this case, to specify the column to map the field to, vendorX uses a value of "column" and vendorY uses a value of "sqlname" for the key attribute. Again, the value for the key attribute is implementation-specific and you can provide extension elements for multiple implementations without any interference.

Type-Mapping

Besides specifying the name of the column, you may also want to indicate the column's datatype. The datatypes that can be used for a specific Java type vary across relational datastores and JDO implementations. The supported column types for each Java datatype in each underlying datastore should be specified in your JDO implementation's documentation. Table 5-2 provides a list of the relational column datatypes commonly supported for the Java types supported by JDO.

Table 5-2. Java types and corresponding column types found in relational databases

Java type	Column datatypes
Boolean, boolean	BIT, TINYINT, SMALLINT, BYTE, INT2
Byte, byte	TINYINT, SMALLINT, BYTE, INT2
Character, char	INTEGER, CHAR, VARCHAR
Short, short	SMALLINT, INTEGER, NUMBER, INT2
Integer, int	INTEGER, NUMBER, INT4
Long, long	BIGINT, DECIMAL, INT8
Float, float	FLOAT, DECIMAL, REAL
Double, double	DOUBLE, NUMBER, DECIMAL
BigInteger	DECIMAL, NUMBER, NUMERIC, BIGINT
BigDecimal	DECIMAL, NUMBER, DOUBLE
String	CHAR, VARCHAR, VARCHAR2, LONGVARCHAR, CLOB
Date	TIMESTAMP, DATE, DATETIME
Locale	VARCHAR

ANSI SQL defines some of these column types. Others are supported by specific relational databases and found in applications' schemas. Some implementations allow you to specify the maximum size of a String stored in the datastore.

BLOBs

You may be using JDO with an existing relational schema that has a column defined as a binary large object (BLOB) and wonder how JDO deals with them. The short answer is that the JDO 1.0.1 Specification does not directly specify the mapping for any datastore-specific datatype. Your JDO implementation defines the mappings it supports from Java types to the datatypes of the underlying datastore.

You should ask yourself what kind of data the BLOB contains and why it is being stored as a BLOB. In some circumstances, a BLOB contains structured data that may be more appropriately and easily represented as persistent objects in JDO. Sometimes BLOBs are used as a denormalizing technique to simplify the modeling and access of a complex graph of data. In other cases, BLOBs and denormalization are used as an optimization technique because a normalized representation of the data cannot be efficiently accessed.

The best approach for dealing with data commonly found in a BLOB depends on the kind of data involved and how effective your JDO implementation and datastore are in dealing with the data.

Indexes

JDO does not define the concept of an index. Indexes can be added to columns independent of the JDO environment. However, some implementations may allow you to specify indexes in the metadata, allowing you to provide the index information relative to the fields in your Java classes. An index on a single field is usually specified as a nested extension of a field element. If the index includes more than one column, it will likely be specified with an extension of the class element, so that you can specify the order of the fields in the index.

Identity

An instance is identified uniquely in the datastore via an identity value. JDO has two durable types of identity: datastore and application. With both types, the identity value is stored in one or more columns of the class's table. Those columns become the table's primary key.

For example, we use datastore identity for the Movie class defined in the com. mediamania.content package. The JDO implementation may represent datastore identity as an INTEGER in the relational schema. Line ❶ of Example 5-1 illustrates the use of the oid column to store the datastore identity value for the Movie table, which is defined as the table's primary key on line ❷.

Example 5-1. Datastore identity stored in a primary-key column

```
CREATE TABLE Movie (
❶    oid          INTEGER,
     title        VARCHAR(24),
     rating       CHAR(4),
     genres       CHAR(16),
❷    PRIMARY KEY(oid)
)
```

Each implementation has its own default name for this column, but you can usually specify the name that should be used.

You may have a table with no primary key defined, but instead have a unique index defined for one or more columns. With either a primary key or a unique index, the associated columns are used for storing the identity value. If you use a unique index for a JDO identity, none of the columns in the index can have a null value.

With datastore identity, either the JDO implementation or the datastore itself provides a unique identity value for each instance. The datastore identity value is separate from the fields you define in your class. The representation of the datastore identity is managed entirely by the JDO implementation.

Some databases automatically generate primary keys when rows are inserted into a table. These columns typically use a special *sequence* type. Essentially, they are read-only columns whose values cannot be changed when they are under application control. Some JDO implementations may allow you to map datastore identity to use these columns.

With application identity, you specify one or more Java fields in a class to be the *primary-key fields*. These fields are mapped onto the columns that serve as the primary key of the class's table. When using application identity you must specify which fields in the class are primary-key fields and define an application-identity class.

Chapter 10 covers identity in detail, but feel free to examine this chapter if you would like more on this now. An understanding of identity does not require any material in the intervening chapters. If you are trying to implement a JDO application as you read this book, and you are using an existing relational database schema that has defined primary keys, you may want to jump ahead and read Chapter 10. Otherwise, just assume while reading this chapter that your table contains one or more columns that serve as *identity columns*, and that they correspond to some specific fields in your class.

JDO implementations often use a unique number to provide a datastore-identity value. These numbers are often generated by a sequence facility. Your application may use a sequence generator in your existing relational schemas to provide unique values for a primary key. Some JDO implementations allow you to identify a specific sequence in the datastore to use for obtaining unique identity values for datastore identity. This sequence is often specified in the metadata using a vendor-specific extension element. Currently, applications cannot directly access such a sequence generator to assist in generating unique values for application identity using a standard JDO syntax. However, some JDO implementations provide facilities for generating unique values for your application-identity classes. If you are using application identity and do not have a real-world identifier that defines the identify for a particular instance, you will need to use an interface provided by the JDO implementation or datastore to obtain unique values. Such a facility is being considered for a future JDO release.

Inheritance

You may have one or more inheritance hierarchies in your object model. JDO implementations provide an assortment of approaches for mapping the Java classes in an inheritance hierarchy into the nonhierarchical relational tables. To understand the different mapping alternatives that are available, consider the inheritance hierarchy in Figure 5-1.

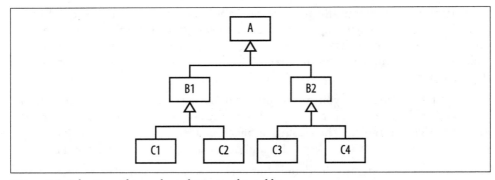

Figure 5-1. Inheritance hierarchy to be mapped to tables

JDO implementations support one or more of the following mapping strategies:

Each class in the hierarchy has a separate table. With this approach, a separate table is used for each class: A, B1, B2, C1, C2, C3, C4. Each table contains only the fields from its associated class. To access all the fields of a C1 instance, including the fields inherited from A and B1, it is necessary to access the tables corresponding to A, B1, and C1. Accessing a B2 instance requires accessing A and B2.

With this approach, typically the primary keys for B1 and B2 are defined as foreign keys on A, the primary keys for C1 and C2 are defined as foreign keys on B1, and the primary keys for C3 and C4 are defined as foreign keys on B2.

Each class in the hierarchy has a separate table, but inherited fields are duplicated in the tables for each subclass. This approach avoids the need to access the tables for A and B1 when accessing an instance of C1; only C1 needs to be accessed. However, when you use this mapping strategy, support for inheritance and polymorphism becomes very cumbersome. Accessing an instance of class A requires a join of all of A's tables.

The hierarchy is flattened into a single table containing all the classes. This is the default approach used for many JDO implementations. All of the classes in the hierarchy are placed in one table, which must have a column for every field of every class in the hierarchy. Essentially, all of the classes in a hierarchy are merged into one table. This approach relies on the datastore's efficient storage-management support of null fields, since a row for an instance of C2 will not use the fields of C1, B2, C3, and C4.

With this approach, the JDO implementation uses an additional *type-discriminator column* that has a unique value for each class stored in the table. When you retrieve the values for an instance, the value of this column determines the class of the instance to be constructed.

Combination of separate classes and flattened hierarchy. This approach combines fields from multiple classes into a number of tables, but the mapping between classes and tables is not one to one. For example, suppose you define three tables: A, B1, and B2.

- Table A contains the primary key, a type-discriminator column, and all the fields declared in class A.
- Table B1 contains a primary key that is also a foreign key to table A, and columns for each field in classes B1, C1, and C2.
- Table B2 contains a primary key that is also a foreign key to table A, and columns for each field in classes B2, C3, and C4.

Leaves of the hierarchy determine the tables. This approach results in four tables, corresponding to the C1, C2, C3, and C4 classes. But there may also be instances of A, B1, and B2. The classes are grouped, by default, into the following tables:

- Table 1 contains the data for the A, B1, and C1 classes.
- Table 2 contains the data for the C2 class.
- Table 3 contains the data for the B2 and C3 classes.
- Table 4 contains the data for the C4 class.

A vendor may support one or more of these inheritance-mapping approaches. All of the approaches are vendor-specific; JDO does not standardize inheritance-mapping. Each approach has performance implications, since an instance's field values may be spread among several tables that must be joined and accessed. If a vendor supports more than one inheritance-mapping approach, the vendor usually will have a meta-data extension that you can use to specify which approach to use. As you can imagine, only one approach can be used for each inheritance hierarchy.

For a class in an inheritance hierarchy, when the fields of an instance are mapped to multiple tables, the columns containing the instance's identity value need to exist in each table used to represent the class. So, when you use the first inheritance-mapping approach, an instance of C1 has the same primary-key value in the tables that correspond to classes A, B1, and C1. Some implementations let you specify the names of the primary-key columns for each table used in the inheritance hierarchy.

References

The datastore's representation of a reference to an instance (either a class or inter-face reference) depends on the identity type defined for the reference's class. The class's identity type determines the primary-key (or unique-key) columns of the class's table. In addition, a class may be mapped to one or more tables. A Java refer-ence is represented in the datastore by a foreign key that refers to the tables associ-ated with the class of the reference. For example, Example 5-1 defined the Movie table. Example 5-2 defines a Role table for the Role class in the com.mediamania. content package. The Role class has a reference, named movie, to the Movie class. On line ❶, the Role table defines a foreign key to reference the primary key of the Movie table.

Example 5-2. Foreign key used to reference a primary-key column

```
CREATE TABLE Role (
     oid      INTEGER,
     name     VARCHAR(20),
     movie    INTEGER,
     PRIMARY KEY(oid),
❶    FOREIGN KEY(movie) REFERENCES Movie(oid)
)
```

Your application does not have to deal with primary and foreign keys; it simply uses standard Java syntax, using the reference to access the object in memory. You also do not need to specify anything specific in the metadata for a reference; its declara-tion in Java provides all of the necessary information.

JDO supports Java's polymorphism, allowing a reference to refer to an instance of any subclass of the reference's declared class. A JDO implementation must be able to determine the type of the instance being referred to, so that it can access the right table (or tables). Implementations employ various techniques to store this type infor-mation. With some inheritance-mapping approaches, the implementation requires a type-discriminator column to identify the type of an instance. Most implementations allow you to specify the name for the type-discriminator column.

Collections and Relationships

In a relational data model, relations are usually *normalized*. A relation is in *first normal form* if the cells of a table contain only a single atomic value, which is nondecomposable as far as the database is concerned. Initially, relational databases supported only simple types, such as integers, strings, and dates. Over time, they have added support for column types that can represent a set of data. But most relational database schema designs represent a collection of values with a set of rows.

You can represent a collection using a foreign key or a join table. We will examine each of these techniques in the following subsections. We'll consider the Movie and Role classes in the com.mediamania.content package and examine alternate ways of representing the relationship between these two classes in Java and a relational schema. For this discussion, we will ignore the inheritance relationship between Movie and MediaContent. We'll focus on the one-to-many relationship that exists between Movie and Role.

This mapping discussion is important when you are mapping between an existing relational schema and Java classes. If you're letting the JDO implementation generate a relational schema for you, or letting it generate your Java classes automatically from a relational schema, you do not need to be as concerned with the following discussion. However, as your object model and relational schema evolve, understanding the following material will become more important.

Using a Foreign Key

A one-to-many relationship between tables A and B usually is represented in a relational schema with a foreign key in B referencing the primary key in A. In the case of Movie and Role, the Role table should contain a foreign key that references the primary key of the Movie table. Example 5-3 uses this technique in the definition of the Movie and Role tables.

Example 5-3. SQL tables using a foreign key to represent a collection

```
CREATE TABLE Movie (
    oid         INTEGER,
    title       VARCHAR(24),
    rating      CHAR(4),
    genres      CHAR(16),
    PRIMARY KEY(oid)
)

CREATE TABLE Role (
    oid         INTEGER,
    name        VARCHAR(20),
❶   movie       INTEGER,
    PRIMARY KEY(oid),
    FOREIGN KEY(movie) REFERENCES Movie(oid)
)
```

Suppose you have Movie and Role tables, defined in SQL as shown in Example 5-3. With this schema, each Role row can reference only one Movie row. Multiple Role rows can reference the same Movie row via their movie column, declared on line ❶. Thus, the foreign-key column movie establishes the one-to-many relationship between Movie and Role in a relational schema.

The following SQL query accesses the Role rows that are associated with a specific Movie:

```
SELECT  name
FROM    Movie, Role
WHERE   title = 'Braveheart' AND Movie.oid = Role.movie
```

The join of the oid column in the Movie table with the movie column in the Role table associates the rows in the Role table with the one row in the Movie table that has a title column equal to 'Braveheart'.

You may have an existing relational schema that represents a collection or relationship using this foreign-key technique, and you may have to use this schema in your JDO application. Alternatively, if you do not have an existing schema, you may want to use a foreign key to represent your collection, as shown in Example 5-3. We will now examine several Java class designs to represent the relationship between Movie and Role with this relational schema.

Isomorphic mapping

Example 5-4 provides our first Java class design, in which we define a direct isomorphic mapping (identical form and structure) with the relational tables in Example 5-3.

Example 5-4. Isomorphic mapping between classes and tables

```
public class Movie {
    private String      theTitle;
    private String      movieRating;
    private String      genres;
}

public class Role {
    private String      name;
❶   private Movie       movie;
}
```

The Java classes do not have the oid table columns that are used to store the datastore identity in the relational tables. The Role class's movie field, declared on line ❶, provides a reference to the associated Movie instance.

The following JDO metadata defines the mapping between the schema defined in Example 5-3 and the Java classes declared in Example 5-4:

```
<jdo>
    <package name="com.mediamania.content" >
        <class name="Movie" >
            <field name = "theTitle" >
                <extension vendor-name="vendorX" key="column" value="title" />
            </field>
            <field name = "movieRating" >
                <extension vendor-name="vendorX" key="column" value="rating" />
            </field>
            <field name = "genres" >
                <extension vendor-name="vendorX" key="column" value="genres" />
            </field>
            <extension vendor-name="vendorX" key="table" value="Movie" />
        </class>
        <class name="Role" >
            <field name="name" >
                <extension vendor-name="vendorX" key="column" value="name" />
            </field>
            <field name="movie" >
                <extension vendor-name="vendorX" key="column" value="movie" />
            </field>
            <extension vendor-name="vendorX" key="table" value="Role" />
        </class>
    </package>
</jdo>
```

However, the Java model in Example 5-4 does not provide a means to navigate from a Movie instance to its associated Role instances. Java and the JVM do not have the join facility found in a relational database. You could implement equivalent functionality in Java by examining all the Role instances to determine which instances reference a specific Movie instance. But this would be very inefficient if there were a large number of Role instances. Furthermore, this is not how you would normally represent and access such a relationship in Java.

If you are interested in accessing all the Role instances associated with a Movie referenced by the variable movie, and pm is initialized to the PersistenceManager, you can execute the following code:

```
Query q = pm.newQuery(Role.class);
q.setFilter("movie == param1");
q.declareParameters("Movie param1");
Collection result = (Collection) q.execute(movie);
```

This query returns an unmodifiable collection of Roles that refer to the Movie. The performance of this query would likely be similar to the performance you would get if the foreign key were represented by a collection, as we will describe in the following section.

You can also implement a method in the Movie class to add a Role to the movie:

```
void addRole(Role role) {
    role.setMovie(this);
}
```

This method removes the Role from whatever Movie it currently refers to and replaces it with the Movie (referenced by this). But this technique does not allow you to execute a portable query that navigates from a Movie to a Role, which can be done by using the contains( ) construct (described in Chapter 9). In order to do this, you would need to define a collection in Movie and map it to the datastore.

Defining a collection

You may want to define a collection in your Movie class that contains the set of associated Role instances, modeled by the foreign key movie (declared on line ❶ in Example 5-3). Example 5-5 shows the Java classes for such a model.

Example 5-5. Using the foreign key to represent a collection

```
public class Movie {
    private String      theTitle;
    private String      movieRating;
    private String      genres;
❶   private Set         cast;
}

public class Role {
    private String      name;
}
```

With this mapping, the movie column in the Role table represents the cast collection in the Movie class, which contains the Roles associated with a movie. Line ❶ of the JDO metadata shown in Example 5-6 identifies the use of the movie column in the Role table for this purpose.

Example 5-6. JDO metadata for Java classes in Example 5-5 and schema in Example 5-3

```
<jdo>
    <package name="com.mediamania.content" >
        <class name="Movie" >
            <field name = "theTitle" >
                <extension vendor-name="vendorX" key="column" value="title" />
            </field>
            <field name = "movieRating" >
                <extension vendor-name="vendorX" key="column" value="rating" />
            </field>
            <field name = "genres" >
                <extension vendor-name="vendorX" key="column" value="genres" />
            </field>
            <field name="cast" >
                <collection element-type="Role"/>
❶               <extension vendor-name="vendorX" key="rel-column" value="movie"/>
            </field>
            <extension vendor-name="vendorX" key="table" value="Movie" />
        </class>
```

Example 5-6. JDO metadata for Java classes in Example 5-5
and schema in Example 5-3 (continued)

```
            <class name="Role" >
                <field name="name" >
                    <extension vendor-name="vendorX" key="column" value="name" />
                </field>
                <extension vendor-name="vendorX" key="table" value="Role" />
            </class>
        </package>
</jdo>
```

The use of the `rel-column` on line ❶ tells the implementation that the relation should be treated as a one-to-many association.

Defining a collection and a reference

Instead of using the Java model shown in Example 5-4, you are more likely to define the Movie class with a collection to contain the set of associated Role instances (as shown in line ❶ of Example 5-7), in addition to the Movie reference in Role.

Example 5-7. Using a foreign key for both a collection and a reference in Java

```
public class Movie {
    private String      theTitle;
    private String      movieRating;
    private String      genres;
❶   private Set         cast;
}

public class Role {
    private String      name;
❷   private Movie       movie;
}
```

The metadata for the Java classes in Example 5-7 would be similar to Example 5-6, except we would also associate the movie field in the Role class with the movie column in the Role table. Adding a Role reference to a particular Movie instance's cast collection establishes a relationship between the Movie and Role instances. You can acquire an Iterator from a Movie instance's cast collection to access each Role instance associated with the Movie instance.

However, this model has a complication. Suppose you have two Movie instances. What happens if your Java application adds the same Role reference to the cast collection in both Movie instances? In Java, each cast collection could easily contain a reference to the same Role instance. But the collection is represented in the datastore via the foreign-key column named movie in the Role table. The movie column for a given Role row can reference only a single Movie row. How would this be handled at commit time? The implementation cannot store the fact that two Movie instances are referencing the same Role, given the schema defined in Example 5-3; it can store only one reference. The implementation should throw an exception at commit, or it may silently store only one of the Movie references. Consider the movie reference in the Role class, which can reference only a single Movie. If the Role instance is in memory, it may reference one of the Movie instances (let's call it M) that reference the Role in their cast collection. This may result in M being the one Movie that gets associated with the Role in the datastore.

However, if a Role can be referenced by multiple Movies and a Movie can reference multiple Roles, this is really a many-to-many relationship. But our design states that there should be a one-to-many relationship between Movie and Role. So, this situation should not occur if your Java application is honoring the cardinality of the relationship. Representing a many-to-many relationship in Java requires a collection in the classes at both ends of the relationship.

Managed relationships

Using a foreign key in the relational datastore to represent a collection in Java becomes especially cumbersome when the foreign key is represented by a reference at one end of the relationship and a collection at the other end. Some JDO implementations handle the mapping of a single foreign key to both sides of a relationship by providing a *managed relationship*. With this capability, if the application updates one side of a relationship, the JDO implementation updates the other side automatically. Some vendors do not support managed relationships, because they result in behavior that differs from the behavior of Java when using references and collections in non-JDO environments.

For example, if the application adds a Role instance to a Movie instance's cast collection, the implementation automatically sets the Role instance's movie reference to the Movie instance. Or, if the application removes a Role from a Movie instance's cast collection, the Role instance's movie reference is set to null automatically. Similarly, if the application sets the Role instance's movie reference to a particular Movie instance A, the implementation automatically removes the Role from the cast collection of the Movie instance currently referenced by movie (unless it is null) and it adds the Role to A's cast collection.

Currently, JDO does not support managed relationships, but some JDO implementations do support them. Implementations that support managed relationships provide a metadata extension that allows you to identify a field's *inverse member*, which is the member at the other end of the relationship. The metadata for specifying a managed relationship between Movie and Role would look like this:

```
<jdo>
    <package name="com.mediamania.content" >
        <class name="Movie" >
            <field name="cast" >
                <collection element-type="Role"/>
❶               <extension vendor-name="vendorX"
                        key="inverse" value="Role.movie"/>
```

```
                    </field>
                    <extension vendor-name="vendorX" key="table" value="Movie" />
                </class>
                <class name="Role" >
                    <field name="movie" >
                        <extension vendor-name="vendorX" key="column" value="movie"/>
                        <extension vendor-name="vendorX"
                                   key="inverse" value="Movie.cast"/>
                    </field>
                    <extension vendor-name="vendorX" key="table" value="Role" />
                </class>
            </package>
        </jdo>
```

On line ❶, an extension element is nested within the field element for Movie.cast to specify that Role.movie is its inverse member in the relationship. On line ❷, an extension element is also nested in the field element for Role.movie to specify that Movies.cast is its inverse member.

Use of managed relationships in a JDO implementation is not portable to other JDO implementations. Many Java developers may consider such automatic maintenance behavior unusual. But it solves the problem of an application attempting to establish a relationship between Java instances that cannot be represented in the datastore with the schema defined in Example 5-3. A future JDO release may add support for managed relationships, if an approach can be designed that preserves JDO's level of transparency and consistency with Java.

Using a Join Table

We have presented three Java class designs that could be used to represent the schema defined in Example 5-3. Now let's consider another datastore representation of the Movie.cast collection. Some JDO implementations represent a collection with a set of rows in a *join table*. Each row contains the value for one collection element. Instead of having a foreign key in the Role table, a separate join table is defined to contain the elements of the cast collection. Example 5-8 provides a schema using a join table named Movie_cast.

Example 5-8. Use of a join table to represent a collection

```
CREATE TABLE Movie (
    oid         INTEGER,
    title       VARCHAR(24),
    rating      CHAR(4),
    genres      CHAR(16),
    PRIMARY KEY(oid)
)

CREATE TABLE Role (
    oid         INTEGER,
    name        VARCHAR(20),
    PRIMARY KEY(oid),
```

Example 5-8. Use of a join table to represent a collection (continued)

```
)

CREATE TABLE Movie_cast (
    movieoid    INTEGER NOT NULL,
    roleoid     INTEGER,
    PRIMARY KEY(movieoid, roleoid),
❶  FOREIGN KEY(movieoid) REFERENCES Movie(oid),
❷  FOREIGN KEY(roleoid)  REFERENCES Role(oid),
❸  CONSTRAINT r UNIQUE(roleoid)
)
```

The Movie_cast join table has two columns: movieoid references the associated Movie row (line ❶), and roleoid references the associated Role row (line ❷). Each element in a Movie.cast collection has a corresponding row in the Movie_cast table.

If a table like Movie_cast is used to represent a one-to-many relationship, you should define a unique constraint on the join table columns that correspond to the many side of the relationship. In this case, the roleoid has a unique constraint, shown on line ❸, because it would be illegal to have the same Role appear more than once in the table. Even though the JDO implementation might allow you to add the Role to two different Movies, the datastore would disallow the operation at commit time.

Most JDO implementations let you specify the name of the join table representing a collection. We would specify the name of the table for the Movie.cast field by nesting a vendor-specific metadata extension within the collection element specified for Movie.cast. Most JDO implementations also let you specify the name of each column in the table.

Example 5-8 actually illustrates how many-to-many relationships normally are represented in a relational schema (except you would not have the UNIQUE constraint specified on line ❸). A given row in the Movie table can be associated with multiple rows in the Movie_cast table via the movieoid foreign key, and a given row in the Role table can be associated with multiple rows in the Movie_cast table. You would represent the many-to-many relationship in Java with a collection in both classes involved in the relationship. However, with this particular relational schema, it would be necessary to define a managed relationship to represent the many-to-many relationship. A single row in the Movie_cast table would represent the existence of an element in the collections of both classes involved in the many-to-many relationship.

One-to-One Relationships

In Java, you represent a one-to-one relationship between two classes by having a reference in each class that refers to an instance of the other class. As an example, consider the one-to-one relationship that exists between the Rental and RentalItem classes in the Media Mania application, illustrated in Figure 4-4. The Rental class has a field named rentalItem that references an instance of RentalItem. Likewise, the RentalItem class has a field named currentRental that references a Rental instance.

We would likely define one or two methods that would preserve the relationship between these two classes and ensure that an instance of Rental and an instance of RentalItem refer to one another with these references.

For this example, we ignore the inheritance relationship between the Rental and Transaction classes. We define two relational tables, named Rental and RentalItem:

```
   CREATE TABLE Rental (
        oid            INTEGER,
❶      item           INTEGER,
        return         TIMESTAMP,
        actualReturn   TIMESTAMP,
        code           INTEGER,
        PRIMARY KEY(oid),
❷      FOREIGN KEY(item)   REFERENCES RentalItem(oid),
        FOREIGN KEY(code)   REFERENCES RentalCode(oid)
❸      CONSTRAINT uniqitem UNIQUE(item)
   )

   CREATE TABLE RentalItem (
        oid            INTEGER,
        mediaItem      INTEGER,
        serial         VARCHAR(16),
❹      currentRental  INTEGER,
        PRIMARY KEY(oid),
❺      FOREIGN KEY(currentRental)  REFERENCES Rental(oid),
        FOREIGN KEY(mediaItem)        REFERENCES MediaItem(oid),
❻      CONSTRAINT uniqcurr UNIQUE(currentRental)
   )
```

The Rental and RentalItem tables each have a foreign key that references the other table. The Rental table has a column named item, declared on line ❶, that is a foreign key (line ❷) that references the RentalItem table. The RentalItem table has a column named currentRental, declared on line ❹, that is a foreign key (line ❺) that references a row in the Rental table.

The uniqitem unique constraint on line ❸ in the Rental table ensures that only a single row in Rental refers to a particular row in the RentalItem table. Likewise, the uniqcurr unique constraint on line ❻ in the RentalItem table ensures that there is only a single row in the RentalItem table that refers to a particular row in the Rental table. While this relational representation directly mirrors our use of references in Java, it is actually redundant to maintain a foreign key in both tables in the relational model.

It is sufficient to define a foreign key in only one of the tables, having it reference the primary key of the other table. The tables could be defined as follows:

```
   CREATE TABLE Rental (
        oid            INTEGER,
        return         TIMESTAMP,
        actualReturn   TIMESTAMP,
        code           INTEGER,
```

```
❶      item            INTEGER,
    PRIMARY KEY(oid),
❷      FOREIGN KEY(item)       REFERENCES RentalItem(oid),
    FOREIGN KEY(mediaItem) REFERENCES MediaItem(oid),
❸      CONSTRAINT uniqitem UNIQUE(item)
)

CREATE TABLE RentalItem (
    oid             INTEGER,
    mediaItem       INTEGER,
    serial          VARCHAR(16),
    PRIMARY KEY(oid)
)
```

The item column declared on line ❶ in the Rental table is a foreign key (line ❷) that references a row in the RentalItem table. The uniqitem unique constraint on line ❸ makes sure that only a single row in Rental refers to a particular row in the RentalItem table. The item column is sufficient to model the one-to-one relationship between Rental and RentalItem.

One-to-one relationships have some of the same issues that we explored with one-to-many relationships, relative to their representation in a relational datastore and how they are mapped into Java. To deal with these issues, some implementations support one-to-one managed relationships.

Representing Lists and Maps

Suppose we decide to use an ordered list of Roles in the Movie class. In Java, a List is used to represent an ordered collection. We redefine the Movie class as follows:

```
public class Movie {
    private String      title;
    private String      rating;
    private String      genres;
    private List         cast;
}
```

A JDO implementation must preserve a List's ordering in the datastore. To do so, it must maintain an ordering column to indicate the relative ordering of each collection element. If the collection is represented by a join table, as in Example 5-8, the ordering column is placed in the join table. The Movie_cast table then has the column declared on line ❶:

```
CREATE TABLE Movie_cast (
    movieoid    INTEGER,
    roleoid     INTEGER,
❶    elementidx INTEGER,
    FOREIGN KEY(movieoid) REFERENCES Movie(oid)
    FOREIGN KEY(roleoid)  REFERENCES Role(oid)
)
```

If the collection is represented by a foreign key (as in Example 5-3), the ordering column is placed in the table containing the foreign key. Thus, the ordering column is placed directly in the Role table. Most implementations let you state the name of this ordering column.

By default, an implementation must preserve the ordering of the elements in a List in the datastore. Java does not provide an unordered collection class that allows duplicate elements. Some JDO implementations allow a List to be used to represent a collection when the ordering of the elements is not preserved in the datastore. You can specify this by nesting an extension element in the List's field or collection metadata element. If you do not need to preserve the order of a collection, this provides a more efficient mapping to the datastore.

If your persistent class has a Map, you must store the key and value of each Map element. The join table requires a column for the key and the value. Implementations usually let you declare the names of these columns. A Map does not require an ordering column.

CHAPTER 6

Class Enhancement

You need to enhance a persistent class before you can use it in a JDO runtime environment. Class enhancement enables the state of a persistent instance in memory to be synchronized with its representation in the datastore. A persistent class must be enhanced so that it implements the `javax.jdo.spi.PersistenceCapable` interface. The `PersistenceCapable` interface defines a set of methods that the JDO implementation uses to manage instances.

You also need to enhance every class that directly accesses a managed field of a persistent class. JDO field-mediation code needs to be inserted to ensure proper access and management of the field. If your persistent class has a managed field that is not private, any class that directly accesses the field needs to be enhanced. Such a class is referred to as a *persistence-aware class*. This is distinct from a class being JDO-aware, which describes a class that makes direct calls to JDO interfaces at the source level. A persistence-aware class may itself be transient or persistent. So, even though you have a class that is transient, if it directly accesses a managed field, you need to enhance it. You would not list a transient persistence-aware class in the metadata, because any class listed in a metadata file is persistent. So, the only place you identify that a transient class is persistence-aware is in your build files that enhance the class.

We recommend that you declare all of your managed fields to be private; this is considered a best practice in object-oriented development. Independent of the need in JDO to enhance persistence-aware classes, such accesses represent a loss of encapsulation and can often lead to data-integrity issues. Fields declared private cannot be accessed directly by another class. Using private fields thus minimizes the number of persistence-aware classes that need to be enhanced. If a nonmediated access occurs because you forgot to enhance a persistence-aware class, your application will likely behave incorrectly. So, always declare your fields to be private.

The JDO specification defines a standard reference-enhancement contract, which thoroughly specifies all the requirements to enhance a class. Enhanced classes are independent of any particular JDO implementation and datastore.

Enhancement Approaches

You may not be familiar with class enhancement, but it is not JDO-specific and it has been applied in other software technologies. There are several approaches that can be used to enhance a class. Enhancement can be performed by:

- Implementing enhancement yourself manually
- Using a source-code enhancer
- Using a byte-code enhancer

Each enhancement approach requires access to the JDO metadata you have defined.

You may explicitly declare that your class implements PersistenceCapable. In this case, you need to implement the PersistenceCapable contract fully, as specified by the JDO specification. An enhancer ignores a class if you have explicitly declared that it implements PersistenceCapable. We do not recommend this approach; it is tedious and error-prone.

A source-code enhancer reads your original source code and adds the source necessary to support the JDO enhancement contract. The revised source is compiled and is then ready for execution in a JDO environment. At the time this book was written, only one vendor supported a source-code enhancer; the vender also supported a byte-code enhancer.

The most common approach for enhancing a class is to use a JDO byte-code enhancer. It reads a class file produced by the Java compiler and generates a new class file that has been enhanced. With a byte-code enhancer, you can make classes persistent even if you do not have the source code. Figure 6-1 illustrates the process of using a byte-code enhancer to enhance the Movie class.

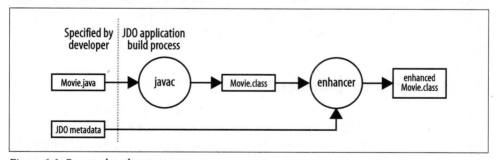

Figure 6-1. Byte-code enhancement process

All persistent and persistence-aware classes need to be enhanced before they can be used in a JDO runtime environment. They must be enhanced before or during their loading into the JVM at runtime. Some implementations may enhance classes in the class loader itself during the class-loading process. Class enhancement is often performed as an additional step in the build process. Most vendors provide an Ant task you can use to enhance your classes in an Ant build file.

Consult your implementation's documentation to determine which technique they use for class enhancement; this will ensure your classes implement the PersistenceCapable interface. At the time this book was written, most JDO implementations supported a byte-code enhancer, so we assume that you are using one.

Reference Enhancer

The JDO reference implementation, implemented by Sun Microsystems, includes a *reference enhancer* that enhances class files according to the reference-enhancement contract.

The following command uses the reference enhancer to enhance the persistent classes in the Media Mania object model:

```
java com.sun.jdori.enhancer.Main -d enhanced -s classes \
    classes/com/mediamania/content/Studio.class \
    classes/com/mediamania/content/MediaContent.class \
    classes/com/mediamania/content/Movie.class \
    classes/com/mediamania/content/Game.class \
    classes/com/mediamania/content/Role.class \
    classes/com/mediamania/content/MediaPerson.class \
    classes/com/mediamania/store/MediaItem.class \
    classes/com/mediamania/store/RentalItem.class \
    classes/com/mediamania/store/RentalCode.class \
    classes/com/mediamania/store/Customer.class \
    classes/com/mediamania/store/Address.class \
    classes/com/mediamania/store/Transaction.class \
    classes/com/mediamania/store/Purchase.class \
    classes/com/mediamania/store/Rental.class
```

This command places the enhanced class files in a separate directory hierarchy named *enhanced*. You can also enhance the class files in place, replacing your original class file with the enhanced form by using the -f command option. Another useful option is -v, which produces verbose output indicating the actions performed by the enhancer.

Vendor-Specific Enhancement

A JDO vendor can use Sun's reference enhancer directly with their implementation, or they can implement their own enhancer that performs the same function. A vendor can extend the enhancements required in the reference-enhancement contract by adding their own methods and fields to be used in their runtime environment. However, these additional implementation-specific enhancements cannot conflict with the reference-enhancement contract.

The reference-enhancement contract establishes guidelines for how a vendor can add enhancements, so the enhanced classes are usable with any other JDO implementation's runtime environment. The reference-enhancement contract adds fields and methods whose names begin with "jdo". Any methods and fields added by another vendor's enhancer do not have a name that begins with "jdo"; they begin with some other string that has a vendor-identifying name followed by the string "jdo".

Binary Compatibility

The standard enhancement interface defined by the JDO reference-enhancement contract provides binary compatibility among all enhancers and runtime environments. It requires that:

- A class enhanced by the reference enhancer is usable with any JDO-compliant runtime environment.
- A class enhanced by a JDO-compliant vendor's enhancer is usable by the reference implementation's runtime environment.
- A class enhanced by a JDO-compliant vendor's enhancer is usable by any other JDO-compliant runtime environment.

Furthermore, an enhanced class file can be shared concurrently in a JVM among several coresident JDO implementations.

An implementation's runtime environment can determine whether a class was enhanced by its own enhancer. If it has, the implementation's runtime environment can use any implementation-specific enhancements that were placed in the class file. Otherwise, it must use the standard reference-enhancement interface contract. Table 6-1 shows which enhancement interface a JDO runtime environment will use, based on the enhancer used to enhance the class.

Table 6-1. Enhancement interfaces used

Enhancer used	Reference runtime	Vendor A runtime	Vendor B runtime
Reference enhancer	Reference enhancement	Reference enhancement	Reference enhancement
Vendor A enhancer	Reference enhancement	Vendor A enhancement	Reference enhancement
Vendor B enhancer	Reference enhancement	Reference enhancement	Vendor B enhancement

You can distribute your classes in either their enhanced or unenhanced form. Both forms are portable across implementations. If you are distributing the classes as a third-party class library that will be used in a variety of applications, you probably should distribute them unenhanced. The developers using your classes can then choose which enhancer to use. In this case, we recommend you provide them with the necessary metadata for your classes, which they may need to customize. If you are deploying an application that uses a specific JDO implementation, you may distribute your persistent classes in their enhanced form. It does not matter though, because a class distributed in its enhanced form can still be used with any JDO-compliant implementation. If you expect your classes will be used with multiple JDO implementations and you wish to distribute them in their enhanced form, we recommend that you use the Sun reference enhancer.

Enhancement Effects on Your Code

It is important for you to understand how enhancement affects your persistent classes. Enhancement does not alter the logic or functional behavior that you have defined. It adds code to mediate all access to a field to ensure that its value has been read from the datastore and that any modifications are tracked. You will not see any behavioral differences between transient instances of enhanced classes and transient instances of the same nonenhanced classes.

The `PersistenceCapable` interface is designed to avoid name conflicts with fields and methods that you define. All of its declared method names are prefixed with "jdo". To avoid selecting a name the enhancer uses, you should not declare a persistent class with fields or methods that start with "jdo". The reference-enhancement contract adds additional methods and fields that begin with "jdo" to your classes.

The enhancer does not change the behavior of introspection. All of the fields and methods added to an enhanced class are exposed when you use the Java reflection APIs.

Your enhanced classes will have dependencies on the JDO `JDOImplHelper`, `StateManager`, and `PersistenceCapable` interfaces, defined in the `javax.jdo.spi` package. Therefore, your enhanced classes need to have the *jdo.jar* file that contains their definitions available in your classpath at runtime.

Class enhancement will not impact source-line-level debugging. You can debug your enhanced classes using the line numbers of your original source code. You will be able to work at the source level as if the class had not been enhanced. If the enhancer makes any code modifications that change the offset of any byte codes within a method, it updates the line number references to reflect the change.

However, as you will learn in this chapter and Chapter 12, a JDO implementation has some flexibility as to when it initializes an instance's persistent fields. The enhancer places field-mediation code in your application classes to ensure the field is loaded before your application classes access a field. But this field mediation is not applied to debuggers or software that uses introspection. These will access the field directly, even when it has not been loaded by the JDO implementation. This may confuse you, because the field's value will change when it is loaded from the datastore. This can even occur if the specific field you are examining in the debugger has not been accessed by the application; it could get loaded as a result of an access to another field in the instance.

Changes Made by the Enhancer

The remainder of this chapter describes in more detail some of the changes made to your class files by the enhancer. We do not cover all the methods added by an enhancer. Nor do we explain all of the functionality added to a class to enable transparent persistence. You do not need to understand all the details of class enhancement; your application should never directly use the fields and methods added by enhancement. But it is useful, though not necessary, to have a basic understanding of how your classes are modified by the process. We list all the fields that are added by class enhancement and some of the methods. To gain a thorough understanding of the enhancement contract, you should read the JDO specification. You do not need to understand the remaining material in this chapter to use JDO. If you are not interested in the details of enhancement, you can skip over the remainder of this chapter.

The enhancer adds an interface, fields, and methods to your persistent classes so that they can be stored in a datastore transparently. The enhancer adds the following line to the definition of a persistent class:

```
implements javax.jdo.spi.PersistenceCapable
```

The PersistenceCapable interface defines methods the JDO implementation uses to manage instances in a JDO runtime environment. The enhancer adds the implementation of these PersistenceCapable methods. It also adds metadata information to each class, which is used by the JDO runtime environment to manage the fields.

A getfield byte-code instruction performs all field-read accesses at the class-file level, and a putfield byte-code instruction performs all field modifications. There is a different getfield and putfield instruction for each type in Java. The JDO implementation mediates all accesses and updates to a managed field to ensure its value has been retrieved from the datastore before your application accesses it and all modifications have been captured. The enhancer replaces each getfield and putfield byte-code instruction for a managed field with a call to a method it generates to provide this mediation.

Metadata

The enhancer generates its own metadata, based on the class declaration and the metadata you have defined. This metadata is added during enhancement to each persistent class as static fields. The JDO runtime environment uses this information to manage the fields of the class. Access of this metadata information is much more efficient than using Java reflection.

Class metadata

The following static fields are added to represent class-level metadata:

```
private final static int      jdoInheritedFieldCount;
private final static Class     jdoPersistenceCapableSuperclass;
private final static long      serialVersionUID;
```

jdoInheritedFieldCount
> Initialized to the number of managed fields inherited from superclasses.

jdoPersistenceCapableSuperclass
> Initialized to the Class instance of the most immediate superclass that is persistent within the hierarchy. It is null if the class is the topmost persistent class in the hierarchy or if it is not in an inheritance hierarchy.

serialVersionUID

Added only if it does not already exist in the class. It is used with serialization and has the same value as the class in its non-enhanced form. This allows you to serialize a persistent instance and later deserialize it into an instance of the class in its unenhanced form.

Field metadata

The following fields provide information about each managed field in the class:

```
private final static String[]  jdoFieldNames;
private final static Class[]    jdoFieldTypes;
private final static byte[]     jdoFieldFlags;
```

Each managed field has an index value that is used to identify it uniquely. A field's index value is used to access its entries in these arrays.

jdoFieldNames

Contains the name of each field.

jdoFieldTypes

Contains the type of each field.

jdoFieldFlags

Contains some flags to indicate the form of access and mediation that should be performed for the fields. It also has a flag to indicate whether the field should be serialized.

Class registration

A static initializer is added to each persistent class. This static initialization code is executed after any other initialization you may have defined in the class. It registers the class with the JDO runtime environment by calling the static registerClass() method defined in the JDOImplHelper class. This class is defined in the javax.jdo.spi package, and it provides utility methods used by JDO implementations. If the persistent class is not abstract, a helper instance of the class is constructed and passed to registerClass().

The generated static metadata fields are passed as arguments to registerClass(). The JDOImplHelper class provides methods that allow this information to be shared by all JDO implementations that manage instances of the class in the JVM.

Instance-Level Data

The reference enhancer adds the following two fields to the least-derived (topmost) persistent class in an inheritance hierarchy:

```
protected transient javax.jdo.spi.StateManager  jdoStateManager;
protected transient byte                         jdoFlags;
```

These are the only two fields added to a class that affect the size of an instance in memory.

jdoStateManager

This field contains a reference to the StateManager that manages the fields of persistent and transient transactional instances. This field is null for nontransactional transient instances.

jdoFlags

This field indicates the state of the fields in the instance.

The StateManager instance referenced by jdoStateManager manages the value of the jdoFlags field. Since these two fields are transient, they do not impact serialization.

Field Mediation

Access to a managed field is mediated by the JDO implementation to ensure its value has been retrieved from the datastore before it is accessed by the application and to capture all application modifications to the field. Nonmanaged fields are ignored by the enhancer. No enhancement is performed on access to nonmanaged fields, because they lie outside the domain of persistence and may be accessed like any normal Java field, obeying the accessibility rules dictated by the public, private, and protected modifiers and default package access.

Generated accessors and mutators

The enhancer generates a get and set method for each managed field in a persistent class. These methods have the following form:

```
final static mmm ttt   jdoGetField(theclass instance);
final static mmm void  jdoSetField(theclass instance, ttt newValue);
```

with the following elements:

Field

This is the name of the field in the class.

mmm

This is the same access modifier (public, private, or protected) as the corresponding field in the nonenhanced class. This ensures the security of instances by preserving the same field access restrictions that are declared in the class.

ttt

This is the type of the field in the nonenhanced class.

theclass

This is the class in which this static method is defined. This parameter is used to pass an instance of the class to the static method.

These generated methods examine the values in jdoFlags and jdoFieldFlags and perform the appropriate behavior to get or set the field's value. These methods provide access mediation of the managed fields.

The enhancer must enhance every class that has a getfield or putfield byte-code instruction for a managed field of a persistent class. Each getfield is replaced with a call to the corresponding jdoGetField( ), and each putfield is replaced with a call to the corresponding jdoSetField( ). The jdoSetField( ) methods enable the StateManager to track which fields in each instance are modified by the application. The PersistenceManager can then automatically propagate all instance modifications to the datastore at transaction commit.

As it turns out, the stack signature required for the getfield and putfield byte codes matches the stack signature needed for the call to jdoGetField( ) and jdoSetField( ). The enhancer needs to replace only a single byte-code instruction—getfield or putfield—without needing to add or alter any other byte-code instructions. So, replacing these byte codes does not increase the size of the byte code in your class.

The timing of managed field accesses, for both transient and persistent instances, will be different from the timing of field accesses in an unenhanced class, because the getfield and putfield byte-code instructions are replaced with calls to these generated static methods. But the methods are defined as static and final, which reduces their method-call overhead. Furthermore, since they are static and final methods, a HotSpot or other Just-In-Time (JIT) environment can optimize the byte code by removing the method call entirely.

Management of field values

The methods described in this section are used to mediate application access to managed fields. The StateManager instance referenced by the jdoStateManager field manages the state of the managed fields in a persistent instance by using the following two methods added by enhancement:

```
public void jdoReplaceField(int field);
public void jdoProvideField(int field);
```

The parameter passed to these methods is the index value that uniquely identifies a field.

Since jdoReplaceField( ) and jdoProvideField( ) are placed in the class, the StateManager can access and alter every managed field, regardless of the field's access modifier (e.g., default package-level, private, and protected). At the same time, it preserves the field-accessibility restrictions for all classes except the StateManager, which must be granted permission explicitly in Java runtime environments that enforce security. You must use the JDOPermission class, described in Chapter 2, to grant permission to the StateManager.

The StateManager uses jdoReplaceField( ) to store values from the datastore in the instance. jdoReplaceField( ) calls the StateManager method replacing*XXX*Field( ) to get a value for the field. The *XXX* corresponds to one of the specific field types handled in JDO. The StateManager has a replacing*XXX*Field( ) method for each field type. The jdoReplaceField( ) method assigns to the field the value that is returned by replacing*XXX*Field( ).

The StateManager uses jdoProvideField( ) to retrieve a field value from an instance. jdoProvideField( ) calls the StateManager method provided*XXX*Field( ) to access a field's value. There is a provided*XXX*Field( ) method for each field type, denoted by *XXX*.

CHAPTER 7

Establishing a JDO Runtime Environment

This chapter describes how to establish a JDO runtime environment. This includes specifying the particular JDO implementation to be used, connecting to the datastore, and setting various properties that control the management of transactions and the cache of persistent instances.

Your primary interface when using JDO is the PersistenceManager interface. You configure a PersistenceManager instance by using a PersistenceManagerFactory instance, which you can create by calling a method defined in JDOHelper. Or, in a Java 2 Platform, Enterprise Edition (J2EE) environment, you would likely use Java Naming and Directory Interface (JNDI) to store and look up one or more PersistenceManagerFactory instances.

You can initialize and set various properties within the PersistenceManagerFactory, including the information needed to connect to the datastore. Once you have established the desired configuration, you call a PersistenceManagerFactory method to create a PersistenceManager instance. You can create multiple PersistenceManagers from a single PersistenceManagerFactory, and you can alter some of the properties in a PersistenceManager once it has been created.

A PersistenceManager instance has a one-to-one relationship with an associated Transaction instance. The PersistenceManager interface provides a method to access this instance. The property settings in the PersistenceManager and Transaction instances control the runtime behavior of the JDO runtime environment.

Figure 7-1 illustrates the relationships among these classes and the methods you can use to access and create the associated instances. This chapter describes the capabilities these interfaces provide, so you can configure your application's runtime environment for accessing the datastore.

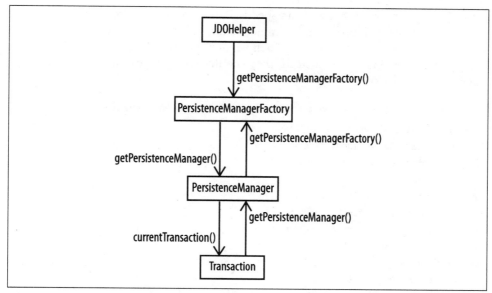

Figure 7-1. Interfaces used to configure and control the JDO runtime environment

Configuring a PersistenceManagerFactory

A PersistenceManagerFactory has a number of properties you can use to configure a PersistenceManager. You should initialize these property values when the PersistenceManagerFactory is first created via the JDOHelper interface. Once you have constructed a PersistenceManagerFactory with the necessary property values, you call getPersistenceManager( ) to construct a PersistenceManager instance. The values of the properties in the PersistenceManagerFactory instance become the default settings for the properties in all the PersistenceManager instances created by the factory.

To create a PersistenceManagerFactory, initialize a Properties instance and pass it as a parameter to one of the following JDOHelper methods:

```
public static PersistenceManagerFactory
                getPersistenceManagerFactory(Properties props, ClassLoader cl);
public static PersistenceManagerFactory
                getPersistenceManagerFactory(Properties props);
```

The second method, without a ClassLoader parameter, uses the ClassLoader in the calling thread's current context to resolve the class name.

Table 7-1 lists the keys that you can specify in the Properties object to initialize the PersistenceManagerFactory. A JDO implementation may have some of its own additional properties that are necessary. Such vendor-specific properties should not have the javax.jdo.option prefix; instead, they should use a prefix that identifies the specific implementation.

Table 7-1 . Standard property keys used to initialize a PersistenceManagerFactory

```
javax.jdo.PersistenceManagerFactoryClass
javax.jdo.option.ConnectionUserName
javax.jdo.option.ConnectionPassword
javax.jdo.option.ConnectionURL
javax.jdo.option.ConnectionDriverName
javax.jdo.option.ConnectionFactoryName
javax.jdo.option.ConnectionFactory2Name
javax.jdo.option.IgnoreCache
javax.jdo.option.Optimistic
javax.jdo.option.NontransactionalRead
javax.jdo.option.NontransactionalWrite
javax.jdo.option.Multithreaded
javax.jdo.option.RetainValues
javax.jdo.option.RestoreValues
```

The keys and values in a Properties instance are represented by String instances. Each property listed in Table 7-1 has a corresponding property value in PersistenceManagerFactory that is either a String or a boolean. The value of a String property is used directly, without change. In the case of a boolean property, the String value in the Properties instance is considered true if it compares equal to "true" (ignoring case); otherwise, it is initialized to false.

You must include the javax.jdo.PersistenceManagerFactoryClass property, which is used to specify the implementation-specific class of the instance this method returns. The name associated with this property should be the fully qualified name of the implementation's class that implements the PersistenceManagerFactory interface. Your implementation's documentation should provide you with the name of this class.

If you do not initialize a property, the implementation can choose the default value. A JDO vendor will likely choose default values that work best with its implementation. Therefore, the default values are not likely to be consistent across different implementations. To ensure that your application is portable and has consistent behavior across implementations, you should initialize the values of all the properties that are relevant to your application.

The following code populates a `Properties` instance with JDO properties and constructs a `PersistenceManagerFactory` using `JDOHelper`. The `RestoreValues` property is initialized to `false`, because its property value is not equal to "true" (ignoring case).

```
import java.util.Properties;
import javax.jdo.JDOHelper;
import javax.jdo.PersistenceManagerFactory;

...

PersistenceManagerFactory pmf = null;
Properties properties = new Properties();
properties.put("javax.jdo.PersistenceManagerFactoryClass",
               "com.sun.jdori.fostore.FOStorePMF");
properties.put("javax.jdo.option.ConnectionURL", "fostore:database/fostore");
properties.put("javax.jdo.option.ConnectionUserName", "dave");
properties.put("javax.jdo.option.ConnectionPassword", "jdo4me");
properties.put("javax.jdo.option.Optimistic", "false");
properties.put("javax.jdo.option.IgnoreCache", "false");
properties.put("javax.jdo.option.RetainValues", "true");
properties.put("javax.jdo.option.RestoreValues", "yes"); // will be set to false
pmf = JDOHelper.getPersistenceManagerFactory(properties);
```

The two `getPersistenceManagerFactory()` methods delegate to a static `getPersistenceManagerFactory()` method, which should exist in the class named in the `javax.jdo.PersistenceManagerFactoryClass` property. If any exceptions are thrown while trying to call this static method, a `JDOFatalUserException` or `JDOFatalInternalException` is thrown, depending on whether the exception is due to your application or the implementation. The nested exception indicates the cause of the exception. A `JDOFatalUserException` is thrown if the class specified by the `javax.jdo.PersistenceManagerFactoryClass` property is not found or accessible. If the class exists, but it does not have a public static implementation of `getPersistenceManagerFactory(Properties)`, a `JDOFatalInternalException` is thrown. If the method does exist, but it throws an exception, it is rethrown by the `JDOHelper` method.

Implementations may manage a map of instantiated `PersistenceManagerFactory` instances that have specific property key values, and return a previously instantiated `PersistenceManagerFactory` instance with the property values you request. The same `PersistenceManagerFactory` instance can be returned when the application makes multiple calls to construct an instance with the same property values, using the same or different `Properties` instances.

The `PersistenceManagerFactory` interface provides methods to get and set the values of its properties. However, since `getPersistenceManagerFactory()` can return a previously constructed `PersistenceManagerFactory` instance, the returned instance is sealed (i.e., its properties cannot be changed), and any call to alter a property with a set method throws an exception. Portable applications should therefore completely initialize the PersistenceManagerFactory with the properties in a Properties instance. If you want to call the set methods to initialize property values, you can construct the PersistenceManagerFactory with a vendor-specific constructor. This will return a nonsealed instance that can have its properties changed, but using such vendor-specific constructors is not portable.

Connection Properties

The following connection properties are used to configure a datastore connection:

javax.jdo.option.ConnectionURL

> The ConnectionURL property identifies the specific datastore to access. The syntax and value of this parameter is determined by the underlying datastore. If you are using a JDO implementation that is layered on top of a JDBC connection, you will likely specify the same value a JDBC application would use to establish a connection. The JDO implementation uses the ConnectionURL property value to establish its internal JDBC connection.

javax.jdo.option.ConnectionDriverName

> The ConnectionDriverName property is used to specify the particular database driver. For example, oracle.jdbc.driver.OracleDriver is a common driver used with Oracle. A ConnectionDriverName is normally required when accessing a relational database with JDBC. Some datastores, such as an object database, do not have multiple drivers. For these datastores, it is not necessary to provide a value for ConnectionDriverName.

javax.jdo.option.ConnectionUserName *and* javax.jdo.option.ConnectionPassword

> Most datastores perform access authentication by requiring a username and password. The ConnectionUserName and ConnectionPassword properties are used to initialize these connection properties. An alternative to providing these two values in the Properties object used to initialize the PersistenceManagerFactory is to call the getPersistenceManager() method that accepts the userid and password as parameters.

javax.jdo.option.ConnectionFactoryName

> The ConnectionFactoryName property identifies the name of the connection factory from which the JDO implementation should obtain datastore connections. JNDI is used to locate the connection factory with the given name.

> Instead of providing the name of the factory, you can directly provide the ConnectionFactory instance by passing it as a parameter to setConnectionFactory().

If you are running in a managed environment that has other connection properties that you can and want to set in your application, you can configure a connection factory. When you use a connection factory, the ConnectionURL, ConnectionUserName, and ConnectionPassword connection properties are overridden by the Connection-Factory and ConnectionFactoryName properties.

If you set multiple connection properties, they are evaluated in order. If you specify ConnectionFactory, all other connection properties are ignored. If you do not specify ConnectionFactory, but you specify ConnectionFactoryName, all other properties are ignored.

If you use a connection factory, you should provide values for the following properties, if the datastore has a corresponding concept:

URL
> The URL of the datastore

UserName
> The name of the user establishing the connection

Password
> The password for the user

DriverName
> The driver name for the connection

ServerName
> The name of the server for the datastore

PortNumber
> The port number for establishing a connection to the datastore

MaxPool
> The maximum number of connections in the connection pool

MinPool
> The minimum number of connections in the connection pool

MsWait
> The number of milliseconds to wait for an available connection from the connection pool before throwing a JDODataStoreException

LogWriter
> The PrintWriter to which messages should be sent

LoginTimeout
> The number of seconds to wait for a new connection to be established to the datastore

The PersistenceManagerFactory instance may also support additional properties that are specific to the datastore or PersistenceManager.

In an application-server environment, a connection factory always returns connections that are enlisted in the thread's current transaction context. Using optimistic transactions requires an additional connection factory that returns connections that are not enlisted in the current transaction context. (Chapter 15 discusses this in detail.) For this purpose, the `ConnectionFactory2Name` property and `setConnectionFactory2( )` method are used:

`javax.jdo.option.ConnectionFactory2Name`
> The `ConnectionFactory2Name` property identifies the name of the connection factory from which nontransactional datastore connections are obtained. JNDI is used to locate the connection factory by name.
>
> Alternatively, you can specify the connection factory instance directly by passing it as a parameter to `setConnectionFactory2( )`.

The following list provides the get and set methods for each of the connection properties:

`javax.jdo.option.ConnectionURL`
Get method: `String getConnectionURL( )`
Set method: `void setConnectionURL(String)`

`javax.jdo.option.ConnectionUserName`
Get method: `String getConnectionUserName( )`
Set method: `void setConnectionUserName(String)`

`javax.jdo.option.ConnectionPassword`
Get method: none
Set method: `void setConnectionPassword(String)`

`javax.jdo.option.ConnectionFactoryName`
Get methods: `String getConnectionFactoryName( )`
              `Object getConnectionFactory( )`
Set methods: `void setConnectionFactoryName(String)`
              `void setConnectionFactory(Object)`

`javax.jdo.option.ConnectionFactory2Name`
Get methods: `String getConnectionFactory2Name()`
              `Object getConnectionFactory2( )`
Set methods: `void setConnectionFactory2Name(String)`
              `void setConnectionFactory2(Object)`

`javax.jdo.option.ConnectionDriverName`
Get method: `String getConnectionDriverName( )`
Set method: `void setConnectionDriverName(String)`

Optional Feature Properties

Properties are also available to initialize the settings of the optional features. Specifically, the following transaction properties can be initialized (they are covered in detail in later chapters):

- `javax.jdo.option.NontransactionalRead`
- `javax.jdo.option.NontransactionalWrite`
- `javax.jdo.option.Optimistic`
- `javax.jdo.option.RetainValues`

These properties affect the runtime behavior of the application. You can provide a value for these flags when you configure your JDO runtime environment. The flags can be initialized in the `Properties` object used to construct the `Persistence-ManagerFactory`. If you attempt to set one of these properties to true and the implementation does not support it, a `JDOUnsupportedOptionException` is thrown.

The following list provides the get and set methods for the optional feature properties:

`javax.jdo.option.NontransactionalRead`
    Get method: `boolean getNontransactionalRead( )`
    Set method: `void setNontransactionalRead(boolean)`

`javax.jdo.option.NontransactionalWrite`
    Get method: `boolean getNontransactionalWrite( )`
    Set method: `void setNontransactionalWrite(boolean)`

`javax.jdo.option.Optimistic`
    Get method: `boolean getOptimistic( )`
    Set method: `void setOptimistic(boolean)`

`javax.jdo.option.RetainValues`
    Get method: `boolean getRetainValues( )`
    Set method: `void setRetainValues(boolean)`

Flags

You can also set some additional flags to control the behavior of your JDO environment. These flags have the following properties, which can be used to configure the `PersistenceManagerFactory`:

- `javax.jdo.option.IgnoreCache`
- `javax.jdo.option.Multithreaded`
- `javax.jdo.option.RestoreValues`

We discuss `Multithreaded` and `RestoreValues` later in this chapter. Chapters 8 and 9 describe `IgnoreCache`.

Flags Settings in Multiple Interfaces

Some features have flags that you can get and set to control the behavior of your JDO environment. These flags are maintained in several JDO interfaces. Table 7-2 lists these features and the JDO interfaces that have associated flags and methods for managing their settings.

Table 7-2. Methods to manage flags for features

Feature	Interfaces with methods to get/set flags
NontransactionalRead	PersistenceManagerFactory, Transaction
NontransactionalWrite	PersistenceManagerFactory, Transaction
Optimistic	PersistenceManagerFactory, Transaction
RetainValues	PersistenceManagerFactory, Transaction
RestoreValues	PersistenceManagerFactory, Transaction
IgnoreCache	PersistenceManagerFactory, PersistenceManager, Query

All of these flags have Boolean values. For example, the following methods are defined in Transaction and PersistenceManagerFactory:

```
void     setOptimistic(boolean flag);
boolean  getOptimistic();
```

If the implementation does not support an optional feature, the value of the associated flag in these interfaces is false. If you attempt to set the flag to true, a JDOUnsupportedOptionException is thrown. For optional features that the implementation does support, it can choose a default value of true or false for the flag. A JDO vendor usually selects a default value most suited to their implementation.

If you want to guarantee that your application behaves consistently across implementations, you should set the values of these flags explicitly (assuming that the implementation supports the feature you wish to enable). Setting a flag to false protects you from unexpected behavior in the future, if the implementation later enables the feature with a default setting of true. You can initialize these flags within the property file that you use to construct the PersistenceManagerFactory.

Determining the Optional Features and Default Flag Settings

You can determine which optional features an implementation supports by calling the following PersistenceManagerFactory method:

```
Collection supportedOptions();
```

This method returns a Collection of String values, where each element represents an optional feature or query language that the implementation supports. If the implementation does not support an optional feature, this method does not return its associated option string.

The string "javax.jdo.query.JDOQL" indicates that the standard JDO query language is supported. An implementation may also support other query languages; if so, a value is returned to identify each supported query language. These alternative, implementation-specific query languages (and their associated names) are not defined in the JDO specification.

Example 7-1 is a small application that lists the optional features and default flag values for the optional features listed in Table 7-2. It extends the MediaManiaApp class used in Chapter 1. To get the implementation's default values, the property file used to initialize the PersistenceManagerFactory should not initialize the properties. The application calls supportedOptions( ) on line ❶ to access the options supported by the implementation. Lines ❷ through ❼ call PersistenceManagerFactory methods to access the default values for the optional feature flags.

Example 7-1. Getting an implementation's optional features and default flag values

```
package com.mediamania;

import java.util.Collection;
import java.util.Iterator;
import javax.jdo.PersistenceManagerFactory;

public class GetOptions extends MediaManiaApp {

    public static void main(String[] args) {
        GetOptions options = new GetOptions( );
        options.print( );
    }

    public void print( ) {
        Collection options = pmf.supportedOptions( );
        Iterator iter = options.iterator( );
        System.out.println("Supported options:");
        while ( iter.hasNext( ) ) {
            String option = (String) iter.next( );
            System.out.println(option);
        }
        System.out.println("\nDefault values for flags:");
        System.out.print("IgnoreCache           ");
        System.out.println( pmf.getIgnoreCache( ) );
        System.out.print("NontransactionalRead  ");
        System.out.println( pmf.getNontransactionalRead( ) );
        System.out.print("NontransactionalWrite ");
        System.out.println( pmf.getNontransactionalWrite( ) );
        System.out.print("Optimistic            ");
        System.out.println( pmf.getOptimistic( ) );
        System.out.print("RestoreValues         ");
        System.out.println( pmf.getRestoreValues( ) );
        System.out.print("RetainValues          ");
        System.out.println( pmf.getRetainValues( ) );
    }
    public void execute( ) {
    }
}
```

Sun's JDO reference implementation produces the following output for this program:

```
Supported options:
javax.jdo.option.TransientTransactional
javax.jdo.option.NontransactionalRead
javax.jdo.option.NontransactionalWrite
javax.jdo.option.RetainValues
javax.jdo.option.Optimistic
javax.jdo.option.ApplicationIdentity
javax.jdo.option.DatastoreIdentity
javax.jdo.option.ArrayList
javax.jdo.option.HashMap
javax.jdo.option.Hashtable
javax.jdo.option.LinkedList
javax.jdo.option.TreeMap
javax.jdo.option.TreeSet
javax.jdo.option.Vector
javax.jdo.option.Array
javax.jdo.option.NullCollection
javax.jdo.query.JDOQL

Default values for flags:
IgnoreCache           true
NontransactionalRead  true
NontransactionalWrite false
Optimistic            true
RestoreValues         true
RetainValues          true
```

Notice that all of the flags in Table 7-2 have a setting maintained in a PersistenceManagerFactory instance. When you call getPersistenceManager() to construct a PersistenceManager instance, the values of the flags in the PersistenceManagerFactory are copied into the PersistenceManager instance. When you call currentTransaction() to access the associated Transaction instance, the transaction-related flags in the Transaction instance get the same values that were set in the PersistenceManagerFactory instance. If you want a flag in the Transaction instance to have a different value, you can call the flag's set method in the Transaction interface. But do not call these methods when a transaction is active.

The value of the IgnoreCache flag in a PersistenceManager affects the behavior of extent iteration and queries. Basically, it determines whether changes you have already made to instances in the application cache should be reflected in extents and the results of queries. The IgnoreCache flag is covered in Chapter 8 and Chapter 9 when we cover extents and queries, respectively.

In a nonmanaged environment, you can use multiple PersistenceManager instances. Each call to PersistenceManagerFactory.getPersistenceManager() returns a new instance for your use. You can change the IgnoreCache flag in a PersistenceManager instance. So, it is possible to have two PersistenceManager instances, where one has its IgnoreCache flag set to true, and the other has it set to false.

The IgnoreCache setting in a PersistenceManager establishes the initial value of the IgnoreCache flag in each Query you construct via a call to PersistenceManager.newQuery( ). So, you can construct multiple Query instances and set the values of their respective IgnoreCache flags independently.

Vendor-Specific Properties

A JDO implementation can define its own property keys. You can use the property keys to initialize implementation-specific properties when you configure a PersistenceManagerFactory. Each such property key should have a prefix that associates it with the vendor's implementation. Implementations silently ignore any properties that they do not recognize. If they recognize a property key that they do not support and you specify a value that enables the feature, a JDOFatalUserException is thrown when you call getPersistenceManagerFactory( ).

Nonconfigurable Properties

A JDO vendor may provide nonconfigurable properties and make them available to your application via a Properties instance, which can be retrieved with the following PersistenceManagerFactory method:

```
Properties getProperties( );
```

Each key and value is a String. All JDO implementations support two standard keys:

VendorName
> The name of the JDO vendor

VersionNumber
> The release number of the vendor's implementation

Other properties returned by getProperties( ) are vendor-specific. This method does not return the configurable properties we covered previously. Your application can modify the returned Properties instance, but the modifications do not affect the behavior of the PersistenceManagerFactory instance.

Acquiring a PersistenceManager

Once you have configured a PersistenceManagerFactory with the appropriate property settings, you can call one of the following PersistenceManagerFactory methods to construct a PersistenceManager instance:

```
PersistenceManager getPersistenceManager( );
PersistenceManager getPersistenceManager(String userid, String password);
```

The returned instance may come from a pool of PersistenceManager instances, but the property values in the returned PersistenceManager instance are equal to their values in the PersistenceManagerFactory instance.

After your first call to getPersistenceManager( ), none of the set methods in the PersistenceManagerFactory will succeed. You may be able to modify the setting of operational parameters dynamically using a vendor-specific interface.

If you acquire the PersistenceManager by calling the getPersistenceManager( ) method that has the userid and password parameters, all of the manager's accesses to get a connection from the connection factory use the provided userid and password. If PersistenceManager instances are pooled, then getPersistenceManager( ) returns only a PersistenceManager instance with the same userid and password.

You may need to access the PersistenceManagerFactory that was used to create a PersistenceManager. You can call the following PersistenceManager method to access it:

```
PersistenceManagerFactory  getPersistenceManagerFactory( );
```

If a PersistenceManagerFactory instance was not used to create the Persistence-Manager instance (e.g., a call to a vendor-specific PersistenceManager constructor was used), this method returns null.

User Object

Your application may use multiple PersistenceManager instances concurrently. You may find it useful to define a class that is responsible for managing and tracking the set of PersistenceManager instances. In such circumstances, it is useful to associate the manager object responsible for each PersistenceManager instance and be able to access the manager object from the PersistenceManager instance. The following PersistenceManager methods allow you to set and get an instance to be associated with a PersistenceManager instance:

```
void    setUserObject(Object object);
Object getUserObject( );
```

You have complete freedom in how this user object is used. The implementation does not inspect or use it in any way.

Closing a PersistenceManager

A PersistenceManager maintains a set of resources that it uses to manage persistent instances. If you are finished using a PersistenceManager, you can close it to free up its resources by calling its close( ) method:

```
void close( );
```

After you call close( ), all methods on the PersistenceManager instance (except isClosed( )) throw a JDOFatalUserException. If the current transaction is active when you call close( ), a JDOUserException is thrown.

When the PersistenceManager instance is closed, it might be returned to a pool of PersistenceManager instances or garbage-collected, at the choice of the implementation. Before it can be used to satisfy another getPersistenceManager() request, its properties are reset to the values specified in its associated PersistenceManager-Factory instance.

You can call the following PersistenceManager method to determine whether a PersistenceManager is closed:

```
boolean isClosed();
```

Once the PersistenceManager instance has been constructed or retrieved from a pool, it returns false. It returns true only after close() has successfully closed the instance.

Closing a PersistenceManagerFactory

A PersistenceManagerFactory also maintains significant resources. If you no longer need a PersistenceManagerFactory, you can close it with the following method:

```
void close();
```

This method disables the PersistenceManagerFactory and relinquishes its associated resources.

Closing a PersistenceManagerFactory prematurely can have a significant impact on the operation of the JDO environment. Therefore, a security check is made for JDOPermission("closePersistenceManagerFactory") to determine whether the caller has been granted permission to close a PersistenceManagerFactory. If the permission check fails, close() does not close the PersistenceManagerFactory and throws a SecurityException.

This close() method automatically closes all PersistenceManager instances that are still open and do not have an active Transaction. If some PersistenceManager instances do have active Transaction instances, a JDOUserException is thrown. The JDOUserException instance thrown to the caller of close() does not have a failed instance. It has a nested exception array that contains a JDOUserException for each PersistenceManager that could not be closed. Each nested JDOUserException references a PersistenceManager as the failed instance.

Transactions

Accesses and updates to persistent instances are performed in the context of a transaction. The JDO Transaction interface provides the methods you use to begin and commit a transaction. It also has methods to manage the settings of transaction flags.

It is similar in functionality to a `javax.transaction.UserTransaction`. Both interfaces have `begin()`, `commit()`, and `rollback()` methods with the same semantics and behavior.

A one-to-one relationship exists between a `PersistenceManager` and its associated `Transaction` instance. A `PersistenceManager` instance represents a single view of persistent data, including persistent instances that have been cached across multiple serial transactions. If your application needs multiple concurrent transactions, each transaction will have its own `Transaction` instance and associated `Persistence-Manager` instance.

You call methods in the JDO `Transaction` interface to perform operations on a transaction. The underlying datastore has its own representation for a transaction, with its own operations and interfaces. JDO supports a type of transaction referred to as a *datastore transaction*. This is not the transaction in the underlying datastore. We refer to the transaction at the datastore level as the *transaction in the datastore*, to distinguish it from the JDO datastore transaction.

Properties of Transactions

Transactions have a set of common properties that are referred to as the ACID (Atomic, Consistent, Isolated, Durable) properties of a transaction. JDO transactions support these properties.

Atomic
> Within a transaction, either *all* or *none* of the changes made to instances are propagated to the datastore.

Consistent
> A change to a value in an instance is consistent with changes to any other values in the same instance and all other instances in the same transaction.

Isolated
> Changes to instances are isolated from changes made in other transactions.

Durable
> Changes to persistent instances survive the end of the Java Virtual Machine context in which they are made.

Transactions and Locking in the Datastore

Instead of attempting to redefine the semantics of datastore transactions, JDO defines operations on persistent instances that use the underlying datastore operations. In order to understand the differences between the JDO transaction modes, it is useful to understand how transaction guarantees are implemented in datastores.

Durability is mainly a datastore-implementation detail, in which changes are guaranteed to be persistent in the face of various failure modes of hardware, software, and the computing environment.

Atomicity means that the datastore manages the changes associated with each instance, such that at commit time all of the changes to each instance are applied, and a failure to apply any change invalidates the entire set of changes. Additionally, all changes are made to the instances, or none are made.

Consistency is a responsibility shared between the application and the datastore. It applies to all of the instances that were accessed during a transaction, whether the access was for read or write. Consistency requires that if multiple instances are related in some way, then changes in one of the instances are made consistently with changes in other instances.

Transaction-isolation levels

Isolation is the most complex of the transaction guarantees, and datastore vendors adopt many strategies to achieve it. Isolation is so complex because there is a significant performance penalty associated with *strict isolation*, which requires that transactions execute as if they operated completely independent of each another. Therefore, datastores provide varying levels of isolation with different performance characteristics, allowing applications to choose a level of isolation that provides an appropriate balance between consistency and performance.

The isolation levels can be characterized as follows:

Level 0 (Dirty Read; Read Uncommitted)
> Transactions might read data from transactions that have not yet committed; therefore, there is no guarantee of consistency, although concurrency is highest.

Level 1 (Cursor Stability; Read Committed)
> Transactions will read data only from committed transactions. Updates in one transaction will not overwrite updates from another transaction. Reading the same data twice might result in different data the second time.

Level 2 (Repeatable Read)
> Updates in one transaction will not overwrite updates from another transaction. Reading the same data twice is guaranteed to return the same results each time, but queries might return different results due to inserted data between the queries (sometimes called *phantom reads*).

Level 3 (Serializable; Isolated)
> Updates in one transaction will not overwrite updates from another transaction. Reading the same data twice is guaranteed to return the same results each time. Reading data prevents other transactions from updating the data. Queries return the same results if they are executed twice.

It is significant to note here that JDO does not mandate any specific isolation level; decisions regarding which isolation level to use, whether to expose the isolation level to applications, and how to expose the level are made by the JDO implementation.

Locking in the datastore

To implement level 1, level 2, and level 3 transaction isolation, datastores often implement isolation of transactions in the datastore using *locking*. Locking is typically implemented by associating a *lock instance* with each datastore operation. The lock instance contains the transaction identifier, the lock mode, and the datastore instance. Locks are stored in a *lock table*.

When an operation is performed to read, write, insert, or delete a datastore instance, the datastore creates a lock instance for the current operation and tries to add the lock to the lock table. The lock addition fails if an incompatible lock already exists in the lock table. Depending on the datastore implementation, the incompatibility might result in the transaction waiting for some timeout period, or immediately failing. During the timeout period, the transaction with the conflicting lock might commit or roll back, thereby allowing the waiting transaction to proceed.

Lock compatibilities are typically implemented using a *lock-compatibility matrix*, a simplified version of which is illustrated in Table 7-3. Most datastores implement a much more sophisticated version of this matrix.

Table 7-3. Lock-compatibility matrix

		Lock Requested	
		Exclusive	Shared
Lock Held	**Exclusive**	No	No
	Shared	No	OK

Read requests use shared locks, while insert, update, and delete requests use exclusive locks. Thus, multiple transactions can read the same datastore instances without conflict, but if a transaction is reading an instance, that instance cannot be updated or deleted by another transaction until all transactions holding the shared lock complete. Similarly, if a transaction deletes an instance, no other transaction can access that instance until the transaction holding the exclusive lock on the deleted instance completes.

The effect of locking with long transactions is significant. While the long transaction is active, all other transactions that attempt to access instances used in it are subject to the compatibility rules of the lock table. Even if the long transaction only holds read locks, other transactions that attempt to update the same instances will wait for completion of the long transaction.

This is a simplified view of datastore locks; for a more detailed understanding of database locking, you should consult your JDO implementation's documentation.

Types of Transactions in JDO

Transactions are a fundamental aspect of JDO. All changes to instances that should be reflected in the datastore are performed in the context of a transaction. JDO supports three transaction-management strategies:

Nontransactional access

> The ability to access instances from the datastore without having a transaction in the datastore in progress is an optional feature in JDO. The NontransactionalRead and NontransactionalWrite features determine whether an application can read and modify instances in memory outside of a transaction. But any modifications you make to instances in memory outside of a transaction cannot be propagated directly to the datastore.

Datastore transaction

> When you use a datastore transaction, all the operations you perform on persistent data are done within a single transaction in the datastore. This means that between the first data access in the transaction and the commit of that transaction, a single active transaction is used in the datastore. Datastore transactions are supported in all JDO implementations.

Optimistic transaction

> When you use an optimistic transaction, operations on instances in memory outside a JDO transaction or before transaction commit are implemented by the JDO implementation with a series of short local transactions in the datastore. If an optimistic transaction has updates that need to be propagated to the datastore, when you commit the optimistic transaction the JDO implementation uses an underlying transaction in the datastore to verify that the proposed changes do not conflict with updates that may have been committed by other, concurrent transactions. Optimistic transactions are an optional feature in JDO.

If you anticipate that you will primarily have concurrent transactions attempting to access and modify the same instances, resulting in lock conflicts, then you should use datastore transactions. If you anticipate that lock conflicts will not occur, you should consider optimistic transactions. In these situations, optimistic transactions place fewer demands on the datastore, because locks are not maintained throughout the duration of the optimistic transaction. We continue to use datastore transactions until we cover nontransactional access in Chapter 14 and optimistic transactions in Chapter 15.

Acquiring a Transaction

You can access the Transaction instance associated with a PersistenceManager by calling the following PersistenceManager method:

```
Transaction currentTransaction( );
```

All calls you make to currentTransaction( ) for a given PersistenceManager instance return the same Transaction instance until you have closed the PersistenceManager instance with a call to close( ). You can use the same Transaction instance to execute multiple serial transactions. If you want to execute multiple parallel transactions in a JVM, then you can use multiple PersistenceManager instances.

You can call the following Transaction method to access its associated PersistenceManager instance:

```
PersistenceManager getPersistenceManager( );
```

Setting the Transaction Type

PersistenceManagerFactory and Transaction instances each maintain a flag that indicates whether to use a datastore or optimistic transaction. If an implementation does not support optimistic transactions, these PersistenceManagerFactory and Transaction flags will always be false. If the application attempts to set the flag to true, a JDOUnsupportedOptionException is thrown. If the implementation supports optimistic transactions, whether the default value is true or false is the implementation's choice.

You can initialize the Optimistic flag when the PersistenceManagerFactory instance is constructed. You can also get and set the Optimistic flag in the Persistence-ManagerFactory and Transaction instances with the following methods:

```
void     setOptimistic(boolean flag);
boolean  getOptimistic( );
```

Calling setOptimistic( ) with a false parameter value indicates that datastore transactions should be used, and calling it with a true value indicates that optimistic transactions should be used. You cannot call these methods when a Transaction instance is active (i.e., after you call begin( ) and before you call commit( ) or rollback( )).

Transaction Demarcation

Your application is responsible for transaction demarcation in a nonmanaged environment. In the managed environment of an application server, transaction demarcation is performed for you automatically. One exception is when you use bean-managed transactions. The following discussion applies only when you are running in a nonmanaged environment or using bean-managed transactions in an EJB environment. Managed environments are covered in Chapter 16 and Chapter 17. If you call these transaction-demarcation methods in a managed environment with container-managed transactions, a JDOUserException is thrown.

You call the following Transaction method to begin a transaction:

```
void begin( );
```

You then call commit( ) or rollback( ) to complete the transaction:

```
void commit( );
void rollback( );
```

Calling commit( ) indicates that you want all the updates that were made in the transaction to be propagated to the datastore. Calling rollback( ) indicates that none of the changes should be made in the datastore.

The following code illustrates the use of begin( ), commit( ), and rollback( ). It also shows that you can use the same Transaction instance to execute multiple transactions serially. In addition, it demonstrates that repeated calls to currentTransaction( ) for a PersistenceManager instance return the same Transaction instance.

```
// assume pmf variable is initialized to a PersistenceManagerFactory
PersistenceManager pm = pmf.getPersistenceManager( );
Transaction tx = pm.currentTransaction( );
try {
    tx.begin( );

    // place application's access of database here

    tx.commit( );
} catch (JDOException jdoException) {
    tx.rollback( );
    System.err.println("JDOException thrown:");
    jdoException.printStackTrace( );
}

// ...

try {
    tx.begin( );

    // place application's access of database here

    tx.commit( );
} catch (JDOException jdoException) {
    tx.rollback( );
    System.err.println("JDOException thrown:");
    jdoException.printStackTrace( );
}

// ...

❶ Transaction trans = pm.currentTransaction( ); // trans and tx reference same instance
try {
    trans.begin( );

    // place application's access of database here

    trans.commit( );
} catch (JDOException jdoException) {
```

```
        trans.rollback();
        System.err.println("JDOException thrown:");
        jdoException.printStackTrace();
    }
```

We call currentTransaction() on line ❶ to get a Transaction instance. We do this here only to point out that the Transaction instance returned on line ❶ is the same instance referenced by the tx variable. All calls you make to currentTransaction() for a given PersistenceManager return the same Transaction instance.

Notification of transaction completion

The javax.transaction package has an interface, called Synchronization, that is used to notify an application when a transaction-completion process is about to begin. And when the completion process has finished, it provides a status indicating whether the transaction committed successfully.

The Synchronization interface has the following two methods:

```
void beforeCompletion();
void afterCompletion(int status);
```

The beforeCompletion() method is called prior to the start of the transaction-commit process; it is not called during rollback. The afterCompletion() method is called after the transaction has been committed or rolled back. The status parameter passed to afterCompletion() indicates whether the transaction committed or rolled back successfully. Its value is either STATUS_COMMITTED or STATUS_ROLLEDBACK; these are defined in the javax.transaction.Status interface. These two methods provide an application with some control over the environment in which the transaction completion executes (for example, to validate the state of instances in the cache before transaction completion) and the ability to perform some functionality once the transaction completes.

JDO supports the Synchronization interface. To use it, you must declare a class that implements it. You can register one instance of the class with the Transaction instance using the following method:

```
void setSynchronization(javax.transaction.Synchronization sync);
```

Calling this method replaces any Synchronization instance already registered. If you need more than one instance to receive notification, then your Synchronization class is responsible for managing this, forwarding callbacks as necessary. If you pass a null to the method, this indicates that no instance should be notified. If you call setSynchronization() during commit processing (within beforeCompletion() or afterCompletion()), a JDOUserException is thrown.

You can retrieve the currently registered Synchronization instance by calling the following Transaction method:

```
javax.transaction.Synchronization getSynchronization();
```

Commit processing

`Transaction.commit( )` performs the following operations:

- It makes a call to `beforeCompletion( )` on the `Synchronization` instance registered with the `Transaction` (if there is one).
- It flushes (propagates) modified persistent instances to the datastore.
- It notifies the underlying datastore to commit the transaction.
- It transitions the states of persistent instances according to the JDO instance lifecycle specification; this is covered in Chapter 11 and Appendix A.
- It makes a call to `afterCompletion( )` for the `Synchronization` instance registered with the `Transaction` (if there is one), passing the results of the datastore commit operation.

Additional steps are taken with optimistic transactions, which are covered in Chapter 15.

Rollback processing

`Transaction.rollback( )` performs the following operations:

- It rolls back changes made in this transaction in the datastore.
- It transitions the states of persistent instances according to the JDO instance lifecycle specification.
- It makes a call to `afterCompletion( )` for the `Synchronization` instance registered with the `Transaction` (if there is one).

Restoring Values on Rollback

The `RestoreValues` feature controls the behavior that occurs at transaction rollback. If it is `true`, persistent and transactional instances are restored to their state as of the beginning of the transaction; if it is `false`, the state of instances is not restored. If `RestoreValues` is `true`, the values of fields of instances made persistent during the transaction are restored to their state as of the call to `makePersistent( )`. If `RestoreValues` is `false`, they keep the values they had when `rollback( )` was called.

You call the following `Transaction` methods to get and set the `RestoreValues` flag:

```
boolean getRestoreValues( );
void    setRestoreValues(boolean flag);
```

The value of the `flag` parameter replaces the currently active `RestoreValues` setting. You can call this method only when the transaction is not active; otherwise, a `JDOUserException` is thrown.

Determining Whether a Transaction Is Active

Call the following Transaction method to determine whether a transaction is active:

```
boolean isActive();
```

It returns true after the transaction has been started and until Synchronization. afterCompletion( ) has been called.

Multiple PersistenceManagers

A PersistenceManager supports one transaction and uses one connection to the underlying datastore at a time. A PersistenceManager might use multiple transactions serially, and it might use multiple connections in the datastore serially.

But you may want to perform multiple transactions concurrently. You can do this by instantiating multiple PersistenceManager instances. Each will have its own Transaction instance. Each call to PersistenceManagerFactory. getPersistenceManager( ) returns a new PersistenceManager instance. Each persistent instance in the JVM is associated with a single PersistenceManager. Multiple PersistenceManager instances may have their own separate copy of the same datastore instance. A common application-programming technique is to have a separate thread or thread group for each PersistenceManager that is managing a set of instances.

You can also use multiple PersistenceManager instances from different JDO implementations in the same JVM. This is how things operate in an application-server environment, where each active session has its own transaction. Each active session has its own PersistenceManager instance. Because of JDO's binary compatibility capabilities, these PersistenceManager instances can manipulate instances of the same persistent classes.

Multithreading

You may have a simple application that requires only a single transaction at a time. It would use a single PersistenceManager and may perform successive transactions using the associated Transaction instance. You may have only a single thread accessing the persistent instances and instances of the JDO interface, but you may want multiple threads to access instances. In this case, you need to inform the JDO implementation that multiple threads are accessing the JDO environment.

A JDO implementation is *thread safe*, which means that its behavior is predictable in the presence of multiple application threads. When the application accesses and modifies persistent or transactional fields of persistent instances, the PersistenceManager performs its operations as if the operations were serialized. It is free to serialize internal data structures and order multithreaded operations in any way it chooses. The only application-visible behavior is that operations might block indefinitely (but not infinitely) while other operations complete.

Synchronizing a `PersistenceManager` instance is a relatively expensive operation. Many applications do not need multiple threads using the same `PersistenceManager` instance. If your application has multiple threads accessing a `PersistenceManager` or the instances it manages (e.g., persistent or transactional instances of persistent classes, instances of `Transaction` or `Query`, query results, etc.), you need to notify the `PersistenceManager` that multiple threads may access it.

You notify a `PersistenceManager` that it may be used by multiple application threads by setting the `Multithreaded` flag to true. This instructs the `PersistenceManager` to synchronize internally to avoid corruption of data structures due to multiple application threads. You call the following methods to get and set the `Multithreaded` flag:

```
boolean getMultithreaded();
void    setMultithreaded(boolean flag);
```

These methods are available in the `PersistenceManagerFactory` and `Persistence-Manager` interfaces. You can also set the flag via the `javax.jdo.option.Multithreaded` property when you construct the `PersistenceManagerFactory`. You can also perform your own synchronization. In this case, you would set the `Multithreaded` flag to false.

JDO implementations do not use user-visible instances (e.g., instances of `PersistenceManagerFactory`, `PersistenceManager`, `Transaction`, `Query`, etc.) as synchronization objects, with one exception. The implementation must synchronize instances of persistent classes during a state transition that replaces the `StateManager`. This occurs if the application attempts to make the same instance persistent concurrently in multiple `PersistenceManager` instances.

If your application needs to serialize its own operations, you must implement your own appropriate synchronizing behavior, using instances visible to the application. This may include JDO interface instances (e.g., `PersistenceManager`, `Query`, etc.) and instances of your persistent classes.

CHAPTER 8

Instance Management

Your object model is usually composed of a set of classes with many interrelationships. The graph of all the related instances of those classes may include the entire contents of the datastore, but typically your applications deal with only a small number of the persistent instances at a time. JDO provides the illusion that your application can access the entire graph of connected instances, while in reality it only instantiates the small subset of instances that the application needs. This concept is called *transparent data access*, *transparent persistence*, or simply *transparency*.

A PersistenceManager manages the persistent instances accessed from a datastore. It provides methods to make instances persistent and to delete instances from the datastore. It also provides factory methods to construct Extent and Query instances, which you use to access instances from the datastore.

A PersistenceManager can manage any number of persistent instances at a time. Each instance of a persistent class is associated with one PersistenceManager or zero PersistenceManagers. A transient instance is not associated with any Persistence-Manager instance. As soon as an instance is made persistent or transactional, it is associated with exactly one PersistenceManager.

You can use a static JDOHelper method to access the PersistenceManager associated with a persistent instance:

```
static PersistenceManager getPersistenceManager(Object obj);
```

It returns null if the obj parameter is null, a transient instance of a persistent class, or an instance of a transient (nonpersistent) class.

This chapter describes how to make instances persistent, access them via an extent, navigate among persistent instances, modify their state, and delete instances from the datastore. These are referred to as the CRUD operations of using a database: Create, Read, Update, and Delete. Chapter 13 covers advanced operations for managing instances.

Persistence of Instances

A class is persistent if it has been specified in a JDO metadata file and enhanced. An instance of a persistent class can be either transient or persistent. The JDO specification refers to a persistent class as *persistence-capable* to emphasize that while a class provides support for persistence, it allows instances to be transient or persistent. We just use the phrase *persistent class* and note that instances can be either transient or persistent. We refer to classes that are not persistent as *transient classes*. All instances of a transient class are transient.

All instances of transient and persistent classes that you construct in your applications are initially transient. They become persistent explicitly when you pass them to makePersistent( ), or implicitly if they are referenced by a persistent instance at transaction commit.

Explicit Persistence

You can call the following PersistenceManager method to make a transient instance persistent explicitly:

```
void makePersistent(Object obj);
```

You must call it in the context of an active transaction, or a JDOUserException is thrown.

Null Parameters

The PersistenceManager interface has methods that are passed references to one or more instances; the parameters are defined as one of the following types: Object, Object[], and Collection. You can pass a null value for these parameters. If you pass a null to a method taking an Object parameter, the method has no effect. If you pass null as the value for a parameter of the Object[] or Collection type, the method throws a NullPointerException. If you pass a non-null Object[] or Collection that contains elements that are null, the operation is applied to the non-null elements and the null elements are ignored.

The following program creates some Studio instances and makes them persistent with makePersistent( ):

```
package com.mediamania.content;

import com.mediamania.MediaManiaApp;
import javax.jdo.PersistenceManager;
```

```
public class LoadStudios extends MediaManiaApp {
    public static void main(String[] args) {
        LoadStudios studios = new LoadStudios();
        studios.executeTransaction();
    }
    public void execute() {
        Studio studio = new Studio("Buena Vista");
        pm.makePersistent(studio);
        studio = new Studio("20th Century Fox");
        pm.makePersistent(studio);
        studio = new Studio("DreamWorks SKG");
        pm.makePersistent(studio);
    }
}
```

You can also call one of the following PersistenceManager methods to make an array or collection of instances persistent:

```
void makePersistentAll(Object[] objs);
void makePersistentAll(Collection objs);
```

These methods have no effect on any of the parameter instances that are already persistent and managed by this PersistenceManager. A JDOUserException is thrown if a parameter instance is managed by a different PersistenceManager.

The following program makes an array of RentalCode instances persistent:

```
package com.mediamania.store;

import com.mediamania.MediaManiaApp;
import javax.jdo.PersistenceManager;
import java.math.BigDecimal;

public class LoadRentalCodes extends MediaManiaApp {
    private static BigDecimal cost6 = new BigDecimal("6.00");
    private static BigDecimal cost5 = new BigDecimal("5.00");
    private static BigDecimal cost4 = new BigDecimal("4.00");
    private static BigDecimal cost2 = new BigDecimal("2.00");
    private static BigDecimal cost1 = new BigDecimal("1.00");

    private static RentalCode[] codes = {
        new RentalCode("Hot",      1, cost6, cost6),
        new RentalCode("New",      2, cost5, cost4),
        new RentalCode("Recent",   4, cost5, cost2),
        new RentalCode("Standard", 5, cost4, cost2),
        new RentalCode("Oldie",    7, cost2, cost1)
    };
    public static void main(String[] args) {
        LoadRentalCodes loadRentalCodes = new LoadRentalCodes();
        loadRentalCodes.executeTransaction();
    }
    public void execute() {
        pm.makePersistentAll(codes);
    }
}
```

It is a common mistake to pass an array or collection to makePersistent( ), which has a single instance parameter and makes it persistent. In this case, makePersistent( ) throws an exception because, although arrays and collections are objects, they cannot be persistent by themselves. So, be sure that you call makePersistentAll( ) when making an array or collection of instances persistent. Each PersistenceManager operation that can accept multiple instances, passed by an array or collection, has a method name that ends with the word All.

Persistence-by-Reachability

Within application memory, instances of transient classes and the transient and persistent instances of persistent classes can reference one another. When a persistent instance is committed to the datastore, transient instances of persistent classes that are referenced by persistent fields of the flushed instance also become persistent. This behavior propagates to all instances in the closure of instances reachable through persistent fields. This behavior is called *persistence-by-reachability*.

Figure 8-1 illustrates persistence-by-reachability in an instance diagram.

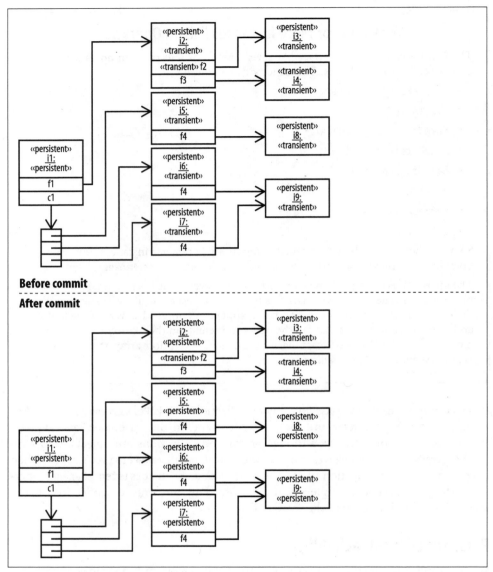

Figure 8-1. Persistence-by-reachability

Each rectangle represents an instance, identified by the names i1 through i9. The UML stereotype notation of «stereotype» is used to indicate whether the class and instance are transient or persistent. The specific class of each instance is not identified, but the topmost stereotype indicates whether the class is persistent or transient. Only i4 is an instance of a transient class; all the others are instances of a persistent class. The stereotype below the instance identifier indicates whether the specific instance is transient or persistent. In the top half of Figure 8-1, i1 is persistent and all other instances are transient. The field c1 is a collection that contains references to i5, i6, and i7. Instance i2 contains a transient field named f2, and it references i3.

The top half of the diagram indicates the persistence of instances in memory prior to commit; the bottom half specifies their persistence after commit. The instances identified as transient in the bottom half of the figure are not in the datastore. Each reference depicted in this model is a persistent field, except for the f2 field in instance i2. The reachability algorithm does not include transient instances referenced by a transient fields. As you can see, the reachability algorithm transitively traverses through references and collections, making all instances of persistent classes persistent. Instance i4 is an instance of a transient class, so it does not become persistent. Instance i3, referenced by the transient field f2, also does not become persistent.

When you explicitly make an instance persistent, any transient instances that are reachable transitively via persistent fields of this instance become *provisionally persistent*. The reachability algorithm runs again at commit. Any instance that was made provisionally persistent during the transaction, but is no longer reachable from a persistent instance at commit, reverts to a transient instance.

The following program loads information about new movies into the database, making extensive use of persistence-by-reachability. In addition, it creates a RentalItem instance for each item that will be rented to customers. A large percentage of the code deals strictly with parsing the input data. Line ❶ creates a Movie instance, which is then made persistent on line ❷. After reading a line of data with movie-content data, the program reads some information about the particular formats of the movie (e.g., DVD and VHS), represented by a MediaItem instance. The parseMediaItemData( ) method reads the information required to initialize a MediaItem instance. Line ❹ creates the MediaItem instance. The input data then contains a line for each rental unit that provides its unique serial number. Line ❺ creates RentalItem instances with the provided serial number and line ❻ associates it with the MediaItem instance. When parseMediaItemData( ) returns the MediaItem instance, line ❸ associates it with the Movie instance.

```
package com.mediamania.store;

import java.io.FileReader;
import java.io.BufferedReader;
import java.io.IOException;
import java.util.Calendar;
import java.util.Date;
import java.util.StringTokenizer;
import java.math.BigDecimal;
import javax.jdo.PersistenceManager;
import com.mediamania.MediaManiaApp;
import com.mediamania.content.*;

public class LoadNewMovies extends MediaManiaApp {
    private BufferedReader  reader;
```

```java
    public static void main(String[] args) {
        LoadNewMovies loadMovies = new LoadNewMovies(args[0]);
        loadMovies.executeTransaction();
    }
    public LoadNewMovies(String filename) {
        try {
            FileReader fr = new FileReader(filename);
            reader = new BufferedReader(fr);
        } catch (Exception e) {
            System.err.print("Unable to open input file ");
            System.err.println(filename);
            System.exit(-1);
        }
    }
    public void execute() {
        try {
            while (reader.ready()) {
                String line = reader.readLine();
                parseMovieData(line);
            }
        } catch (IOException e) {
            System.err.println("Exception reading input file");
            System.err.println(e);
        }
        // when execute returns and the transaction commits, each of the
        // transient Studio, MediaPerson, MediaItem, RentalItem instances
        // associated with the Movie instance we explicitly made persistent
        // will become persistent through reachability
    }

    public void parseMovieData(String line) throws IOException {
        StringTokenizer tokenizer = new StringTokenizer(line, ";");
        String title = tokenizer.nextToken();
        String studioName = tokenizer.nextToken();
        Studio studio = ContentQueries.getStudioByName(pm, studioName);
        if (studio == null)
            studio = new Studio(studioName);  // creates a transient Studio
        String dateStr = tokenizer.nextToken();
        Date releaseDate = Movie.parseReleaseDate(dateStr);
        String rating = tokenizer.nextToken();
        String reasons = tokenizer.nextToken();
        String genres = tokenizer.nextToken();
        int runningTime = 0;
        try {
            runningTime = Integer.parseInt(tokenizer.nextToken());
        } catch (java.lang.NumberFormatException e) {
            System.err.print("Exception parsing running time for ");
            System.err.println(title);
        }
        String directorName = tokenizer.nextToken();
        MediaPerson director = ContentQueries.getMediaPerson(pm, directorName);
        if (director == null) {
            System.err.print("Director named ");
            System.err.print(directorName);
            System.err.print(" for movie ");
```

```
                    System.err.print(title);
                    System.err.println(" not found in the database");
                    director = new MediaPerson(directorName); //creates transient MediaPerson
                }
❶       Movie movie = new Movie(title, studio, releaseDate, rating, reasons,
                                genres, runningTime, director); // creates transient Movie
❷       pm.makePersistent(movie);

                int numFormats = 0;
                try {
                    numFormats = Integer.parseInt(tokenizer.nextToken( ));
                } catch (java.lang.NumberFormatException e) {
                    System.err.print("Exception parsing number of formats for ");
                    System.err.println(title);
                }
                for (int i = 0; i < numFormats; ++i) {
                    MediaItem mediaItem = parseMediaItemData(movie);
❸               movie.addMediaItem(mediaItem); // adds transient MediaItem
                }
            }
    // the following method returns a transient MediaItem
    // and a set of associated transient RentalItems
        private MediaItem parseMediaItemData(MediaContent content)
          throws IOException {
            String line = reader.readLine( );
            StringTokenizer tokenizer = new StringTokenizer(line, ";");
            String format = tokenizer.nextToken( );
            String priceString = tokenizer.nextToken( );
            BigDecimal price = new BigDecimal(priceString);
            String rentalCodeName = tokenizer.nextToken( );
            RentalCode rentalCode = StoreQueries.getRentalCode(pm, rentalCodeName);
            int Nrentals = 0;
            try {
                Nrentals = Integer.parseInt(tokenizer.nextToken( ));
            } catch (java.lang.NumberFormatException e) {
                System.err.print("Exception parsing # of rentals for ");
                System.err.println(content.getTitle( ));
            }
            int NforSale = 0;
            try {
                NforSale = Integer.parseInt(tokenizer.nextToken( ));
            } catch (java.lang.NumberFormatException e) {
                System.err.print("Exception parsing # for sale of ");
                System.err.println(content.getTitle( ));
            }
❹       MediaItem mediaItem = new MediaItem(content, format, price,
                                            rentalCode, NforSale);
            for (int r = 0; r < Nrentals; ++r) {
                String serialNumber = reader.readLine( );
❺           RentalItem rentalItem = new RentalItem(mediaItem, serialNumber);
❻           mediaItem.addRentalItem(rentalItem); // add transient RentalItem
            }
            return mediaItem;
        }
    }
```

When the Movie instance is made persistent on line ❷, a MediaPerson and Studio instance are created and referenced by the Movie instance if they are not found in the database. In this case, when the call is made to makePersistent( ) on line ❷, the MediaPerson and Studio instances become provisionally persistent. References are established from the newly persistent Movie instance to MediaItem instances. References are then established from these MediaItem instances to RentalItem instances on line ❻. The reachability algorithm runs when the transaction commits. If a MediaPerson or Studio instance is still associated with the Movie instance at commit, it becomes persistent. Further, each MediaItem instance associated with the Movie instance and each RentalItem instance associated with each such MediaItem instance are reachable from the Movie instance and become persistent.

A major benefit of persistence-by-reachability is that most of your application can be written entirely independent of JDO, without making any explicit calls to JDO interfaces. Most of your application can use standard Java practices to create and associate instances in memory, without knowing that a datastore or transaction is involved. The JDO implementation automatically handles all the work of storing new persistent instances and associations that you have established established between persistent instances.

Extent Access

An extent provides you with access to all the persistent instances of a class and, optionally, its subclasses. You can iterate over the elements of the extent or perform a query on the extent. The JDO Extent interface represents the extent of a class. Later in this chapter, we will discuss the IgnoreCache flag, which controls whether instances made persistent or deleted during the current transaction are contained in the extent.

You control whether an extent is maintained for a class in the metadata. You use the metadata class element's requires-extent attribute to indicate whether the persistent class has an extent. It has a default value of "true".

If your application does not need to iterate over the instances of a class or perform a query on the extent, you can set the requires-extent attribute to "false" explicitly. Even if a class does not have an extent, you can still make instances persistent, establish references to them, and navigate to them in your application and queries.

JDO 1.0.1 requires that if a class has a requires-extent set to "true", none of its subclasses can set requires-extent to "false". If your application specifies the subclass's parameter to be true when calling the getExtent( ) method for a base class, all subclass instances are included in the iteration of the extent.

Accessing an Extent

You access the Extent associated with a class by calling the following PersistenceManager method:

```
Extent getExtent(Class persistentClass, boolean subclasses);
```

It returns an Extent that contains all the instances in the class specified by the persistentClass parameter and all the instances of its subclasses, if the subclasses parameter is true. If the class identified by the persistentClass parameter does not have an extent, a JDOUserException is thrown. This occurs only if the metadata for the class has the requires-extent attribute set to "false".

The Extent interface has methods you can use to access the components that were used initially to construct the Extent:

```
PersistenceManager getPersistenceManager();
Class              getCandidateClass();
boolean            hasSubclasses();
```

An Extent is not a Java collection instance that has all the instances of the class populated in memory. This is a common misunderstanding. Common Collection behaviors are not possible. For example, you cannot determine whether one Extent contains another, the size of the Extent, or whether the Extent contains a specific instance. Such operations are performed by executing a query against the Extent. An Extent instance is logically a holder of the following information:

- The class of the instances in the Extent
- Whether subclasses are part of the Extent
- A collection of active iterators over the Extent

No datastore action is taken when you construct an Extent. The contents of the Extent are accessed when a query is executed or you use an Iterator to iterate over its elements. An Extent is often used as a parameter to a Query instance. When you perform a query on an Extent, the Extent is used only to identify the prospective datastore instances; its elements are typically not instantiated in the JVM. Chapter 9 covers queries in detail.

Extent Iteration

You call the following Extent method to acquire an Iterator to iterate over all the instances in the Extent:

```
Iterator iterator();
```

You can call iterator() multiple times to construct multiple Iterator instances that can iterate over the extent independently. Extent does not provide any other

Collection methods. If you call any mutating Iterator method, including remove( ), an UnsupportedOperationException is thrown. If you have already accessed a specific instance in the Extent and it is in memory, it is returned. This instance also contains any updates you may have made to it.

An Extent can have a very large number of instances. It might be common for you to iterate over the elements of an Extent. Extents are supposed to be implemented such that you do not get out-of-memory conditions during iteration. If your application does have limitations on the number of instances that can reside in memory, Chapter 13 describes the ability to evict instances from the cache as a means of limiting memory growth.

When you have finished using an extent Iterator, you should close it to free all its associated resources. You can call the following Extent method to close an Iterator acquired from the Extent:

```
void close(Iterator iterator);
```

After this call, the Iterator returns false to hasNext( ) and throws NoSuchElementException if next( ) is called. The Extent itself can still be used to acquire other iterators and perform queries. You can also call the following Extent method to close all of the iterators acquired from the Extent:

```
void closeAll( );
```

The following program demonstrates the use of an Extent. It accesses the MediaContent extent on line ❶ and acquires an Iterator on line ❷. It then iterates through the extent, accessing each MediaContent instance on line ❸.

```
package com.mediamania.store;

import java.util.Iterator;
import javax.jdo.PersistenceManager;
import javax.jdo.Extent;
import com.mediamania.MediaManiaApp;
import com.mediamania.content.MediaContent;

public class GetMediaContent extends MediaManiaApp {
    public static void main(String[] args) {
        GetMediaContent content = new GetMediaContent();
        content.executeTransaction();
    }
    public void execute( ) {
        Extent mediaExtent = pm.getExtent(MediaContent.class, true);
        Iterator iter = mediaExtent.iterator();
        while (iter.hasNext( )) {
            MediaContent media = (MediaContent) iter.next();
            System.out.println(media.getDescription( ));
        }
    }
}
```

Ignoring the Cache

The IgnoreCache flag in the PersistenceManager controls whether instances made persistent or deleted in the current transaction are included during Extent iteration or queries. We cover the effect of IgnoreCache on queries in Chapter 9. If you have set the IgnoreCache flag to false, an implementation that performs queries in the datastore server will need to flush the instances in the application cache to the datastore, so their currently cached state can be reflected in the query result. You can set IgnoreCache to true as a performance-optimizing hint, so the implementation can avoid flushing the cache when a query is executed or an Extent is iterated.

You can use the following PersistenceManager methods to get and set the IgnoreCache flag associated with a PersistenceManager:

```
boolean getIgnoreCache( );
void    setIgnoreCache(boolean flag);
```

The IgnoreCache flag affects the extent Iterators for all Extents obtained from the PersistenceManager.

If you have the IgnoreCache flag set to false in the PersistenceManager when you call iterator( ) to obtain an Iterator instance from an Extent, then:

- The Iterator *will return* instances that were made persistent in the transaction prior to calling iterator( ).
- The Iterator *will not return* instances deleted in the transaction prior to the call to iterator( ).

Setting the IgnoreCache flag to true is only a hint that the Extent can return approximate results by ignoring persistent instances that have been added, modified, or deleted in the current transaction. If IgnoreCache is set to true in the PersistenceManager when an Iterator is obtained, new and deleted instances in the current transaction *might* be ignored by the Iterator, but it is at the option of the implementation. That is, new instances might not be returned, and deleted instances might be returned. Iterating an Extent with IgnoreCache set to true can differ among implementations. Therefore, to be portable you should set the IgnoreCache flag to false.

Accessing and Updating Instances

Once you have accessed some instances by iterating an Extent or executing a query, you can access related instances by traversing references and iterating through collections contained in the accessed instances. The JDO implementation ensures that the related objects are instantiated and read from the datastore. All classes that can access a field—based on its access modifier (public, private, etc.)—can directly access and modify the field, just as they would if the application were not running in a JDO environment.

The following program accesses a specific Movie instance and determines how many DVD copies of the Movie are currently available for rent. It accesses a specific Movie instance and then navigates to related instances. Line ❶ accesses the Movie, based on its title. Appendix E contains the implementation of the StoreQueries class. Line ❷ accesses the set of associated MediaItem instances. We access each MediaItem instance on line ❸ and determine if it is a DVD format on line ❹. If so, line ❺ accesses its set of associated RentalItem instances. We acquire a reference to each RentalItem instance on line ❻. On line ❼, we determine whether the RentalItem is currently being rented. If it is currently rented to a customer, the value of rental will not be null. If rental is null, then it should be in stock and available for rent. In this case, we increment the dvdRentalsInStock counter. Once all the instances have been accessed, we print the value of dvdRentalsInStock on line ❽.

```
        package com.mediamania.store;

        import java.util.Iterator;
        import java.util.Set;
        import javax.jdo.PersistenceManager;
        import javax.jdo.Extent;
        import com.mediamania.MediaManiaApp;
        import com.mediamania.content.Movie;

        public class DVDMovieInStock extends MediaManiaApp {
            private String  title;

            public DVDMovieInStock(String title) {
                this.title = title;
            }
            public static void main(String[] args) {
                DVDMovieInStock inStock = new DVDMovieInStock(args[0]);
                inStock.executeTransaction();
            }
            public void execute() {
                int dvdRentalsInStock = 0;
❶              Movie movie = StoreQueries.getMovieByTitle(pm, title);
❷              Set items = movie.getMediaItems();
                Iterator iter = items.iterator();
                while (iter.hasNext()) {
❸                  MediaItem item = (MediaItem) iter.next();
❹                  if (item.getFormat().equals("DVD")) {
❺                      Set rentals = item.getRentalItems();
                        Iterator rentalIter = rentals.iterator();
                        while (rentalIter.hasNext()) {
❻                          RentalItem rentalItem = (RentalItem) rentalIter.next();
                            Rental rental = rentalItem.getCurrentRental();
❼                          if (rental == null) dvdRentalsInStock++;
                        }
                    }
                }
❽              System.out.print(dvdRentalsInStock);
                System.out.print(" DVD copies of the movie ");
```

```
            System.out.print(title);
            System.out.println(" are in stock");
        }
    }
```

When you modify the field of a persistent instance, the instance is automatically marked as modified. When you commit the transaction, all of the updates are propagated to the datastore.

The following method is defined in the MediaItem class. It is called whenever one or more copies of a particular item are sold to a customer. An application calls this method to update the count of the quantity in stock and the number of items sold year-to-date.

```
public void sold(int qty) {
    if (qty > quantityInStockForPurchase) {
        // report error
    }
    quantityInStockForPurchase -= qty;
    soldYTD += qty;
}
```

These MediaItem field updates are propagated to the datastore at commit.

Explicit Marking of Modified Instances

Instances are automatically marked as modified when a field is changed, except for array fields. An array is a Java system object, and there is no means to associate it with a particular persistent instance that should be notified when it is updated. Some implementations may be able to track changes to an array in the enhanced code of the persistent class. Furthermore, some may track changes to an array that is passed as a reference outside the owning class to another class that has not been enhanced. But these are advanced capabilities that most implementations cannot support, and they are not required by JDO. Thus, if you change an array field in a persistent instance, the changes might not be flushed to the datastore. If you would like your applications to be portable and work correctly across all JDO implementations, you should not depend on the automatic tracking of array changes.

You can call the following JDOHelper method to mark a specific field as being dirty (modified), so that its values are propagated to the datastore when the instance is flushed:

```
static void makeDirty(Object obj, String fieldName);
```

The fieldName parameter identifies the field to be marked as dirty; it can optionally include the field's fully qualified package and class name. This method has no effect if the obj parameter is transient, null, or not a persistent class, or if the field identified by fieldName is not a managed field.

Deleting Instances

You can call one of the following `PersistenceManager` methods to delete one or more persistent instances from the datastore:

```
void deletePersistent(Object obj);
void deletePersistentAll(Object[] objs);
void deletePersistentAll(Collection objs);
```

They must be called in the context of an active transaction, or a `JDOUserException` is thrown. The representation of the instance in the datastore is deleted when it is flushed to the datastore (via `commit( )` or `evict( )`). Chapter 13 covers the `evict( )` method. These methods have no effect on instance parameters that are already deleted in the transaction. They throw a `JDOUserException` if a parameter is transient or managed by a different `PersistenceManager`.

The following application is used to delete a customer from the datastore. This includes deleting all the customer's transactions. Line ❶ accesses the `Customer` instance. If line ❷ determines that `Rental` instances are still associated with the `Customer` instance, the application prints an error message and returns without removing any data. Otherwise, it deletes the `Customer` instance and its associated `Address` and `Transaction` instances.

```
package com.mediamania.store;

import java.util.Set;
import java.util.List;
import com.mediamania.MediaManiaApp;

public class DeleteCustomer extends MediaManiaApp {
    private String lastName;
    private String firstName;

    public DeleteCustomer(String fname, String lname) {
        lastName = lname;
        firstName = fname;
    }
    public static void main(String[] args) {
        DeleteCustomer deleteCustomer = new DeleteCustomer(args[0], args[1]);
        deleteCustomer.executeTransaction();
    }
    public void execute( ) {
        Customer customer = StoreQueries.getCustomer(pm, firstName, lastName);
        Set rentals = customer.getRentals();
        if (!rentals.isEmpty()) {
            System.err.print(firstName); System.err.print(" ");
            System.err.print(lastName);
            System.err.print(" cannot be deleted until current rentals ");
            System.err.println("are returned");
            return;
        }
```

```
        List transactions = customer.getTransactionHistory();
        Address address = customer.getAddress();
        pm.deletePersistent(address);
        pm.deletePersistentAll(transactions);
        pm.deletePersistent(customer);
    }
}
```

Some datastores and JDO implementations support integrity constraints—similar to referential integrity constraints—that could prevent the deletion of an instance. If your application uses these non-JDO facilities, it is implementation-defined whether an exception is thrown at commit or the delete operation is simply ignored. Explicit support for automatic relationship maintenance, delete propagation, and referential integrity constraints are being considered as a possible feature in the next release of JDO.

The behavior of deletePersistent() and deletePersistentAll() is not exactly the inverse of makePersistent() and makePersistentAll(), due to the transitive nature of persistence-by-reachability, which is not used when you delete instances. You need to call deletePersistent() or deletePersistentAll() explicitly for all instances that need to be deleted. Any instances that are referenced by the deletePersistent() and deletePersistentAll() parameters are not deleted, unless they are also parameters to these methods.

Delete Propagation

Some implementations support delete propagation. On a persistent class basis, you would indicate which references and collections should be traversed to establish a set of related instances to be deleted. When the application deletes an instance of the class, the JDO implementation automatically deletes the specified set of related instances. This capability is similar to the persistence-by-reachability algorithm, except it performs the inverse operation.

This relies on implementation-specific facilities that are not covered by the JDO specification. Some implementations allow you to specify this behavior in the metadata and invoke it automatically when the application calls deletePersistent() or deletePersistentAll(). If you want your application to be portable, you should use deletePersistent() or deletePersistentAll() for all deletions from the datastore, and you should not depend on implementation-specific reachability algorithms that automatically delete related instances.

A portable approach for delete propagation is to use the jdoPreDelete() callback, defined in the JDO InstanceCallbacks interface. If your persistent class has declared that it implements InstanceCallbacks, this method is called during the execution of deletePersistent():

```
    public void jdoPreDelete();
```

This method is useful when you have a *composite-aggregation association*, where the related instances are considered *existence-dependent components* of the *composite object*. The deletion semantics of the composite aggregate can be defined by deleting the dependent instances in this method. This method can reference and use any of the fields in the class. But when the method completes, you cannot access any of the deleted instance's fields, or a JDOUserException is thrown.

CHAPTER 9

The JDO Query Language

In Chapter 8 we learned how to access all the instances of a class by using an Extent. Once we have accessed some instances from the datastore, we can navigate to other related instances in Java by traversing references and iterating through collections. This allows us to access an application-specific closure of related instances to perform the functionality provided by the application.

But when you iterate an Extent, you potentially access all the instances of a class. We may only care about one or a small number of instances of the class that meet certain criteria. Once these initial instances have been accessed, we typically then navigate to instances related to those initial instances. However, getting to the first few persistent instances is a bootstrap issue. JDO provides a query language, called JDO Query Language (JDOQL), that is used to access persistent instances based on specified search criteria.

You perform queries in JDO by using the Query interface. The PersistenceManager interface is a factory for creating Query instances, and queries are executed in the context of the PersistenceManager instance used to create the Query instance. JDO queries allow you to filter out instances from a set of candidate instances specified by either an Extent or a Collection. A filter consisting of a Boolean expression is applied to the candidate instances. The query result includes all of the instances for which the Boolean expression is true.

The JDO query facility was designed with the following goals:

Query language neutrality. The underlying query language might be a relational query language such as SQL, an object database query language such as the Object Data Management Group's (ODMG) Object Query Language (OQL), or a specialized API to a hierarchical database or mainframe EIS system.

Optimization to a specific query language. The query interface must be capable of optimizations; therefore, enough information should be specified so that the implementation can exploit datastore-specific query features. In particular, JDO specifies JDOQL so that all queries can be executed by a standard SQL-92 backend datastore.

Accommodation of multitier architectures. A query may be executed entirely in application memory, delegated to a query engine running in a back-end datastore server, or executed using a combination of processing in the application and datastore server processes.

Large result set support. A query might return a massive number of instances. The query architecture must be able to process the results within the resource constraints of the execution environment.

Compiled query support. Parsing a query may be resource intensive. In many applications, the parsing can be done during application development or deployment prior to execution. The query interface must allow you to compile queries and bind values to parameters at runtime for optimal query execution.

The execution of a query might be performed by the PersistenceManager or it might be delegated to the underlying datastore. Thus, the actual underlying datastore query executed might be implemented in a language very different from Java, and it might be optimized to take advantage of a particular query-language implementation.

Query Components

The JDO query facility applies a Boolean filter to a collection of candidate instances and returns the instances that evaluate to true. The collection of candidate instances can be either an Extent or a Collection. The class of candidate instances is another query component. Instances are returned in the query result only if they are instances of the candidate class.

Let's begin by examining a method that performs a query that accesses Customer instances in the Media Mania model. We assume that an application has started a transaction and called queryCustomers( ), passing the PersistenceManager instance and values to filter the Customer instances to those whose addresses are in a specific city and state.

```
      public static void queryCustomers(PersistenceManager pm,
                                 String city, String state) {
❶     Extent customerExtent = pm.getExtent(Customer.class, true);
❷     String filter = "address.city == city && state == address.state";
❸     Query query = pm.newQuery(customerExtent, filter);
❹     query.declareParameters("String city, String state");
❺     query.setOrdering(
          "address.zipcode ascending, lastName ascending, firstName ascending");
❻     Collection result = (Collection) query.execute(city, state);
      Iterator iter = result.iterator( );
❼     while (iter.hasNext( )) {
          Customer customer = (Customer) iter.next( );
          Address address = customer.getAddress( );
          System.out.print(address.getZipcode( ));       System.out.print(" ");
          System.out.print(customer.getFirstName( ));    System.out.print(" ");
          System.out.print(customer.getLastName( ));     System.out.print(" ");
```

```
                    System.out.println(address.getStreet( ));
            }
❽       query.close(result);
    }
```

This code performs a query on the Customer extent, which we access on line ❶. When we create the Query instance on line ❸, we provide the Customer extent as the collection of candidate instances to be evaluated in the query. When you use an Extent, as we have here, it also identifies the class of the candidate instances. We use the candidate class to establish the namespace for the identifiers used in the query filter. Line ❷ specifies the filter for the query. It uses the Customer field address and navigates to the associated Address instance to access the city and state fields. The city and state identifiers in the filter are query parameters, which are declared on line ❹. We access all Customer instances that live in a specific city and state. The Java == operator expresses equality, and the Java operator && performs a conditional AND operation. You will find JDOQL very easy to learn, because it uses Java operators and syntax. You also express your queries using the identifiers in your object model. On line ❺, we establish an ordering for the instances that are in the query result. First we order customers based on their ZIP code; we then order all customers in the same ZIP code by their last name and then first name, all in ascending order. This ordering specification is similar to SQL's ORDER BY clause.

Line ❻ executes the query. We pass the city and state method parameters to execute( ) as query parameters, which are also named city and state. It is not necessary for the method parameters to have the same names as the query parameters, but we do so to make it clear to anyone reading the code that they are associated. Line ❹ declares the query parameters and their order. The order in this declaration establishes the order that the query parameter values should be passed to execute( ) on line ❻.

The result of the query must be cast to a Collection in JDO 1.0.1. The execute( ) method is defined to return Object, to allow for future extensions that may return a single instance. In general, you should call iterator( ) only on the return value of execute( ). Once we have an Iterator, we can iterate through all the returned Customer instances. The code also navigates from the returned Customer instance to its associated Address instance. Once we are done with the query result, we close it on line ❽.

Every query requires three components:

Class of candidate instances
> This specifies the class of the instances that should be included in the query result. All of the candidate instances should be of this class or one of its subclasses. The class provides a scope for the names in the query filter, similar to the scope established for field names in a Java class definition. In the previous example, the Customer extent established the class of candidate instances when we called newQuery( ).

Collection of candidate instances

The collection of candidate instances is either a java.util.Collection or an Extent. We used the Extent for the Customer class in the previous example. We use the Extent when we intend the query to be filtered by the datastore, not by in-memory processing. The Collection might be a previous query result, allowing for subqueries. If you do not explicitly provide the collection of candidate instances but you do provide the class of candidate instances, the candidate collection defaults to the extent of the class of candidate instances, including subclass instances.

Any instances in the collection of candidate instances that are not of this class are silently ignored and are not included in the query result. This can occur when the set of candidate instances is a Collection containing instances of multiple classes.

Query filter

The query filter is a String that contains a Boolean expression that is evaluated for each instance in the candidate collection. The query result returns the candidate instances that have a true result for the query filter. If the query filter is not specified, the filter results in a true value for all of the candidate instances. The query filter in the previous example is specified on line ❷.

The collection and class of the candidate instances and the query filter can be initialized when a Query is constructed by calling one of several newQuery( ) methods defined in the PersistenceManager interface (as we did on line ❸). Once a Query has been constructed, all of the query components can be set; each has an associated set method.

A query may also include the following components:

Parameters

A parameter provides a means of passing a value to be used in the query filter expression. Parameters serve a role similar to formal method parameters in Java. The query in our example had query parameters named city and state, declared on line ❹. The declaration of query parameters' name and type has the same syntax as method parameters. You provide a value for the query parameters when the query is executed.

Variables

A variable is used in a query filter to reference the elements of a collection. The use and declaration syntax of query variables is similar to the local variables in a method. Our example did not access elements of a collection, so we did not use a query variable. A variable is bound to the elements of a collection by a contains( ) expression (covered later in this chapter). Some implementations allow a variable that is not bound to a collection to be associated with an Extent. In this case, the variable is referred to as an *unbound variable*, and it may represent any instance in the extent of the class in the datastore.

Import statements

Parameters and variables can be of a class different from the candidate class; an import statement declares their type names. Types supported by JDO and defined in the java.lang package do not need to be imported. This includes the String class, the type of the query parameters in our example, so we did not need to import any types. Examples of import are provided later in this chapter.

Ordering specification

You can specify the order of the instances returned in the query result by providing an ordering specification, which is a list of expressions with an indicator to specify whether the values should be in ascending or descending order. We provided an ordering specification on line ❺ in our example.

You need to create and initialize these query components before you execute a query. Query components can be initialized when a Query is constructed or via a set method provided for the query component. The order in which you initialize the query components before the Query is executed does not matter.

Creating and Initializing a Query

The PersistenceManager interface contains a set of Query factory methods used to construct Query instances. They mainly differ in which query components are initialized. Query instances may be constructed at any time before a PersistenceManager is closed.

The following PersistenceManager method constructs an empty Query instance with none of the components initialized:

```
Query newQuery();
```

The following PersistenceManager methods construct a Query instance with an Extent as the collection of candidate instances:

```
Query newQuery(Extent candidates);
Query newQuery(Extent candidates, String filter);
```

The candidate class is initialized with the class of the Extent. The second method also initializes the query filter. We used this second method when we constructed the Query on line ❸ in our example.

Alternatively, a collection can serve as the set of candidate instances in a query. The following PersistenceManager methods construct a Query instance with a Collection as the set of candidate instances:

```
Query newQuery(Class candidateClass, Collection candidates);
Query newQuery(Class candidateClass, Collection candidates, String filter);
```

When performing a query on a collection, it is necessary to specify the class of the candidate instances explicitly.

The elements in the collection should be persistent instances associated with the same `PersistenceManager` as the `Query` instance. If the collection contains instances associated with another `PersistenceManager`, a `JDOUserException` is thrown during `execute()`. An implementation might allow you to perform a query on a collection of transient instances, but this is a nonportable, implementation-specific capability.

You can also construct a `Query` instance without initializing the set of candidate instances by calling one of the following `PersistenceManager` methods:

```
Query newQuery(Class candidateClass);
Query newQuery(Class candidateClass, String filter);
```

Once the `Query` is constructed, the collection of candidate instances can be set by calling one of its two `setCandidates()` methods, or it will default to the extent of the candidate class (including subclasses) identified by the `candidateClass` parameter passed to one of these two `newQuery()` methods. This allows you to perform a query without having to deal with an `Extent`.

A `Query` instance can be serialized. This allows you to create queries, serialize them, store them on disk, and later use them in a different execution environment. The serialized fields include the candidate class, the filter, parameter declarations, variable declarations, imports, the `IgnoreCache` setting, and the ordering specification. Of course, the candidate collection is not serialized with the `Query` instance. When a serialized `Query` instance is restored, it is no longer associated with its former `PersistenceManager`.

The following `PersistenceManager` method is used to construct a new `Query` instance from an existing or deserialized `Query` instance:

```
Query newQuery(Object query);
```

The query parameter might be a restored `Query` instance that was serialized from the same JDO implementation but a different execution environment, or it might be currently bound to a `PersistenceManager` from the same implementation. All of the query components from the query parameter are copied to the new `Query` instance, except for the candidate `Collection` or `Extent`. You can initialize this query component with a call to `setCandidates()`.

Lastly, you can use the following `PersistenceManager` method to construct a `Query` that uses a query language different than JDOQL:

```
Query newQuery(String language, Object query);
```

The `Query` instance is constructed using the specified `language` and query parameters. The `language` parameter specifies the query language used by the query parameter. The query instance must be an instance of a class defined by the query language. For JDOQL, the value of the `language` parameter is `"javax.jdo.query.JDOQL"`. The JDO specification does not specify other query languages that can be specified and used by this method; it is implementation-specific.

Once you have constructed a Query, you can access the PersistenceManager instance you originally used to create the Query instance by calling the following Query method:

```
PersistenceManager getPersistenceManager();
```

A null is returned if the Query was restored from a serialized form.

You can have multiple Query instances active simultaneously in the same PersistenceManager instance. The queries may be executed simultaneously by different threads, but the implementation may execute them serially. In either case, the execution is thread-safe.

The Query interface provides methods to bind query components before the query is executed. Their parameters replace the previously set query component (i.e., the methods are not additive). For example, if a query needs multiple variables, they all must be specified in the same call to declareVariables().

You can use the following Query methods to set the required components of the query, including the candidate class, candidate set, and filter:

```
void setClass(Class candidateClass);
void setCandidates(Collection candidates);
void setCandidates(Extent candidates);
void setFilter(String filter);
```

If you specify an Extent as the set of candidate instances, the candidate class defaults to the class of the Extent. When you perform a query on a collection, you need to specify the class of the candidate instances explicitly. In other words, if you pass a Collection to setCandidates(), you must also call setClass() before compiling or executing the query.

If you specify the class of candidate instances but do not provide the collection of candidate instances, the collection defaults to the Extent of the candidate class, with subclass instances included. Therefore, each of the following approaches produces an equivalent Query initialization:

```
// Approach 1
Query query = pm.newQuery(MediaContent.class);

// Approach 2
Query query = pm.newQuery();
query.setClass(MediaContent.class);

// Approach 3
Query query = pm.newQuery(pm.getExtent(MediaContent.class, true));

// Approach 4
Query query = pm.newQuery();
query.setCandidates(pm.getExtent(MediaContent.class, true));
```

If a collection serving as the set of candidates has an element that has been deleted by a call to deletePersistent( ), the element is ignored. If instances are added or removed from the candidates collection after setCandidates( ) is called, it is implementation-specific whether those elements take part in the query or a NoSuchElementException is thrown during execution of the query. So, you should not alter the collection once it has been passed to setCandidates( ).

You declare query parameters, variables, and their types after the Query has been constructed by calling the following methods:

```
void declareParameters(String parameters);
void declareVariables(String variables);
void declareImports(String imports);
```

The following method initializes the ordering specification:

```
void setOrdering(String ordering);
```

We cover each of these methods and their parameter syntax later in this chapter.

Changes in the Cache

When you use an Extent for the set of candidate instances in a query, the instances you retrieve depend on the setting of the IgnoreCache flag. This flag indicates whether changes you have made to instances during the transaction should be reflected in the query results.

If IgnoreCache is false, instances that were made persistent in the current transaction are *included* in the set of candidate instances; instances deleted in the current transaction are *not included* in the set of candidate instances. Furthermore, instances changed in the transaction are evaluated with their current values.

Setting IgnoreCache to true tells the query engine that you would like queries to be optimized and to return approximate results by ignoring any changes in the cache. Instances made persistent in the current transaction might not be considered part of the candidate instances, and instances deleted in the current transaction might not be considered part of the candidate instances.

For portability, you should set the IgnoreCache flag to false. An implementation may choose to ignore the setting of the IgnoreCache flag, always returning exact results that reflect current cached values, just as if the value of the flag were false. The results of iterating Extents and executing queries may differ among implementations when IgnoreCache is set to true.

The PersistenceManager interface has the following methods to get and set the value of the IgnoreCache flag for all Query instances created by the PersistenceManager:

```
boolean getIgnoreCache( );
void    setIgnoreCache(boolean flag);
```

The initial value of the IgnoreCache setting in a Query instance is set to the value that the IgnoreCache flag in the PersistenceManager had when the Query was constructed. It is also possible to get and set the IgnoreCache option on a specific Query instance by using the following Query methods:

```
void    setIgnoreCache(boolean flag);
boolean getIgnoreCache( );
```

The IgnoreCache flag is preserved when you construct a query instance from another query instance.

Query Namespaces

Two namespaces exist in JDOQL queries; they contain:

- The names of types
- The names of fields, parameters, and variables

Parameters and variables are given a name and type when they are declared. The types of the parameters and variables are placed in the first namespace; the parameter and variable names are placed in the latter namespace.

Type Names

When a type name is used (e.g., in a parameter or variable declaration), it must be one of the following:

- The name of the candidate class
- The name of a class or interface declared in the java.lang package
- The name of a class or interface imported by a call to declareImports( )
- The name of a class or interface in the same package as the candidate class
- A name imported by a type-import-on-demand declaration, as in "import <package>.*;"

The type namespace automatically includes the name of the candidate class and the names of other classes in the same package. It also automatically includes the names of the public types declared in the java.lang package, just as if there had been a type-import-on-demand declaration (import java.lang.*).

You must include any additional types names necessary for the types of parameters and variables. You import the types into a Query instance by calling the following Query method:

```
void declareImports(String imports);
```

The String parameter imports contains one or more import statements, separated by a semicolon. The syntax of the parameter is identical to Java's import statements. All imports must be declared in the same call to declareImports( ).

For example, we may have a query that accesses the Transaction instances associated with a Customer, returning those with an acquisitionDate field that is greater than a specific Date value. This query would have a Transaction variable used to reference the elements of the transactionHistory collection in Customer. It would also have a query parameter of type Date. We would specify the following import declaration:

```
query.declareImports(
        "import com.mediamania.store.Transaction; import java.util.Date");
```

The declareImports() method adds the names of the imported class or interface types into the type namespace. It is valid to specify the same import multiple times. When a query is compiled, an error occurs if you have more than one type-import-on-demand declaration and the same type name (excluding the package name) is imported from more than one package. In this case, the specific type to which a type name refers would be ambiguous. This error is reported when you call compile() or execute().

Field, Parameter, and Variable Names

The other query namespace contains the names of fields, parameters, and variables. The names of the fields in the candidate class are automatically placed in this namespace. The declareParameters() method introduces the parameter names, and the declareVariables() method introduces the variable names. The parameter and variable names must be unique, so their use is not ambiguous in the query filter.

The this keyword can be used in the query filter to denote the current candidate instance being evaluated. This reference can be used as an operand of the expressions in the query filter. It is possible to have a parameter or variable name with the same name as a field in the candidate class. In this case, the candidate class field is hidden. You can use this to access any fields of the candidate class that may be hidden by a parameter or variable of the same name. The hidden field is accessed by using the this qualifier: this.fieldName. However, we recommend that you use parameter and variable names that are unique and distinct from the field names. Your queries will be shorter and easier for others to understand.

Keywords

JDOQL defines keywords in the following categories:

- Primitive type names: boolean, byte, short, int, long, char, float, double
- Boolean literals: true, false
- Expressions: null, this
- Import declarations: import
- Ordering specification: ascending, descending

You cannot use these keywords as field names, though most of them are Java keywords anyway. The exceptions are ascending and descending; you will not be able to use fields with these names in a query.

Literals

Expressions in a query filter can include literals of the following types:

- int, long (42, -7, 2048L, 4096l)
- float, double (3.14, 3.14f, 3.14F, 0.6180339887d, 1.6180339887D)
- boolean (true, false)
- char ('J')
- String ("JDO is great!")
- null

The syntax used for these literals is identical to their syntax in Java, as described in the Java Language Specification.

Query Execution

When a query executes, the query filter is evaluated for each element of the candidate collection. Those instances that evaluate to true for the filter are included in the query result, which is a subset of the instances in the candidate collection. The query result should be cast to a Collection (execute( ) is declared to return an Object). You should then aquire an Iterator to access the instances in the result.

Parameter Declarations

When you execute a query, you often need to provide one or more values to be used in the query filter's expressions. One technique is to generate the query filter string dynamically, providing the necessary values directly in the filter. But this approach does not allow the same query to be compiled and reused in subsequent query executions, which are likely to require the same filter expressions but with different values.

Query parameters allow you to specify such values dynamically when the query is executed. The parameter names are used in the filter expression to specify constraints. A parameter name can be used zero, one, or multiple times in the query filter. When you execute the query, each parameter must be provided a value; these values are substituted for each use of the parameter name in the filter. You can use parameters to minimize the need to construct a unique query filter dynamically each time you execute a query.

You need to declare a name and type for each query parameter. In addition, you may need to import the type of the parameter using declareImports( ). The parameter declaration is a `String` containing one or more parameter type declarations, separated by commas. This follows the Java syntax for declaring the parameters of a method. All the query parameters are declared in a single `String`. The following `Query` method binds the parameter declarations to the `Query` instance:

```
void declareParameters(String parameters);
```

Each parameter must be bound to a value when the query is executed. They are passed to the query execute( ) methods as Java `Objects`; these values might be of simple wrapper types or more complex object types. The first example in this chapter had the following query parameter declaration:

```
query.declareParameters("String city, String state");
```

You may want to have a parameter of a primitive type, such as `int`. You can declare a parameter to have type `int`, but the value passed in the call to execute( ) must be the primitive's wrapper type, since it is passed as an `Object`. So, a query parameter declared with type `int` requires an `Integer` value to be passed to execute( ). In addition, the parameter value passed to execute( ) for primitive type parameters cannot be `null`, because there would not be a valid value for the parameter in the query expressions. A query parameter can be used in the filter as an operand of any query operator that accepts a value of the parameter's type.

You can also have a query parameter that is an instance of a persistent class. Such a parameter and the fields it references can be used with any of the supported query expressions, including the ability to navigate to other instances. The instances should be persistent or transactional and be associated with the same `PersistenceManager` as the `Query` instance. If a persistent instance associated with another `PersistenceManager` is passed as a parameter, a `JDOUserException` is thrown during execute( ). Some implementations may support a query parameter that is a transient instance of a persistent class, but implementations are not required to support this.

Executing a Query

The `Query` interface provides methods to execute a query with zero or more parameters. The execute( ) method has been overloaded so you can pass zero, one, two, or three parameters:

```
Object execute( );
Object execute(Object parameter1);
Object execute(Object parameter1, Object parameter2);
Object execute(Object parameter1, Object parameter2, Object parameter3);
```

Two other methods, described later in this section, allow you to pass more query parameters using a different parameter-passing technique. Each query parameter is an `Object`. As discussed earlier, you use a wrapper type (`Integer`) to pass the value for a primitive parameter (`int`). The parameters passed to execute( ) are associated with the declared parameters, based on their order. The parameters passed to the execute methods are used only for the current execution and are not preserved for use in subsequent query executions. If the PersistenceManager that constructed a Query is closed when an execute method is called, a JDOUserException is thrown.

In the following example, we access all the Movie instances with a specific rating, a running time shorter than a specific duration, and a particular director:

```
public static void queryMovie1(PersistenceManager pm,
                                String rating, int runtime, MediaPerson dir) {
    Extent movieExtent = pm.getExtent(Movie.class, true);
    String filter =
        "rating == movieRating && runningTime <= runTime && dir == director";
    Query query = pm.newQuery(movieExtent, filter);
    query.declareParameters("String movieRating, int runTime, MediaPerson dir");
    Collection result = (Collection)
                        query.execute(rating, new Integer(runtime), dir);
    Iterator iter = result.iterator();
    while (iter.hasNext()) {
        Movie movie = (Movie) iter.next();
        System.out.println(movie.getTitle());
    }
    query.close(result);
}
```

❶ query.declareParameters line
❷ query.execute line

We declare three parameters on line ❶. The second parameter is of type int, and the third parameter is of type MediaPerson, one of our persistent classes. Since MediaPerson is in the same package as the Movie candidate class, we do not need to import MediaPerson explicitly with an import declaration. The JDOQL implementation will convert the Integer parameter passed on line ❷ to the int declared on line ❶. The query would also have been valid if we had declared the runTime query parameter to be an Integer. Even though we compare runTime with the int field runningTime, JDOQL handles such conversions automatically (see the "Promotion of Numeric Operands" sidebar in this chapter).

The execute() methods execute the query with the supplied parameters and return a result. An element of the candidate collection is returned in the result if it is assignment-compatible with the candidate class of the Query, and for all variables in the query there exists a value for which the query filter expression evaluates to true. We will cover variables later in this chapter. If the query filter is not specified when the query is executed, then the filter defaults to true and the input collection is filtered to include only instances of the candidate class.

The return type of the execute() methods is Object. In JDO 1.0.1, the execute() methods return an object that supports the operations of an unmodifiable Collection; the value returned should be cast to a Collection. A future JDO release may support queries that return a single instance; the method has been defined to return Object to allow for this future extension. An implementation of a non-JDOQL query language might return a value of a different type (e.g., java.sql.ResultSet).

You can iterate the unmodifiable Collection returned by the execute( ) methods to access the query results. Executing any operation that might change the Collection causes an UnsupportedOperationException. Although the object returned by execute( ) is declared to implement Collection, most implementations do not return a collection that has been fully populated with the results of the query. The primary use of the returned object is to acquire an Iterator via the iterator( ) method defined in the Collection interface. The returned Collection can also serve as the set of candidate instances for an additional query, supporting a form of subqueries.

The execute( ) methods described in this section support a maximum of three parameters. It is also possible to pass parameters via a Map:

```
Object executeWithMap(Map parameters);
```

The executeWithMap( ) method is similar to execute( ), but it takes its parameters from a Map instance. The Map contains key/value pairs, where the key is the parameter's declared name and the value is the actual value to use for the parameter in the query. Unlike execute( ), you can pass an unlimited number of parameters to executeWithMap( ).

The following example extends the previous example to return only Movie instances that were released after a specified date. This query requires four parameters, so we will use executeWithMap( ). At line ❶, we begin populating a HashMap with the query parameters. The Map entry's key is the parameter name, as specified in declareParameters( ), and its value is the value to use for the parameter.

```
    public static void queryMovie2(PersistenceManager pm,
                                String rating, int runtime, MediaPerson dir, Date date) {
        Extent movieExtent = pm.getExtent(Movie.class, true);
        String filter = "rating == movieRating && runningTime <= runTime && " +
                        "dir == director && releaseDate >= date";
        Query query = pm.newQuery(movieExtent, filter);
        query.declareImports("import java.util.Date");
        query.declareParameters(
            "String movieRating, int runTime, MediaPerson dir, Date date");
        HashMap parameters = new HashMap();
❶      parameters.put("movieRating", rating);
        parameters.put("runTime", new Integer(runtime));
        parameters.put("dir", dir);
        parameters.put("date", date);
❷      Collection result = (Collection) query.executeWithMap(parameters);
        Iterator iter = result.iterator();
        while (iter.hasNext()) {
            Movie movie = (Movie) iter.next();
            System.out.println(movie.getTitle());
        }
        query.close(result);
    }
```

Parameters can also be passed with an array:

```
Object executeWithArray(Object[] parameters);
```

The executeWithArray( ) method is also similar to execute( ), but it takes its parameters from an array instance. The array contains Objects; the position of parameters in the parameter declaration determines the position of their corresponding values in the array. The number of elements in the array must be equal to the number of parameters that have been declared. Similar to executeWithMap( ), the number of parameters is not limited.

The following example performs the same query as the previous one, except this time we use executeWithArray( ). The order in which the parameters are declared on line ❶ must correspond with the order in which the values are populated in the array on line ❷.

```
    public static void queryMovie3(PersistenceManager pm,
                                String rating, int runtime, MediaPerson dir,
                                Date date) {
        Extent movieExtent = pm.getExtent(Movie.class, true);
        String filter = "rating == movieRating && runningTime <= runTime && " +
                        "dir == director && releaseDate >= date";
        Query query = pm.newQuery(movieExtent, filter);
        query.declareImports("import java.util.Date");
        query.declareParameters(
❶          "String movieRating, int runTime, MediaPerson dir, Date date");
❷      Object[] parameters = { rating, new Integer(runtime), dir, date };
        Collection result = (Collection) query.executeWithArray(parameters);
        Iterator iter = result.iterator();
        while (iter.hasNext()) {
            Movie movie = (Movie) iter.next();
            System.out.println(movie.getTitle());
        }
        query.close(result);
    }
```

The result of a query can be very large, depending on the size of the candidate collection and filter. An application can iterate through the result or pass it to another Query as its candidate instances. The size( ) method defined in Collection might return Integer.MAX_VALUE if the actual size of the result is not known. A portable application should not use size( ).

You can call any of these execute methods repeatedly for the same Query instance. All of the query components, including the candidate collection, are maintained by the Query instance after execution. This allows you to reexecute the same query with different query parameter values. You can also change any of the query components of a Query after it has been executed. The Query will be recompiled before it is executed.

Compiling a Query

Before you can execute a query, it is compiled to verify its correctness. Compiling a Query validates its components and reports any inconsistencies by throwing a

JDOUserException. When execute( ) is called, if the Query has not compiled or if a query component has been changed since the Query was last compiled, the Query compiles automatically.

You can verify the correctness of a query before executing it by compiling it directly. The following Query method compiles a query:

```
void compile( );
```

Calling compile( ) tells the Query instance to prepare and optimize an execution plan for the query. Once a Query is compiled, it can be executed repeatedly without incurring the initial parsing and optimization overhead.

The Query Filter

The query filter is a Boolean expression that is evaluated for each candidate instance; the query result includes only those instances that are true. The filter contains expressions supported by the JDO Query Language (JDOQL). Appendix D contains the Backus-Naur Form (BNF) syntax for JDOQL.

The query filter is specified with respect to the object model defined by your persistent classes, using the field names in your persistent classes. You do not use the names and representation found in the underlying datastore. You write your applications using the single data model of your persistent classes.

The filter can access the fields in your classes directly, even though they may be declared private. Some developers say that this breaks encapsulation, but database query languages express constraints on the values of fields. A JDOQL query will never modify the value of a field, and only the JDO implementation can access these fields in your application directly, which it needs to do anyway to manage their state. Those that argue this breaks encapsulation believe that only the methods of a class should access its fields. JDOQL has been designed so that query execution can take place in either the application's execution environment or the datastore server. Requiring the use of methods would require the datastore server to support Java and the loading of your application classes. This would severely limit the number of datastores that JDO could support. In most cases, the Java field names used in the query filter get remapped to the names of data constructs in the underlying datastore, which are then accessed in the datastore server environment.

The names of persistent fields are supported as identifiers in query expressions. You may find some implementations supporting nonpersistent fields (including final and static fields), but implementations are not required to support these fields. So, if you want to write queries that will be portable across all implementations, do not use nonpersistent, final, or static fields in your filter expressions.

You can provide the query filter to a Query when it is constructed, by using one of the newQuery( ) methods that takes a filter as a parameter, as we have done in the previous examples. Or, you can set the filter by calling the following Query method:

```
void setFilter(String filter);
```

General Characteristics of Expressions

The identifiers in the filter should be in the namespace of the specified candidate class, with the addition of declared imports, parameters, and variables. As in the Java language, this is a reserved word that refers to the current candidate instance being evaluated from the collection or extent.

JDOQL uses operators taken directly from the Java language, so Java developers will be familiar with them. Parentheses can be used to mark operator precedence explicitly. Whitespace—nonprinting characters, including space, tab, carriage return, and line-feed—in the filter is a separator and is otherwise ignored.

Query expressions are nonmutating and have no side effects. The assignment operators (=, +=, etc.), pre- and post-increment, and pre- and post-decrement are not supported. JDOQL defines a few methods on String and Collection instances. But methods defined by the application, including object construction, are not supported. Nonmutating method calls may be supported in an implementation as a nonstandard extension.

Query Operators

A subset of Java's operators can be used in the filter expression. The operators apply to all the types as defined in the Java language, except for a few cases that we will note in this section. You can use operator composition to construct arbitrarily complex expressions. You can use parentheses to control the precedence of multiple operators and make the expressions easier for others to read and understand.

Equality and inequality operators

Table 9-1 specifies the equality operators. These expressions have a Boolean result. We have used these in our previous query examples.

Table 9-1. Equality operators

Operator	Description
==	Equal
!=	Not-equal

The equal and not-equal operators are valid for all the operand types that are valid in Java. In addition, you can use them with the following operands:

- Primitives and instances of wrapper classes (see the "Promotion of Numeric Operands" sidebar)
- Date values (fields and parameters)
- String values (fields, parameters, literals, and results of String expressions)

Promotion of Numeric Operands

Numeric operands are promoted when you use equality, comparison, and arithmetic operations. The promotion rules follow the rules defined in the Java Language Specification (see Chapter 5.6, "Numeric Promotions") and have been extended to support BigDecimal, BigInteger, and the numeric wrapper classes:

- If either operand is of type BigDecimal, the other is converted to BigDecimal.
- Otherwise, if either operand is a BigInteger and the other is a floating-point type (float, double) or one of its wrapper classes (Float, Double), both operands are converted to BigDecimal.
- Otherwise, if either operand is a BigInteger, the other is converted to a BigInteger.
- Otherwise, if either operand is a double, the other is converted to a double.
- Otherwise, if either operand is a float, the other is converted to a float.
- Otherwise, if either operand is a long, the other is converted to a long.
- Otherwise, both operands are converted to int.

An operand that is one of the numeric wrapper classes is treated as its corresponding primitive type. If one operand is an instance of a numeric wrapper class and the other operand has a primitive numeric type, the rules in this sidebar apply and the result type is the corresponding numeric wrapper class.

In Java, the this.rating == movieRating expression compares the identity (references) of the String instances. In JDOQL, an expression evaluating the equality of Date and String values does not compare the object references as in Java. Instead, it tests the equality of their values.

Comparisons between floating-point values are, by nature, inexact. Therefore, you should be cautious when using equality comparisons (== and !=) with floating-point values. If you need precise comparisons, use the type BigDecimal instead.

Persistent instances compare equal if they have the same identity (i.e., they are the same instance in the datastore). Equality of references for nonpersistent types uses the equals( ) method defined for the class. A persistent and nonpersistent instance are never considered equal.

If a datastore supports null values for Collection types, it is valid to compare a collection field to null. If you are using a datastore that does not support a null value for a Collection type, then a subexpression that compares a collection field to null evaluates false. If the datastore supports null values for Collection types, the javax.jdo.option.NullCollection option should be included in the list of supported options.

Comparison operators

Table 9-2 lists the comparison operators, which have a Boolean result.

Table 9-2. Comparison operators

Operator	Description
<	Less-than
<=	Less-than or equal
>	Greater-than
>=	Greater-than or equal

These comparison operators are valid for all the operand types defined in Java. In addition, they are valid for the following operands:

- Primitives and instances of wrapper classes (see the "Promotion of Numeric Operands" sidebar)
- Date values (fields and parameters)
- String values (fields, parameters, literals, and results of String expressions)

The comparison of two Date instances or two String instances compares the values represented by the instances. The ordering used in String comparisons is not defined in JDO. This allows implementations to order them according to a datastore-specific ordering, which might be locale-specific.

Boolean operators

Table 9-3 lists the supported Boolean operators. These expressions have Boolean operands and compute a Boolean result.

Table 9-3. Boolean operators

Operator	Description
&	Boolean logical AND (not bitwise)
&&	Conditional AND
|	Boolean logical OR (not bitwise)
||	Conditional OR
!	Logical complement (negate)

The following example uses these Boolean operators to access all the Movie instances that have a rating other than G or PG and a running time between an hour and an hour and 45 minutes:

```
public static void queryMovie4(PersistenceManager pm) {
    Extent movieExtent = pm.getExtent(Movie.class, true);
    String filter = "!(rating == \"G\" || rating == \"PG\") && " +
                    "(runningTime >= 60 && runningTime <= 105)";
    Query query = pm.newQuery(movieExtent, filter);
    Collection result = (Collection) query.execute();
    Iterator iter = result.iterator();
    while (iter.hasNext()) {
        Movie movie = (Movie) iter.next();
        System.out.println(movie.getTitle());
    }
    query.close(result);
}
```

You can use these Boolean operators and parentheses to compose query expressions as nested and complex as necessary to express your filter.

The previous example also demonstates the use of String and int literals. Since String literals in a JDOQL filter use Java's syntax of double-quote delimiters, you need to use the backslash character (\) when specifying your filter with a Java String literal in your application. These back-quotes are not needed in JDOQL's syntax, and they are not placed in this String filter we have declared. Query filters are simpler if you use a query parameter instead of a String literal. A parameter also provides more flexibility than a literal, because it allows you to provide an alternative value in the query.

The operators listed in Table 9-3 lists correspond to Java's Boolean (&, |) and conditional (&&, ||) operators. In Java, the Boolean operators always evaluate both operands, but the conditional operators first evaluate the left operand and evaluate the right operand only if necessary to determine the Boolean result. In Java, && evaluates the right operand only if the value of the left operand is true, and || evaluates the right operand only if the value of the left operand is false. This aspect of Java's conditional operators is not preserved in JDOQL. There are no side effects of operators in JDOQL, which could be leveraged by such conditional evaluations. JDOQL implementations may or may not evaluate the right operand based on the evaluation of the left operand; this is purely an optimization decision. Some underlying datastores, such as those based on SQL, do not have such conditional operators. A SQL implementation would likely map both & and && to the SQL AND operator.

Arithmetic operators

Table 9-4 lists the supported arithmetic operators.

Table 9-4. Arithmetic operators

Operator	Description
+	Binary and unary addition
-	Binary subtraction or numeric-sign inversion
*	Multiplication
/	Division
~	Integral unary-bitwise complement

The result type of these expressions depends on the operand types, as explained in the "Promotion of Numeric Operands" sidebar.

Let's examine a query that uses these arithmetic operators:

```
     public static void queryProfits(PersistenceManager pm, BigDecimal value,
                                     BigDecimal sellCost, BigDecimal rentCost) {
❶       Query query = pm.newQuery(MediaItem.class);
        query.declareImports("import java.math.BigDecimal");
❷       query.declareParameters(
            "BigDecimal value, BigDecimal sellCost, BigDecimal rentCost");
❸       query.setFilter("soldYTD * (purchasePrice - sellCost) + " +
                        "rentedYTD * (rentalCode.cost - rentCost) > value");
        Collection result = (Collection) query.execute(value, sellCost, rentCost);
        Iterator iter = result.iterator();
        while (iter.hasNext()) {
            MediaItem item = (MediaItem) iter.next();
            // process MediaItem
        }
        query.close(result);
     }
```

We initialize a Query instance on line ❶, where we set the candidate class. Notice that we do not explicitly specify the candidate collection. If we specify the candidate class but not the candidate collection (as we do here), the candidate collection defaults to the Extent of the candidate class, with subclasses included (the Extent component that indicates subclasses should be included is true). In this query we retrieve all the MediaItem instances whose profit this year exceeds the value parameter. There are costs associated with the selling and renting of an item; the values for these costs are passed via the sellCost and rentCost query parameters, declared on line ❷. These values are subtracted from the price charged to purchase or rent the item in the filter specified on line ❸. We multiply the per-item profits by the number of items sold and rented year-to-date. We then determine whether the profits for an item exceed the threshold specified by the value query parameter. The query returns only those items whose profits exceed the value parameter.

The precedence of the arithmetic operators in the JDOQL filter is identical to their precedence in Java. We have used parentheses to override the precedence. We could add additional parentheses to make the expression more clear for those that are not always certain of the operator precedences.

String expressions

Two String methods are defined, startsWith( ) and endsWith( ):

```
boolean startsWith(String str);
boolean endsWith(String str);
```

These methods operate on a String within a query. The startsWith( ) method returns true if the String begins with the value in the str argument. The endsWith( ) method returns true if the String ends with the value in the str argument.

These methods provide support for wild card queries. However, no special semantics are associated with the str argument; in particular, no specific wild-card characters are supported.

A typical nonstandard implementation based on a SQL datastore would map the JDOQL query expression:

```
name.startsWith("%Tina")
```

to the SQL LIKE operation:

```
NAME LIKE ('%Tina%')
```

The '%' wild-card character represents zero or more characters. The startsWith( ) method adds a '%' at the end of its parameter's value when it is mapped to SQL.

The + operator can be used to specify String concatenation, but it is supported only for String operands. Thus, this is supported:

```
"Movie: " + title
```

But this expression is not:

```
title + 5
```

References

You can use the . (dot) operator to navigate through reference fields, as in Java. You can also use the . operator to navigate through multiple references in your object model. For example, the following expression assumes that we have a filter operating on a set of RentalItem candidate instances:

```
currentRental.customer.address.city
```

We navigate from the RentalItem to the Rental instance by using the currentRental field, then use the customer field inherited from Transaction to access the specific Customer that has rented the RentalItem. We then use the address field to get the customer's address and access the city. This example also illustrates that your expressions can access inherited fields; we access the customer field in Transaction, the base class of Rental.

Using such navigations does not change the candidate class; you cannot return the instances accessible via navigation. If your main goal is to query and return instances

---

of a class accessible via such a navigation, the class of the instances that you want in your result should be your candidate class and you should provide a filter that may include a navigation that performs the inverse of your original navigation expression.

In Java, when you navigate through a null reference, a NullPointerException is thrown. But if a subexpression in a query traverses through a null reference, the subexpression does not throw an exception; it evaluates as false. Only the subexpression is false, not the entire filter. Other subexpressions in the filter or other values for variables may still qualify the candidate instance for inclusion in the result set.

Cast expression

Java and JDO allow a base class reference to contain a reference to an instance of a subclass. In addition, Java and JDO allow you to declare a reference to an interface and initialize it with a reference to an instance of any class that has been declared to implement the interface. We have demonstrated that when you have a reference to a subclass (Rental), you can directly use fields in a base class (Transaction). But suppose you have a reference to a base class and want to have a query expression that determines whether the reference is to a particular subclass and, if so, accesses a field of the subclass. Likewise, suppose you have an interface reference. You cannot call the methods of the Java interface in a query expression, but you may want to determine whether the reference refers to an instance of a specific class and, if so, have a query expression using a field of that class.

You can express such queries in JDOQL by using a *cast expression*. The syntax of the cast expression is identical to its use in Java. Precede the reference expression with a type name, enclosed in parentheses. If you cast a reference to a specific class, an attempt is made to convert the reference to the class. If the cast fails (which would throw a ClassCastException in Java), the most-nested Boolean subexpression in which the cast was performed is false. This behavior also occurs if you navigate through a null reference in JDOQL. If the cast succeeds, then the reference can be used to access the referenced instance as an instance of the type used in the cast.

The following example uses the collection of historical transactions associated with a particular Customer as its candidate set of instances:

```
    public static void queryTransactions(PersistenceManager pm, Customer cust) {
❶       Query query = pm.newQuery(com.mediamania.store.Rental.class,
                            cust.getTransactionHistory());
❷       String filter = "((Movie)(rentalItem.mediaItem.content)).director." +
                        "mediaName == \"James Cameron\"";
❸       query.declareImports("import com.mediamania.content.Movie");
❹       query.setFilter(filter);
        Collection result = (Collection) query.execute();
        Iterator iter = result.iterator();
        while (iter.hasNext() ){
            Rental rental = (Rental) iter.next();
            MediaContent content =
```

```
                    rental.getRentalItem().getMediaItem().getMediaContent();
        System.out.println(content.getTitle());
    }
    query.close(result);
}
```

The `transactionHistory` collection in `Customer` contains `Transaction` instances, which are either `Rental` or `Purchase` instances. We only want to process the `Rental` instances in the collection, so we set the `Rental` class as the candidate class in the call to `newQuery()` on line ❶. In the filter, declared on line ❷, we navigate from the `Rental` instance to the `RentalItem`, from the `RentalItem` to the `MediaItem`, and from the `MediaItem` to the `MediaContent` instance. The `MediaContent` instance can be either a `Movie` or a `Game` instance. We want to determine which movies the customer is currently renting that were directed by James Cameron. So, we cast the `MediaContent` reference to a `Movie` instance on line ❷. This allows us to access the `director` field defined in the `Movie` class. We then determine whether this movie was directed by James Cameron. Line ❹ sets the filter for the query. Since our `Rental` candidate class is defined in the `com.mediamania.store` package and we are casting to the `Movie` class, which is defined in the `com.mediamania.content` package, it is necessary to import the `Movie` class on line ❸.

In this example, we constrain the `transactionHistory` collection to `Rental` instances by specifying `Rental` as the candidate class. An alternative, less-elegant approach would be to cast to `Rental` in the filter itself. Lines ❶ and ❷ could be replaced with the following lines:

```
Query query = pm.newQuery(com.mediamania.store.Transaction.class,
                          cust.getTransactionHistory());
String filter = "((Movie)(((Rental)this).rentalItem.mediaItem.content))." +
                "director.mediaName == \"James Cameron\"";
```

But the use of multiple casts results in a more-complex filter. The first solution is simpler. As we noted previously, we could simplify the filter by passing the director's name as a parameter instead of using the `String` literal.

Collections

You can also use collections in your query expressions. The `isEmpty()` and `contains()` methods are defined for use with a collection in a query.

The method `isEmpty()` determines whether a collection is empty:

```
boolean isEmpty();
```

Not all datastores allow a null-valued collection to be stored. Portable queries on these collections should use `isEmpty()` instead of comparing to `null`. A null collection field is treated as if it is empty if a method is called on it. In particular, `isEmpty()` returns `true`, and `contains()` returns `false`.

You can also have a query expression that examines a collection to determine whether an element exists in the collection that has a true value for a provided query expression. This allows you to navigate to a set of related instances in the datastore. You navigate by using the contains( ) method, which lets you associate a variable with the elements of a collection. The variable can then be used to express constraints on the collection elements.

Variable declaration

To access the elements of a collection, you must declare the variable with its name and type. Variables are declared in a String containing one or more variable declarations, separated by a semicolon if there there is more than one variable declaration. It uses the same syntax you use in Java to declare a method's local variables.

The following Query method binds a variable declaration to the Query instance:

```
void declareVariables(String variables);
```

You will need to import the type using declareImports( ) if the variable's type is not already in the query's type namespace.

The contains( ) method

The contains( ) method is used in conjunction with an AND expression to determine whether an element of a collection results in a true result for at least one element of the collection. You associate a variable with the elements of a collection by passing the variable to contains( ). The contains( ) method must be the left operand of an AND expression in which the variable used is the right operand:

```
boolean contains(Object o);
```

The contains( ) method returns true if at least one collection element results in a true result for the right operand of its associated AND expression.

A portable query filter must constrain all of its variables that are used in any of its expressions, by applying the contains( ) clause to a persistent field of a persistent class. That is, each occurrence of an expression in the filter using the variable includes a contains( ) clause ANDed with an expression using the variable.

The following example finds all Movie instances for which the director also played an acting role in the movie:

```
      Extent movieExtent = pm.getExtent(Movie.class, true);
❶     String filter = "cast.contains(role) && role.actor == director";
      Query query = pm.newQuery(movieExtent, filter);
❷     query.declareVariables("Role role");
      Collection result = (Collection) query.execute();
```

In this query, we declare a variable, named role, on line ❷ to reference the Role instances in the cast collection. We use the contains( ) method on line ❶ to associate the role variable with the elements of cast. The contains( ) expression is the left operand of &&, and the right operand has an expression using the role variable. The right operand's expression checks to see whether the MediaPerson referenced by the actor field is equal to the director field in the Movie instance.

You use the contains( ) method to see whether at least one element exists in the collection that is true for the expression in the right operand. Since only one collection element needs to have a true result for the right operand, not all of the collection elements need to be processed. Evaluation can stop once the first collection element is found with a true result for the right operand. The contains( ) method and its associated ANDed right operand are considered an expression. Negating this expression with the ! operator asks if it is true that *no* element exists in the collection that is true for the right operand (i.e., that there is no element in the collection for which the right operand is true).

The following example illustrates the use of multiple variables. In fact, it navigates through multiple collections by using the second variable to access elements of a collection accessed by the first variable. This query finds all the Movie instances currently being rented by customers that live in a city with a given name.

```
    public static void queryMoviesSeenInCity(PersistenceManager pm, String city) {
❶       String filter = "mediaItems.contains(item) &&" +
❷                           "(item.rentalItems.contains(rentalItem) && " +
❸                           "(rentalItem.currentRental.customer.address.city == city))";
        Extent movieExtent = pm.getExtent(Movie.class, true);
        Query query = pm.newQuery(movieExtent, filter);
❹       query.declareImports("import com.mediamania.store.MediaItem; " +
                                "import com.mediamania.store.RentalItem");
❺       query.declareVariables("MediaItem item; RentalItem rentalItem");
        query.declareParameters("String city");
        Collection result = (Collection) query.execute(city);
        Iterator iter = result.iterator();
        while (iter.hasNext()) {
            Movie movie = (Movie) iter.next();
            System.out.println(movie.getTitle());
        }
        query.close(result);
    }
```

Line ❺ declares the variables item and rentalItem. Line ❶ associates the item variable with the MediaItem instances of the current Movie candidate instance. The rest of the filter is the right operand of the associated AND operator. We access the RentalItem instances associated with the MediaItem instances (referenced by item) by binding the rentalItem variable with the rentalItems collection. We then use the rentalItem variable to access the current Rental transaction and navigate to access the city of the customer renting the movie.

For a portable query, the contains( ) clause must be the left expression of an AND expression in which the variable is used in the right expression. The filter specified on line ❶ illustrates a situation where you need to use parentheses to override Java's left-associativity rule that applies when there are two or more operators with the same precedence in a filter expression. If we had declared the filter as:

```
    String filter = "mediaItems.contains(item) &&" +
                        "item.rentalItems.contains(rentalItem) && " +
                        "(rentalItem.currentRental.customer.address.city == city)";
```

it would have been evaluated as:

```
String filter = "(mediaItems.contains(item) &&" +
                "item.rentalItems.contains(rentalItem)) && " +
                "(rentalItem.currentRental.customer.address.city == city)";
```

which is not valid, because `rentalItem` on the third line is not the right operand of an AND expression whose left operand binds `rentalItem` with a `contains()`.

A portable query will constrain all of its variables with a `contains()` method in each OR expression the filter may have. A variable that is not constrained with an explicit `contains()` method is constrained by the extent of the persistent class (including subclasses) in the database, based on the variable's declared class. Such a variable is referred to as an *unbound variable*. If the variable's class does not manage an `Extent`, then no results will satisfy the query.

For example, the following query returns all movies from the same director that were released after a particular movie, specified by title:

```
public static void queryRecentMovies(PersistenceManager pm, String title) {
    Extent movieExtent = pm.getExtent(Movie.class, true);
    String filter = "this.releaseDate > movie.releaseDate && " +
                    "this.director == movie.director && movie.title == title";
    Query query = pm.newQuery(movieExtent, filter);
    query.declareParameters("String title");
    query.declareVariables("Movie movie");
    Collection result = (Collection) query.execute(title);
    Iterator iter = result.iterator();
    while (iter.hasNext()) {
        Movie movie = (Movie) iter.next();
        // process Movie
    }
}
```

The `movie` variable of type `Movie` is unconstrained, so it is evaluated relative to the `Movie` extent. In this particular query, the unbound variable accesses the same extent as the query, but this just a coincidence, as the extent accessed by an unconstrained variable is based on the variable's declared type.

Ordering Query Results

An application can specify an order for the query result by providing an ordering statement, specified by a `String` that contains one or more ordering declarations, separated by commas. Each ordering declaration is a Java expression of an orderable type, followed by either ascending or descending. Your ordering expression may use the `.` operator to navigate references.

Each ordering expression must be one of the following types:

- Any primitive type except boolean
- Any wrapper type except Boolean

- BigDecimal
- BigInteger
- String
- Date

We mentioned earlier that JDO does not define the ordering of Strings when you use the comparison operators (<, <=, >, and >=). This also applies for the ordering of query results.

The following Query method binds the ordering statement to the Query instance:

```
void setOrdering(String ordering);
```

The ordering statement may include multiple ordering expressions. The result of the leftmost expression is used first to order the results. If the leftmost expression evaluates to the same value for two or more elements, then the second expression is used to order those elements. If the second expression also evaluates to the same value, then the third expression is used, and so on, until the last expression is evaluated. If the values of all of the ordering expressions are equal for two or more elements, then the ordering of those elements is unspecified.

The following example demonstrates the use of ordering:

```
public static void queryTransactionsInCity(PersistenceManager pm,
                           String city, String state, Date acquired) {
    Extent transactionExtent =
        pm.getExtent(com.mediamania.store.Transaction.class, true);
    Query query = pm.newQuery(transactionExtent);
❶  query.declareParameters("String thecity, String thestate, Date date");
❷  query.declareImports("import java.util.Date");
❸  String filter = "customer.address.city == thecity && " +
            "customer.address.state == thestate && acquisitionDate >= date";
    query.setFilter(filter);
❹  String order =  "customer.address.zipcode descending, " +
                   "customer.lastName ascending, " +
                   "customer.firstName ascending, acquisitionDate ascending";
❺  query.setOrdering(order);
    Collection result = (Collection) query.execute(city, state, acquired);
    Iterator iter = result.iterator();
    while (iter.hasNext()) {
        com.mediamania.store.Transaction tx =
            (com.mediamania.store.Transaction) iter.next();

        // process Transactions
    }
    query.close(result);
}
```

The query returns all Transaction instances that occurred on or after a specified date for customers in a given city and state. Line ❶ declares these necessary parameters. We also need to import the Date class for the date parameter on line ❷. The filter declared on line ❸ uses these parameters to limit the Transaction instances returned by the query. We specify the ordering expression on line ❹ and set it on line ❺. The Transaction instances are ordered first in descending order, based on the customer's ZIP code. All instances in the same ZIP code are placed in ascending order, based on the customer's last and first name. Transaction instances for specific customers with unique last and first names are placed in ascending order, based on the date they acquired the media content. The ordering declarations are separated by a comma in the ordering expression.

The ordering of instances is not specified when the fields used in the ordering expression have null values. Implementations may differ in how they perform the ordering; they may place the instances containing null-valued fields either before or after instances whose fields contain non-null values.

Closing a Query

When you are finished with the result of a query, you can close the results, allowing the release of resources used in implementing the query (e.g., database cursors or iterators). You can use the following Query methods to close query results:

```
void close(Object queryResult);
void closeAll();
```

The close( ) method closes the result that was returned by one call to execute( ). You use closeAll( ) to close all the results from calls to execute( ) on the Query instance. Both methods release the query result's resources. After they complete, you cannot use the query result (e.g., to iterate the returned elements). Closing a query result does not affect the state of its instances. Once you have closed a result, any Iterator that was acquired returns false to hasNext( ) and throws NoSuchElementException if next( ) is called. But the Query instance is still valid and can be used to execute more queries. Each query example in this chapter closed its query result.

CHAPTER 10

Identity

Java defines two concepts that determine whether two instances are the same: *identity* and *equality*. Two instances have the same Java identity if and only if they occupy the same memory location within the Java Virtual Machine (JVM). Java identity is managed entirely by the JVM, whereas Java equality is determined by the class. Two distinct instances with different identities are equal if they represent the same value, based on the abstraction being modeled. For example, two distinct instances of Integer with separate Java identities may have the same integer-abstraction value; they are considered equal. Or, two distinct HashSet instances may contain the same elements and be considered equal, even though they may have a completely different organization of their internal data structures, as a result of the order in which elements were added and removed. If you are a Java developer, you likely understand the Java concepts of identity and equality already.

JDO has its own requirements for uniquely identifying a persistent instance. The same datastore instance can be in multiple transactions in the JVM at the same time, so the Java notion of identity cannot be used. The application doesn't necessarily implement equals( ), so it cannot be used.

Therefore, JDO defines its own identity abstraction to identify an instance uniquely in the datastore. This identity is used in the datastore to establish a reference to an instance. It is also used to determine if two in-memory instances represent the same object in the datastore. We refer to this new form of identity as *JDO identity*, when necessary, to distinguish it from Java identity. JDO identity is defined differently from both Java identity and Java equality.

The JDO implementation manages a cache of persistent instances for each PersistenceManager, such that each instance from the datastore is represented by a single instance in the cache of the PersistenceManager. This cache is not a specific region of memory; it simply consists of the set of all instances managed by the PersistenceManager. The JDO implementation allows an application to navigate through persistent references and collections of references accessed from the datastore by using simple Java references. The JDO identity of the persistent class determines the representation of these references in the datastore and how the implementation accesses an instance in the datastore when your application uses a reference.

If the JVM has multiple `PersistenceManager` instances, each has its own associated cache of persistent instances. Two or more of these `PersistenceManager` instances may have their own distinct copy of the same datastore instance. In this case, each copy of the datastore instance has a distinct Java identity, but they all have an identical JDO identity.

Overview

JDO has several types of identity. You must select the type of identity to use for each persistent class. An identity class represents an identity value, and its form depends on the type of identity. Each persistent class has an associated identity class that represents a unique identity value for each persistent instance. If you have two instances of identity classes for two persistent instances, they will compare equal if and only if the persistent instances have the same JDO identity. JDO provides methods to map between a persistent instance and its associated identity.

JDO Identity Types

JDO defines three types of identity:

Datastore identity
> The identity is managed by the JDO implementation or the datastore and is not associated with the values of any fields in the instance.

Application identity
> The identity is managed by the application, and its uniqueness is enforced by the JDO implementation or datastore. The identity is composed of one or more fields of the class, referred to as the *primary-key fields*. The composite value of the primary-key fields must uniquely identify each persistent instance in the datastore. You must define an application identity class with fields that correspond, in name and type, to the primary-key fields in the persistent class.

Nondurable identity
> Some datastores do not support a unique identifier for some of their data. For example, a log file or a table in a relational database may not have a primary-key constraint. For the JDO implementation to manage instances that do not have a durable identity, nondurable identity provides a unique identity for each instance while it is in the JVM; but this identity is not preserved or used in the datastore.

JDO uses these three different types of identity to model existing datastores. Many relational databases use application-visible primary-key columns in which the values of the columns represent real-world concepts. For example, a purchase order's line item table contains an purchase-order number and a line number as a composite primary key, and these columns have significance in the application domain. Most object databases provide identity for persistent instances that do not depend on application-visible values. In order to support natural mappings for both of these styles of identity, JDO provides both application identity and datastore identity.

There are other cases, primarily from the relational-database domain, where there is no identity associated with a row in a table. For example, there is no natural key for a log-file entry, and although there may be queryable columns, there is no uniqueness requirement. Support for these kinds of tables is provided by nondurable identity.

Each type of identity is an optional feature in JDO, but a JDO implementation must support either datastore or application identity and may support both. They have the following property names:

- `javax.jdo.option.DatastoreIdentity`
- `javax.jdo.option.ApplicationIdentity`
- `javax.jdo.option.NondurableIdentity`

You can call `supportedOptions( )`, defined in `PersistenceManagerFactory`, to determine which types of identity your implementation supports.

Metadata

You need to select an identity type for each persistent class. You declare the identity type in the metadata using the `identity-type` attribute in the `class` element for the persistent class. It can be given one of the following values:

- `"datastore"`
- `"application"`
- `"nondurable"`

The application can explicitly specify a value for `identity-type` or let it have a default value. If you decide to use application identity for a persistent class, you need to define an application identity class and specify it in the metadata in the `class` element's `objectid-class` attribute. Some implementations can generate this class for you. Only application identity uses the `objectid-class` attribute. So, if you specify the `objectid-class` attribute for a persistent class, its `identity-type` attribute defaults to `"application"`; otherwise, it defaults to `"datastore"`. Furthermore, the identity type you select for the least-derived persistent class in an inheritance hierarchy is used as the identity type for all the persistent classes in the inheritance hierarchy. Once you have enhanced a persistent class, its identity type is fixed.

Table 10-1 summarizes which type of identity you will get based on the values you provide for these metadata attributes. The `MyAppId` class denotes an application identity class that you have defined.

Table 10-1. Identity types, based on value of identity-type and objectid-class metadata attributes

Value of identity-type	Value of objectid-class	Identity type used for the class
No value provided	No value provided	Datastore identity
No value provided	"MyApplId"	Application identity
"datastore"	No value provided	Datastore identity
"datastore"	"MyApplId"	Error
"application"	No value provided	Error
"application"	"MyApplId"	Application identity
"nondurable"	No value provided	Nondurable identity
"nondurable"	"MyApplId"	Error

If you have a class C that extends class B, where B has a value specified for the objectid-class attribute, class C must also use application identity and must either use class B's objectid-class (if the objectid-class is concrete) or define its own objectid-class that extends B's objectid-class. You never specify the objectid-class attribute for subclasses of concrete classes.

Identity Class

Every persistent class has an associated identity class that is used to represent the unique identity of each persistent instance. The JDO implementation defines the classes used to represent datastore and nondurable identity. The implementation may use the same identity class for multiple persistent classes, or a different identity class for each persistent class. On the other hand, when you use application identity, you must define an application identity class yourself.

Every persistent instance has a unique identity value, which can be represented by an instance of the identity class. You can acquire a copy of the identity instance associated with a persistent instance; you can save it, retrieve it later from durable storage (by serialization or some other technique), and use it to obtain a reference to the same persistent instance. The JDO implementation does not necessarily maintain an instantiation of the identity instance in the cache for each persistent instance in the cache, but it can construct an instance for use by your application.

When you make an instance persistent via makePersistent( ), the instance is assigned an identity. If the metadata states that the instance's class has an identity type that the implementation does not support, a JDOUserException is thrown for that instance. The enhancer in some implementations may also produce a warning or error when the class is enhanced if the implementation does not support the identity type.

The identity of a persistent instance is managed by the JDO implementation. For classes with a durable identity (datastore or application identity), each

PersistenceManager instance manages at most one instance in the memory cache for a given object in the datastore, regardless of how your application accessed the persistent instance.

Datastore Identity

Datastore identity can be used with datastores that provide an identifier that does not depend on the values of fields in an instance. This is the form of identity that object databases have provided for years. It is also supported in a relational JDO implementation by managing an additional primary-key column that is distinct from the columns containing field values.

Existing relational schemas often have a primary-key column that contains a value provided by a *sequence* or some other facility that can generate unique values for the application. This is especially useful when the entity being modeled does not have an attribute that is a natural real-world identifier, or when the number of attributes necessary to identify an instance uniquely becomes excessive.

The implementation guarantees that the identity value is unique for all instances. You cannot change the identity of an instance if its class uses datastore identity. Datastore identity is the easiest type of identity to use, because the implementation and datastore handle everything automatically; it does not require any additional development on your part.

A JDO implementation's datastore identity class has the following characteristics:

- It is public.
- It implements Serializable, allowing you to serialize identity instances.
- The type of all its nonstatic fields are serializable.
- All of its serializable fields are public.
- It has a public no-arg constructor.
- It overrides toString( ), returning a String that can be used as the parameter for the following String constructor.
- It has a constructor with a String parameter that creates an identity instance that compares equal to any other identity instance whose toString( ) returns a String that is equal to the String parameter.

The last two characteristics are necessary to create a String representation of an identity and later reconstruct an identity instance with the String by using newObjectIdInstance( ), covered later in this chapter. You cannot test the equality of two datastore identity instances if they were acquired from different JDO implementations.

Application Identity

You can use application identity with a datastore that allows the values in an instance to determine its identity. The values of one or more persistent fields in the instance form a unique value that is referred to as the *primary key*; the fields are referred to as the *primary-key fields*. The application is responsible for generating the values of the primary-key fields to ensure they collectively have a unique value for each instance in the datastore. The primary-key fields must have a unique value for a given class and its subclasses that use the same application identity class.

Primary-Key Fields

You indicate that a Java field is a component of the primary key in the metadata by setting the primary-key attribute of the field's associated field element to "true". Each field of the primary key must have this attribute set to "true"; it has a default value of "false". The primary-key fields of a persistent class must be persistent. Therefore, the persistence-modifier attribute of the field metadata element cannot be set to "transactional" or "none". The primary-key fields become a property of the persistent class that cannot be changed after the class is enhanced. If you need to change the set of fields in a primary key, you will need to enhance the class again. Read access to primary-key fields is never mediated.

The type of primary-key fields must be serializable and should be one of the primitive types, String, Date, Byte, Short, Integer, Long, Float, Double, BigDecimal, or BigInteger. JDO implementations are required to support these types and might support other reference types.

When a transient instance is made persistent, the implementation uses the values of the primary-key fields to construct an identity for the instance. A JDOUserException is thrown during makePersistent() if an instance in the PersistenceManager cache already has the same primary key, or during the flush of the new instance to the datastore if the datastore already has an instance with the same primary key.

The primary-key fields of a persistent class uniquely identify an instance in the datastore. Your Java object model will likely contain references and collections of references to instances of the class. The declaration and use of these references is performed with standard Java syntax. The JDO implementation automatically maps the references used at the Java level to primary keys when things are mapped to the underlying datastore. Your application does not need to know that application identity is being used, nor does it need to know what the primary-key fields are for a particular persistent class. You simply use the Java references.

Persistent Class equals() and hashCode( ) Methods

It is important for you to understand the interaction between JDO identity and equality. The equals( ) method in Object simply uses the Java identity based on the address of the instance in the JVM. The Java identity of a persistent instance is guaranteed neither between PersistenceManagers, nor across space and time. You should implement equals( ) for your persistent classes that use application identity differently from the default implementation in Object.

If you store persistent instances of classes using application identity in the datastore and query them using the == query operator, or refer to them by a persistent collection that enforces equality (Set, Map), then the implementation of equals( ) should exactly match the JDO implementation of equality, using the identity value (primary-key fields). To be portable, the equals( ) and hashCode( ) methods of any persistent class using application identity should depend on all of the primary-key fields.

This policy is not enforced, but if it is not correctly implemented, the semantics of standard transient collections and the persistent collections may differ. Specifically, the Set and Map collections call the equals( ) and hashCode( ) methods of their elements to enforce uniqueness constraints and manage their element look up mechanisms. The identity (represented by the primary-key fields) to identify an instance uniquely in the datastore must be used in the management of these collections in the cache.

The Application-Identity Class

You need to implement an application-identity class for your classes that use application identity. You can either define it by hand or use a tool some vendors provide to generate the class for you. The identity class needs to have fields that correspond, in name and type, with the primary-key fields in the persistent class. It should also have all of the characteristics of an RMI remote object for the class that will be used as a primary-key class in EJB. Specifically, the application identity class should have the following characteristics:

- It must be public.
- It must implement Serializable.
- If it is an inner class, it must be static.
- It must have nonstatic fields with the same name and type as each of the primary-key fields in the persistent class.
- The type of these fields must be serializable and should be one of the primitive types, String, Date, Byte, Short, Integer, Long, Float, Double, BigDecimal, or BigInteger. JDO implementations are required to support these types and might support other reference types.

- All of its serializable, nonstatic fields must be public.

- Its equals( ) and hashCode( ) methods must use the values of all the fields that correspond to the primary-key fields in the persistent class. The implementation of these methods in the identity class must match the implementation in the persistent class.

- It must have a public no-arg constructor, which may be the default constructor.

- It must override toString( ), as defined in Object, and return a String that can be used as the parameter of the following String constructor.

- It must provide a String constructor that returns an instance that compares equal to another instance that returned the String parameter via toString( ).

These restrictions allow you to construct an instance of the application identity class by providing only the values for the primary-key fields or, alternatively, by providing the result of toString( ) from an existing application identity instance.

The names and types of the primary-key fields in the persistent class must be the same as the fields in the application identity class, and the fields in the application identity class must have a public access modifier. But you can choose any access modifier that you want for the primary-key fields in the persistent class. In particular, we recommend that you declare your primary-key fields private, since changing them is dependent on the implementation supporting the optional ChangeApplicationIdentity feature, covered later in this chapter.

You must specify the application identity class in the metadata with the objectid-class attribute class element of the persistent class. You should use Java's rules for naming when specifying the objectid-class value: if you do not include a package in the name, it is assumed to be in the same package as the persistent class. If you use an inner class, use the $ marker before the inner class name.

An implementation is permitted to extend the application-identity class to include additional fields not provided by the application, to further identify the instance in the datastore. Thus, the identity instance returned by an implementation might be a subclass of the user-defined application identity class. An implementation must be able to use an application identity instance from any other JDO implementation.

A Single-Field Primary Key

Let's start with a simple example. We'll create a new version of the RentalCode class that we defined in the com.mediamania.store package and place it in a new package called com.mediamania.store.appid. The sole reason we place the RentalCode class and its application identity class in a separate package is to distinguish between the class that uses datastore identity and the class that uses application identity. Your object model would normally have one class with one type of identity. The fields and a few of the methods of the new RentalCode class are declared as follows:

```
package com.mediamania.store.appid;

import java.math.BigDecimal;

public class RentalCode
{
❶      private String      code;
       private int         numberOfDays;
       private BigDecimal  cost;
       private BigDecimal  lateFeePerDay;

       RentalCode( )
       { }

    // methods, etc...

❷      public boolean equals(Object obj) {
           return  obj instanceof RentalCode &&
                   ((RentalCode)obj).code.equals(code);
       }
❸      public int hashCode( ) {
           return code.hashCode( );
       }
}
```

The code field declared on line ❶ should contain a unique String value for each RentalCode instance, providing a natural primary-key. We also define equals( ) and hashCode( ) in terms of the primary-key field code on lines ❷ and ❸.

We specify the following metadata for the class:

```
<package name="com.mediamania.store.appid">
    <class name="RentalCode"
        objectid-class="com.mediamania.store.appid.RentalCodeKey" >
        <field name="code" primary-key="true" />
    </class>
</package>
```

The metadata specifies the code field as the one primary-key field in RentalCode.

We also specify the RentalCodeKey class as the application identity class for RentalCode. Let's examine the class in detail:

```
package com.mediamania.store.appid;

import java.io.Serializable;

❶ public class RentalCodeKey implements Serializable {
❷      static {
           RentalCode code = new RentalCode( );
       }
❸      public String       code;
```

```
❹       public RentalCodeKey(String code) {
            this.code = code;
        }
❺       public RentalCodeKey( ) {
            code = new String("");
        }
❻       public String toString( ) {
            return code;
        }
❼       public boolean equals(Object obj) {
            return  obj instanceof RentalCodeKey &&
                    ((RentalCodeKey)obj).code.equals(code);
        }
❽       public int hashCode( ) {
            return code.hashCode( );
        }
    }
```

On line ❶, we declare that RentalCodeKey implements Serializable. The application identity class must have public fields that correspond to the primary-key fields in the persistent class; line ❸ declares the code field. The class needs to have a public, no-arg constructor, which we define on line ❺. We also define a constructor on line ❹, which takes a String argument. In the case of RentalCodeKey, only a single String field corresponds to the primary-key, so we can just assign the String argument to the code field. As we will see in the next example, if there are multiple primary-key fields, you will need to parse the values in the String argument to this constructor. Having the single code field of type String also makes our required toString( ) trivial as well. We also define equals( ) and hashCode( ) on lines ❼ and ❽, respectively. These methods delegate to the code field and call the corresponding String methods.

Class registration code is placed in the static initialization method that the enhancer adds to your persistent class. The association between a persistent class and its application identity class is established when the persistent class is registered in the JDO environment. The JDO implementation does not know the specific application identity class for a persistent class until the persistent class has been loaded into the JVM and had this static initialization method executed.

Often, the first time an application accesses a persistent instance via its identity, the application has not yet used the persistent class. The application creates and initializes an application identity instance, passing it to getObjectById( ). But the persistent class may not be loaded in the JVM yet, so the registration of the persistent class and its identity class has not occurred. The JDO implementation may throw an exception, indicating that you have passed an invalid identity value.

To prevent this from happening, we must make sure that the persistent class has been loaded before we use an instance of the identity class to access an instance. By placing the static initialization block at line ❷ in RentalCodeKey, we force the loading of RentalCode when RentalCodeKey is loaded. The RentalCode instance created in the static initialization block is garbage-collected once the block has finished, but this has the effect of loading the RentalCode class when the identity class is loaded.

A Compound Primary Key

The application identity can consist of multiple primary-key fields. Now let's cover another example that illustrates additional approaches and techniques that can be used when defining an application identity class.

We will now consider the following persistent Customer class that we have placed in the com.mediamania.store.appid package. This is a simplied version of the Customer class defined in the com.mediamania.store package. To provide a unique primary key, we use a combination of the firstName, lastName, and phone fields.

With this persistent class, we define the application identity class as a static inner class, named Id, on line ❷. Since there is a tight coupling between an application identity class and its persistent class, it makes sense to define it as an inner class. But the inner class must be static; you cannot use a nonstatic inner class for the application identity class. Adopting this approach across all of your persistent classes simplifies development by instituting a single consistent naming mechanism for all your application identity classes.

```
package com.mediamania.store.appid;

import java.io.Serializable;
import java.util.StringTokenizer;

public class Customer {
    private String  firstName;  // primary-key field
    private String  lastName;   // primary-key field
    private String  phone;      // primary-key field
    private String  email;

// other fields removed for brevity in the example

    Customer()
    { }
    public Customer(String firstName, String lastName,
                    String phone, String email) {
        this.firstName = firstName;
        this.lastName = lastName;
        this.phone = phone;
        this.email = email;
    }
    public String getFirstName() {
        return firstName;
    }
    public String getLastName() {
        return lastName;
    }
    public String getPhone() {
        return phone;
    }
```

```java
    public String getEmail() {
        return email;
    }
❶  public boolean equals(Object obj) {
        if(!(obj instanceof Customer)) return false;
        Customer c = (Customer)obj;
        Id id1 = new Id(firstName, lastName, phone);
        Id id2 = new Id(c.firstName, c.lastName, c.phone);
        return id1.equals(id2);
    }
    public int hashCode() {
        Id id = new Id(firstName, lastName, phone);
        return id.hashCode();
    }

❷  public static class Id implements Serializable {
        static {
            Customer customer = new Customer();
        }
        public String  firstName;
        public String  lastName;
        public String  phone;

❸      public Id(String fname, String lname, String phone) {
            firstName = fname;
            lastName = lname;
            this.phone = phone;
        }
❹      public Id() {
            firstName = "";
            lastName = "";
            phone = "";
        }
❺      public Id(String val) {
            StringTokenizer tokenizer = new StringTokenizer(val, "|");
            firstName = tokenizer.nextToken();
            lastName  = tokenizer.nextToken();
            phone     = tokenizer.nextToken();
        }
❻      public String toString() {
            StringBuffer buffer = new StringBuffer();
            buffer.append(firstName);
            buffer.append("|");
            buffer.append(lastName);
            buffer.append("|");
            buffer.append(phone);
            return buffer.toString();
        }
❼      public boolean equals(Object obj) {
            if (!(obj instanceof Id)) return false;
            Id id = (Id) obj;
            if (!phone.equals(id.phone)) return false;
```

```
                if (!lastName.equals(id.lastName)) return false;
                return firstName.equals(id.firstName);
            }
❽          public int hashCode( ) {
                return toString().hashCode( );
            }
        }
    }
```

We need to define equals( ) and hashCode( ) in Customer, and they must be based on the values of the primary-key fields. Line ❶ defines these methods. Since the functionality that manages the composite value of the three primary-key fields is defined in the Id class, equals( ) and hashCode( ) delegate to temporary Id instances already in Id, instead of duplicating the code. This strategy also makes sure they implement the same functionality. This may or may not always make sense for your persistent classes.

The Id class provides three constructors. The constructors defined on lines ❹ and ❺ are required of all application identity classes. Since this persistent class has multiple primary-key fields, the constructor defined on line ❺ must parse the String to initialize each component of the primary key. An application identity class does not require the constructor defined on line ❸, but it provides a useful means of initializing all the primary-key components. We define the required application identity method toString( ) on line ❻; its result can be used by the String method on line ❺ to initialize a new Id instance.

We need to define equals( ) and hashCode( ) in our application identity classes, and they should be based on the values of all the primary-key fields. On line ❼, we define equals( ) for Id. We define hashCode( ) on line ❽, and it uses Id's toString( ) method to construct a String containing all the primary-key field values and then calls String's hashCode( ) to compute the hash code for Id.

Let's examine the metadata for Customer:

```
<package name="com.mediamania.store.appid">
    <class name="Customer" identity-type="application"
           objectid-class="Customer$Id" >
        <field name="firstName" primary-key="true" />
        <field name="lastName"  primary-key="true" />
        <field name="phone"     primary-key="true" />
    </class>
</package>
```

We provide field elements to specify each of the primary-key fields. Since we provide a value for objectid-class, inclusion of the identity-type attribute is optional. We let the package of the objectid-class attribute value default to the same package as the persistent class, since we do not include the package name. Since Id is an inner class, we use $ between the class name and inner class name to denote Id.

A Compound Primary Key That Contains a Foreign Key

It is common in relational schemas to have a compound primary key that includes a foreign key column. For example, assume you have a table in your relational database, called Order, to represent an order placed by a customer. The Order table has a primary-key column containing a unique order number. A separate table, called LineItem, contains the individual items in the customer's order. There is a one-to-many relationship between Order and LineItem, represented by the LineItem table having a foreign key reference to a row in the Order table. To identify a particular LineItem row uniquely, we define a primary key for LineItem that consists of the order number, which is a foreign key reference to Order, and a line-item number that is unique within the particular order. A primary key, like the one defined for the LineItem table, is very common in relational schemas.

Let's examine the Java classes and metadata necessary to represent such a model. An Order class could be defined as follows:

```java
package com.mediamania.store;

import java.io.Serializable;

public class Order {
    private int          orderNumber; // primary-key field
    private Customer     customer;

    public Order( ) {
        orderNumber = 0;
    }
    public Order(Customer cust, int orderNum) {
        customer = cust;
        orderNumber = orderNum;
    }
    public boolean equals(Object obj) {
        return obj instanceof Order && ((Order)obj).orderNumber == orderNumber;
    }
    public int hashCode( ) {
        return orderNumber;
    }

    public static class Id implements Serializable {
        static {
            Order order = new Order( );
        }
        public int       orderNumber;

        public Id( ) {
            orderNumber = 0;
        }
        public Id(int orderNum) {
            orderNumber = orderNum;
        }
```

```
        public Id(String orderNum) {
            orderNumber = 0;
            try {
                Integer.parseInt(orderNum);
            } catch(NumberFormatException e) { }
        }
        public String toString() {
            return Integer.toString(orderNumber);
        }
        public boolean equals(Object obj) {
            return obj instanceof Id && ((Id)obj).orderNumber == orderNumber;
        }
        public int hashCode() {
            return orderNumber;
        }
    }
}
```

In a real application, the class would likely have more fields and methods, but we primarily want to describe the application identity classes that are appropriate for this model. The orderNumber field in Order has a unique value that uniquely identifies an Order instance. We define the application identity class for Order as a static inner class named Id. The Id class has a corresponding orderNumber field. The application needs to have a means of acquiring a unique value for orderNumber. JDO does not currently provide a facility for generating unique application values, but it is being considered for a future release. Some JDO implementations provide such a facility now. The Order.Id class implements all the functionality necessary in an application identity class.

Now let's examine the LineItem class. As in the Order class, we do not provide all the fields and functionality a real application would have, but we include fields and methods relevant to our discussion.

```
package com.mediamania.store;

import java.io.Serializable;
import java.math.BigDecimal;

public class LineItem {
    private int        orderNumber;    // primary-key field
    private int        itemNumber;     // primary-key field
    private String     description;
    private BigDecimal price;
// other fields

    LineItem() {
        orderNumber = 0;
        itemNumber = 0;
    }
    public LineItem(int orderNum, int itemNum, String desc, BigDecimal price) {
        orderNumber = orderNum;
        itemNumber = itemNum;
```

```
            description = desc;
            this.price = price;
        }
        // other methods

        public static class Id implements Serializable {
            static {
                LineItem item = new LineItem( );
            }
            public int  orderNumber;
            public int  itemNumber;

            public Id( ) {
                orderNumber = 0;
                itemNumber = 0;
            }
            public Id(int orderNum, int itemNum) {
                orderNumber = orderNum;
                itemNumber = itemNum;
            }
            public Id(String val) {
                int separatorIndex = val.indexOf('|');
                orderNumber = 0;
                itemNumber = 0;
                try {
                    orderNumber = Integer.parseInt(val.substring(0,separatorIndex));
                } catch (NumberFormatException e) { }
                try {
                    itemNumber = Integer.parseInt(val.substring(separatorIndex+1));
                } catch (NumberFormatException e) { }
            }
            public String toString( ) {
                return  Integer.toString(orderNumber) + "|" +
                        Integer.toString(itemNumber);
            }
            public boolean equals(Object obj) {
                if (!(obj instanceof Id)) return false;
                Id id = (Id) obj;
                return orderNumber == id.orderNumber && itemNumber == id.itemNumber;
            }
            public int hashCode( ) {
                return orderNumber*1000 + itemNumber;
            }
        }
    }
}
```

LineItem has two primary-key fields: orderNumber and itemNumber. Again, we define the application identity class as a static inner class Id. It contains the two fields of the primary key: orderNumber and itemNumber.

You may consider it more appropriate to declare the primary-key fields as follows:

```
    private Order      order;       // primary-key field
    private int        itemNumber;  // primary-key field
```

Since the LineItem table in the database has a foreign-key reference to the Order table, this would seem to be the natural mapping. But the type of primary-key fields in JDO should be one of the primitive, String, Date, or Number types. The fields in the application identity class and the application identity class itself must be serializable. But if we use the preceding order field, when the identity instance is serialized it will also serialize the Order and possibly other persistent instances.

You may still want to have a reference to Order that you can use to navigate to the instance. You could declare the following fields in the LineItem class:

```
private int        orderNumber;   // primary-key field
private int        itemNumber;    // primary-key field
private Order       order;
private String      description;
private BigDecimal  price;
```

How this gets mapped to the underlying datastore depends on the capabilities of the JDO implementation you are using. Some implementations would require the underlying datastore to have a redundant orderNumber field, since the order field declared in this example would be represented in the datastore by the primary key of Order, declared to be an order number. There are some implementations that would allow the orderNumber and order fields to be mapped onto the same column in a relational database. These implementations also ensure that these two fields are always kept in sync, as a change to one of the fields necessitates a change to the other.

Here is the metadata for the Order and LineItem classes:

```
<package name="com.mediamania.store" >
    <class name="Order" objectid-class = "Order$Id" >
        <field name="orderNumber" primary-key="true" />
    </class>
    <class name="LineItem" objectid-class="LineItem$Id" >
        <field name="orderNumber" primary-key="true" />
        <field name="itemNumber"  primary-key="true" />
    </class>
</package>
```

Application Identity in an Inheritance Hierarchy

There are special considerations when using application identity for persistent classes in an inheritance hierarchy. Only certain persistent classes in the inheritance hierarchy can have primary-key fields, and there are restrictions on the definition and metadata specification of their associated application identity classes. Every class in the hierarchy must have exactly one nonabstract (concrete) application identity class. A least-derived (topmost), concrete persistent class must have an associated application identity class, specified either in the objectid-class attribute of its own persistent class's metadata, or in the objectid-class attribute of one of its abstract superclasses. The persistent class and all its subclasses use this concrete application identity class. The subclasses must not specify a value for the objectid-class attribute. You can declare primary-key fields only in abstract superclasses and in the topmost, concrete classes in an inheritance hierarchy. You need to define an application identity class for each persistent class in the hierarchy that has a primary-key field. Each of these application identity classes must declare fields that correspond to the primary-key fields in their respective persistent class. Within an inheritance hierarchy, you can have intermediate classes between two persistent classes that have primary-key fields, in which the intermediate classes do not have any primary-key fields.

The simplest design is to define one application identity class for the entire inheritance hierarchy, specified at the least-derived persistent class in the hierarchy, regardless of whether it is concrete or abstract. If you require multiple application identity classes for the persistent classes in an inheritance hierarchy, the application identity classes form an inheritance hierarchy that corresponds to the inheritance hierarchy of their associated persistent classes.

Let's look at an example, illustrated in Figure 10-1. If a Component abstract class declares a masterId primary-key field, the ComponentKey application identity class (which should be abstract as well) must also declare a field of the same name and type.

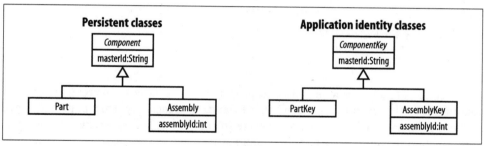

Figure 10-1. Inheritance of application identity classes in inheritance hierarchies

The following code declares a subset of the Component class:

```
package productdesign;

public abstract class Component {
    private String  masterId; // primary-key field
    private int      x;
    private int      y;
// other fields

    protected Component( )
    { }
    protected Component(String id) {
        masterId = id;
        x = 0;
        y = 0;
    }
// other methods
}
```

We define the ComponentKey class as follows:

```java
package productdesign;

import java.io.Serializable;

public abstract class ComponentKey implements Serializable {
    static {
        Component comp = new Component( );
    }
    public String    masterId;

    public ComponentKey( ) {
        masterId = "";
    }
    public ComponentKey(String id) {
        masterId = id;
    }
    public String toString( ) {
        return masterId;
    }
    public boolean equals(Object obj) {
        return   obj instanceof ComponentKey &&
                ((ComponentKey)obj).masterId.equals(masterId);
    }
    public int hashCode( ) {
        return masterId.hashCode( );
    }
}
```

A concrete Part class that extends Component must declare a concrete application identity class (for example, PartKey) that extends ComponentKey. Part might not have its own primary-key fields, as we illustrate in this example. Persistent subclasses of Part must not have their own application identity class.

We define the Part class as follows:

```java
package productdesign;

public class Part extends Component {
    private String   designer;
// other fields

    protected Part( )
    { }
    public Part(String assemId, String designer) {
        super(assemId);
        this.designer = designer;
    }
    public String getDesigner( ) {
        return designer;
    }
// other methods
}
```

Here is a portion of the associated PartKey class:

```
package productdesign;

public class PartKey extends ComponentKey {
    static {
        Part part = new Part( );
    }
    public PartKey(String id) {
        super(id);
    }
    public PartKey( ) {

    }
// other identity methods
}
```

The concrete Assembly class that extends Component must declare a concrete application identity class (for example, AssemblyKey) that extends ComponentKey. If Assembly has a assemblyId primary-key field, the assemblyId field must also be declared in AssemblyKey with the same name and type.

Here is a part of the Assembly class declaration:

```
package productdesign;

import java.util.HashSet;

public class Assembly extends Component {
    private int        assemblyId; // primary-key field
    private HashSet     components;

    private Assembly( )
    { }
    public Assembly(String componentId, int aid) {
        super(componentId);
        assemblyId = aid;
        components = new HashSet( );
    }
    public int getAssemblyId( ) {
        return assemblyId;
    }
}
```

We define the AssemblyKey class as follows:

```
package productdesign;

public class AssemblyKey extends ComponentKey {
    static {
        Assembly assembly = new Assembly( );
    }
    public int  assemblyId;
```

```java
    public AssemblyKey( ) {
        assemblyId = 0;
    }
    public AssemblyKey(String id) {
        super(id.substring(0, id.indexOf('|')));
        assemblyId = 0;
        try {
            assemblyId = Integer.parseInt(id.substring(id.indexOf('|')+1));
        } catch(Exception e) { }
    }
    public AssemblyKey(String master, int id) {
        super(master);
        assemblyId = id;
    }
    public String toString( ) {
        return super.toString( ) + "|" + Integer.toString(assemblyId);
    }
    public boolean equals(Object obj) {
        if (!(obj instanceof AssemblyKey)) return false;
        AssemblyKey assemKey = (AssemblyKey) obj;
        if (assemblyId != assemKey.assemblyId) return false;
        return super.equals(assemKey);
    }
    public int hashCode( ) {
        return assemblyId * super.hashCode( );
    }
}
```

Persistent subclasses of Assembly must not have their own application identity class.

There might be other abstract or nonpersistent classes in the inheritance hierarchy between Component and Part, or between Component and Assembly. The application identity classes and primary-key fields ignore these classes.

Here is the metadata for these classes:

```xml
<jdo>
    <package name="productdesign" >
        <class name="Component" objectid-class="ComponentKey" >
            <field name="masterId" primary-key="true" />
        </class>
        <class name="Part" objectid-class="PartKey"
                persistence-capable-superclass="Component"/>
        <class name="Assembly" objectid-class="AssemblyKey"
                persistence-capable-superclass="Component" >
            <field name="assemblyId" primary-key="true" />
            <field name="components" >
                <collection element-type="Part" />
            </field>
        </class>
    </package>
</jdo>
```

❶

There is an interesting modeling issue to consider in the Assembly class. It contains a collection named components. An Assembly abstraction models a set of components

---

that should be treated as a single design unit in a product design. On line ❶ in the metadata we declare that components contains Part instances. We may also want to allow an Assembly to contain references to Component instances, which could include references to other Assembly instances. But in the object model we have defined here, Component introduces only a *partial primary key*. Though the Part class is the first concrete class in its branch of the inheritance hierarchy and it does not add any additional fields to identify a Part instance, the Assembly class does introduce additional fields that are necessary to reference an Assembly instance. Many other classes may extend Component and introduce their own additional primary-key fields. In general, you should not rely on support of partial primary keys to represent references when using application identity (though some implementations may support it). If your model needs support of such references, you should either have the persistent class at the root of the inheritance hierarchy completely define the primary key for its class and all subclasses, or you should use datastore identity, which does not have this issue.

Nondurable Identity

Some datastores cannot provide a unique identity that can be used to locate a specific piece of data. This limitation can be common in log files, history files, and similar files, where performance is a primary concern and there is no need for the overhead associated with managing a durable identity for each datastore instance. Objects are typically inserted into the datastore with transactional semantics, but they are not accessed by key. They may have references to instances elsewhere in the datastore, but often they have no keys or indexes themselves. They might be accessed by other attributes, and they might be deleted in bulk. JDO defines a nondurable identity type for use when accessing instances in such datastores.

Multiple objects in the datastore might have the same values; we refer to them as *duplicate objects*. An application may want to treat the duplicate objects individually. For example, the application should be able to count the persistent instances to determine how many have the same values. In addition, if the application changes a single field of one duplicate instance, exactly one instance has its field changed in the datastore. If multiple duplicate instances are modified in memory, then instances in the datastore are modified to correspond with the instances modified in memory. Similarly, if an application deletes a specific number of duplicate objects, it should delete this same number of objects in the datastore.

As another example, a single datastore instance using nondurable identity may be loaded twice into the JVM by the same PersistenceManager. Since there is no durable identity to distinguish instances from the datastore, two separate instances are instantiated in memory with two different nondurable identities, even though all of the values in the instances are the same. Only one of these instances can be updated or deleted. If only one instance is updated or deleted, then the changes made to that instance are reflected in the datastore at commit by changing the single datastore instance. However, if both instances are changed, the transaction fails at commit because changes to distinct instances in memory can be applied only to different datastore instances. In this case, there are multiple instances in memory and only one instance in the datastore.

Because nondurable identity is not visible in the datastore, it has special behaviors:

- After a transaction terminates (via commit or rollback), neither an instance in memory with nondurable identity nor its identity can be accessed, and any attempt to access them causes a JDOUserException to be thrown.
- A nondurable identity cannot be used in a different PersistenceManager instance than the one that issued it, and attempts to use it, even indirectly, throw a JDOUserException.
- The results of a query in the datastore always create and return new instances that are not already in the JVM. So, if the results of multiple queries contain the same instances in the datastore, additional instances of the datastore instances are instantiated in memory with the same values, but with different identities.
- makePersistent( ) succeeds even if another instance has the same values for all its persistent fields.

The implementation's class that implements nondurable identity has the following characteristics:

- It is public.
- All of its fields are public.
- The types of all of its fields are serializable.
- It has a public no-arg constructor, possibly the default constructor.

You should be aware that, at the time of this writing, there has been very limited support of nondurable identity (just one vendor supports it). The level of support may improve over time, but it obviously has not been a vendor priority.

Identity Methods

JDO provides methods to map between identity instances and their associated persistent instances, and between an identity instance and a String value. You can acquire an identity instance for a persistent instance by using getObjectId( ), and you can access a persistent instance if you have an identity instance with getObjectById( ). Figure 10-2 shows these methods.

You can also convert an identity instance to a String by using toString( ). You can then use the returned String to reconstruct a corresponding identity instance with newObjectIdInstance( ). These capabilities are the reasons why you need to define

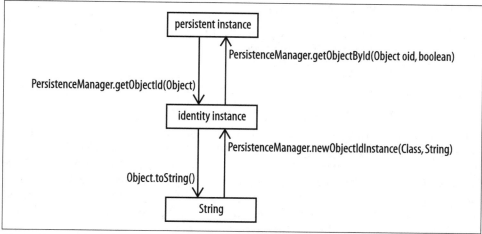

Figure 10-2. Methods to map between a persistent instance and its identity

toString( ) and a constructor that accepts a single String argument. Now let's describe the functionality of these methods in detail. These methods work for each identity type.

Get the Identity Class

You can access the identity class of a persistent class by calling the following PersistenceManager method:

```
Class getObjectIdClass(Class persistentClass);
```

Passing the Class of a persistent class that uses datastore or nondurable identity returns the implementation-defined identity class. Passing the Class of a persistent class that uses application identity returns your application identity class. The method returns null if the parameter is null, the class referenced by persistentClass is abstract or not persistent, or the metadata specifies that the persistent class uses application identity and the implementation does not support application identity.

When using the JDO reference implementation, the following lines of code:

```
Class c1 = pm.getObjectIdClass(com.mediamania.store.Customer.class);
System.out.println(c1.toString( ));
Class c2 = pm.getObjectIdClass(com.mediamania.store.appid.Customer.class);
System.out.println(c2.toString( ));
```

produce the following output:

```
class com.sun.jdori.fostore.OID
class com.mediamania.store.appid.Customer$Id
```

Get the Identity of an Instance

JDO provides two methods to access the identity of a persistent instance. You can use either the PersistenceManager method:

```
Object getObjectId(Object obj);
```

or the JDOHelper method:

```
static Object getObjectId(Object obj);
```

These methods return null if the obj instance is transient, null, or not of a persistent class. Otherwise, they return an identity instance for the obj parameter. The identity instance returned is guaranteed to be unique only in the context of the PersistenceManager that created the identity and only for datastore and application identity. Within a transaction, the identity returned will be unique when compared with the identity of all the other persistent instances associated with the PersistenceManager, regardless of their type of identity.

There are only a small number of RentalCode instances in our example; this is reference data that rarely changes in the datastore. Suppose a MediaMania store application needs to establish references to RentalCode instances quickly. Here we deal specifically with the RentalCode class defined in the com.mediamania.store package. For example, consider the application that creates new MediaItem instances when the store receives new DVDs. The application wants to reference them by their code value. Instead of performing a query to access a specific RentalCode instance, the following utility class maintains a mapping from the code value to the RentalCode instance:

```
package com.mediamania.store;

import java.util.Iterator;
import java.util.HashMap;
import javax.jdo.PersistenceManager;
import javax.jdo.Extent;

public class RentalCodeAccessor {
    private static HashMap              rentalCodes;
    private static PersistenceManager   pm;

    public static synchronized void initialize(PersistenceManager thePM) {
        pm = thePM;
        rentalCodes = new HashMap();
        Extent rentalCodeExtent = pm.getExtent(RentalCode.class, true);
        Iterator iter = rentalCodeExtent.iterator();
        while (iter.hasNext()) {
            RentalCode rentalCode = (RentalCode) iter.next();
            Object id = pm.getObjectId(rentalCode);
            rentalCodes.put(rentalCode.getCode(), id);
        }
        rentalCodeExtent.close(iter);
    }
```

❶

```
❷       public static Object getId(String code) {
            return rentalCodes.get(code);
        }
    }
```

The class has a static initialize( ) method that is called to read the RentalCode instances from the datastore and populate a Map, where the key of an entry is the code value of a RentalCode, and the entry's value is the identity of the RentalCode instance. We acquire the identity for a RentalCode instance on line ❶ and place an entry into the Map on the next line. On line ❷, we define getId( ), which returns the identity instance associated with a particular code value, or null if there is no entry for the provided code.

The application can then make calls to getId( ) to access identity instances:

```
Object id = RentalCodeAccessor.getId("Hot");
System.out.println(id.toString( ));
id = RentalCodeAccessor.getId("Recent");
System.out.println(id.toString( ));
id = RentalCodeAccessor.getId("Oldie");
System.out.println(id.toString( ));
```

When using the reference implementation, these lines of code produce the following output:

```
OID: 102-11
OID: 102-13
OID: 102-15
```

The RentalCode class defined in the com.mediamania.store package uses datastore identity. This output shows the reference implementation's representation of a datastore identity value. The String representation of datastore identity is different with each JDO implementation. The value 102 denotes a specific class (RentalCode) and the numbers 11, 13, and 15 identify specific instances.

The identity value returned by getObjectId( ) is the identity of the instance at the beginning of the transaction. Later in this chapter, we'll discuss the case where you can change the application identity of an instance during a transaction. In this situation, you use another method to return the current identity of an instance.

An identity instance does not necessarily contain any of the internal state of a persistent instance, nor is it necessarily an instance of the class the implementation uses internally to manage identity. The returned instance represents the identity for the application to use. Multiple identity instances obtained from the same PersistenceManager for the same persistent instance have the same identity value, and a call to equals( ) on two such instances returns true. The identity instances used as parameters or returned by getObjectId( ), getTransactionalObjectId( ), and getObjectById( ) are not saved internally; rather, they are copies of the implementation's internal representation, or they are used to find instances of the internal representation. Therefore, you can modify the instance returned by getObjectId( ); you will not affect the persistent instance or its identity.

Getting an Instance via Its Identity

The following PersistenceManager method attempts to find an instance in the cache with the specified identity:

```
Object getObjectById(Object oid, boolean validate);
```

The oid parameter is an identity instance that might have been returned by an earlier call to getObjectId( ) or getTransactionalObjectId( ), or it might be an application identity instance constructed by the application. We use the validate flag to tell the implementation whether or not it should verify that the instance associated with the oid identity parameter currently exists in the datastore.

We add the following method to the RentalCodeAccessor utility class:

```
    public static RentalCode getRentalCode(String code) {
❶       Object id = rentalCodes.get(code);
        if (id == null) return null;
❷       RentalCode rentalCode = (RentalCode) pm.getObjectById(id, true);
        return rentalCode;
    }
```

On line ❶, we look up the code value in the Map, returning null if it is not found. Otherwise, we call getObjectById( ) on line ❷ to access the RentalCode instance associated with the identity value. RentalCodeAccessor provides access to RentalCode instances defined in the com.mediamania.store package, which use datastore identity. You should declare Object references to refer to instances of a vendor's datastore identity class.

Now let's look at an example of using getObjectById( ) to access instances that use application identity. In the com.mediamania.store.appid package we declared RentalCode and Customer persistent classes, with RentalCodeKey and Customer.Id identity classes, respectively. The following lines of code create instances of these application identity classes and access the associated instances:

```
RentalCodeKey key = new RentalCodeKey("High Demand");
RentalCode code = (RentalCode) pm.getObjectById(key, true);

Customer.Id id = new Customer.Id("Brian", "Mathie", "330-555-2020");
Customer cust = (Customer) pm.getObjectById(id, true);
```

If the PersistenceManager cannot convert the oid parameter passed to getObjectById( ) to a valid identity instance, then it throws a JDOUserException. This could occur if the parameter is an instance of an application identity class and the implementation does not support application identity. Or, the instance may be of a class that is different from the one specified in the metadata.

If you pass a value of false for the validate parameter, the following behavior occurs:

- If there is already an instance in the cache with the same identity as the oid parameter, the instance is returned. No change is made to the state of the returned instance.

- If there is not already an instance in the cache with the same identity as the oid parameter, then an instance with the specified identity is created and returned.

- If the instance does not exist in the datastore, this method may or may not fail. An implementation may immediately throw a JDODataStoreException, or it may return an instance. However, if it returns an instance, a subsequent access of its fields causes a JDODataStoreException to be thrown if the instance does not exist at that time. Further, if a relationship is established to this instance and the instance does not exist when the instance is flushed to the datastore, the transaction in which the association was made will fail.

The implementation decides whether to access the datastore, if required to determine the exact class of the persistent instance. This is the case with inheritance, where multiple persistent classes can share the same identity class.

If you pass true for the validate parameter, the following behavior occurs:

- If a transactional instance is already in the cache with the same identity as the oid parameter, the instance is returned. The state of the returned instance is not changed.

- If a nontransactional instance is in the cache with the same identity as the oid parameter, a transaction is active, and the instance exists in the datastore, a transactional instance is returned with a state consistent with the datastore.

- If an instance with the same identity as the oid parameter is not in the cache but it does exist in the datastore, an instance with the specified identity is created and returned.

- If an instance is already in the cache with the same identity as the oid parameter, the instance is not transactional, and the instance does not exist in the datastore, then a JDOObjectNotFoundException is thrown.

- If an instance with the same identity as the oid parameter is not in the cache and it does not exist in the datastore, then a JDOObjectNotFoundException is thrown.

No change is made to the status of a transaction if JDOObjectNotFoundException is thrown. You will never get this exception as a result of executing a query. You can retrieve the failed instance by calling the exception's getFailedObject( ) method. Of course, the fields of the failed instance will not be initialized, since the instance does not exist in the datastore. But you can access the identity of the instance by calling getObjectId( ), which may be useful to debug the application.

All calls to getObjectById( ) with the same identity value and the same PersistenceManager instance return the same instance with the same Java identity (assuming the instances were not garbage-collected between calls). So, the following code outputs "same instance" to the output stream:

```
RentalCodeKey key = new RentalCodeKey("High Demand");
RentalCode code = (RentalCode) pm.getObjectById(key, true);
RentalCodeKey key2 = new RentalCodeKey("High Demand");
RentalCode code2 = (RentalCode) pm.getObjectById(key2, true);
if (code == code2) System.out.println("same instance");
```

Suppose we use different `PersistenceManager` instances (from the same `PersistenceManagerFactory`) in calls to `getObjectById()` with the same identity value. The instances returned will represent the same persistent instance, but they will have a different Java identity, because each `PersistenceManager` manages its own copy of persistent instances.

Changing the Application Identity of an Instance

If you change the value of a primary-key field during a transaction, this action constitutes an attempt to change the identity of the instance. Changing the identity of an instance is supported only for application identity, and it is an optional JDO feature. The `javax.jdo.option.ChangeApplicationIdentity` option property indicates whether an implementation supports this feature. If it is not supported, the implementation throws a `JDOUnsupportedOptionException` whenever you attempt to change a primary-key field. Since this feature is optional, your application is more portable if it never changes a primary-key field.

For implementations that support the changing of an application identity, the implementation detects changes to primary-key fields. Changing the value of a primary-key field changes the identity value. The new identity value is either unique or already in use by another instance. If another persistent instance already has the identity value, a `JDOUserException` is thrown and the statement that attempted to change the field does not complete. If the resulting identity is unique, it is associated with the instance immediately upon completion of the statement that changed the primary-key field. If the transaction commits successfully, the existing instance in the datastore is updated with the values of any primary-key fields that have changed.

You need to take into account the fact that a change to the value of a primary-key field changes the identity of an instance in the datastore. This might result in a loss of integrity in a production environment that keeps an audit trail of all changes, as the historical record of all changes would not reflect the current identity of the instance in the datastore. In these environments it is best if you do not change the value of a primary-key field.

Get the Current Application Identity of an Instance

The `PersistenceManager` method `getObjectId()` returns the identity of an instance as of the beginning of a transaction. If the application changes the identity of an instance during a transaction, `getObjectId()` continues to return the identity as of the beginning of the transaction until `afterCompletion()` has been called, at which point it returns a different identity value if the transaction commits successfully. Chapter 7 describes the `afterCompletion()` method of the `Synchronization` interface.

The PersistenceManager method:

```
Object getTransactionalObjectId(Object obj);
```

and the JDOHelper method:

```
static Object getTransactionalObjectId(Object obj);
```

return the current identity of an instance, taking into account any changes that may have been made to primary-key fields. These methods return null if the instance is transient, null, or not of a persistent class. If no transaction is in progress or if none of the primary-key fields have been modified, then these methods have the same behavior as getObjectId( ).

The String Representation of Identity

The getObjectId( ) method returns an identity instance, declared to be of type Object. You can call toString( ) on the identity instance to obtain a String representation of the identity value. This String can be written to a file or passed to some other software outside the current JVM context. If the persistent class has application identity, the toString( ) you defined for the application identity class will determine the form of the String's value. If the persistent class uses datastore or nondurable identity, the String value is implementation-specific.

You can later use the String value to construct an identity instance. The following PersistenceManager method returns an identity instance, given the Class and String parameters:

```
Object newObjectIdInstance(Class persistentClass, String str);
```

The str parameter should be the result of a previous call to toString( ) on an identity instance. The persistentClass parameter specifies the class of the instance identified by the str parameter. The newObjectIdInstance( ) method calls the identity class's public constructor that takes a String argument to initialize the identity instance.

In some development projects, we have passed the String representation of identity to an HTML screen to serve as a handle for referencing a persistent object in the browser's separate process context. The string representation of the identity value can be kept in a hidden element in the HTML. Each persistent instance rendered in the user interface can have its associated identity value. Then, when some user action in the browser requires an action to be performed on the instance in the cache, you can pass the identity string back to the application and use newObjectIdInstance( ) and getObjectById( ) to access the instance in the cache quickly.

Advanced Topics

There are a few advanced identity topics, which we will consider in this section.

Choosing an Identity Type

If you are not mapping your JDO object model onto an existing relational schema and you are using an implementation that supports both datastore and application identity, you frequently have the freedom to choose the form of identity. Datastore identity is the logical choice if there is not a natural primary key to identify instances of the class. It is also useful if you prefer to have the JDO implementation generate a unique identity value. Datastore identity also requires less development work on your part. But for some entities being modeled, a primary key is the most suitable solution because of a natural primary-key value that is used to identify the data.

The primary difference between datastore and application identity in your persistent class is the need to define equals( ) and hashCode( ) methods for your persistent classes that use application identity. The only other difference is the specification of the identity type in your metadata. You can develop a persistent class and define an application identity class for it, but then in the metadata you could switch between datastore and application identity. If you do change the identity in the metadata, you need to enhance your classes again, as the enhanced class contains identity-specific information.

Using Identity Versus a Query

If you want to have the flexibility of changing the type of identity used for a persistent class, you should insulate your applications from the particular identity type you choose. When you access an instance with application identity, you initialize an instance of the application identity class with values for the primary-key fields and call getObjectById( ).

As an alternative to getObjectById( ), you could execute a Query, where the filter tests the equality of query parameters with fields in the class. Such a query will work regardless of whether the class uses datastore or application identity. You could define a method for this purpose, possibly a static method of your persistent class. It would have a parameter for each field needed to identify an instance and the PersistenceManager to use. Internally, the method could issue a query, or, if you eventually decide to use application identity, it could call getObjectById( ). Be aware, though, that calling getObjectById( ) will likely perform better than a query.

Identity Across PersistenceManagers

Under some circumstances, you can use identity instances across different PersistenceManager instances from the same or different implementations. For example, when using multiple PersistenceManager instances retrieved from the same

PersistenceManagerFactory, you can use the following code to get an instance in a PersistenceManager (referenced by the pm variable) with the same identity as an instance from a different PersistenceManager:

```
pm.getObjectById(JDOHelper.getObjectId(obj), validate);
```

If multiple PersistenceManager instances (which have been returned by the same PersistenceManagerFactory instance) have their own copy of the same persistent instance in their cache, all the identity instances that are returned by calls to getObjectId() return true to equals(), since they all refer to the same persistent object, even though the identity instances were acquired from distinct copies of the same persistent instance.

You can use getObjectById() only for instances of persistent classes using application identity when you are working with PersistenceManager instances of different JDO implementations. Since each implementation has its own representation for datastore identity, you cannot pass a datastore identity value from one implementation to a PersistenceManager of a different implementation in a call to getObjectById().

CHAPTER 11

Lifecycle States and Transitions

An instance of a persistent class has a lifecycle state that the JDO implementation manages. This lifecycle state is used to determine whether the instance is persistent, loaded, modified, or deleted. During a persistent instance's lifetime in memory, as operations are performed on it, it transitions among various lifecycle states, until it is finally garbage-collected by the JVM.

This chapter describes the lifecycle states required in all JDO implementations. We assume that the RetainValues flag is set to false. Chapter 14 covers the effect of having RetainValues set to true. We discuss the methods available to determine the lifecycle state of an instance. We conclude by discussing the various state transitions that occur to instances during a transaction, when a transaction completes, and between transactions.

As a developer using JDO, you do not really need to understand these lifecycle states and transitions or directly use their related APIs to write your application. These lifecycle states primarily concern JDO implementations, to ensure they correctly implement the JDO APIs. You may occasionally want to determine the state of an instance in more complex usage scenarios; knowing the state of an instance may be useful during debugging. Being aware of these states will give you a better understanding of how an implementation manages instances and the in-memory cache. Some of the early JDO adopters focused considerable attention on these states, giving many the impression that they were a fundamental aspect of using JDO. In reality, most applications never need to deal with these states directly.

Lifecycle States

JDO has a total of 10 lifecycle states. The following 7 states are required:

- Transient
- Persistent-new
- Hollow
- Persistent-clean

- Persistent-dirty
- Persistent-deleted
- Persistent-new-deleted

There are also three optional states:

- Transient-clean
- Transient-dirty
- Persistent-nontransactional

If a JDO implementation does not support the transaction-related optional features that allow transient transactional and persistent-nontransactional instances, these three optional states are not reachable. This chapter focuses on the required states. Chapters 13 and 14 discuss these optional features and associated lifecycle states.

Transient

When you call a constructor to create an instance of a class, the instance is placed in the *transient* state. Each instance created by the application starts its life as a transient instance. Transient instances do not have a JDO identity, because identity is only a characteristic of persistent instances. A transient instance should behave exactly as an instance of the class would if the class were not persistent. No JDO exceptions are thrown for a transient instance.

Many developers wonder how much overhead is involved when transient instances of an enhanced class are manipulated. Fields of transient instances have slightly slower access and modification than they would if the class were not persistent and enhanced. No mediation of access or modification of fields is performed on instances in the transient state. In particular, a transient instance never makes a call to a method of the JDO implementation, specifically those defined in the StateManager interface. To understand the exact overhead involved, read the sidebar "Overhead of Accessing a Field of a Transient Instance."

JDO does not support the demarcation of transaction boundaries for instances in the transient lifecycle state. Indeed, transient instances have no transactional behavior, unless they are referenced by persistent instances at commit time. In that case, they transition to the persistent-new state. Transient-transactional instances are instances that are transient and have transactional behavior. Chapter 13 covers transient-transactional instances.

Persistent-New

Instances that have been made persistent in the current transaction are placed in the *persistent-new* state. This occurs if the application makes an instance persistent explicitly by passing it as a parameter to makePersistent( ), or implicitly through persistence-by-reachability. Thus, instances that become provisionally persistent via the

Overhead of Accessing a Field of a Transient Instance

The enhancer replaces the `getfield` and `putfield` instructions that access a field at the byte-code level with a call to a generated static method. The code generated for these static methods has different logic, depending on whether the specific field is in the default fetch group. Chapter 12 discusses field fetch groups and the default fetch group.

For a field in the default fetch group, the first line of the generated static method checks the `jdoFlags` field (generated by the enhancer) for equality with the `PersistenceCapable` constant `READ_WRITE_OK`. If they are equal, the field is accessed and the method returns. A transient instance has its `jdoFlags` field set to `READ_WRITE_OK`, so this one equality comparison with `jdoFlags` is the only additional software executed for fields in the default fetch group.

For a field that is not in the default fetch group, the first line of the generated static method checks to see whether the `jdoStateManager` field is `null`; if so, the field access or modification is performed and the method returns. Transient instances have their `jdoStateManager` field set to `null`, so this one equality comparison with the `jdoStateManager` field is the only additional software executed for a field that is not in the default fetch group.

reachability algorithm also transition to the persistent-new state. Only transient instances (which include transient, transient-clean, and transient-dirty instances) can transition to the persistent-new state, and this only occurs as a result of making them persistent.

During the transition from transient to persistent-new, the following actions are performed:

- The associated `PersistenceManager` becomes responsible for implementing state interrogation and all further state transitions. This is implemented by setting the `jdoStateManager` field in the instance to reference the associated `StateManager`.

- If the `RestoreValues` flag is `true`, the values of persistent and transactional nonpersistent fields are saved in a before image to be used during transaction rollback.

- The implementation assigns an identity to the instance. This identity uniquely identifies the instance inside the `PersistenceManager` and might uniquely identify the instance in the datastore. The instance must have a unique identity at transaction commit for classes with a durable identity.

Hollow

The JDO implementation instantiates every object accessed from the datastore in memory. The implementation constructs a *hollow* instance by calling the no-arg constructor. An instance in memory is in the hollow state if it represents a specific object in the datastore whose values have not yet been loaded from the datastore into the instance. Instances transition to the hollow state at transaction commit when RetainValues is false.

An instance can be in the hollow state if it is:

- Committed from a previous transaction
- Acquired by getObjectById( )
- Returned by iterating an Extent
- Returned in the result of a query
- Accessed by navigating a persistent field reference

However, with these operations an implementation may choose to return the instances in a different state that is reachable from hollow. An implementation can transition an instance from the hollow state to another state at any time, just as if a field were read. Therefore, the hollow state might not be visible to the application.

Primary-key fields are always available in an instance, regardless of its state. So, the primary-key fields of a hollow instance are initialized. Read access of primary-key fields is never mediated. The JDO implementation is not required to load values into any other field until the application attempts to read or modify the field.

Once the JDO implementation has initialized a reference or collection of references to persistent instances in the cache, these references need to refer to actual Java instances in memory. So, the JDO implementation needs to instantiate instances to refer to; it instantiates instances and places them in the hollow state. It is important for you to know that these hollow instances exist and that they consume memory resources in the JVM. If your application never accesses them, their state may never be initialized from the datastore.

A hollow instance maintains its identity and association with its PersistenceManager instance. A PersistenceManager must not hold a strong (nonweak) reference to a hollow instance. Thus, if your application does not hold a strong reference to a hollow instance, it might be garbage-collected during or between transactions.

Furthermore, instances transition to hollow at transaction commit. If your application still has a strong reference to a hollow instance after transaction commit, the JVM garbage collector will not free up its associated memory resources. If the instances your application refers to have their own references that refer to additional instances in the cache, those instances cannot be freed either. So, it is very important that your application does not refer to such instances after transaction commit, unless you intend to continue using them after commit, between transactions, or in a subsequent transaction. Chapter 14 covers the access and use of persistent instances after commit.

Persistent-Clean

An instance in the *persistent-clean* lifecycle state represents a specific instance in the datastore whose values have not been changed in the current transaction. If any persistent field other than a primary-key field of a hollow instance is read, the instance transitions to persistent-clean. The field values of a persistent-clean instance in memory are identical to their values in the datastore.

Persistent-Dirty

When a field is modified, an instance may become inconsistent with the state it had in the datastore at the beginning of the transaction. This includes instances that have been modified or deleted. These instances are referred to as *dirty*.

If the value of a managed field is modified, the instance is marked as dirty and placed in the *persistent-dirty* state. If your application does not modify any managed field of an instance, the instance is not marked as dirty. In one special circumstance, the application modifies a managed field, but the new value is equal to the old value. If the field is of an array type, the implementation marks the field as modified and makes the instance dirty. Otherwise, the implementation decides whether to consider the instance dirty.

During the commit of a transaction in which a dirty instance's values have changed (including a new persistent instance), the underlying datastore is changed to have the transactionally consistent values from the instance and the instance transitions to hollow.

A JDO implementation might store the state of persistent instances in the datastore at any time; this process is called *flushing*. This does not affect the dirty state of the instances. This flushing behavior is not visible to the application and does not impact the rollback of a transaction.

Persistent-Deleted

A persistent instance that has been deleted in the current transaction by a call to deletePersistent() is in the *persistent-deleted* state. You can read the primary-key fields of a deleted instance, because the primary-key fields always have their values populated. But accessing any other persistent field throws a JDOUserException.

Persistent-New-Deleted

An instance that has been made newly persistent and also deleted in the current transaction is placed in the *persistent-new-deleted* state. You can read its primary-key fields, but any other persistent field access throws a JDOUserException.

State Interrogation

The JDOHelper class provides the following methods to interrogate the state of an instance:

```
static boolean isPersistent(Object obj);
static boolean isTransactional(Object obj);
static boolean isDirty(Object obj);
static boolean isNew(Object obj);
static boolean isDeleted(Object obj);
```

Each of these methods returns false if the instance is null, transient, or of a class that is not persistent. Otherwise, these methods return the following:

isPersistent( )

Returns true for an instance that represents a persistent object in the datastore

isTransactional( )

Returns true for an instance whose state is associated with the current transaction

isDirty( )

Returns true for an instance whose state has changed in the current transaction

isNew( )

Returns true for an instance made persistent in the current transaction

isDeleted( )

Returns true if the instance has been deleted in the current transaction

Table 11-1 specifies the values these methods return for each required lifecycle state. You could write a method that calls each of these methods and returns a String denoting the instance's lifecycle state. This can be useful if you are debugging or would like to know the lifecycle state of instances.

Table 11-1. State interrogation method return values

State of Instance	isPersistent( )	isTransactional( )	isDirty( )	isNew( )	isDeleted( )
Transient	false	false	false	false	false
Hollow	true	false	false	false	false
Persistent-new	true	true	true	true	false
Persistent-clean	true	true	false	false	false
Persistent-dirty	true	true	true	false	false
Persistent-deleted	true	true	true	false	true
Persistent-new-deleted	true	true	true	true	true

Table A-1 in Appendix A provides a complete listing of the values these methods return for all the lifecycle states.

State Transitions

An instance transitions from one lifecycle state to another as the application or JDO implementation performs various operations on it. These state transitions occur during a transaction and at the completion of a transaction. A transition can occur as a result of the passing of an instance as a parameter to a method, such as makePersistent( ). An instance can also transition from one state to another without the application performing any direct operations on the instance. For example, an instance made persistent via reachability changes state without the application directly passing the instance to a method. An instance in the hollow or persistent-clean state will transition to persistent-dirty if it contains a collection field and you add or remove an element from the collection.

State Transitions During a Datastore Transaction

Figure 11-1 illustrates the state transitions that occur when you make a call to makePersistent( ) or deletePersistent( ), or when you access a managed field. In the figure, Start State 1 represents the application calling a constructor to create an instance, and Start State 2 occurs when the JDO implementation calls the no-arg constructor to instantiate an instance from the datastore.

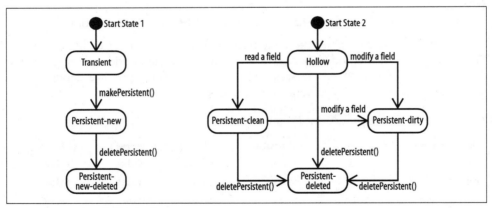

Figure 11-1. Lifecycle-state transitions

If any persistent field of a hollow instance other than a primary-key field is read, the instance transitions to persistent-clean. If a managed field of a hollow or persistent-clean instance is modified, the instance transitions to persistent-dirty. Once an instance enters the persistent-deleted or persistent-new-deleted state during a transaction, no further state transitions occur until transaction completion.

State Transitions When a Transaction Completes

When a transaction completes via a call to commit( ) or rollback( ), instances in every lifecycle state, except hollow and transient, transition to a new lifecycle state; hollow and transient instances remain in their current state. Figure 11-2 illustrates the state transitions that occur when you call commit( ) or rollback( ) and the RetainValues flag is set to false. Chapter 14 covers the behavior that occurs when the RetainValues flag is true.

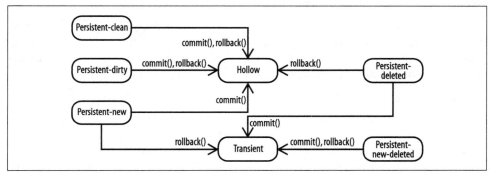

Figure 11-2 . State transitions at transaction completion with RetainValues = false and RestoreValues = false

As illustrated in Figure 11-2, persistent-clean, persistent-dirty, and persistent-new instances transition to hollow at commit. In addition, instances that were persistent at the beginning of the transaction (including those in the hollow, persistent-clean, persistent-dirty, or persistent-deleted state) transition to hollow at rollback, and they retain their identity and association with their PersistenceManager instance.

A persistent-deleted instance transitions to transient at commit. Since it has been deleted from the datastore, it is not associated with a datastore instance. During its transition to the transient state, it loses its identity and association with its PersistenceManager, and its persistent fields are initialized with their Java default values.

A persistent-new-deleted instance transitions to transient at commit and rollback. During these transitions, it also loses its identity and association with its PersistenceManager. When a transaction commits, its persistent fields are initialized with their Java default values.

All instances that transition to transient lose their identity and association with their PersistenceManager, whereas all instances transitioning to hollow retain their identity and association with their PersistenceManager. Primary-key fields are always accessible, regardless of the state of the instance. Read access to these fields is never mediated.

States Between Transactions

A hollow instance maintains its identity and association with its PersistenceManager instance. Between transactions, the hollow state guarantees that there is a single, unique copy of a persistent instance with a specific identity in the cache. Furthermore, if the application makes a request (via query, navigation, or look up by identity) for the same instance in a subsequent transaction, using the same PersistenceManager instance, the identical Java instance in memory is returned, assuming it has not been garbage-collected.

If the instance's class uses application identity, the primary-key fields are maintained. These fields can be accessed between transactions. If the implementation does not support the NontransactionalRead or NontransactionalWrite optional features, access of any other fields between transactions throws a JDOUserException.

CHAPTER 12

Field Management

JDO provides interfaces that allow you to have some control over the management of the fields in a persistent class, including their access and storage. In addition, you can specify how a field with a null value is handled if the underlying datastore does not support null values. JDO metadata controls many of these field-management capabilities.

Transactional Fields

A JDO implementation manages two kinds of fields: persistent fields that are stored in the datastore and *transactional fields*. A transactional field is not persistent, but it participates in a transaction by having its values restored if a rollback occurs. Persistent and transactional fields are referred to collectively as *managed fields*. The state of a transactional field is saved before certain lifecycle-state transitions, so it can be restored if a transaction rollback occurs. The JDO implementation modifies a transactional field only during rollback for instances that have been modified by your application.

You specify that a field is transactional by setting its persistence-modifier attribute to "transactional" in the metadata. A transactional field can be of any type; there are no restrictions. The JDO implementation mediates the modification of a transactional field, but it does not mediate field reads.

null Values

A field of an object type can have a null value in Java. The datastore you access may or may not support null values, and the support may vary depending on the type of the data. Therefore, you should specify how the JDO implementation should handle a field with a null value when it is written to a datastore that cannot store a null value.

The field element's null-value attribute in the metadata specifies how this situation should be handled. This attribute can be given one of the following values:

"none"
> Indicates that a Java null value should be stored as a null in the datastore. If the datastore cannot store a null value, a JDOUserException is thrown.

"exception"
> Indicates that a JDOUserException should always be thrown when a field has a null value, even if the datastore can store a null value for the field.

"default"
> Indicates the implementation should convert the Java null value to the datastore's default value for the field's datatype.

If you do not provide a value for the null-value attribute, it defaults to "none". If you never want to store a field with a null value, then you should set the null-value attribute to "exception".

If the null-value attribute for a field is set to "default" and the field is null in a transaction, the datastore's default value is stored, based on the field's datastore datatype. The next transaction that accesses the instance will obtain this datastore default value. You will have lost the fact that the field was originally null.

For example, if an Integer field that is null is mapped to the datastore's representation of an integer value, you may get a value of zero stored in the datastore. The next transaction accessing the field will also get a zero and it will not know the field was originally null. Similarly, a String field with a null value could be written as a zero-length string in the datastore. There is no good way to represent a null collection in a relational database, but a collection field with a null value could be represented in the datastore as an empty collection. Furthermore, the default value used for a datatype may vary across datastores.

Retrieval of Fields

You should not be concerned about how and when the JDO implementation accesses fields from the datastore. When you access a field, the JDO implementation provides the field's value. But some facilities let you instruct the JDO implementation to load all or a particular subset of fields of an instance together. You can analyze your application's field-access requirements and optimize the performance of accessing fields from the datastore.

Default Fetch Group

A *fetch group* is a group of fields retrieved together from the datastore. JDO implementations usually can retrieve a group of fields as a unit more efficiently than they can retrieve each field individually. In addition, you may have a specific subset of fields that your applications always use together; in this case, accessing these fields as a unit may be more efficient. Conversely, fields that are rarely accessed could be placed in a separate fetch group that is retrieved only when necessary. When fields that are not contained in any fetch group are accessed, they can be retrieved from the datastore individually.

JDO defines one fetch group, called the *default fetch group* (DFG). A `field` element's `default-fetch-group` attribute specifies whether a field should be in the default fetch group. This attribute defaults to "true" for nonkey fields of the following types:

- Primitive types
- `java.util.Date`
- Fields in the `java.lang` package of the types listed in Table 4-2
- `java.math.BigDecimal` and `java.math.BigInteger`

An instance in the hollow state does not have its default fetch group fields loaded, but they get loaded when the instance transitions to persistent-clean or persistent-dirty.

The default fetch group can only contain persistent fields, so you cannot set the `default-fetch-group` attribute to "true" for fields whose `persistence-modifier` is "transactional" or "none". You cannot place a primary-key field in the default fetch group; a primary-key field is always loaded in an instance. When an instance is first instantiated from the datastore and placed in the hollow state, the primary-key fields are set. Since they uniquely identify an instance in the datastore, they are used to fetch the other field values when they are needed.

In fact, the following field-level metadata declarations are mutually exclusive; only one can be specified:

- `default-fetch-group = "true"`
- `primary-key = "true"`
- `persistence-modifier = "transactional"`
- `persistence-modifier = "none"`

An implementation can support other fetch groups in addition to the default fetch group. A class can have multiple fetch groups, which you must specify in the metadata using vendor-specific metadata extensions. Such additional fetch groups allow you to partition a class's fields into separate groups that should be processed as distinct units.

Retrieving All Fields

In some situations, you need to fetch all the field values for one or more instances from the datastore. For example, when you execute a query, a `Collection` is returned that you can iterate through to access each of its elements. The instances in the query result might not be fetched from the datastore. It will probably be more efficient to access them from the datastore as a group, rather than individually.

You can call the following `PersistenceManager` methods to make sure that all of the persistent fields have been loaded into the parameter instances:

```
void retrieve(Object obj);
void retrieveAll(Collection objs);
void retrieveAll(Object[] objs);
```

These methods do not read and set any fields that have been modified in the transaction; any updates you may have made to fields will not be lost. Furthermore, if an instance in the persistent-dirty state is passed to `retrieve()` or `retrieveAll()`, it will be persistent-dirty upon return. These `retrieve()` and `retrieveAll()` methods load *all* of the fields that have not been loaded already.

Suppose you want to load only the fields in the default fetch group. You can do so by calling one of the following methods, passing `true` for the `DFGonly` parameter:

```
void retrieveAll(Collection objs, boolean DFGonly);
void retrieveAll(Object[] objs, boolean DFGonly);
```

This tells the JDO implementation that you need to retrieve only the fields in the default fetch group. After you call this method, if you access any of the default fetch group fields of the parameter instances, the implementation will not need to access the datastore to retrieve the field value. Passing a value of `false` for the `DFGonly` parameter is equivalent to calling `retrieve()` or `retrieveAll()` without the `DFGonly` parameter. Since these methods are just a hint, the implementation may still retrieve all the fields, regardless of the `DFGonly` parameter value. You may notice that there is no method named `retrieve()` that accepts the `DFGonly` parameter. We omitted this deliberately, because in most of the cases where you want to retrieve only the fields in the default fetch group, you have a collection of instances.

Using the `retrieveAll()` methods with the `DFGonly` parameter optimizes performance in applications that need to retrieve a large number of instances in the cache, when you need only the fields in the default fetch group and do not want to incur the overhead of retrieving all the fields. A common example is passing a partial result (e.g., the first 10 instances of the query result) of a JDOQL query to `retrieveAll()` with a value of "true" for `DFGonly`.

Figure 12-1 illustrates the state transitions that occur when you call these methods. In addition, `jdoPostLoad()` is called if the instance's class implements the `InstanceCallbacks` interface. We cover the `InstanceCallbacks` interface later in this chapter.

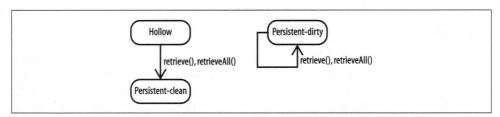

Figure 12-1. State transitions when retrieve methods are called in a datastore transaction

If you call `retrieve( )` for an instance that contains references to other persistent instances, the references are initialized to refer to the related instances. The referenced instances must be instantiated in the cache, if they are not already resident in the cache. They may be in the hollow state; their fields do not need to be fetched.

Some implementations support a preread policy that you can use to instruct the JDO implementation to fetch the field values of related instances when an instance is accessed. You usually specify preread policies with vendor-specific metadata, since JDO 1.0.1 does not specify them. The JDO expert group is considering this as a possible feature in JDO 2.0.

The Management of Fields

The JDO implementation completely controls whether the fields of a persistent instance are fetched from the datastore. During enhancement, the `jdoFlags` field is added to a persistent class to indicate the state of the default fetch group. The value of the `jdoFlags` field directly affects the behavior of default-fetch-group field accesses.

An implementation can choose from a variety of field-management strategies:

- Never cache any field values in an instance, but fetch a field's value each time it is accessed by the application.
- Selectively fetch and cache the values of specific fields in the instance.
- Fetch the values for all the fields in the default fetch group at one time, taking advantage of this performance optimization when managing the instance.
- Manage updates to fields in the default fetch group individually. This results in the instance always delegating field changes to the `PersistenceManager`. With this strategy, the `PersistenceManager` can reliably tell when any field changes, and it can optimize the writing of data to the datastore.

Your application is insulated from the specific techniques an implementation uses to manage fields. Class enhancement makes your application binary-compatible across all implementations, with an interface that gives implementations a lot of flexibility in how they manage fields. Be aware that each implementation employs one or more field-management strategies that can affect the performance of your application.

Serialization

When an instance is serialized in Java, the graph of instances reachable via non-transient fields is written to an output stream. In this context, non-transient refers to fields that have not been declared transient in Java. Java's transient fields and JDO's managed fields are independent concepts, so any combination of Java's transient or non-transient fields with JDO's persistent, transactional, or transient fields is possible in your persistent classes.

You can serialize and deserialize instances of your persistent classes. You do not need to do anything special for serialization to work. In fact, the JDO implementation automatically fetches the graph of instances, even if they have not yet been loaded into the JVM from the datastore.

However, you should be aware that the instances reachable from the instance being serialized might include a large number of instances from the datastore. If your persistent classes are highly interconnected, you may unintentionally serialize a large percentage of your datastore. You can use Java's transient modifier to prevent the serialization of referenced instances. Chapter 4 showed how to make Java transient fields persistent in JDO by setting the persistent-modifier attribute to "persistent". This lets you serialize persistent instances in JDO without extracting and serializing a large portion of the data from your datastore.

JDO enhancement allows you to serialize transient and persistent instances of persistent classes to a format that can later be deserialized with an enhanced or unenhanced form of the class. Deserializing a serialized graph of instances that are persistent in JDO results in a graph of transient instances. So, no JDO-specific functionality is necessary to deserialize the instances. Subsequently, you can make these instances persistent, but they will not have any association with the original persistent instances that were serialized.

Managing Fields During Lifecycle Events

While a persistent instance is in memory, it transitions through certain lifecycle events, as we described in Chapter 11. You may want to execute some functionality when these events occur. For example, if you have a persistent class with nonpersistent fields, you may want to initialize the values of the fields when instances from the datastore are instantiated in memory. This is enabled in JDO by a mechanism called an *instance callback*.

JDO defines the InstanceCallbacks interface to support instance callbacks. This interface has four methods, each of which is called when a particular lifecycle event occurs. If you declare that a persistent class implements the InstanceCallbacks interface, the following methods must be defined and are called when their associated lifecyle event occurs:

void jdoPostLoad( )
> Called for an instance after the values have been loaded into its default fetch group fields. This occurs when the instances transition from hollow to persistent-clean or persistent-dirty. In this method, you should initialize nonpersistent fields that depend on fields in the default fetch group. Another use for this method is to register it with other objects in the runtime environment.
>
> The enhancer does not add field mediation code to this method; so, you should access only fields in the default fetch group, since you are not guaranteed that

the other fields have been fetched. The context in which jdoPostLoad( ) is called does not allow access to other persistent instances.

void jdoPreStore( )

Called before the field values of persistent-new and persistent-dirty instances are flushed to the datastore during commit or to perform a query in the datastore server. It is not called for instances being deleted, which are in the persistent-deleted or persistent-new-deleted state. If you want the stored value for a persistent field to be based on the value of another field that is not persistent, you should set the persistent field's value in this method. The enhancer modifies this method so that the changes you make to persistent fields are propagated to the datastore. You can also access the instance's PersistenceManager and other persistent instances in the method.

void jdoPreClear( )

Called before an instance's persistent fields are cleared (set to their Java default value). This occurs during commit when persistent-new, persistent-clean, and persistent-dirty instances transition to the hollow state. In this method, you should clear nonpersistent fields, nontransactional fields, and associations that exist between the instance and other objects in the runtime environment. The enhancer does not add the field-mediation code to this method, and you can access only transient, transactional, and default fetch group fields.

void jdoPreDelete( )

Called during the execution of deletePersistent( ) for an instance, before the state of the instance transitions to persistent-deleted or persistent-new-deleted. The enhancer adds the field-mediation code to this method, so you can access all the fields. But once this method completes, you can no longer access the fields. In Chapter 8, we described the use of this method to implement a composite-aggregation association, which would propagate the deletion to existence-dependent instances. This is also referred to as a *cascading delete*.

You can use jdoPostLoad( ) and jdoPreClear( ) in concert to establish and remove relationships between your persistent instances and transient instances in the application environment as the persistent instances enter and leave the cache. The jdoPostLoad( ) method could initialize a transient field to some transient instance in the application, which could also reference the persistent instance. In jdoPreClear( ), you could remove the reference to the persistent instance held by the transient instance.

First- and Second-Class Objects

JDO provides a natural mapping of your object model to an underlying datastore using different architectures. Most of the differences between datastores are handled for you automatically. In JDO, you identify the classes of your object model that should be stored in the datastore. Instances of these classes are stored with unique identifiers and can be queried efficiently using the values of their fields. Relationships between instances are modeled as references or collections.

In Java, your application classes, such as Movie and Role, and system-defined classes, such as java.util.Date and java.lang.Integer, are not treated differently. They are all referenceable objects in memory. However, there is a fundamental difference between these objects from the standpoint of JDO and most datastores.

The instances of your persistent classes that you would like to be referenced by two or more instances in the datastore are called *first-class objects* (FCOs). They each have a unique identity in the datastore, they can be queried, and they can be deleted under application control. In addition, the JDO runtime environment guarantees that only a single instance of an FCO with a durable identity is instantiated in memory for a given PersistenceManager cache.

JDO also supports *second-class objects* (SCOs), which represent values. They do not represent entities that you would want to reference in the datastore. A second-class object is associated and stored as part of a single first-class object. The second-class object is embedded in the first-class object that references and owns it. The class of a first-class object has a field that references the second-class object. This field is declared in the metadata as embedded to indicate that it refers to a second-class object.

An SCO instance represents a value. It may have an object representation in Java, but in the datastore it is not a distinct, referenceable piece of data. In a relational datastore, an SCO usually is mapped to one or more columns of a table. These columns are placed in the table in which the owning FCO is stored. Java types such as int, Integer, String, Date, and BigInteger represent values. Except for int, these types are all considered objects in Java. They are used as the types of fields in your persistent classes. In the datastore, they are stored as values with their associated persistent class instance.

An SCO instance tracks all changes that are made to itself and notifies its owning FCO that it has been changed. A change to an SCO is reflected as a change to its owning FCO. If an FCO instance is in the persistent-clean state, when one of its associated SCO instances changes, it transitions to the persistent-dirty state. When an FCO instance is instantiated in the JVM, fields declared as embedded are assigned SCO instances that track changes made to themselves and notify their owning FCO that they have been changed.

If a persistent class has a field of type int and you change the value of this field in an instance, the JDO implementation automatically marks the instance as dirty. Similarly, if the persistent class has a Date field that references a Date object, and you change the Date object's value via setTime( ), the Date object notifies the persistent class instance that its value has been changed. In the datastore, the Date field is stored as a value in the instance (e.g., in a TIMESTAMP column in a relational datastore). In

JDO, an SCO allows specific instances of classes to behave more like primitive values that are contained in an object, rather than as separate referenceable objects. While they are still separate referenceable objects in Java, they are not separate and referenceable in the datastore.

Some of the system-defined classes that are used as field types in your object model are most naturally modeled as second-class objects when stored in the datastore. Table 12-1 identifies the system-defined classes that all JDO implementations support as second-class objects. Fields of these types are embedded by default and many implementations support them only as second-class objects.

Table 12-1. System-defined types that default to second-class objects

Primitives	java.lang	java.util	java.math
boolean	Boolean	Date	BigInteger
byte	Byte	Locale	BigDecimal
short	Short	ArrayList	
char	Character	Collection	
int	Integer	HashMap	
long	Long	HashSet	
float	Float	Hashtable	
double	Double	LinkedList	
	String	List	
	Number	Map	
		TreeMap	
		TreeSet	
		Set	
		Vector	

When discussing second-class objects, there are two kinds of classes to consider: *mutable* and *immutable*. A mutable class provides methods to change the value of an instance; an immutable class maintains a value that cannot be changed. JDO supports the following immutable classes:

java.lang *package*
    Boolean, Character, Byte, Short, Integer, Long, Float, Double, and String

java.util *package*
    Locale

java.math *package*
    BigDecimal and BigInteger

JDO and Java support and encourage sharing instances for fields of these immutable classes. However, you should compare the equality of the fields with the equals() method; you should not compare them by applying the == operator to their references.

Setting or defaulting the embedded attribute to "true" for fields of the system-defined types listed in Table 12-1 implies *containment*. You should not delete instances of these classes from the datastore; the JDO implementation deletes them automatically when the owning instance is deleted. In fact, passing an instance of one of these types to deletePersistent( ) causes a JDOUserException to be thrown. You should only pass instances of your persistent classes to deletePersistent( ).

Implementations support mutable system-defined classes by defining a new class that extends the system-defined class. The new class provides its own implementation of each method that alters the state of the object in the base class. These redefined methods notify the owning FCO instance that the SCO instance has changed and call the corresponding method in the base class to perform the state change (e.g., Date.setTime( )). Therefore, you should not depend on knowing the exact class of a system-defined class instance. The JDO implementation may substitute an SCO instance with an instance of a subclass that has the same value when they are compared by calling equals( ). But you are guaranteed that the actual class of the instance is assignment-compatible with the field's declared type.

In order to make your application code and persistent classes portable across multiple JDO implementations, there are a few simple rules to follow:

- Do not assign the same instance of a system-defined mutable class to multiple persistent fields. Instead, make a copy of a mutable instance before assigning it to another persistent field.

- Initialize collection fields in a class's constructor and do not assign a new value to the collection field. To clear the contents of the collection, call the clear( ) method to remove the elements instead of assigning an empty collection, or null, to the field.

- Do not expose second-class objects as public fields or have a method that returns a reference to a field, because you cannot control when they may be used, in or out of a transaction.

Specifying a Second-Class Object

An instance becomes a second-class object if it is referenced by a field that you have declared in the metadata as embedded. You specify whether a field is embedded by using the field element's embedded attribute. When a reference field has an embedded attribute value of "true", the referenced object is a second-class object and its state is embedded within the owning object that refers to it. The embedded attribute defaults to "true" for a field of a type listed in Table 12-1.

Let's consider the following revisions to the metadata for some of the classes in the com.mediamania.store package, which we illustrated in Figure 4-4:

```
<package name="com.mediamania.store" >
    <class name="Customer" >
        <field name="currentRentals">
            <collection element-type="Rental"/>
```

```
            </field>
            <field name="transactionHistory">
                <collection element-type="Transaction"/>
            </field>
❶          <field name="address" embedded="true" />
        </class>
        <class name="Address" />
        <class name="Rental"
                persistence-capable-superclass="Transaction">
❷          <field name="rentalCode" embedded="true" />
        </class>
        <class name="MediaItem" >
            <field name="rentalItems">
                <collection element-type="RentalItem"/>
            </field>
        </class>
        <class name="RentalCode" />
    </package>
```

Line ❶ declares that the address field should be embedded. Both the Rental and
MediaItem classes have a reference to a RentalCode instance. On line ❷, we declare
that the rentalCode field in the Rental instance is embedded. However, we do not
declare that the rentalCode field is embedded in MediaItem. The RentalCode instances
referenced by MediaItem instances will be found in the extent maintained for the
RentalCode class. A Rental instance will have its own copy of a RentalCode instance
referenced by its rentalCode field; this RentalCode instance does not have an identity
and may have the same value as a RentalCode instance in the extent. Such an
approach may be valuable to this application, because it can preserve for historical
record-keeping purposes the specific RentalCode value used for a Rental, yet have all
the MediaItem instances reference the latest values of a RentalCode instance that is
shared by all MediaItem instances in the datastore.

In a relational JDO implementation, an embedded object may be represented by columns for its fields in the table of the referencing class. For example, the Rental class
declares that the rentalCode field, referring to an instance of RentalCode, should be
embedded. The RentalCode class contains several fields: code, numberOfDays, cost,
and lateFeePerDay. The table that contains the fields of the Rental class would have a
column for each of these RentalCode fields.

Embedding Collection Elements

You specify a collection field as embedded by using the embedded attribute in the collection's field element. You can also specify that the collection's elements should be
embedded within the collection.

The collection and array metadata elements have an embedded-element attribute to
specify whether the collection elements' values should be embedded with the collection instance in the datastore, instead of as separate FCO instances. This attribute
defaults to "false" for persistent classes and interface types and "true" for other types.

You use the embedded-key and embedded-value attributes in the map metadata element to specify whether the map's key and value should be embedded. These attributes default to "false" for persistent classes and interface types and "true" for other types.

Persistent Classes as Second-Class Objects

Many JDO implementations can support your persistent classes as second-class objects, but this support is not a required feature in JDO 1.0.1. For implementations that support SCO instances of your persistent classes, both FCO and SCO instances of a specific persistent class may be possible, but this depends on the implementation. The persistent classes that you define can be either mutable or immutable.

The behavior of SCOs for your persistent classes may not be consistent relative to extents and queries. If the persistent class has a maintained extent, the FCO instances will be in the extent, but an implementation may or may not place the SCO instances in the extent. Furthermore, if a field of one of your persistent classes is an SCO instance, an implementation may or may not be able to access it in a query.

You cannot rely on the automatic deletion of SCO instances for embedded fields of your persistent classes; some implementations will delete them, while others will not. You can always delete instances of your persistent classes explicitly, whether or not they are embedded. We recommend that you delete them explicitly; this will be portable across all JDO implementations.

Using one of your persistent classes as an SCO may offer you some performance and modeling advantages, but there is a tradeoff: they will lack portability and consistency, relative to extents and queries. If you intend to use them, you should verify that your JDO implementation supports them. Here, we describe the behavior of second-class objects with the assumption that the JDO implementation supports them for your persistent classes. If you do not have a specific need to define a persistent class and use it as a second-class object and you want to have a portable application, then you should avoid using instances of your persistent classes as second-class objects, in which case you can skip the remainder of this chapter.

Sharing of Instances

The most visible difference to your application between a field that is an FCO or an SCO is in *sharing*. Multiple FCO instances can have a reference to the same FCO instance and share it. If the referenced FCO instance changes, its changes are visible to all the FCO instances that refer to it.

For example, consider Figure 12-2. If FCO1 is assigned to a persistent field in FCO2 and FCO3, then any changes to instance FCO1 will be visible to FCO2 and FCO3. FCO2 and FCO3 will continue to reference FCO1 in the datastore after the transaction commits and will refer to it when they are accessed by subsequent transactions (until the reference to FCO1 is changed).

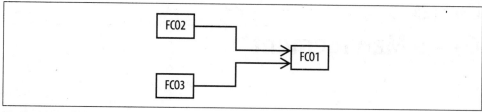

Figure 12-2. Sharing of an FCO instance

The same instance of a mutable class can be assigned to the embedded field of multiple FCO instances, but this is nonportable and strongly discouraged. If you assign an instance to an embedded field of multiple persistent-new, persistent-clean, or persistent-dirty FCO instances, the Java identity of the referenced SCO instances might change when the transaction commits. If an assignment is made to an embedded field of a transient instance and the instance subsequently becomes persistent by being passed to makePersistent( ) or through persistence-by-reachability, the embedded field is replaced immediately with a copy of the SCO instance and the instance is no longer shared. Figure 12-3 illustrates the copying that is performed with SCO instances.

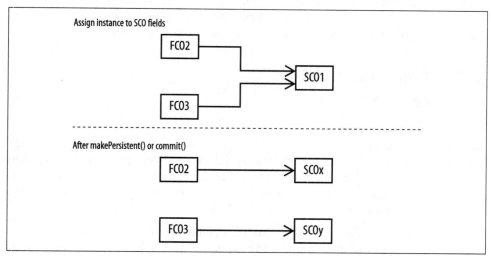

Figure 12-3. SCOs can be shared from assignment only until commit or makePersistent( )

CHAPTER 13

Cache Management

This chapter covers additional operations that you can perform on instances in the cache. In fact, the operations this chapter describes affect only the cache and the instances in the cache; they do not affect the datastore.

First, we describe some operations you can perform to explicitly control the management of instances in the cache. We discuss what occurs when you make a clone of a persistent instance. We introduce *transient-transactional instances*, which are transient instances that have transactional behavior. The chapter concludes by describing how you can convert a persistent instance into a transient instance.

Explicit Management of Instances in the Cache

Normally, a persistent instance is managed in the cache automatically and this management is completely transparent to the application. When you query instances, navigate to instances, or modify instances, the instances are instantiated and their field values are fetched from the datastore. The implementation determines when to fetch a field's value from the datastore, which can occur at any time prior to the application's access of the field.

Instances that are no longer referenced in memory are garbage-collected without requiring your application to perform any explicit action. When you commit a transaction in which persistent instances were created, deleted, or modified, the transaction-completion mechanisms automatically handle the eviction of instances from the cache. So, you usually do not need to evict instances explicitly. By *eviction*, we mean that the PersistenceManager no longer holds a strong reference to the instances, allowing them to be garbage-collected. The JVM is still responsible for reclaiming the memory held by the instances.

Refreshing Instances

JDO provides a means to refresh instances in the cache with their current values in the datastore. This can be useful outside of a transaction (Chapter 14 covers non-transactional access). It is also useful when you use optimistic transactions (covered in Chapter 15). Refreshing an instance can also be used with datastore transactions. If you use a transaction-isolation level of read-committed, the values in the datastore might change between reads. (If you do not want this behavior, then the JDO implementation should use a repeatable-read isolation level). If you really want to guarantee that you have the current state of the object, you can refresh the instance. However, be aware that right after you refresh the instance, it can be changed in the datastore by another transaction.

You can use the following `PersistenceManager` methods to refresh the state of instances in memory with their current state in the datastore:

```
void refresh(Object obj);
void refreshAll();
void refreshAll(Object[] objs);
void refreshAll(Collection objs);
```

These methods perform the following actions on each instance:

- Load the state of the instance in the datastore into the instance
- Call the `jdoPostLoad()` method if the class implements `InstanceCallbacks` and the default fetch group fields have not been loaded yet
- Transition persistent-dirty instances to persistent-clean in a datastore transaction or persistent-nontransactional in an optimistic transaction (Chapter 14 covers the persistent-nontransactional lifecycle state and Chapter 15 covers optimistic transactions)

Since these methods refresh an instance with its current state in the datastore, any changes you may have made to an instance will be lost. This is different from `retrieve()`, which does not overwrite fields that have been modified.

The `jdoPostLoad()` method is only called after the default fetch group has been loaded. So, if the default fetch group had already been loaded prior to invoking `refresh()` or `refreshAll()`, `jdoPostLoad()` is not executed again.

Evicting Instances

Your application may run in a memory-constrained environment. Or, it may access a large number of instances and need to access them only once in the transaction. In these situations, it could be useful to evict from the cache instances that you no longer need. Eviction allows the instances to be subsequently garbage-collected, freeing memory resources.

You can call the following `PersistenceManager` methods to evict instances from the cache:

```
void evict(Object obj);
void evictAll();
void evictAll(Object[] objs);
void evictAll(Collection objs);
```

If you call `evictAll()` with no parameters, all of the persistent-clean instances in the cache will be evicted. Calling these methods is only a hint to the `PersistenceManager` that your application no longer needs the instances in the cache. The implementation is not required to evict the instances.

The `PersistenceManager` performs the following actions for each evicted instance:

- Calls the `jdoPreClear()` method if the class implements `InstanceCallbacks` and the instance is not in the hollow state
- Clears the persistent fields by setting them to their Java default value
- Sets the instance's lifecycle state to hollow

An implementation may evict a persistent-dirty instance, but it needs to flush the state to the datastore. The `PersistenceManager` needs to keep only a weak reference to the persistent-dirty instances that have been evicted; it does not need to maintain a reference to any evicted persistent-clean instances. Once instances have been evicted, they can be garbage-collected.

The values of evicted instances are not retained after transaction completion, regardless of the setting of the `RetainValues` and `RestoreValues` flags. If you want to evict all the transactional instances at transaction commits, set the `RetainValues` flag to `false` (Chapter 14 covers the `RetainValues` flag). If you want them to be evicted on rollback, set the `RestoreValues` flag to `false` (Chapter 7 covers the `RestoreValues` flag). In these cases, you do not need to call the `evict()` and `evictAll()` methods.

Cloning

If you make a clone of a persistent instance, the clone is a separate transient instance. The clone does not have a JDO identity and it is not associated with the `PersistenceManager` of the instance that was cloned. The clone is a shallow copy of the original instance, without regard for the persistent fields. Therefore, the fields might not have been fetched from the datastore yet, causing you to get a `null` for fields that are references, including types like `Integer` and references to other persistent instances. Normally, the fields in the default fetch group have been fetched from the datastore, but not always. You should therefore call `retrieve()` to make sure the field values have been fetched from the datastore.

Another issue to consider is that the persistent instance may have references to other persistent instances. For example, a `RentalItem` has a reference to a `MediaItem`. If we retrieve all the fields of a `RentalItem` instance and then create a clone of it, the clone will have a reference to the MediaItem, but this clone is transient and does not really have a relationship with the MediaItem instance. JDO has a well-defined behavior that allows implementations to create a clone of a persistent instance properly, but we recommend that you do not clone persistent instances.

Transient-Transactional Instances

You can cause transient instances to observe transaction boundaries, such that their state is preserved at commit and restored on rollback. A transient instance that observes transaction boundaries is called a *transient-transactional instance*. Support for transient-transactional instances is optional; their use requires support of the optional TransientTransactional feature. If your implementation does not support TransientTransactional, it will not include the functionality that causes the state transitions associated with transient-transactional instances.

You can use the following PersistenceManager methods to make transient instances transactional:

```
void makeTransactional(Object obj);
void makeTransactionalAll(Object[] objs);
void makeTransactionalAll(Collection objs);
```

After these methods complete, the instances observe transaction boundaries. If the transaction commits, the transient-transactional instances retain their values. The makeTransactional() method throws a JDOUnsupportedOptionException if you pass a transient instance as a parameter and the implementation does not support the optional TransientTransactional feature.

If the call to makeTransactional() is made within the current transaction and the transaction is rolled back, the fields of the transient-transactional instances are restored to the values they had when makeTransactional() was called, using their captured before image (discussed in Chapter 14). If the call to makeTransactional() is made before the beginning of the current transaction and the transaction is rolled back, the fields are restored to their values as of the beginning of the transaction.

The PersistenceManager also provides makeNontransactional() to make a persistent instance nontransactional. Chapter 14 covers this in detail.

Transient-Transactional Lifecycle States

Transient-transactional instances are either clean or dirty, based on whether they have been modified in the current transaction. If a clean instance is not modified, it remains clean. If a clean instance is modified, its field values are saved. If the transaction rolls back, field values of dirty instances are restored from the saved field values. If the transaction commits, the saved field values are discarded. For either commit or rollback, dirty instances become clean.

Managing the behavior of transient-transactional instances requires additional lifecycle states and state transitions. Similar to persistent instances, transient-transactional instances have the transient-clean and transient-dirty lifecycle states to indicate their change status. An instance can be in the transient-clean or transient-dirty state only if the implementation supports the optional TransientTransactional feature.

Transient-clean

A transient-transactional instance that has not been changed in the current transaction is in the transient-clean state. When a transient instance is passed as a parameter to makeTransactional( ), it transitions to the transient-clean state. You can make changes to a transient-clean instance outside of a transaction without changing its lifecycle state. Chapter 14 covers nontransactional access.

Transient-dirty

If you change any managed field of a transient-clean instance in a transaction, it transitions to the transient-dirty state. This is similar to a persistent-clean instance transitioning to persistent-dirty. When you first modify a managed field of a transient-clean instance, before the field's value is changed, the PersistenceManager saves the instance's fields in a before image that is used if a rollback occurs.

State Interrogation

Table 13-1 specifies the values that the JDOHelper lifecycle-state interrogation methods return for the three transient lifecycle states.

Table 13-1. Values returned by the state interrogation methods for all the transient states

State of Instance	isPersistent( )	isTransactional( )	isDirty( )	isNew( )	isDeleted( )
Transient	false	false	false	false	false
Transient-clean	false	true	false	false	false
Transient-dirty	false	true	true	false	false

State Transitions

Figure 13-1 illustrates the state transitions that occur with transient-transactional instances.

If you pass a transient-clean instance to makeNontransactional( ), it transitions to transient; but if you pass a transient-dirty instance, a JDOUserException is thrown.

At commit, a transient-dirty instance transitions to transient-clean and it retains its values. If a transaction rollback occurs and the instance was made transactional in the current transaction, the instance's field values are restored with the before image to the values they had when makeTransactional( ) was called.

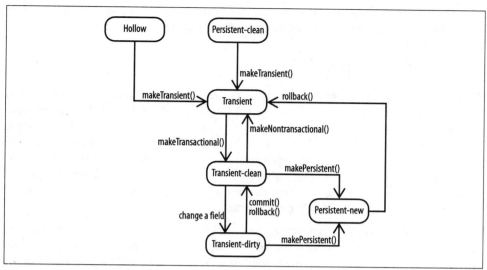

Figure 13-1. State transitions of transient transactional instances

If an instance was made transactional in a previous transaction and a transaction rollback occurs, the instance's fields are restored to their values as of the beginning of the current transaction. When transaction-rollback processing completes, the before images of transient-transactional instances are discarded and the instances transition to transient-clean.

If you pass a transient-dirty instance to makePersistent( ), it transitions to persistent-new. What happens if a transaction rollback occurs? The before image that was saved when the instance transitioned to transient-dirty is used to restore the instance. However, as with any persistent-new instance, the instance reverts to transient at rollback, even if it was previously a transient-transactional instance.

Making a Persistent Instance Transient

Suppose you have a persistent instance that you want to make accessible to a client application via Remote Method Invocation (RMI). Suppose your code is executing in a Common Object Request Broker Architecture (CORBA) or application-server environment, where the transaction context will no longer exist once your servlet or session bean returns from a client invocation. When RMI serializes your instance, the transaction is no longer active. You do not want the PersistenceManager to mediate access to a persistent instance outside of a transaction context. So, to pass the persistent instance to a remote client, you must convert it into a transient instance. This is necessary to disassociate the instance with the PersistenceManager, so field access is not mediated.

You do this by making the persistent instance transient. You can use the following PersistenceManager methods to make persistent instances transient:

```
void makeTransient(Object obj);
void makeTransientAll(Object[] objs);
void makeTransientAll(Collection objs);
```

When the instances transition to transient, they lose their identity and association with the PersistenceManager. They are no longer associated with their representation in the datastore, so their in-memory state does not affect the persistent state in the datastore. Even though the instance in memory is transient, the instance still exists in the datastore. Making a persistent instance transient is not equivalent to calling deletePersistent(). The effect of these methods is immediate and permanent; if a transaction rollback occurs, the instances remain transient. If a parameter is already transient, these methods have no effect.

A persistent-dirty instance has changes to field values that are not committed to the datastore until transaction commit. You do not want to lose these changes, which occurs when an instance is disassociated with its PersistenceManager. Therefore, if you pass a persistent-dirty instance to these methods, a JDOUserException is thrown.

Before calling makeTransient( ), you should call retrieve( ) or retrieveAll( ) to fetch all the field's values from the datastore. Otherwise, some of the fields may not be fetched. The makeTransient( ) methods do not change the values of the fields in the parameter instances.

Another use for makeTransient( ) is to copy an instance from one transaction to another that is running in the same JVM. The following code copies a persistent instance from one PersistenceManager instance (pm1) to another (pm2):

```
RentalCodeKey key = new RentalCodeKey("High Demand");
RentalCode code = (RentalCode) pm1.getObjectById(key, true);
pm1.retrieve(code);
pm1.makeTransient(code);
pm2.makePersistent(code);
```

The PersistenceManager referenced by pm2 might be from the same JDO implementation as pm1 but a different datastore. Or, pm1 and pm2 could be from different JDO implementations and datastores.

If you want the instances to remain transient at transaction commit, you must make sure that all references to them from other persistent instances in memory are changed; you should also make the referring persistent instances transient. Otherwise, the persistence-by-reachability algorithm will cause the instances to become persistent again at commit. Since the original persistent instance still exists in the datastore, if the instance becomes persistent again as a result of persistence-by-reachability, there might be two copies of the instance in the datastore. If the class uses datastore identity, the new transient instance is assigned a new identity value. However, if the class uses application identity and you did not change the value of the primary key, you get an exception indicating that you have a duplicate primary-key value.

CHAPTER 14

Nontransactional Access

Transactional management of persistent data is a core feature of JDO. Using transactions helps guarantee the consistency of data in the datastore. However, there are many cases where transactional consistency is not important to the application. Data that is known to be relatively static can be used outside of a transaction without harm. For example, having the most up-to-date description of movies in the Media Mania datastore isn't critical to the integrity of the database.

Using nontransactional data may make your application perform better, because you don't need to begin and complete transactions in order to access the persistent data in the datastore. This is especially noticeable when the application is in one process and the datastore is in a different process. Beginning and completing transactions often require one or more messages to be passed from one process to the other, in addition to the messages to retrieve the data itself. Avoiding transactions in this environment results in fewer messages.

Nontransactional Features

As you have seen earlier, the JDO runtime contains an instance cache managed by the PersistenceManager, and in the transaction modes we have presented thus far, instances in the cache have always been transactional. We now introduce the behavior of the cache and the instances contained in the cache in light of nontransactional behavior. There are five independent flags that govern this behavior.

NontransactionalRead

> This flag enables your application to iterate extents, perform queries, access persistent values of persistent instances, and navigate the entire graph of persistent instances, without having a transaction active.

NontransactionalWrite

> This flag enables your application to make changes to the cache that will never be committed to the datastore. Most applications expect that changes made to

persistent instances will be stored in the datastore at some point. NontransactionalWrite caters to applications that manage a cache of persistent instances where the changes to the datastore are made by a different application.

Optimistic

This flag enables your application to execute transactions that improve the concurrency of datastore access, by deferring locking of data until commit. We discuss optimistic transactions in detail in Chapter 15; we introduce it here because instances used in an optimistic transaction are read nontransactionally, so they share common characteristics of data that is read with NontransactionalRead.

RetainValues

This flag enables your application to retain the field values of instances in the cache at the end of committed transactions, to improve performance. Subsequent nontransactional accesses to cached values do not need to access the datastore.

RestoreValues

This flag enables your application to retain the field values of instances in the cache at the end of rolled-back transactions, to improve performance. Subsequent nontransactional accesses to cached values do not need to access the datastore.

The JDO implementation governs the availability of these features. Except for RestoreValues, the features are optional, and an implementation might support any or all of them, although if an implementation supports any of Optimistic, RetainValues, or NontransactionalWrite, it will logically support NontransactionalRead as well.

Attempts to use an unsupported feature result in the JDO implementation throwing an exception. For example, if an implementation does not support NontransactionalRead, attempting to set the NontransactionalRead option to true throws a JDOUnsupportedOptionException.

The runtime behavior of the PersistenceManager depends on the current settings of these flags, which are accessed via the Transaction instance associated with the PersistenceManager. You can read the current settings by using the property access method for the flag of interest. This example shows an application-specific method that returns the current setting for a given PersistenceManager instance:

```
boolean retrieveNontransactionalReadSetting(PersistenceManager pm) {
    Transaction tx = pm.currentTransaction();
    return tx.getNontransactionalRead();
}
```

You can set the property values using the property access methods. Once set, they remain unchanged until they are set to a different value. This example shows an application-specific method that changes the NontransactionalRead setting for the given PersistenceManager:

```
void setNontransactionalReadSetting(PersistenceManager pm, boolean value) {
    Transaction tx = pm.currentTransaction();
    tx.setNontransactionalRead(value);
}
```

The settings for the flags are initialized from the PersistenceManagerFactory that created the PersistenceManager. You can read the default settings from the PersistenceManagerFactory. This example shows an application-specific method that returns the default setting for a given PersistenceManagerFactory instance:

```
boolean retrieveNontransactionalReadSetting(PersistenceManagerFactory pmf) {
    return pmf.getNontransactionalRead();
}
```

The default values for these PersistenceManagerFactory flags are JDO implementation–specific. You can configure the PersistenceManagerFactory to have specific default values by using the property access methods with an existing PersistenceManagerFactory, or by including the appropriate values in the Properties instance used to configure the PersistenceManagerFactory.

For example, to guarantee that the PersistenceManagerFactory used by your application has the NontransactionalRead property set to true, you can use one of the following techniques:

```
PersistenceManagerFactory createPMF() {
    PersistenceManagerFactory pmf;
    pmf = new com.sun.jdori.fostore.FOStorePMF();
    // set other required properties
    // the following might throw JDOUnsupportedOptionException
    pmf.setNontransactionalRead(true);
    return pmf;
}
```

Note that this code refers to a JDO implementation–specific class that is not part of the JDO specification. The advantage of the following technique is that you can compile this code without reference to any JDO implementation–specific class:

```
PersistenceManagerFactory createPMF(Properties props) {
    // other required properties are already in the props instance
    PersistenceManagerFactory pmf;
    props.put("javax.jdo.option.NontransactionalRead", "true");
    // the following might throw an Exception
    pmf = JDOHelper.getPersistenceManagerFactory(props);
    return pmf;
}
```

If your application depends on any of the optional features, you should make sure that the JDO implementation that you are using supports them, either by constructing the PersistenceManagerFactory with the property set to true, or by dynamically querying the optional features of the PersistenceManagerFactory during initialization using supportedOptions(). This will avoid exceptions in your application logic that might be awkward to handle.

You might execute your application in an environment where a different component constructs the PersistenceManagerFactory and you must use it. For example, the PersistenceManagerFactory might be constructed and registered as a named entry in a Java Naming and Directory Interface (JNDI) context. Your application looks up the entry and verifies that it supports the required feature.

The required feature can be verified by a simple contains( ) check:

```
PersistenceManagerFactory pmf;
pmf = (PersistenceManagerFactory)ctx.lookup("MoviePMF");
Collection supportedOptions = pmf.supportedOptions( );
if (!supportedOptions.contains("javax.jdo.option.NontransactionalRead")) {
    throw new ApplicationCannotExecuteException
        ("NontransactionalRead is not supported");
}
```

Reading Outside a Transaction

NontransactionalRead allows your application to access the datastore without ever beginning a transaction; it also allows you to access the datastore and read cached instances and fields between completing one transaction and beginning the next. This allows read-only applications nearly full access to the features of JDO, without the overhead of beginning and completing transactions. Access in the NontransactionalRead case includes iterating extents, querying the datastore, accessing persistent field values, and navigating among instances using persistent relationships.

Note that you must always have an active transaction in order to insert new persistent instances, delete existing instances, or change existing data in the datastore.

One use for the NontransactionalRead mode of operation is to access slowly changing information. For example, access to the MediaContent instances can be nontransactional, because in most cases the information is static. At times, the datastore might be updated with new MediaContent instances, but for the most part, the information does not change.

When executing your application outside a transaction, the cache contains persistent instances whose field values came from the datastore, but there is no guarantee that the field values are consistent with the current datastore contents, or are even consistent with other field values from the same persistent instance. This is because field values are retrieved from the datastore on demand.

For example, if you query the datastore and access a field in a persistent instance, the JDO implementation might retrieve only the field accessed. A subsequent read of a different field might come from the cache or might result in a datastore access to retrieve the current value from the datastore. None of the field values retrieved earlier will be refreshed from the datastore, so the persistent instance might contain fields that represented the datastore at different times.

Therefore, before using this mode, make sure that dirty reads are acceptable for correct operation of your application.

Another common pattern is to use nontransactional read to navigate an object graph to locate a particular instance, and then begin a transaction to update the instance. This is possible because the identity of every instance in the cache is known, even though the field values are nontransactional.

Nontransactional instances in the cache will remain nontransactional even if a transaction is subsequently begun. If they are not accessed during subsequent transactions, they will remain nontransactional.

If your application accesses nontransactional instances during a datastore transaction, they become transactional at the time of the first access in the transaction. When this happens, the JDO implementation discards the cached field values and, just as for hollow instances, retrieves transactionally consistent field values from the datastore.

If your application accesses nontransactional instances for read during an optimistic transaction, they will remain nontransactional and might not be refreshed unless your application explicitly refreshes them by calling `PersistenceManager.refresh()`.

Persistent-Nontransactional State

The use of instances outside a transaction introduces another instance lifecycle state: *persistent-nontransactional*. From the application program perspective, this state is indistinguishable from the hollow state. That is, the results of executing the interrogatives in `JDOHelper` (`isNew()`, `isDirty()`, etc.) are the same for instances in both states. Your application generally should not be aware of the difference between instances in the hollow and persistent-nontransactional states.

From a performance perspective, your application might run faster, because accessing field values of instances in the persistent-nontransactional state might be done without a datastore access. Your application can retrieve field values cached in the instance and navigate the object graph to other instances, relying only on the cached values. The only time the datastore must be accessed is when a field that has not yet been loaded from the datastore is read.

With datastore transactions, existing persistent instances begin their lifecycle in the cache as persistent-clean or persistent-dirty. With the first access to persistent instances outside a transaction, they begin their lifecycle in the cache in the persistent-nontransactional state. This can be the result of an Extent iteration, a query execution, or navigation from another persistent-nontransactional instance.

With NontransactionalRead set to true, outside a transaction:

- Your application can read field values, navigate the object graph, execute queries, and iterate extents. The JDO implementation decides whether the instances returned to your application are in the hollow or persistent-nontransactional state. Key fields are instantiated regardless of the instances' states.

- The first time your application accesses a managed, nonkey field of a hollow instance, the instance transitions to persistent-nontransactional. This state transition is shown in Figure 14-1.

- Persistent-nontransactional instances remain in this state until they are accessed in a subsequent transaction.

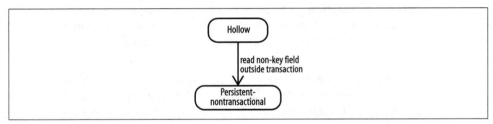

Figure 14-1. State transitions outside a transaction

With NontransactionalRead set to false, outside a transaction:

- If your application attempts to read field values, navigate the object graph, execute queries, or iterate extents, the JDO implementation throws a JDOUserException.

- Persistent instances remain in the hollow state until accessed in a transaction.

We will now discuss a more complete example, based on the Media Mania application. MediaManiaApp declares an abstract method, execute( ), which is implemented by a derived class. In the derived classes, we have seen examples of main( ), which calls executeTransaction( ). This method then begins a transaction, calls execute( ), and commits the transaction.

For this example, we will implement main( ) to call execute( ) instead of executeTransaction( ), which will make the program run without a transaction. The program is PrintMovies in the com.mediamania.nontx package:

```
package com.mediamania.nontx;
import com.mediamania.MediaManiaApp;
import com.mediamania.content.Movie;
public class PrintMovies {
```

We don't define a constructor, so the compiler generates a no-arg constructor that calls the superclass to construct the PersistenceManagerFactory. The superclass constructor calls getPropertyOverrides( ), which is implemented in this class to specify the required NontransactionalRead property:

```
protected static Map getPropertyOverrides() {
    Map overrides = new HashMap();
    overrides.put("javax.jdo.option.NontransactionalRead", "true");
    return overrides;
}
```

In this class, main( ) constructs a new instance of PrintMovies and calls execute( ):

```
public static void main(String[] args) {
    PrintMovies printMovies = new PrintMovies();
    printMovies.execute();
}
```

The superclass defines the pmf and pm fields and initializes them in the constructor. The execute( ) method gets an Extent of Movie and iterates it, calling Utilities.printMovie( ) to display the contents on System.out:

```
public void execute() {
    Extent extent = pm.getExtent(Movie.class, true);
    Iterator iter = extent.iterator();
    while (iter.hasNext()){
        Movie movie = (Movie) iter.next();
        Utilities.printMovie(movie, System.out);
    }
}
```

As an alternative to using getPropertyOverrides( ), execute( ) could be slightly different, setting the NontransactionalRead property of the Transaction instance to true.

```
public void execute() {
    pm.currentTransaction().setNontransactionalRead(true);
    Extent extent = pm.getExtent(Movie.class, true);
    Iterator iter = extent.iterator();
    while (iter.hasNext()){
        Movie movie = (Movie) iter.next();
        Utilities.printMovie(movie, System.out);
    }
}
```

Retaining Values at Transaction Commit

We have seen how reading data outside a transaction results in caching nontransactional instances. Another way for nontransactional instances to exist in the cache is to execute a transaction and then retain the field values at commit time. You can specify this behavior by setting the RetainValues property to true. This is shown in Figure 14-2.

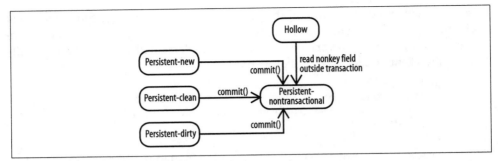

Figure 14-2. RetainValues at transaction commit

With `RetainValues` set to `true`, persistent transactional instances transition to persistent-nontransactional at commit. But with `RetainValues` set to `false`, fields of persistent transactional instances are cleared at transaction commit, and the instances transition to hollow.

The result is that your application can use the cached instances between transactions, and the instances used in the transaction retain their last-committed values. Instances not used in transactions remain nontransactional.

Since the `RetainValues` flag only affects the behavior of transaction `commit()`, your application can change it at any time, using `setRetainValues()` in `Transaction`. Regardless of how many times the value changes, the value currently in effect at commit is used.

Restoring Values at Transaction Rollback

We have seen how an application can retain persistent field values in cached instances across transactions by using the `RetainValues` property. But this property is effective only at commit. If you want to preserve cached values even if a transaction rolls back, you need to use the `RestoreValues` property. Unlike `RetainValues`, `RestoreValues` is not an optional feature, and the property setting affects the treatment of new instances as well as persistent-clean and persistent-dirty instances.

With `RestoreValues` set to `false`, persistent transactional instances have their values cleared at transaction rollback, and the instances transition to hollow. This is shown in Figure 14-3. Subsequent reads of fields in these instances require access to the datastore. In order to allow accesses of the values in the instances without accessing the datastore, the application sets the `RestoreValues` flag to `true`.

Similar to `RetainValues`, there are several ways to set the `RestoreValues` property:

- Your application can include the `javax.jdo.option.RestoreValues` property with a value of `true` or `false` in the `Properties` instance used to construct the `PersistenceManagerFactory`.

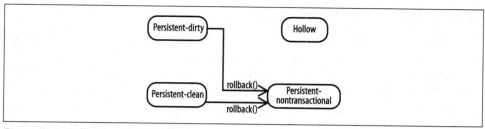

Figure 14-3. Rollback with RestoreValues true

- Your application can set the property using `setRestoreValues()` in `PersistenceManagerFactory`.
- Your application can set the property using `setRestoreValues()` in `Transaction`.

Since this flag affects the way persistent fields are managed during a transaction, the property must be changed only between transactions. If an attempt is made to execute `setRestoreValues()` during an active transaction, a `JDOUserException` is thrown.

Before Image

With `RestoreValues` set to `true`, the JDO implementation must make a *before image* of instances that are made persistent and persistent instances that are changed or deleted during the transaction. The before images contain the state of persistent and transactional fields as of the first access of the fields in the transaction, and they supply the field values restored during rollback. The before image contains a *shallow copy* of all the fields in the instance as of the call to `makePersistent()`, `deletePersistent()`, or a method that changes a managed field.

A shallow copy means that the field values are copied exactly as they are stored in the instance; values of primitive fields are copied, and references are copied. There is no copy made of the contents of reference types.

Making a before image can adversely affect performance, as there is extra work for the JDO implementation to do when the instance is made persistent, deleted, or made dirty. Therefore, applications should carefully consider the use of this flag.

With `RestoreValues` set to `false`, the JDO implementation does not need to remember the state of fields of transient instances that are made persistent. If the transaction is rolled back, the instances revert to transient, and the state of the fields is unchanged. Normally, your application will discard these instances and allow them to be garbage-collected. Similarly, there is no requirement to remember the state of instances that are changed or deleted. At transaction rollback, the instances transition to hollow, and the field contents are cleared.

Restoring Persistent Instances

At rollback, with RestoreValues set to true, persistent-clean, persistent-dirty, and persistent-deleted instances transition to persistent-nontransactional. Persistent-clean instances retain their values as of the end of the transaction. Persistent-dirty and persistent-deleted instances are restored as follows:

- Fields of primitive types (int, float, etc.), wrapper types (Integer, Float, etc.), immutable types (Locale, etc.), and PersistenceCapable types are restored to their values as of the beginning of the transaction.

- Fields of mutable types (Date, Collection, etc.) are marked by the JDO implementation as not loaded. Subsequent accesses of these fields will cause the JDO implementation to read the values from the datastore.

Restoring Persistent-New Instances

At rollback, with RestoreValues set to true, persistent-new and persistent-new-deleted instances transition to transient and all fields are restored to their values in the before image.

The before image allows the JDO implementation to restore the instance to the state it had at the time the instance was made persistent. But consider that the state of reference type fields is also part of the state of the instance and cannot necessarily be restored to its state as of the time the referring instance was made persistent.

For example, consider the following code, which makes an instance of Movie persistent and rolls back the transaction:

```
          Calendar calendar = Calendar.newInstance();
          calendar.set(Calendar.YEAR, 1965);
          Date released = calendar.getTime();
          Movie movie = new Movie("Sound of Music", released, 174, "G", "musical,
          biography");
          tx.setRestoreValues(true);
          tx.begin();
❶        pm.makePersistent(movie);
          calendar.set(Calendar.YEAR, 1987);
❷        released.setTime(calendar.getTimeInMillis()); // AVOID
          calendar.set(Calendar.YEAR, 1999);
❸        released = calendar.getTime();
          tx.rollback(); // movie.released now is 1987; released is 1999
```

❶ During makePersistent(), a shallow copy of movie is made and the copy becomes the before image. The releaseDate field in the persistent movie instance is replaced with a new instance of a JDO implementation–defined subclass of Date, containing the same millisecond value of the original released instance. There are now two instances of Date; both represent the year 1965.

Any change to the Date instance referred to by released after makePersistent() does not affect the persistent instance, but it changes the instance in the before image.

❷ In the preceding example, the instance referred to by the before image is changed to represent the year 1987. Similarly, any change to the value of the field in the persistent instance does not affect the value of released or the before image.

❸ When a new Date is created and assigned to released, there is now a third instance of Date, which contains a value representing the year 1999.

At rollback, the value of the field releaseDate in instance movie is restored to its original value of released, but because the released object was modified to represent the year 1987, these modifications remain. Thus, even though the fields in the movie instance itself were restored, the releaseDate field contains changes made subsequent to makePersistent( ).

After rollback, the original instance of released becomes the restored value of releaseDate in the movie instance; the JDO implementation–defined subclass of Date, representing 1965, is not referenced and can be garbage-collected; and the third instance, representing 1999, is now the value of the released variable.

To avoid this situation, you should never modify instances referred by fields of persistent instances once they are made persistent; instead you should replace the fields or use accessor/mutator methods defined in the persistent class. Replacing the fields leaves the instance in the before image as it was, and using mutator methods in the persistent class modifies the copy of the original instance.

Modifying Persistent Instances Outside a Transaction

JDO manages updates to the datastore by tracking changes made to persistent instances during a transaction. To avoid losing updates, you should have an active transaction when changing fields of persistent instances. When the transaction commits, the changes are made in the datastore.

However, you can write applications that manage a cache of nontransactional persistent instances, where the datastore is updated outside your application. With these applications, the cache becomes stale relative to the current state in the datastore. But if your application is made aware of these changes—for example, by receiving a stream of change notifications—your application can update the cache to reflect the current state of the datastore instances. The stream might consist only of the keys of the instances, in which case the application can simply invalidate the cached instances by calling evict( ) or refresh( ).

But if the stream contains not only the keys but also the changed values for persistent fields, your application can use the stream values to update the cached instances to reflect the current contents of the datastore.

With the NontransactionalWrite property set to false, the only way to update nontransactional instances is to invalidate them in the cache and then fetch the instances from the datastore when they are next needed. But with NontransactionalWrite set to true, your application can update the persistent instances in the cache without beginning a transaction and updating the instances. Your application can make updates to any values, but the most useful approach updates the values in the cache to reflect the current values in the datastore.

Note that the values of fields in persistent-nontransactional instances that have been modified outside a transaction will never be stored in the datastore by the JDO implementation. Any changes made outside of a transaction are lost.

This is due to the behavior of transactional instances. In a subsequent datastore transaction, if the instance is accessed (by field access, extent iteration, query, or navigation), a fresh copy of the instance will be fetched into the cache and the values written outside the transaction will simply be discarded without notice.

With NontransactionalWrite set to false, if your application attempts to make a change to any persistent instance outside a transaction, the JDO implementation will throw a JDOUserException. This includes executing any method that changes a field in the instance and executing JDOHelper.makeDirty( ), referencing a field of any persistent instance.

Hot Cache Example

For example, consider an application that executes in multiple JVMs, each of which manages a hot cache of Movie instances that track changes to a Movie's web site via a live feed. One of the JVMs executes MasterDriver, the application responsible for updating the datastore; the others execute SlaveDriver, an application that updates its copy of the instances in its cache when updates arrive.

Both MasterDriver and SlaveDriver extend AbstractDriver. The constructor of AbstractDriver connects to the source of cache updates and cache requests. We open the request and update input streams from a URL, which might be a file, or in a more realistic application, a stream from an external source. The results of a request are output to System.out, which is not realistic but demonstrates the concept:

```
public class AbstractDriver {
    protected BufferedReader requestReader;
    protected BufferedReader updateReader;
    protected CacheAccess cache;
    protected int timeoutMillis;
    protected AbstractDriver(String updateURL, String requestURL,
        String timeout) {
        updateReader = openReader(updateURL);
        requestReader = openReader(requestURL);
        timeoutMillis = Integer.parseInt(timeout);
    }
```

The BufferedReader allows us to read lines from the input source:

```
protected BufferedReader openReader (String urlName) {
    try {
        URL url = new URL(urlName);
        InputStream is = url.openStream();
        Reader r = new InputStreamReader(is);
        return new BufferedReader(r);
    } catch (Exception ex) {
        return null;
    }
}
```

ServiceReaders will service the updateReader and requestReader until there is no work to do for a specified timeout period, or until it is interrupted:

```
protected void serviceReaders() {
    boolean done = false;
    boolean lastTime = false;
    try {
        while (!done) {
            if (updateReader.ready()) {
                handleUpdate();
                done = false;
                lastTime = false;
            } else if (requestReader.ready()) {
                handleRequest();
                done = false;
                lastTime = false;
            } else {
                try {
                    Thread.sleep (timeoutMillis);
                    if (lastTime) done = true;
                    lastTime = true;
                } catch (InterruptedException ex) {
                    done = true;
                }
            }
        }
    } catch (Exception ex) {
        return;
    }
}
```

HandleRequest reads a line from the requestReader and prints the title of the movie to System.out. A more realistic application would return the results to the requester.

```
protected void handleRequest() throws IOException {
    String request = requestReader.readLine();
    Movie movie = cache.getMovieByTitle(request);
    System.out.println("Movie: " + movie.getTitle());
}
```

HandleUpdate reads a line from the updateReader, parses it into a movie title and a web site, and then calls updateWebSite.

```
protected void handleUpdate() throws IOException {
    String update = updateReader.readLine();
    StringTokenizer tokenizer = new StringTokenizer(update, ";");
    String movieName = tokenizer.nextToken();
    String webSite = tokenizer.nextToken();
    cache.updateWebSite (movieName, webSite);
}
}
```

The interface to the cache is defined by com.mediamania.hotcache.CacheAccess. There are two implementations of this interface: MasterCache and SlaveCache, with a common AbstractCache implementation.

MasterCache performs the updates to the datastore as well as updating the cache. It will retrieve the Movie into the cache if it is not already cached. SlaveCache updates the cache only if the Movie is already cached.

MasterCache needs the NontransactionalRead option set to true because lookups are done outside a transaction, and the RetainValues option set to true so values are retained in the cache at the end of an update transaction. SlaveCache needs the NontransactionalRead and NontransactionalWrite options set to true, because reads and updates are done without a transaction active. Both classes use getPropertyOverrides() to initialize the PersistenceManagerFactory with the correct options.

AbstractCache implements the CacheAccess interface:

```
public interface CacheAccess {
    Movie getMovieByTitle (String title);
    void updateWebSite (String title, String website);
}
```

MasterCache and SlaveCache use the same lookup method implemented in AbstractCache to find a Movie with a particular title. If the Movie does not exist in the cache, it is loaded (outside a transaction) into the cache.

```
public abstract class AbstractCache extends MediaManiaApp
    implements com.mediamania.hotcache.CacheAccess {
    protected Map cache; // key:name value:Movie
    public Movie getMovieByTitle(String title) {
        Movie movie = (Movie)cache.get(title);
        if (movie == null) {
            movie = super.getMovie(title);
            if (movie != null) {
                cache.put(title, movie);
            }
        }
        return movie;
    }
}
```

The difference between MasterCache and SlaveCache is in how the update is handled. MasterCache first loads the Movie into the cache if it isn't already there, and then uses a transaction to perform the update:

```
public class MasterCache extends AbstractCache
    implements CacheAccess {
    protected static Map getPropertyOverrides() {
        Map overrides = new HashMap();
        overrides.put ("javax.jdo.options.NontransactionalRead", "true");
        overrides.put ("javax.jdo.options.RetainValues", "true");
        return overrides;
    }

    public void updateWebSite(String title, String website) {
        Movie movie = getMovieByTitle(title);
        if (movie != null) {
            tx.begin();
            movie.setWebSite(website);
            tx.commit();
        }
    }
}
```

SlaveCache locates the movie in the cache. If the Movie is not in the cache, SlaveCache ignores the message. If the Movie is in the cache, SlaveCache updates it:

```
public class SlaveCache extends AbstractCache
    implements CacheAccess {

    protected static Map getPropertyOverrides() {
        Map overrides = new HashMap();
        overrides.put ("javax.jdo.options.NontransactionalRead", "true");
        overrides.put ("javax.jdo.options.NontransactionalWrite", "true");
        return overrides;
    }

    public void updateWebSite(String title, String website) {
        Movie movie = (Movie)cache.get(title);
        if (movie != null) {
            movie.setWebSite(website);
        }
    }
}
```

To complete the example, MasterDriver initializes the cache to be a MasterCache:

```
public class MasterDriver extends AbstractDriver {
    protected MasterDriver(String updateURL, String requestURL,
        String timeout) {
            super(updateURL, requestURL, timeout);
            cache = new MasterCache();
    }
```

```
    public static void main(String[] args) {
        MasterDriver master = new MasterDriver(
            args[0], args[1], args[2]);
        master.serviceReaders();
    }
}
```

SlaveDriver initializes the cache to be a SlaveCache; otherwise, the implementation is the same as MasterDriver:

```
public class SlaveDriver extends AbstractDriver {
    protected SlaveDriver(String updateURL, String requestURL,
        String timeout) {
            super(updateURL, requestURL, timeout);
            cache = new SlaveCache();
    }

    public static void main(String[] args) {
        SlaveDriver slave = new SlaveDriver(
            args[0], args[1], args[2]);
        slave.serviceReaders();
    }
}
```

CHAPTER 15

Optimistic Transactions

Earlier in this book, we discussed using datastore transactions to guarantee the following properties: atomicity, consistency, isolation, and durability. All operations between begin( ) and commit( ) of a JDO transaction are performed in the context of an underlying datastore transaction.

The datastore transaction model assumes that the duration of JDO transactions is relatively short. For longer transactions, JDO defines *optimistic transactions*, in which some of the transaction properties are implemented by JDO instead of the datastore.

Optimistic transactions are most useful for long-running transactions that rarely affect the same instances. These applications exhibit higher performance and better concurrency by deferring datastore locking on modified instances until commit. Whether you use optimistic or datastore transactions for your applications is a complex issue, because if there is significant contention for transactional instances, optimistic transactions can be less efficient than datastore transactions.

For example, JDO transactions performed in an application server with very high throughput and high concurrency are probably best implemented as datastore transactions. However, if JDO transactions include user "think time," then optimistic transactions are a good choice. The changes made to the cache might be made over a long period of time, during which no locks associated with any of the retrieved instances will be held in the datastore.

In the following summary, "transactional datastore context" refers to the transaction context of the underlying datastore, while "transaction," "datastore transaction," and "optimistic transaction" refer to the JDO transaction concepts.

JDO datastore transactions perform all datastore operations using the same transactional datastore context, which the JDO application delimits using the JDO Transaction methods. Thus, persistent instances accessed within the scope of an active JDO transaction are guaranteed to be associated with the transactional datastore context.

Prior to commit, JDO optimistic transactions perform all datastore operations using short transactional datastore contexts. Thus, persistent instances accessed within the scope of an active JDO transaction prior to commit are only briefly associated with a transactional datastore context. At JDO transaction commit, a transactional datastore context is used to perform all datastore modification operations.

Verification at Commit

With optimistic transactions, instances queried or read from the datastore are not treated as transactional unless they are modified, deleted, or marked by the application as transactional. At commit time, the transactional datastore context is used for verification of inserted, deleted, and updated datastore instances involved in the transaction.

The verification algorithm is not part of the JDO specification, although updates to the same field in the same instance by different transactions must cause a verification failure. The verification can be implemented by different strategies, based on the support provided by different datastores:

- A JDO implementation might use a special timestamp field in each datastore instance and compare this field for verification. Some datastores provide a special timestamp type that automatically updates its value with every transaction that changes any value in the instance. If such a type is not available, an implementation might simply use an extra field, not visible to the application, to track these changes and manage the values itself.

- An implementation might use an application-specific set of fields whose values are compared.

- An implementation might allow your application to aggregate fields into groups and compare all of the values in each affected group to verify that no field in any group has changed.

- An implementation might allow you to choose a different policy for each persistent class in your model.

Thus, it is possible for different optimistic transactions to perform updates to different fields of the same instance without resulting in an optimistic conflict. The JDO implementation provides a default policy for treating this situation and might allow some application control over the policy.

The JDO implementation verifies that the optimistic assumptions are true before permanently making changes to the datastore. For each transactional instance in the cache, the JDO implementation verifies that the values of the instances in the datastore match the assumed values of the optimistic transaction:

- Unmodified instances that have been made transactional are verified against the current contents of the datastore. As noted earlier, the verification might be done by comparing timestamps or field values.

- For application identity, new instances are verified in the datastore to ensure that they do not have the same identity as existing datastore instances. There is no such checking in the case of datastore identity, as this situation cannot occur.

- Deleted instances are verified to ensure that they have not been deleted or modified by a concurrent transaction.

- Updated instances are verified to ensure that they have not changed since being fetched into the cache.

If any instance fails verification, the JDO implementation throws a JDOOptimistic-VerificationException, which contains an array of JDOExceptions, one for each instance that failed the verification. In this case, the optimistic transaction fails.

Recovery from a Failed Transaction

If an optimistic transaction fails verification at commit time, the transaction rolls back, just as if your application had called rollback( ). The changes made to cached instances revert to their pre-transaction state. Since the optimistic failure indicates that the cache is inconsistent with the state of the datastore, you should refresh the failed instances identified in the exception if you intend to continue to use the cache to retry the failed transaction or to perform new transactions.

After refreshing the cached instances, your application can report the failure to the user or it might attempt to replay the transaction. Replaying is only possible if your application has maintained a change list to reapply changes.

In order to replay the transaction, all instances involved in the transaction must be updated. After beginning a new optimistic transaction, the changes to each instance can be replayed:

- Unmodified instances that failed verification can be reloaded from the datastore using PersistenceManager.refresh( ).

- New instances that failed verification can be loaded from the datastore by performing a query or by getting the instance by its primary key.

- New instances that did not fail verification can be made persistent again.

- Deleted instances that failed verification because they were already deleted can simply be ignored.

- Deleted instances that did not fail verification can be deleted again.

- Updated instances that failed verification can be loaded from the datastore using PersistenceManager.refresh( ).

- Updated instances that did not fail verification can be updated again.

Note that you must reapply inserts, updates, and deletes using application-consistency rules; otherwise, the consistency guarantees of the datastore are meaningless.

Setting Optimistic Transaction Behavior

Optimistic transactions are an optional feature of a JDO implementation. If an implementation does not support optimistic transactions, it will throw JDOUnsupportedOptionException when you attempt to set the value of the Optimistic property to true.

The Optimistic flag that activates optimistic transactions is a property of PersistenceManagerFactory and Transaction. You can set the property in the Properties instance used to create the PersistenceManagerFactory and access it via getOptimistic( ) and setOptimistic( ). The setting of the property in Persistence-ManagerFactory is used as the default for all PersistenceManager instances obtained from it.

Setting the Optimistic flag to true changes the lifecycle-state transitions of persistent instances; therefore you can change the flag only when a transaction is not active. If you attempt to change the flag while a transaction is active, the implementation will throw JDOUserException.

Optimistic Example

To illustrate the programming techniques used in optimistic transactions, we'll modify the UpdateWebSite program to use optimistic transactions. First, we need to set the Optimistic property to true before beginning the transaction. We define executeOptimisticTransaction( ) to set the Optimistic property to true before calling execute( ). We return a boolean to indicate whether the transaction commits successfully:

```
public boolean executeOptimisticTransaction() {
    try {
        tx.setOptimistic(true);
        tx.begin();
        execute();
        tx.commit();
        return true;
    } catch (JDOException exception){
        analyzeJDOException(exception, System.out);
        return false;
    } catch (Throwable throwable) {
        throwable.printStackTrace(System.out);
        return false;
    } finally {
        if (tx.isActive()) {
            try {
                tx.rollback();
            } catch (Exception ex) {
            }
        }
    }
}
```

When execute( ) locates the movie by title, the movie is not transactional. When the movie is updated in setWebSite( ), it transitions to transactional and the JDO implementation saves information about the movie to be used at commit:

```
public void execute()
    {
        Movie movie = PrototypeQueries.getMovie(pm, movieTitle);
        if( movie == null ){
            System.err.print("Could not access movie with title of ");
            System.err.println(movieTitle);
            return;
        }
        movie.setWebSite(newWebSite);
    }
```

At commit, the saved information is used to verify that the update did not conflict with a concurrent transaction; if the verification succeeds, the update is performed and the transaction completes.

Define the analyzeJDOException( ) method to analyze failed optimistic transactions:

```
public void analyzeJDOException(JDOException jdoException, PrintStream p) {
        p.println("JDOException thrown:");
        p.println(jdoException.toString());
        Throwable[] nestedExceptions = jdoException.getNestedExceptions();
        int numberOfExceptions = nestedExceptions.length;
        p.println("Number of nested exceptions: " + numberOfExceptions);
        for (int i = 0; i < numberOfExceptions; ++i) {
            Throwable thrown = nestedExceptions[i];
            if (thrown instanceof JDOException) {
                JDOException instanceException = (JDOException)thrown;
                Object instance = instanceException.getFailedObject();
                Object objectId = JDOHelper.getObjectId(instance);
                p.println("Failed instance objectId: " + objectId);
            } else {
                p.println("Nested exception: " + thrown);
            }
        }
    }
```

We change main( ) to execute the optimistic transaction and, if it fails, retry once:

```
public static void main (String[] args) {
        String title = args[0];
        String website = args[1];
        UpdateWebSite update = new UpdateWebSite(title, website);
        if (!update.executeOptimisticTransaction()) {
            System.out.println("Optimistic transaction failed; retrying");
            if (!update.executeOptimisticTransaction()) {
                System.out.println("Failed again.");
            }
        }
    }
```

Figure 15-1 shows what happens during another example of an optimistic transaction, in which the application queries for movies, accesses the director of a movie, and then changes the web site of the movie. There is no datastore transactional context established at optimistic transaction begin( ). A short datastore transactional context is established in order to retrieve information to satisfy iterator.hasNext( ).

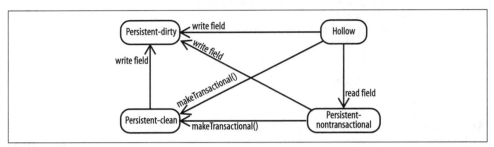

Figure 15-1. Optimistic transaction time line

When the name of the director is accessed, another datastore transactional context is established. At commit time, the final datastore transactional context is established, in which the JDO implementation performs all verification and updates, and commits the changes to the datastore.

Optimistic Transaction State Transitions

With the Optimistic flag set to true, some of the behavior of the cache changes, due to the requirements of verification at commit time. Primarily, the JDO implementation saves the state of the instances that are updated or deleted, so it can verify the instances at commit.

If a persistent field other than one of the primary-key fields is read, a hollow instance transitions to persistent-nontransactional instead of persistent-clean. Subsequent reads of any of these fields in the same transaction do not cause a transition from persistent-nontransactional.

Note that the fields in persistent-nontransactional instances might be read from the datastore at different times, either outside transactions or during transactions where the RetainValues property is set to true.

If the first access to a hollow instance in an optimistic transaction is a write access, the hollow instance transitions to persistent-dirty. During the transition, the JDO implementation fetches the instance from the datastore and saves the state of the instance for verification at commit. These state transitions are shown in Figure 15-2.

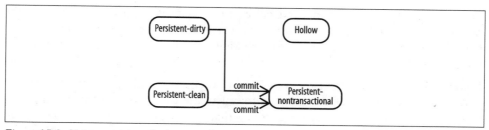

Figure 15-2. State transitions during optimistic transactions

Deleting Instances

A persistent-nontransactional instance transitions to persistent-deleted if it is a parameter of deletePersistent( ). The values of the fields of the instance in memory are unchanged but are saved for verification during commit. To minimize the possibility of a conflict at commit, you can load fresh values from the datastore by calling refresh( ) or refreshAll( ) with the instance as a parameter.

A hollow instance transitions to persistent-deleted if it is a parameter of deletePersistent( ). Since there is no state loaded into the instance, the instance will not be verified during commit. To force verification at commit, you should first call refresh( ) or refreshAll( ) with the instance as a parameter.

Making Instances Transactional

When an optimistic transaction is in progress, a persistent-nontransactional instance transitions to persistent-clean if it is a parameter of makeTransactional( ). The values in managed fields of the instance in memory are unchanged. To minimize the possibility of a verification failure at commit, you can first call refresh( ) or refreshAll( ) with the instance as a parameter before making the instance transactional.

It does not matter at what time during the transaction the instance is made transactional. If the verification policy is to compare field values, the values that are compared include at a minimum all of the fields accessed during the transaction.

Modifying Instances

A persistent-nontransactional instance transitions to persistent-dirty if your application modifies a managed field while an optimistic transaction is in progress. The JDO implementation saves the values of the fields of the instance in memory for use during rollback and for verification during commit. The saved values of fields in the instance in memory are unchanged before the update is applied. To minimize the possibility of a verification failure at commit, you can call refresh() or refreshAll() with the instance as a parameter before making the first change to the instance in the transaction.

If you make changes to instances outside a transaction using the Nontransactional-Write feature, the changes are assumed to reflect the current state of the field values in the datastore. Therefore, with a policy that uses field-value verification, if you make changes to the same instances in a subsequent optimistic transaction, the changes made outside the transaction will be the values used for comparison. With a policy that depends on a special field in the object, the only way to avoid a verification failure is to refresh the instance prior to making the changes.

Commit

At commit, persistent-nontransactional instances do not change their state. Once instances have been read nontransactionally, they remain in the persistent-nontransactional state until they transition to a transactional or hollow state.

At commit, transactional instances transition to new states, based on the setting of the RetainValues flag. There is no difference between datastore and optimistic transactions in this regard.

With RetainValues set to true, persistent-clean and persistent-dirty instances transition to persistent-nontransactional and the instances retain their values as of the end of the transaction.

Rollback

At rollback, persistent-nontransactional instances do not change their state. If instances have been read nontransactionally, they remain in the persistent-nontransactional state at rollback.

At rollback, persistent transactional instances transition to new states, based on the setting of the RestoreValues flag. There is no difference between datastore and optimistic transactions in this regard.

CHAPTER 16

The Web-Server Environment

Up to this point, we have focused on using JDO to write applications in one- and two-tier environments. We now turn to distributed environments, with an emphasis on writing applications in which your JDO application code runs in a server.

The two most popular server environments in which Java is the implementation language for applications are the web server and the application server. A web server provides a web container in which servlets and JSP pages execute. Typically, a web server also provides support for serving static web content (HTML, GIF, and JPEG files, etc.) in addition to dynamic content. Both web servers and application servers support remote clients using a variety of protocols, including HTTP (Hypertext Transfer Protocol), HTTPS (HyperText Transfer Protocol over SSL), and SOAP (Simple Object Access Protocol). In addition, application servers support CORBA IIOP/RMI (Common Object Request Broker Architecture Internet Inter-Orb Protocol/Remote Method Invocation) protocols. We cover application servers in more detail in Chapter 17.

With either of these types of servers, the implementation of remote services is opaque to the client; the services could be implemented by any kind of host running any language that supports the protocols. JDO fits into these environments to provide access to persistent data for applications that implement dynamic content.

Web Servers

In order to describe where JDO fits into a web server, we start with a brief overview of the web container and how the container handles requests. The application components that handle the requests can use JDO to provide access to persistent information used to service the requests.

There is no standard for all the characteristics of web servers and the services they support, but most implementations support applications written to implement HTTP and HTTPS messages. Since the details of security and secure access to these services are not important to the implementation using JDO, we will use HTTP to describe both HTTP and HTTPS protocols. The use of HTTPS is transparent to the application.

HTTP is a request/response protocol in which a browser sends a request to a server at a specific Internet address and waits for a response from the server. The server parses the request and delegates its handling to the responsible component, based on policy files used to configure the server.

HTTP responses can be *static* (i.e., their content never changes). Graphics, web-page templates, banners, and other artifacts of web pages are primarily static, and web servers typically cache these items and deliver them to users on request.

Other HTTP responses are *dynamic*. The response is generated only upon receipt of the request and may depend on current information (time of day, current price of a stock, etc.) or the requester (contents of a shopper's cart, value of a portfolio, etc.). These requests must be handled by a program, which in current web servers might be a script-based component like Common Gateway Interface (CGI) or "PHP: Hypertext Preprocessor," or a programming component.

In a Java-based web server, the programming component that handles the request is either a servlet or a JSP page. Application developers implement programs that adhere to either the servlet or JSP programming contracts to handle requests and generate responses to clients.

SOAP is a remote-object protocol that uses HTTP to transmit requests and receive responses. A web server that supports SOAP provides a layer of processing that interprets SOAP messages, presents them to servlets for processing, and formats the responses for clients.

A server that supports servlet and JSP pages implements a web container that is responsible for managing the lifecycle of servlets and JSP pages, receiving and decoding MIME-type HTTP requests, and formatting MIME-type HTTP responses.

The details of parsing requests and formatting responses will vary based on whether the servlet uses pure HTTP or SOAP, but these details are beyond the scope of this book. Here, we focus on the programming interface to the JDO persistence layer.

To implement a servlet that handles HTTP requests, you extend a base class, HttpServlet, provided by the container implementation. You implement init( ) and destroy( ) and override one or more service methods, typically doGet( ) and/or doPost( ). These methods handle the HTTP-protocol GET and POST requests.

The web container calls init( ) once per servlet instance it creates, and, upon successful completion of the method, it places the servlet into service. This is your application's chance to perform any one-time initialization that is required. You can implement your servlet as a SingleThreadModel, in which multiple requests are dispatched to multiple servlet instances. The SingleThreadModel should be avoided, because the servlet container has to create multiple instances for multiple simultaneous requests.

For SingleThreadModel servlets, if the web container needs to reduce the number of active servlet instances, it selects a servlet instance for destruction and calls destroy( ).

This is your last chance to clean up any resources that might have been allocated to this servlet. After this method completes, the servlet will no longer be used and might be garbage-collected by the JVM. Figure 16-1 shows the lifecycle of a servlet.

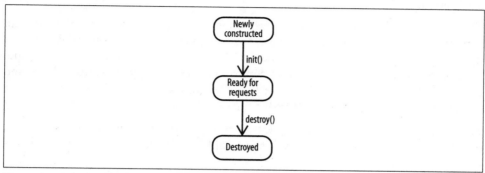

Figure 16-1. Servlet lifecycle

Accessing the PersistenceManagerFactory

The servlet programming model is inherently flexible and, theoretically, servlets could dynamically determine which JDO resource contains the information needed to service a request. But most servlets use the same PersistenceManagerFactory instance to service all the user requests, and this resource does not change during the lifetime of the servlet. Therefore, the best time to acquire the PersistenceManagerFactory and save it for future use is during the init( ) call. There are a number of alternate techniques that you can use to initialize the reference to the PersistenceManagerFactory, depending on the support for services provided by the web container.

Looking up the PersistenceManagerFactory in JNDI

If the web container is part of a J2EE server, or if it supports the JNDI (Java Naming and Directory Interface) lookup service, you should use the JNDI lookup method and save the result in a servlet field. The container configures the PersistenceManagerFactory at server startup and stores it by name in the JNDI namespace.

To use this facility in a J2EE server, you need to define a resource reference in the deployment descriptor of your web application. This resource reference is part of the servlet specification. The resource-ref element is one of the elements contained in the web-app element (the root of the web-application deployment descriptor):

```
<resource-ref>
<res-ref-name>jdo/MediaManiaPMF</res-ref-name>
<res-type>javax.jdo.PersistenceManagerFactory</res-type>
<res-auth>Container</res-auth>
</resource-ref>
```

Your application performs the lookup by using the initial context provided by the container. This initial context is specific to your deployed application, so the name is scoped to your application and you can locate resources that are bound to your application.

The name you look up uses one level of indirection. At deployment time, the deployer makes the association between the name you specify in your application—in this case, java:comp/env/jdo/MediaManiaPMF—and the actual resource that is registered in the server. The details of this deployment step are not standardized, but the indirection allows you to hardcode the resource name and allow the server to bind it to a resource dynamically at deployment time.

This indirection allows multiple applications to use the same hardcoded JNDI name to refer to different resources, as well as multiple applications to use different hardcoded JNDI names to refer to the same resource:

```
PersistenceManagerFactory persistenceManagerFactory;
String pmfName = "java:comp/env/jdo/MediaManiaPMF";
public void init(ServletConfig config) throws ServletException {
    try {
        super.init(config);
        Context ic = new InitialContext();
        persistenceManagerFactory = (PersistenceManagerFactory)
            ic.lookup(pmfName);
    } catch (NamingException ex) {
        throw new ServletException("Unable to locate PMF resource: " +
            pmfName);
    }
}
```

The server configures the PersistenceManagerFactory at server startup by a server-specific process. Typically, you configure the URL, username, password, and other properties in an XML-formatted file, and when you look up the resource by name, you get the configured resource. You cannot use any of the set( ) methods of PersistenceManagerFactory to change the properties. If you need to set specific properties, you use the set( ) methods of the individual components (Transaction, Query, or PersistenceManager) after you get the PersistenceManager.

Constructing the PersistenceManagerFactory from Properties

If you run your servlet outside a J2EE environment and the web container does not support JNDI, you construct and initialize a PersistenceManagerFactory much as you would in a two-tier environment. Instead of hardcoding the properties of the PersistenceManagerFactory, we recommend that you load a Properties instance identified by a configuration file stored in the *WEB-INF* directory in the deployed application. This way, you can change the resource without changing any code in your servlet. Simply change the properties file packaged in the war file. This example of initialization is from the servlet named MovieInfo in the com.mediamania.appserver package:

```
public class MovieInfo extends HttpServlet {
    PersistenceManagerFactory persistenceManagerFactory;
    PersistenceManager pm;

    public void init() throws ServletException {
        try {
            ServletContext ctx = getServletContext();
            InputStream in = ctx.getResourceAsStream("WEB-INF/pmf.properties");
            Properties props = new Properties();
            props.load(in);
            persistenceManagerFactory =
                JDOHelper.getPersistenceManagerFactory(props);
        } catch (IOException ex) {
            throw new ServletException("Unable to locate PMF resource.");
        }
    }
}
```

The *pmf.properties* file in this example has the same contents as the properties file used in a two-tier application:

```
javax.jdo.PersistenceManagerFactoryClass:com.sun.jdori.fostore.FOStorePMF
javax.jdo.option.ConnectionURL:fostore:/shared/databases/jdo/dbdir
javax.jdo.option.ConnectionUserName:craig
javax.jdo.option.ConnectionPassword:faster
javax.jdo.option.Optimistic:true
javax.jdo.option.NontransactionalRead:true
```

Servicing Requests

After your servlet has been initialized, the web container sends incoming requests to it. The web container dispatches each incoming HTTP request to service( ), which is implemented by the HttpServlet base class to call one of the HTTP service methods (doGet( ) or doPost( )) implemented by your servlet class. The following is a typical implementation of doGet( ) and doPost( ), which both delegate to processRequest( ). This implementation is not standard, but it is a common pattern used by tools that create servlets; it is part of the MovieInfo class.

```
protected void doGet(HttpServletRequest request,
    HttpServletResponse response)
        throws ServletException, java.io.IOException {
    processRequest(request, response);
}
protected void doPost(HttpServletRequest request,
    HttpServletResponse response)
        throws ServletException, java.io.IOException {
    processRequest(request, response);
}
protected void processRequest(HttpServletRequest request,
    HttpServletResponse response)
        throws ServletException, java.io.IOException {
    pm = persistenceManagerFactory.getPersistenceManager();
    response.setContentType("text/html");
```

```
java.io.PrintWriter out = response.getWriter();
out.println("<html>");
out.println("<head>");
out.println("<title>Servlet</title>");
out.println("</head>");
out.println("<body>");
out.print(formatMovieInfo());
out.println("</body>");
out.println("</html>");
out.close();
pm.close();
}
```

PersistenceManager per Request

The following method actually performs the application-specific processing that requires the PersistenceManager. Implementing JDO datastore access as a method in the servlet is not recommended; it is presented only as an example. Note that the PersistenceManager is obtained from the PersistenceManagerFactory at the beginning of the processRequest( ) method and is closed at the end of the method. This pattern, known as *PersistenceManager per Request*, is a typical use of PersistenceManager in managed environments. If the request contained multiple methods, they would all use the same PersistenceManager.

```
protected String formatMovieInfo( ) {
    StringBuffer result = new StringBuffer();
    Extent movies = pm.getExtent(Movie.class, true);
    Iterator it = movies.iterator();
    while (it.hasNext()) {
        result.append("<P>");
        Movie movie = (Movie)it.next();
        result.append(movie.getDescription());
    }
    return result.toString();
}
```

PersistenceManager per Application

The PersistenceManager per Request pattern is the most common and arguably the most scalable approach to managing PersistenceManager instances. Another approach, *PersistenceManager per Application*, may offer better performance in certain situations.

With this pattern, there is a single PersistenceManager for all servlets and all requests in the application. This approach might be good for read-only applications that use a relatively small number of persistent instances and don't need transactions. Since multiple threads can execute request methods simultaneously, access to the PersistenceManager must be carefully controlled. Either the application needs to serialize access, or the PersistenceManager needs to have the Multithreaded property set to true.

You should keep the number of instances small to avoid growing the cache. With the PersistenceManager per Request pattern, most objects can be garbage-collected as soon as the request is done. But with a single `PersistenceManager`, newly instantiated instances in the cache tend to stay around for a long time. While the JDO implementation holds only a weak reference to persistent instances in the cache, managing the weak references might be a challenge for the garbage collector.

You should avoid transactions, because while one thread is committing a transaction, no other thread can access the cache. Even with the `Multithreaded` property set to true, only one thread can access the `PersistenceManager` during commit. The benefits of having cached instances can be overshadowed by poor concurrency during commit.

PersistenceManager per Transactional Request

If most requests are nontransactional, with a small number of transactional requests (insert, delete, or update), you can consider combining the common `PersistenceManager` approach with *PersistenceManager per Transactional Request*. This allows you to navigate the graph of persistent instances in the common cache to find the instance that needs to be updated, and then use a new `PersistenceManager` obtained from the same `PersistenceManagerFactory` to perform the transaction.

PersistenceManager per Session

Another approach for managing the `PersistenceManager` is to create a `PersistenceManager` and store it in a session attribute. While this makes some of the programming easier, it has significant disadvantages.

Implementations of the `PersistenceManager` generally do not support serialization, which is the specified implementation of a persistent session state. Therefore, the application cannot be distributable; all of the requests that are part of a session must be handled by the same server. Further, migration of sessions in case of system failure is not possible.

These aspects of the runtime environment reduce the scalability and robustness of your application, and we recommend that you carefully evaluate your reasons to use this pattern. As an alternative, you can store the identity instances of persistent instances in session attributes and obtain the persistent instances by using `getObjectById()` from the `PersistenceManager` obtained for the request. This is a scalable technique that avoids the problems associated with storing the `PersistenceManager` itself in the session state.

Transactions

For many requests, transactions are not required. Looking up information, browsing a datastore, or even displaying certain types of data for particular users does not necessarily require transactional guarantees. Thus, many requests can simply use the PersistenceManager to perform a query, navigate to some instances of interest to satisfy the request, retrieve some persistent fields, and close the PersistenceManager. But to add new instances, update instances in the datastore, or delete instances, you must begin and commit a transaction.

If you are deploying your servlet outside a J2EE server and don't have access to a UserTransaction, then you use the JDO Transaction to delimit transactions, using the begin( ), commit( ), and rollback( ) methods discussed in earlier chapters. In this environment, you cannot combine operations from multiple data sources into a single global transaction.

If you are deploying your servlet in a J2EE server, there are two mechanisms that you can use for managing transactions. The first is to use the JDO Transaction discussed previously. Using the JDO Transaction, your application is responsible for performing all the operations that are part of the same transaction using the same PersistenceManager. With this approach, you cannot coordinate transactions that involve multiple resources.

The second mechanism is to use a UserTransaction, available from the server via the JNDI lookup method. The instance that implements a UserTransaction is created and managed by the server. With a UserTransaction, you can demarcate J2EE transactions that span multiple data sources, and any operations done between the beginning and completion of the J2EE transaction will be coordinated with other operations. This allows you to use multiple resources (more than one JDO PersistenceManager, JDBC DataSource, EJB bean method, etc.) and combine all of their operations into one global transaction.

In order for the PersistenceManagerFactory to give you the PersistenceManager associated with the proper J2EE transaction, you call begin( ) on the UserTransaction prior to getting the PersistenceManager from the PersistenceManagerFactory. During the execution of getPersistenceManager( ), the PersistenceManagerFactory discovers that the UserTransaction is active and automatically begins the JDO transaction for you. The JDO Transaction is marked so that calling any of the JDO transaction completion methods is a user error. Instead, you must complete the J2EE transaction via UserTransaction commit( ) or rollback( ). The PersistenceManager is also marked so that, when it is closed by your application, it waits for the UserTransaction completion before being reused or discarded.

JavaServer Pages

JavaServer Pages technology provides an easy way to generate dynamic web content by embedding actions into HTML pages. The actions are either callouts to the Java language or references to library routines that encapsulate commonly needed functions, such as datastore access.

JSP pages allow construction of dynamic web content by using HTML editors to create prototype web pages. The dynamic content is interpreted by the HTML editor as just another tag that can be edited without further interpretation. With this approach, web content designers can use WYSIWYG (what you see is what you get) web-page editors, in which the dynamic content is displayed as text.

Using JSP pages effectively requires libraries of functions, called *tag libraries*. There are standard tag libraries, which include functions to access request parameters, access cookies, create and access scoped variables, query a JDBC database, iterate collections of transient or persistent instances, parse and transform XML documents, and display information from beans used in the JSP page.

At the time of this writing, there is no standard tag library to define access to JDO. The effort is underway, however.

The shape of a standard tag library for JDO can be seen by examining the JDBC tag library. There are tag elements to establish the factory, query the datastore, and demarcate transactions.

Until a standard tag library is available for JDO, code JSP pages using JDO with native Java code callouts from the page.

Struts with JDO

Struts is a component framework developed as an open source project (under the auspices of the Jakarta Apache project) to ease development of scalable web-tier applications. Struts defines an updated Model-View-Controller pattern (called MVC2) for implementing web-based applications. It also defines servlet and JSP components as either views or controllers, with the model implemented as business objects accessible to both view and controller components.

Views are either servlets or JSP pages that provide the HTML-generation end of the process. *Controllers* are usually servlets and provide the flow control and delegation to the business objects. Many common patterns for generating web-based forms are implemented in Struts as base classes, making construction of complex forms-based applications easy.

When using JDO with Struts, the issues are the same as with generic servlet and JSP pages. The PersistenceManagerFactory (or multiple instances of PersistenceManagerFactory) used with the application is constructed at server or application startup, and each component that needs JDO services needs to access the PersistenceManagerFactory in order to get the PersistenceManager used in the business logic.

Struts 1.1 does not include direct support for JDO, but it provides a flexible way to configure the controller servlet: by defining PlugIn classes that are initialized when the web container loads the Struts servlet. You can exploit this Struts feature by writing a

JDOPlugIn class for JDO that manages the PersistenceManagerFactory. A Struts PlugIn class has an init( ) method invoked at servlet initialization, a destroy( ) method invoked at server shutdown, and an arbitrary number of configuration methods.

At servlet initialization, the Struts framework creates an instance of PlugIn for each plug-in element found in the *struts-config.xml* file in the application's war file. For each set-property element found in the plug-in element, the framework configures the PlugIn by calling the corresponding PlugIn method, following the JavaBeans get/set pattern. After configuring the PlugIn, the framework calls init( ) to have the PlugIn perform the initialization.

The following sample implementation of JDOPlugIn uses three properties: name, path, and jndiName, corresponding to the methods setName(String), setPath(String), and setJndiName(String), respectively. name is the name under which the PlugIn registers the PersistenceManagerFactory; it is required. path is the pathname where the properties file is located in the war file. jndiName is the JNDI name under which the PersistenceManagerFactory was registered by a server-specific process at server startup. One of path and jndiName is required. The following code shows the field declarations and the set( ) methods:

```
public class JDOPlugIn implements PlugIn {
    private ServletContext ctx;
    private String name;
    private String path;
    private String jndiName;
    public JDOPlugIn( ) {
    }
    public void setName(String name) {
        this.name = name;
    }
    public void setPath(String path) {
        this.path = path;
    }
    public void setJndiName(String jndiName) {
        this.jndiName = jndiName;
    }
```

The init( ) method uses these helper methods to locate or construct the PersistenceManagerFactory:

```
    private PersistenceManagerFactory
            getPersistenceManagerFactoryFromPath(String path)
                throws IOException {
        Properties props = new Properties( );
        InputStream in = ctx.getResourceAsStream(path);
        props.load(in);
        return JDOHelper.getPersistenceManagerFactory(props);
    }
    private PersistenceManagerFactory
            getPersistenceManagerFactoryFromJndi(String jndiName)
                throws NamingException {
```

```
                Context ic = new InitialContext();
                return (PersistenceManagerFactory) ic.lookup(jndiName);
        }
```

The init() method determines whether to load the PersistenceManagerFactory from a properties file using the path property or to look up the PersistenceManagerFactory from JNDI. It then puts the PersistenceManagerFactory into the servlet context using the given name:

```
public void init(ActionServlet servlet, ModuleConfig config)
        throws ServletException {
    ctx = servlet.getServletContext();
    if (name == null || name.length() == 0) {
        throw new ServletException
            ("You must specify name.");
    }
    try {
        PersistenceManagerFactory pmf;
        if (path != null) {
            pmf = getPersistenceManagerFactoryFromPath(path);
        } else if (jndiName != null) {
            pmf = getPersistenceManagerFactoryFromJndi(jndiName);
        } else {
            throw new ServletException
                ("You must specify either path or jndiName.");
        }
        ctx.setAttribute(name, pmf);
    } catch (Exception ex) {
        throw new ServletException(
            "Unable to load PMF: name:" + name +
            ", path: " + path +
            ", jndiName: " + jndiName,
            ex);
    }
}
```

To use the JDOPlugIn, add elements to the *struts-config.xml* file. For each PersistenceManagerFactory you want to use in your Struts application, add a new plug-in element to the file, with set-property elements:

```
<plug-in className="com.mediamania.appserver.JDOPlugIn">
  <set-property property="name" value="jdo.Movies"/>
  <set-property property="path" value="WEB-INF/jdoMovies.properties"/>
</plug-in>
<plug-in className="com.mediamania.appserver.JDOPlugIn">
  <set-property property="name" value="jdo.Accounting"/>
  <set-property property="path" value="WEB-INF/jdoAccounting.properties"/>
</plug-in>
```

Once the PlugIn has initialized one or more PersistenceManagerFactory instances, any Struts Action component associated with the ActionServlet can access them by name. Typically, these will be classes acting as controllers executing business logic. The execute() method in these classes gets the PersistenceManagerFactory by name from the servlet context, gets the PersistenceManager, performs whatever business logic is required, commits or rolls back the transaction, closes the PersistenceManager, and returns control to the Struts framework. For example, the execute( ) method might take a Movie name from the context as a movieName attribute, look up its description, and put the description into the context as a movieDescription attribute:

```java
public class LookupMovieAction extends Action {
    PersistenceManagerFactory pmf = null;
    PersistenceManager pm = null;
    public ActionForward execute(ActionMapping mapping,
        ActionForm form,
        HttpServletRequest request,
        HttpServletResponse response)
        throws Exception {
        try {
            ServletContext ctx = getServlet().getServletContext();
            pmf = (PersistenceManagerFactory)ctx.getAttribute("jdo.Movies");
            pm = pmf.getPersistenceManager();
            Query q = pm.newQuery(Movie.class, "title == param1");
            q.declareParameters ("String param1");
            String movieName = request.getParameter("movieName");
            Collection movies = (Collection)q.execute(movieName);
            Movie movie = (Movie)movies.iterator().next();
            String description = movie.getDescription();
            ctx.setAttribute("movieDescription", description);
        } catch (JDOException e) {
        } finally {
            if (pm != null) {
                pm.close();
            }
            pm = null;
        }
        return (mapping.findForward("success"));
    }
}
```

A typical cycle of Struts processing in the web server involves several interactions between the browser and the web server. In the following sequence, "ACTION" represents a Struts Action component and "JSP" represents a JSP page:

1. HTTP request arrives at server.

2. ACTION—initialize session (no JDO access).

3. JSP—display page (includes an input form).

4. HTTP response sent back to user.

5. User fills in form.

6. HTTP request arrives at server.

7. ACTION—update datastore based on the submitted form (transactional update).

8. ACTION—read datastore and set up for next page (possibly nontransactional access).

9. JSP—display page (includes another input form).

10. HTTP response sent back to user.

11. Repeat steps 5 through 10 until the logical conclusion of the interaction ("Thank you for your order") or the user goes away and the session expires.

12. User fills in form.

13. HTTP request arrives at server.

14. ACTION—update datastore based on the submitted form (transactional update).

15. JSP—display page (no input form).

16. HTTP response sent back to user.

With this pattern, each ACTION gets the configured `PersistenceManagerFactory` appropriate for the usage (transactional or nontransactional) and executes the business logic appropriate for that action.

CHAPTER 17

J2EE Application Servers

Application servers provide a reliable, scalable, and secure environment in which applications execute. In the Java context, an application server is a platform that implements the J2EE (Java 2 Enterprise Edition) contracts to support applications.

Because of security concerns, many web sites do not allow servers directly facing the Internet to handle business transactions directly. Instead, web servers delegate the more important transactions to an application server isolated from the Internet by firewalls and/or additional layers of code. This architecture minimizes the threat of attacks on the core business infrastructure.

Application servers provide functionality defined strictly by the J2EE platform, typically a superset of functionality provided by web servers. In addition to supporting applications written to the Servlet and JSP contracts, application servers support the EJB (Enterprise JavaBeans) architecture, allowing application-server components to be written as distributed objects. Trusted clients and servlets and JSP pages running in the same or different servers can access these objects directly.

An application server that implements the J2EE contracts also provides a number of services required by applications. There are many more services available, but the following are the most important from the JDO developer's viewpoint:

JDBC
> Provides access to datastores via a standard protocol.

JNDI (Java Naming and Directory Interface)
> Provides a binding between names of services and the instances that implement those services. For example, the name of a JDBC DataSource resource might be java:comp/env/jdbc/HumanResources and its implementation might be a DataSource bound to the human-resources database.

JTS (Java Transaction Service)
> Coordinates local and distributed transactions to guarantee the atomicity of transactions that span different resources and processes.

JavaMail
> Provides a programming interface to create and send email messages.

JMS (Java Message Service)
> Offers a means for applications to send and receive asynchronous messages in transactional contexts.

The EJB architecture is a component architecture for developing and deploying distributed business applications. In this chapter, we take a look at some common design patterns for implementing multitier applications. This book is not intended to be a reference for patterns, but the examples illustrate some popular access methods.

Enterprise JavaBeans Architecture

EJB components are similar to servlets/JSP pages in that remote access is built-in. You don't need to write any remote infrastructure to implement multitier architecture designs. Declaring a bean to be remote generates all of the code required to make the bean run remotely. Just as the HTTP protocol mediates remote access for web-based clients, the SOAP and/or RMI/IIOP protocols enable remote access for EJB components. Using standard remote protocols allows you to focus development on the application logic instead of protocol-handling.

But there are two significant differences between servlets/JSP pages and EJB components.

First, declarative transactions and distributed transactions are built into EJB components. As an application developer, you don't need to code transactions explicitly into your application logic. Transactions are applied to applications declaratively, not embedded into code. During application assembly, the assembler specifies the transaction attributes of each method. Assembly combines application components into larger applications and preserves transaction semantics. Distributed transactions (transactions that include multiple *resource managers*) are handled for your application as transparently as local transactions (those that involve only one resource manager).

Second, security is built into EJB components. You don't need to write security protocols or worry about credentials. Methods and resources are declared to require security checks; these are administration issues, not programming concerns. Similar to method-transaction associations, methods that require a specific security context are identified during application assembly.

The flexibility of transaction and security associations come at a cost. Each time a method is executed via the local or remote interface, the container checks the transaction and security requirements of the method against the current thread's transaction and security context.

EJB components come in four flavors:

Stateless session beans

Stateless session beans are the simplest enterprise beans. They have no fixed association with any particular client. They serve as message endpoints to service clients for execution of remote or local methods defined in an interface. The interface typically defines a service contract with clients. Each business method is self-contained and doesn't rely on the results of any previous method.

Stateful session beans

Stateful session beans are service endpoints created on behalf of specific clients for execution of remote or local methods defined in an interface. They implement conversational behavior with clients. Results of business methods can be stored in the bean for use by subsequent business methods.

Entity beans

Entity beans model a persistent entity, which might be a record or row in an enterprise information system (EIS) or relational database, or a collection of related records. Entity beans are identified by a *primary key*.

Message-driven beans

Message-driven beans serve as the endpoint for a queue or topic to a Java Message Service (JMS) or some other messaging implementation. They implement synchronous or asynchronous queued service requests.

Your applications can exploit JDO as a component for integration into EJB architecture servers in conjunction with other components. Servlets, JSP pages, session beans (both stateful and stateless), and message-driven beans can use JDO persistent classes to implement business objects, either directly as *data-access objects* (DAO) or through *business delegates*.

We start the discussion of high-level architecture by reviewing two aspects of our Media Mania application: casual browsing of the offerings in the store and business transactions, such as purchase or rental of media. The front end to both of these is the Web, but for business transactions we delegate to the EJB tier.

In Chapter 16, we discussed some techniques for accessing persistent data from JDO instances. Using a combination of servlets and JSP pages, clients can browse the offerings of the store, and the servlets/JSP pages maintain persistent information about their items while shopping. Once a collection of items has been selected for purchase or rental, we want to complete the transaction and we choose to implement the business logic using EJB components.

Stateless Session Beans

For our example, we assume that the web tier of the Media Mania store handles the interactions with the customer while he is browsing and shopping. The web tier manages the customer's name and contents of his cart. The web tier might manage the cart using persistent classes or simply maintain the cart as a session state. When the customer chooses to check out, the web tier delegates this important function to the EJB tier of the application.

For this purpose, we implement a stateless session bean, called CashierBean, with a checkout( ) business method. We use the stateless-session-bean pattern because it best models the semantics of a store cashier. During the time a customer is checking out, the cashier devotes all of her time to that customer. Once a customer walks away from the cashier, the cashier forgets all about that customer in order to help the next one. Any information needed from the transaction must be stored persistently during the interaction with the customer.

A stateless session bean is the most efficient type of bean for this purpose because there is no client state that needs to be maintained between business methods. Any currently idle bean can service any incoming request from any client. Therefore, these beans can be managed by the application server easily, based on workload. If more requests arrive for a particular type of bean than there are beans available, the server can create more quickly. Similarly, if there are too many idle beans, they can quickly be destroyed because there is no persistent state to save.

Configuring the PersistenceManagerFactory

When you develop a session bean that uses JDO, you associate each instance of the bean with an instance of the PersistenceManagerFactory that you look up when you initialize the session bean during setSessionContext( ).

The bean class contains instance variables that hold the associated PersistenceManager and PersistenceManagerFactory.

```
public class CashierBean implements javax.ejb.SessionBean {
    private javax.ejb.SessionContext context;
    private PersistenceManagerFactory pmf;
    private PersistenceManager pm;
    private static String pmfName = "java:comp/env/jdo/MediaManiaPMF";
```

When the container calls setSessionContext( ) to initialize the bean, we look up the PersistenceManagerFactory via JNDI. The name of the PersistenceManagerFactory is hardcoded into the bean, but JNDI uses an indirection to find the actual PersistenceManagerFactory. The PersistenceManagerFactory represents the same datastore for all beans sharing the same datastore resource. This allows the PersistenceManagerFactory to manage the association between the distributed transaction and the PersistenceManager:

```
public void setSessionContext(javax.ejb.SessionContext aContext) {
    context = aContext;
    try {
        Context ic = new InitialContext();
        pmf = (PersistenceManagerFactory)ic.lookup(pmfName);
```

```
        } catch (NamingException ex) {
            throw new EJBException("setSessionContext", ex);
        }
    }
```

This simple bean uses only one PersistenceManagerFactory. If your application requires more than one PersistenceManagerFactory, each of them should be looked up during setSessionContext() and saved into its own field.

During assembly of the application, the assembler defines the resource-ref element in the session element that describes the CashierBean in the *ejb-jar.xml* file. The resource-ref identifies the PersistenceManagerFactory as a resource; the res-ref-name is the JNDI name in the session bean's JNDI context:

```
<resource-ref>
  <res-ref-name>jdo/MediaManiaPMF</res-ref-name>
  <res-type>javax.jdo.PersistenceManagerFactory</res-type>
  <res-auth>Container</res-auth>
</resource-ref>
```

During deployment of the bean, the deployer associates the res-ref-name given in the deployment descriptor with the actual PersistenceManagerFactory constructed by a server implementation–specific process. The association is indirect; the name coded into the application is in the session bean's JNDI context and is mapped to the actual resource name. This allows different applications to use the same name to refer to different resources or to use different names to refer to the same resource.

The server-resource configuration process, while not standard, typically requires the deployer to write a server-resource definition file containing the PersistenceManagerFactory class name, properties, and JNDI lookup name. For example:

```
<persistence-manager-factory-resource>
  <jndi-name>jdo/MediaManiaPMF</jndi-name>
  <factory-class-name>com.sun.jdori.FOStorePMF</factory-class-name>
  <property key="ConnectionURL" value="fostore://mmserv/MediaManiaDB"/>
  <property key="ConnectionUserName" value="fortune"/>
  <property key="ConnectionPassword" value="silence"/>
</persistence-manager-factory-resource>
```

The server typically implements the resource configuration at server initialization by getting the factory class name as a String and obtaining a corresponding class instance using Class.forName(). The server turns each property's name in the property list into a method name by using the JavaBeans pattern of capitalizing the first character of the property name and prepending set to the name. Then, the server looks up the method using Class.getMethod() and invokes the method with the property value as a parameter. After the server sets all properties, it binds the configured object to the name specified in the jndi-name element. This binding allows the bean's Context.lookup() method in setSessionContext() to find the resource during server operation.

We continue the implementation of our bean with the business method. The signature of the checkout( ) method is complex, but it illustrates a best practice for remote methods. Instead of decomposing the checkout process into several methods, the single checkout( ) method takes as parameters all the information needed to perform the operation. The benefit of this decomposition is that the transaction and security checks occur only once per checkout, regardless of the number of items checked out.

The only initialization we assume in Example 17-1 is that the pmf field has the appropriate PersistenceManagerFactory for this application.

Example 17-1. The CashierBean checkout method

```
public void checkout(
    java.lang.String lastName,
    java.lang.String firstName,
    java.util.Collection rentals,
    java.util.Collection purchases)
    throws java.rmi.RemoteException {
    PersistenceManager pm = pmf.getPersistenceManager( );
    Customer customer = StoreQueries.getCustomer(pm, firstName, lastName);
    Iterator it = rentals.iterator( );
    while (it.hasNext()) {
        RentalValueObject rvo = (RentalValueObject)it.next( );
        RentalItem ri = StoreQueries.getRentalItem
            (pm, rvo.serialNumber);
        Rental rental = new Rental(customer, new Date( ), ri);
        customer.addTransaction(rental);
        customer.addRental(rental);
    }
    it = purchases.iterator( );
    while (it.hasNext()) {
        PurchaseValueObject pvo = (PurchaseValueObject)it.next( );
        MediaItem mediaItem = StoreQueries.getMediaItem(
            pm, pvo.title, pvo.format);
        Purchase purchase = new Purchase(customer, new Date( ), mediaItem);
        customer.addTransaction(purchase);
    }
    pm.close( );
}
```

We use static methods defined in StoreQueries to find the Customer by first and last name (line ❷), find a RentalItem by serial number (line ❸), and find a MediaItem by title and format (line ❹). This static-method pattern allows us to keep the application classes free of any references to the JDO interfaces. Of course, when you design your persistent classes, you may find it useful to put these finder methods directly into the persistent classes.

In the checkout( ) method, the customer is identified uniquely by first name and last name, and the rentals and purchases are represented by collections of value objects.

A *value object* is a design pattern for representing complex data that can be serialized and sent by value from one process to another. In our case, the value objects are used only to hold data values; all the information needed to identify a specific rental or purchase item is contained in the corresponding value object. Since the data elements need no abstraction, the value-object classes are implemented to have no behavior and all their fields are public. The compiler generates a public no-arg constructor for each class:

```
public class MediaValueObject
        implements java.io.Serializable {
    public String title;
}
public class RentalValueObject extends MediaValueObject {
    public String serialNumber;
}
public class PurchaseValueObject extends MediaValueObject {
    public String format;
}
```

The strings and value objects in the parameter list of the checkout( ) method can be serialized and sent by value using any of a number of protocols, including SOAP, RMI, and IIOP. The details of which protocol is used are not important to the implementation of the business logic.

Stateless Session Beans with Container-Managed Transactions

In the checkout( ) method, we update the datastore and insert new instances. Therefore, we need to have an active JDO transaction. The simplest implementation technique is to use *container-managed transactions*, in which the container manages the transactions for us. In order for the container to begin a new transaction for the business method automatically, the deployer must declare in the deployment descriptor that the business method requires transactions. This descriptor specifies that checkout( ) requires an active transaction, and the container will start a transaction if one is not already active. The container-transaction element is contained in the assembly-descriptor element of the ejb-jar element in the *ejb-jar.xml* file:

```
<container-transaction>
    <method>
        <ejb-name>CashierBean</ejb-name>
        <method-name>checkout</method-name>
    </method>
    <trans-attribute>Required</trans-attribute>
</container-transaction>
```

Because we marked the checkout( ) method in the deployment descriptor of the CashierBean with trans-attribute given the value Required, the checkout( ) method has transactional behavior. Before the container calls the method, it automatically obtains a UserTransaction and begins a transaction if one is not already in progress. This gives maximum flexibility for the reuse of components. If a new component is implemented with a method defined as requiring transactions, the new method can call the checkout( ) method and the container will simply verify that there is already a transaction in progress.

When the checkout( ) method calls getPersistenceManager( ) on the Persistence-ManagerFactory (on line ❶ of Example 17-1), the JDO implementation determines the UserTransaction associated with the thread of control of the caller and checks if there is an active transaction. If there is already a PersistenceManager associated with an active UserTransaction, the JDO implementation returns it. If not, the JDO implementation constructs a new PersistenceManager, associates it with the active UserTransaction, and begins the JDO Transaction in which we perform all of the queries and updates.

When we close the PersistenceManager (on line ❺ of Example 17-1), all of the changed and new instances remain in the PersistenceManager cache. The PersistenceManager will remain active until the container completes the transaction. In this case, the container completes the transaction as soon as the checkout( ) method returns. Since we are using container-managed transactions, we never use the JDO Transaction methods.

Now, we fill in the required methods according to the EJB specification for stateless session beans. The ejbActivate( ) and ejbPassivate( ) methods are used for stateful session beans, and the ejbCreate( ) and ejbRemove( ) methods are empty since there is no special behavior required when creating or removing our stateless session bean:

```
public void ejbActivate( ) {
}
public void ejbPassivate( ) {
}
public void ejbRemove( ) {
}
public void ejbCreate( ) {
}
```

Now that we have seen how to implement a simple session bean using JDO, we will describe the lifecycle and special requirements for all kinds of session beans. Figure 17-1 shows the lifecycle for stateless session beans.

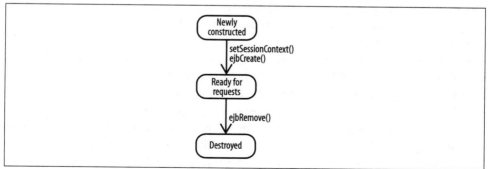

Figure 17-1. Stateless session bean lifecycle

The fields of a JDO session bean of any type include:

- A reference to the `PersistenceManagerFactory`, which is initialized by the `setSessionContext()` method. This method looks up the `Persistence-ManagerFactory` by JNDI access to the object identified in the deployment descriptor.

- A reference to the `PersistenceManager`, which is acquired by each business method and closed at the end of the business method.

- A reference to the `SessionContext`, which is initialized by the method `setSessionContext()`.

Stateful Session Beans with Container-Managed Transactions

Stateful session beans are service objects that are created for a particular user, and they may have a state associated with that user between business methods. A business-method invocation on a reference to a stateful session bean is dispatched to the specific instance created by the user.

The timeworn example of a stateful session bean is the online shopping cart; the cart that keeps track of all the items purchased at an online purveyor contains all the information needed when you go to check out. Every item you have picked from the shelves and all the special discounts you've chosen are put into the cart. No matter when you stop shopping or when you return, your cart still contains the items that you put into it.

But the burden of managing the cart belongs to the server. And, since stateful session beans are created for a specific user, the beans' state takes up precious memory space. If the cart's owner doesn't use the cart for an extended period of time, the server has to deal with storing the contents persistently.

There are a number of other implications that you should consider before using stateful session beans:

- The create method for the stateful session bean can take parameters specific to the intended use, so you can create beans with different behavior based on create parameters. A stateless session bean has only one create method, and therefore only one type of bean may be created.

- The bean is dedicated to the particular user and is therefore bound to a specific server process. Load-balancing techniques, if implemented by the server at all, are complicated and may require special deployment descriptors.

- If the server needs to manage memory usage in the JVM, it can passivate the bean, but only after a potentially expensive serialization process to persistent storage (usually a file in a local directory). Management of this memory and persistent storage can be a significant resource drain on the server. Because memory and persistent storage are scarce resources, the lifecycle allows the server to destroy a bean that has not been used for some amount of time, called the *timeout period*. After the timeout period expires, your bean might be destroyed without notice.

- Implementing the ejbActivate( ) and ejbPassivate( ) methods is your responsibility as the bean developer. Any state that can't simply be serialized must be saved at ejbPassivate( ) and restored at ejbActivate( ). Although ejbPassivate( ) will not be called while a transaction is active, the bean might time out, and your implementation must take this into account.

- You can't preserve a JDO state using serialization, as JDO implementations don't support serialization for JDO-implementation artifacts such as those that implement PersistenceManager and Transaction. This means that your bean can save only the object identities of persistent instances, not object references, and your bean then has to restore them using getObjectById( ) in business methods.

Otherwise, the behavior of stateful session beans using container-managed transactions is the same as for stateless session beans. In particular, all business methods in the bean interface acquire a PersistenceManager at the beginning of the method and close it at the end of the method.

Figure 17-2 shows the lifecycle of a stateful session bean.

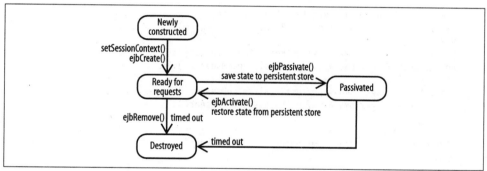

Figure 17-2. The lifecycle of a stateful session bean

Bean-Managed Transactions

Bean-managed transactions offer the stateless session bean developer additional flexibility, but at the cost of additional complexity.

There are two alternate techniques for demarcating transaction boundaries in your bean code: use the server's javax.transaction.UserTransaction or use the PersistenceManager's javax.jdo.Transaction. If you use UserTransaction, you can begin and complete distributed transactions managed by the server's TransactionManager. If you use JDO's Transaction, you begin and complete local transactions that are managed completely by the JDO implementation, without any help (or interference) from the container.

javax.transaction.UserTransaction

To use `UserTransaction`, you obtain it via `getUserTransaction()` from the `SessionContext` instance, begin the transaction, and then obtain the `PersistenceManager` from the `PersistenceManagerFactory`. During `getPersistenceManager()`, the `PersistenceManagerFactory` will automatically associate the `PersistenceManager` with the active `UserTransaction`.

When your bean invokes methods of beans that use container-managed transactions, the container automatically associates transactional resources used by the other beans in the current `UserTransaction`. The transactional resources can be JDO `PersistenceManagers`, `JDBC` `Connections`, or connector resources.

If you require nontransactional access to JDO, you must obtain the `PersistenceManager` when the `UserTransaction` is not active. After beginning a `UserTransaction`, if your application needs a `PersistenceManager` for transactional access, a different `PersistenceManager` must be obtained for this purpose. Your application must keep track of which `PersistenceManager` is being used for which purpose. Once you complete the `UserTransaction` by calling `commit()` or `rollback()`, the `PersistenceManager` associated with that transaction can no longer be used.

Consider the following code fragment, in which `ctx` is the `SessionContext` instance:

```
UserTransaction utx = ctx.getUserTransaction();
PersistenceManager pm1 = pmf.getPersistenceManager();
utx.begin();
PersistenceManager pm2 = pmf.getPersistenceManager();
PersistenceManager pm3 = pmf.getPersistenceManager();
utx.commit();
PersistenceManager pm4 = pmf.getPersistenceManager();
PersistenceManager pm5 = pmf.getPersistenceManager();
utx.begin();
PersistenceManager pm6 = pmf.getPersistenceManager();
PersistenceManager pm7 = pmf.getPersistenceManager();
utx.commit();
```

In this example, `pm1`, `pm4`, and `pm5` are references to unique instances of `PersistenceManager`, and transaction completion is managed independently by each of the associated `Transaction` instances. `pm2` and `pm3` are references to the same instance, and transaction completion is controlled by the `utx` instance. `pm6` and `pm7` are references to the same instance, and transaction completion is controlled by the `utx` instance.

javax.jdo.Transaction

As the bean developer, if you choose to use the same `PersistenceManager` for multiple serial transactions, you must demarcate transaction boundaries by using the `javax.jdo.Transaction` instance associated with the `PersistenceManager`. Obtaining a `PersistenceManager` without having an active `UserTransaction` results in your being able to manage transaction boundaries via begin( ), commit( ), and rollback( ) of javax.jdo.Transaction. In this mode, the JDO implementation does not access UserTransaction.

Your bean can invoke methods of beans that use container-managed transactions, but since the container doesn't know about JDO transactions, it cannot automatically associate transactional resources used by the other beans in the transaction.

Stateless Session Beans with Bean-Managed Transactions

You establish transaction boundaries using one of the techniques detailed in the previous section, but the bean's state (including the PersistenceManager) cannot be retained across business-method boundaries. Therefore, each business method must obtain a PersistenceManager and close it before it returns.

Stateful Session Beans with Bean-Managed Transactions

The major difference between stateful and stateless session beans with bean-managed transactions is that with stateful session beans you can save states between method invocations, including PersistenceManager, and you can even keep transactions active. However, we recommend that you do not keep transactions open between business methods.

If you use UserTransaction, the server knows that the transaction is open at the end of the business method and it will leave the bean in a state that cannot be passivated. Since the bean can't be passivated, it will continue to tie up server resources until the timeout period elapses. If the server does time out the bean, the server automatically rolls back the transaction and you lose everything in the current transaction.

If you use JDO Transaction instead, the server might not even be aware of your transaction and might passivate the bean. In this case, you have to close the PersistenceManager in ejbPassivate( ), since the PersistenceManager cannot be serialized. Again, you lose the current transaction.

Message-Driven Beans

Message-driven beans are quite similar to stateless session beans. Both are stateless, and with each method call, the container establishes a transaction context based on the deployment-descriptor transaction attribute for the message-listener methods.

Message-driven beans implement the MessageDrivenBean interface for lifecycle callbacks and a message-listener interface for business methods that is specific to the type of message provider with which the bean is used. Message-driven beans used with the JMS MessageListener interface have only one business method, onMessage( ), that takes one parameter: an instance of javax.jms.Message. Those that are used with another message provider must implement all of the methods of the corresponding message-listener interface. The interaction with JDO is the same in all cases.

The lifecycle of a message-driven bean (shown in Figure 17-3) is as simple as a stateless session bean. To use JDO with message-driven beans, your application uses the `setMessageDrivenContext()` method to save the context and look up and save the `PersistenceManagerFactory`.

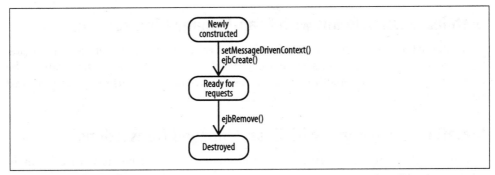

Figure 17-3. The lifecycle of a message-driven bean

To process the message-listener method, your application code obtains a `PersistenceManager` from the `PersistenceManagerFactory` and handles the message, performing JDO accesses as required. At the end of the business method, you close the `PersistenceManager`.

Persistent Entities and JDO

In the J2EE environment, you have a choice of using native file I/O, serialization, JDBC, entity beans, session beans, or JDO persistent classes as the implementation strategy for persistence of your application object model (persistent entities). In many cases, you can use more than one strategy in the same application.

File I/O and serialization based on files are not robust or scalable enough for application-server use beyond trivial storage of a simple class state, and we will not describe these options further. The choice between the other strategies depends on your requirements for the persistence abstraction.

Local Persistent Storage

Using JDBC or JDO directly allows your application to store entities using a local-persistence interface with minimum security and transaction-association options. That is, the security context of the caller of each business method governs access to the resources, and the transaction context of the caller is the transaction context of all the calls made to the local-persistence interface. In our example implementation of CashierBean, the transaction and security checks are performed only when the container receives an invocation on checkout( ) and calls your application code.

The local-persistence alternatives do not allow transparent execution of the implementation methods in different tiers of the architecture. All calls are local and use resource managers in the same JVM as the caller.

JDO

We have already seen how using JDO as your implementation strategy allows you to use your application-domain object model directly, including features such as inheritance, polymorphic relationships, dynamic queries, and modeling List and Map types. And we have already discussed in detail the requirements of the EJB components that use JDO directly to implement business methods.

JDBC

JDBC gives you the most flexibility to customize database access and the most work to do. With JDBC, you implement every JDBC call to create, read, update, and delete instances in the datastore. Thus, you can handcraft the model and the datastore accesses to use all features of the datastore, including generation of primary keys, extensions to SQL, datastore-specific types, and stored procedures.

But this flexibility comes at a significant cost. Much of the code you write is repetitive and error-prone. The server cannot help you by caching data, because it doesn't know the data-access patterns of your application.

You might reasonably choose to use JDBC in some specific part of your application that has requirements that are not satisfied by other alternatives. For example, JDO doesn't provide for UNION or GROUP BY functions available in SQL. You can implement queries that need these features by coding the queries in SQL and using JDBC as the connection vehicle to the database.

To implement our CashierBean using JDBC, the first task is to understand the entity-relationship model implemented in the relational database. The most interesting part of the model involves the relationships between the Customer, MediaContent, Movie, Game, RentalItem, Transaction, Rental, and Purchase entities. Since JDBC does not support inheritance, in order for your application to access any of the classes modeled as subclasses, you need to code the appropriate joins into the SQL code used for the queries, deletes, updates, and inserts.

An equally important part of the modeling task involves defining the type mapping between the SQL types and the Java types. Most primitive types are easy to map, but others are deceptively difficult. Strings might have as many as four natural mappings in a vendor's implementation of SQL, depending on the access patterns and the maximum length of the string. For example, CHAR, VARCHAR, VARCHAR2, or CLOB might be the best column-type representation for a string.

Another task is to map the database accesses into native SQL. The number of SQL statements that you need to code can be estimated by multiplying the number of persistent classes by four or more, and adding the number of business queries. Typically, you need at least four SQL statements per class:

1. SELECT columns for specific rows from the table.
2. INSERT a row into the table. For subclasses, this might be multiple INSERT statements, depending on how the inheritance is modeled.
3. DELETE a row from the table.
4. UPDATE some columns in certain rows.

Without going into much more detail, creating the SQL statements and corresponding result analysis for each class in your application domain is repetitive and error-prone. Many application programmers faced with a reasonably complex domain model try to write a tool to help with this part of the programming. Unfortunately, the result of the tool typically must be adjusted and optimized by hand, and the resulting production classes are not easily reused in different applications.

Remote Persistent Storage

Your domain-model entities may have requirements that cannot be satisfied by direct access to local persistent classes or JDBC. These requirements include:

Location independence
> The location of the datastore might be different from the location of the calling business method. This might be a factor in the scalability of the system, since adding new server resources might require splitting the access of some datastores across servers. Defining access to certain entities as possibly remote gives more flexibility in the system design.

Transaction association per method
> When defining the domain model, you might want to define different transaction contexts for different methods of persistent classes.

Security association per method
> When defining the domain model, you might have different security requirements for different methods of persistent classes.

Entity beans

Entity beans are used for modeling large-scale persistent instances that have a natural (intrinsic) identity and are accessed via business methods. Entity beans have a lifecycle mandated by the EJB specification. The lifecycle governs whether the bean has a persistent state associated with it and whether the state might need to be synchronized with the datastore.

Entity beans use a pattern in which information from persistent storage is accessed from the datastore, cached in the bean, and stored back in the datastore under the direction of the container. The cached data is identified by a key, and the key can be used to access the bean from local or remote clients.

In terms of complexity, entity beans present a more difficult challenge to the container than stateless session beans do, but less difficult than with stateful session beans. Entity beans have a state that has to be managed, but since the state is not associated with a specific user, the container can use pooling techniques to maximize reuse of the beans for different transactions. Because of the difficulty of managing the state efficiently, most container implementations offer a range of tuning options for entity beans far beyond the options available for session beans.

Implementing the lifecycle of a bean-managed persistence (BMP) entity bean is a complex task for the bean developer. For each required method, you need to know whether there is an identity (primary key) associated with the bean, whether there is already a resource manager associated with the bean, and how to represent relationships to other entity beans. Even though the lifecycle of the bean is defined elaborately in the EJB specification, container vendors have chosen quite different strategies to optimize performance, and some of the lifecycle events are implemented differently by different containers. These differences are important if you want to optimize the performance of your bean.

For example, the lifecycle defines ejbLoad() to indicate that the state of the bean should be loaded from persistent storage. And ejbStore() indicates that the state of the bean should be stored into persistent storage. But there is no lifecycle method to indicate that the transaction context of the bean is changing. And the container does not indicate whether the bean's state has changed, and therefore whether the state really needs to be stored.

Additionally, the container doesn't indicate to the bean developer why ejbStore() is called. It might be to flush the cache so that query results are consistent, or it might be the last flush before transaction end. The absence of information makes it impossible for the bean developer to implement load/store optimizations.

Another example is the definition of the bean context for finder methods. In the bean's implementation of ejbFindByPrimaryKey(), the bean contract requires that the developer establish whether or not the bean exists in the database, which requires a database query to execute successfully. An implementation might want to retrieve other information (e.g., state) from the database as long as a query is required. However, there is no way in the defined lifecycle to cache the information retrieved by the existence query. Therefore, it is difficult to eliminate the extra query.

Once you understand the strategy of entity-bean development, the complexity of the code is somewhat predictable and therefore lends itself to code generation. This is why we recommend that if you choose to use entity beans to implement your persistent object model, you should use container-managed persistence (CMP) entity beans instead of writing your own BMP entity beans.

When using CMP beans, you need to implement more methods and deployment descriptors than you need with session beans, but fewer compared to BMP beans. And while CMP beans offer significant portability of the code and deployment descriptors you write, there is no standard to describe the mapping between CMP beans and the corresponding datastore persistent-data description.

To implement our CashierBean using CMP beans as delegates, the first task is to understand the entity-relationship model implemented in the relational database. As with JDBC, the most interesting part of the model involves the relationships between the Customer, MediaContent, Movie, Game, RentalItem, Transaction, Rental, and Purchase entities. Since CMP beans do not directly support the polymorphic relationships inherent in this object model, you need to change the object model to remove these relationships.

CMP beans provide for type mapping, so you don't need to hand-code the transformations as you do in JDBC. The container provides mapping tools that allow you to declare the association between cmp-fields and database columns. The container handles the type conversions for you.

When using CMP beans with session beans, the application-assembly and deployment processes become more complex. For each CMP bean used by the session bean, the deployment descriptor must identify the bean's home and local and/or remote interfaces. The initialization of the session bean itself in the setSessionContext( ) method must look up and save references to the home interfaces for all beans that need to be accessed by finder methods.

Session beans as façades

When you have a requirement that cannot be implemented by a local persistent class directly, often you can model an entity bean's semantics by a stateless session bean façade that itself delegates to a JDO business delegate or data access object. In this model, each business method in the remote interface identifies not only the operation to be performed, but also the identity of the object upon which to perform it.

Using this pattern provides all the benefits of EJB components, with a small amount of extra work (compared to using JDO directly). You can use this pattern to implement inheritance that maps directly to JDO inheritance and polymorphism.

To use this pattern, analyze each method in the JDO persistent class and decide the category to which it belongs:

Private methods

These should not be exposed to outside callers, as they might cause inconsistent state changes if not performed as part of a larger operation. For example, city, state, and ZIP code should be updated together in the same business method, although the individual set methods can be implemented as private methods. The method that updates all three fields can be exposed as a local or remote instance method.

Local instance methods

These change the state of the instance in some trivial way or retrieve some trivial information. For example, getName( ) and setName( ) should be exposed only as local instance methods.

Remote instance methods

These change the state of the instance in a large-scale way or retrieve a substantial amount of information from the instance. You should use value objects as parameters to these methods.

Local static methods

These usually are defined in the persistent class as static and operate on a number of instances, instead of just one. For example, query methods that find one or more instances and return them to the caller operate on the extent of instances in the datastore. Other methods might take a collection of instances as a parameter and perform a similar operation on each of them.

Remote static methods

These have characteristics similar to local static methods. They include methods that operate on multiple instances, but they exclude methods that simply find instances.

Define the remote interface to the session bean façade, if needed, to include all remote instance methods and remote static methods of the persistent class. Declare each method to throw a RemoteException. Modify each instance method to add an extra parameter that is the JDO identity instance of the instance to which it applies.

Define the local interface to the session bean, if needed, to include all local instance methods and local static methods of the persistent class. Modify each instance method to add an extra parameter that is the JDO indentity instance of the instance to which it applies.

Implement each session-bean method that models a persistent-class instance method to obtain the PersistenceManager, obtain the persistent instance via a call to getObjectById( ), and delegate to the persistent-class instance method. Wrap the entire method in a try-catch block. For remote methods, if an exception is caught, throw a RemoteException with the caught exception as a nested exception.

Implement each session-bean method that models a persistent-class static method to obtain the PersistenceManager and delegate to the persistent class method. Wrap the entire method in a try-catch block. For remote methods, if an exception is caught, throw a RemoteException with the caught exception's toString( ) as part of the message text.

Modify methods that return references to persistent instances to return String instead, and in the session-bean method body, translate the return instance by calling getObjectId( ).toString( ). Similarly, modify methods that take persistent instances as parameters to take String instead, and look up the persistent instance in the method body by calling newObjectIdInstance( ) and getObjectById( ).

JDO or CMP?

Both CMP beans and JDO persistent classes have features that you should consider before committing your project to use either strategy.

JDO persistent classes are suitable for modeling both coarse-grained and fine-grained persistent instances and in an application server are typically used behind session beans. CMP beans are typically used behind session beans; their remote behavior is seldom exploited.

JDO persistent classes can be used without recompilation in any tier of a distributed architecture and can be debugged in a one- or two-tier environment prior to integration into a web or application server. CMP beans can be debugged only after deployment into the application server.

Unlike servlets, JSP pages, and EJB components, there is no built-in remote behavior with JDO classes. All of the distributed, transaction, and security policies are based on the single persistence manager that manages all of the persistent instances of your model. This means that JDO persistent classes can be used in any tier of a distributed application and remote behavior is implemented by the container, not the JDO implementation.

CMP beans give you a high degree of portability across application servers. The bean class and required deployment descriptor are standard. Most of the incompatibilities between implementations are found in unspecified areas of mapping beans to the underlying datastore, optional features such as read-only beans, and extensions in deployment and management of beans. JDO implementations vary with regard to the optional features that they support.

With CMP, you identify every bean class, persistent field, and persistent relationship in the deployment descriptor. Using JDO, you identify every persistent class in the metadata, but you can usually take the default for the persistence of fields, including relationships.

With CMP, relationships are managed; this means that during the transaction a change to one side of the relationship immediately affects the other side, and the change is visible to the application. JDO does not support managed relationships, although some vendors offer them as optional features.

Inheritance is a common paradigm for modeling real-world data, but CMP beans do not support inheritance. CMP makes a distinction between the implementation class and the bean. The abstract bean-implementation classes and the local and remote interfaces can form inheritance relationships, but the CMP beans that model the application's persistent classes cannot. Relationships in CMP are between CMP beans, not implementation classes, and these relationships cannot be polymorphic. In our example, it would be impossible for a MediaItem CMP bean to have a relationship with a MediaContent CMP bean, because MediaContent has no instances. In order to implement this kind of model, you would need to change the MediaItem CMP bean to have two different relationships: one between MediaItem and Movie, and another between MediaItem and Game. You would need to treat the relationships separately in every aspect of the bean.

The programming model used to access fields is very different between CMP beans and JDO. With CMP beans, all persistent fields and relationships are defined by abstract get and set methods in the abstract bean class, plus a declaration in the deployment descriptor. Access to the field value is the responsibility of the concrete implementation class generated by the CMP code-generation tool. With JDO, persistent fields and relationships are declared or defaulted in the metadata, and access to the field values is provided by the code in the class for transient instances or by the JDO implementation for persistent instances. The JDO enhancer generates the appropriate field-access code during the enhancement process.

JDOQL and EJBQL provide similar access to data in the datastore. Both allow you to select persistent instances from the datastore to use in your programs. Both use the read-modify-write pattern for updating persistent data. Neither language is a complete data-manipulation language; both are used only to select instances for manipulation by the programming language.

CMP beans require active transactions for all business methods. Nontransactional access is not standard or portable. JDO allows you to choose whether transactions are required. JDO requires inserts, deletes, and updates to be performed within transactions, but read-only applications, including caching, can be implemented portably without transactions.

Table 17-1 is a summary comparing CMP beans with JDO persistent classes.

Table 17-1. Comparison of CMP beans and JDO

Characteristic	CMP beans	JDO persistent classes
Environmental		
Portability of applications	Few portability unknowns	Documented portability rules
Operating environment	Application server	One-tier, two-tier, web server, application server
Independence of persistent classes from environment	Low: beans must implement EJB interfaces and execute in server container	High: persistent classes are usable with no special interface requirements and execute in many environments
Metadata		
Mark persistent classes	Deployment descriptor identifies all persistent classes	Metadata identifies all persistent classes
Mark persistent fields	Deployment descriptor identifies all persistent fields and relationships	Metadata defaults persistent fields and relationships

Table 17-1. Comparison of CMP beans and JDO (continued)

Characteristic	CMP beans	JDO persistent classes
Modeling		
Domain-class modeling object	CMP bean (abstract schema)	Persistent class
Inheritance of domain-class modeling objects	Not supported	Fully supported
Field access	Abstract get/set methods	Any valid field access, including get/set methods
`Collection, Set`	Supported	Supported
`List, Array, Map`	Not supported	Optional features
Relationships	Expressed as references to CMP local interfaces	Expressed as references to JDO persistent classes or interfaces
Polymorphic references	Not supported	Supported
Programming		
Query language	EJBQL modeled after SQL	JDOQL modeled after Java Boolean expressions
Remote method invocation	Supported	Not supported
Required lifecycle methods	`setEntityContext,` `unsetEntityContext,` `ejbActivate, ejbPassivate,` `ejbLoad, ejbStore, ejbRemove`	no-arg constructor (may be private)
Optional lifecycle callback methods	`ejbCreate, ejbPostCreate,` `ejbFind`	`jdoPostLoad, jdoPreStore,` `jdoPreClear, jdoPreDelete`
Mapping to relational datastores	Vendor-specific	Vendor-specific
Method security policy	Supported	Not supported
Method transaction policy	Supported	Not supported
Nontransactional access	Not standard	Supported
Required classes/interfaces	`EJBLocalHome`, local interface (if local interface supported); `EJBHome`, remote interface (if remote interface supported); Abstract beans must implement `EJBEntityBean`; Identity class (if nonprimitive identity)	Persistent class; `objectid` class (only for application identity)
Transaction synchronization callbacks	Not supported	Supported

Lifecycle States and Transitions

Table A-1 specifies the values returned by the JDOHelper lifecycle state interrogation methods for all the JDO lifecycle states.

Table A-1. Lifecycle-state interrogation methods

State of instance	isPersistent()	isTransactional()	isDirty()	isNew()	isDeleted()
Transient	false	false	false	false	false
Transient-clean	false	true	false	false	false
Transient-dirty	false	true	true	false	false
Hollow	true	false	false	false	false
Persistent-nontransactional	true	false	false	false	false
Persistent-new	true	true	true	true	false
Persistent-clean	true	true	false	false	false
Persistent-dirty	true	true	true	false	false
Persistent-deleted	true	true	true	false	true
Persistent-new-deleted	true	true	true	true	true

Table A-2 contains the state transitions for every lifecycle state.

Table A-2. Lifecycle-state transitions

Method	Current state				
	Transient	P-new	P-clean	P-dirty	Hollow
makePersistent	P-new	unchanged	unchanged	unchanged	unchanged
deletePersistent	error	P-new-del	P-del	P-del	P-del
makeTransactional	T-clean	unchanged	unchanged	unchanged	P-clean
makeNontransactional	error	error	P-nontrans	error	unchanged
makeTransient	unchanged	error	Transient	error	Transient
commit with RetainValues = false	unchanged	Hollow	Hollow	Hollow	unchanged
commit with RetainValues = true	unchanged	P-nontrans	P-nontrans	P-nontrans	unchanged
rollback with RestoreValues = false	unchanged	Transient	Hollow	Hollow	unchanged
rollback with RestoreValues = true	unchanged	Transient	P-nontrans	P-nontrans	unchanged
refresh with active datastore transaction	unchanged	unchanged	unchanged	P-clean	unchanged
refresh with active optimistic transaction	unchanged	unchanged	unchanged	P-nontrans	unchanged
evict	n/a	unchanged	Hollow	unchanged	unchanged
read field outside of a transaction	unchanged	impossible	impossible	impossible	P-nontrans
read field with active optimistic transaction	unchanged	unchanged	unchanged	unchanged	P-nontrans
read field with active datastore transaction	unchanged	unchanged	unchanged	unchanged	P-clean
write field or makeDirty outside of a transaction	unchanged	impossible	impossible	impossible	P-nontrans
write field or makeDirty with active transaction	unchanged	unchanged	P-dirty	unchanged	P-dirty
retrieve outside of a transaction or with active optimistic transaction	unchanged	unchanged	unchanged	unchanged	P-nontrans
retrieve with active datastore transaction	unchanged	unchanged	unchanged	unchanged	P-clean

error: a JDOUserException is thrown; the state does not change

| Current state | | | | | |
T-clean	T-dirty	P-new-del	P-del	P-nontrans	Method
P-new	P-new	unchanged	unchanged	unchanged	**makePersistent**
error	error	unchanged	unchanged	P-del	**deletePersistent**
unchanged	unchanged	unchanged	unchanged	P-clean	**makeTransactional**
Transient	error	error	error	unchanged	**makeNontransactional**
unchanged	unchanged	error	error	Transient	**makeTransient**
unchanged	T-clean	Transient	Transient	unchanged	**commit with RetainValues = false**
unchanged	T-clean	Transient	Transient	unchanged	**commit with RetainValues = true**
unchanged	T-clean	Transient	Hollow	unchanged	**rollback with RestoreValues = false**
unchanged	T-clean	Transient	P-nontrans	unchanged	**rollback with RestoreValues = true**
unchanged	unchanged	unchanged	unchanged	unchanged	**refresh with active datastore transaction**
unchanged	unchanged	unchanged	unchanged	unchanged	**refresh with active optimistic transaction**
unchanged	unchanged	unchanged	unchanged	Hollow	**evict**
unchanged	impossible	impossible	impossible	unchanged	**read field outside of a transaction**
unchanged	unchanged	error	error	unchanged	**read field with active optimistic transaction**
unchanged	unchanged	error	error	P-clean	**read field with active datastore transaction**
unchanged	impossible	impossible	impossible	unchanged	**write field or makeDirty outside of a transaction**
T-dirty	unchanged	error	error	P-dirty	**write field or makeDirty with active transaction**
unchanged	unchanged	unchanged	unchanged	unchanged	**retrieve outside of a transaction or with active optimistic transaction**
unchanged	unchanged	unchanged	unchanged	P-clean	**retrieve with an active datastore transaction**

unchanged: no state change takes place; no exception is thrown due to the state change

JDO Metadata DTD

The following XML DTD describes the form of JDO metadata.

```
<?xml version="1.0" encoding="UTF-8"?>
<!--
Copyright (c) 2002 Sun Microsystems, Inc.,
901 San Antonio Road,
Palo Alto, California 94303, U.S.A.
All rights reserved.

This is the DTD defining the Java Data Objects 1.0 metadata.
-->

<!NOTATION JDO.1_0 PUBLIC
          "-//Sun Microsystems, Inc.//DTD Java Data Objects Metadata 1.0//EN">
<!--
This is the XML DTD for the JDO 1.0 Metadata.
All JDO 1.0 metadata descriptors must include a DOCTYPE of the following form:
  <!DOCTYPE jdo
    PUBLIC "-//Sun Microsystems, Inc.//DTD Java Data Objects Metadata 1.0//EN"
    "http://java.sun.com/dtd/jdo_1_0.dtd">
-->


<!ELEMENT jdo ((package)+, (extension)*)>

<!ELEMENT package ((class)+, (extension)*)>
<!ATTLIST package name CDATA #REQUIRED>

<!ELEMENT class (field|extension)*>
<!ATTLIST class name CDATA #REQUIRED>
<!ATTLIST class identity-type (application|datastore|nondurable) #IMPLIED>
<!ATTLIST class objectid-class CDATA #IMPLIED>
<!ATTLIST class requires-extent (true|false) 'true'>
<!ATTLIST class persistence-capable-superclass CDATA #IMPLIED>
```

```
<!ELEMENT field ((collection|map|array)?, (extension)*)?>
<!ATTLIST field name CDATA #REQUIRED>
<!ATTLIST field persistence-modifier (persistent|transactional|none) #IMPLIED>
<!ATTLIST field primary-key (true|false) 'false'>
<!ATTLIST field null-value (exception|default|none) 'none'>
<!ATTLIST field default-fetch-group (true|false) #IMPLIED>
<!ATTLIST field embedded (true|false) #IMPLIED>

<!ELEMENT collection (extension)*>
<!ATTLIST collection element-type CDATA #IMPLIED>
<!ATTLIST collection embedded-element (true|false) #IMPLIED>

<!ELEMENT map (extension)*>
<!ATTLIST map key-type CDATA #IMPLIED>
<!ATTLIST map embedded-key (true|false) #IMPLIED>
<!ATTLIST map value-type CDATA #IMPLIED>
<!ATTLIST map embedded-value (true|false) #IMPLIED>

<!ELEMENT array (extension)*>
<!ATTLIST array embedded-element (true|false) #IMPLIED>

<!ELEMENT extension (extension)*>
<!ATTLIST extension vendor-name CDATA #REQUIRED>
<!ATTLIST extension key CDATA #IMPLIED>
<!ATTLIST extension value CDATA #IMPLIED>
```

JDO Interfaces and Exception Classes

This appendix describes the interfaces and exception classes defined in the `javax.jdo` package. The name, parameters, and return type of each method is provided here and its description can be found in one or more chapters of this book. The index contains an entry for each method so you can locate relevant content.

Interfaces

An application uses the following Java interfaces and `JDOHelper` class in a JDO environment.

Extent

An Extent is used to access all of the instances of a particular class and, optionally, its subclasses. An application can either iterate over all the instances or use the extent as the set of candidates instances filtered with a `Query`.

```
public interface Extent {
    public void              close(Iterator it);
    public void              closeAll();
    public Class             getCandidateClass();
    public PersistenceManager getPersistenceManager();
    public boolean           hasSubclasses();
    public Iterator          iterator();
}
```

Returned by   `PersistenceManager.getExtent()`

Passed to   `PersistenceManager.newQuery()`, `Query.setCandidates()`

InstanceCallbacks

A persistent class can implement the InstanceCallbacks interface so that the following callback methods are called when particular lifecycle events occur:

```
public interface InstanceCallbacks {
    public void         jdoPostLoad();
    public void         jdoPreClear();
    public void         jdoPreDelete();
    public void         jdoPreStore();
}
```

JDOHelper

This helper class provides applications with several utility methods. It provides methods to perform the following functions:

- Construct a PersistenceManagerFactory instance via a Properties object
- Interrogate the lifecycle state of an instance
- Get the object identifier of an instance
- Mark a field of an instance as modified

```
public class JDOHelper {
    public                      JDOHelper();
    public static Object        getObjectId(Object obj);
    public static PersistenceManager
                                getPersistenceManager(Object obj);
    public static PersistenceManagerFactory
                                getPersistenceManagerFactory(Properties props);
    public static PersistenceManagerFactory
                                getPersistenceManagerFactory(Properties props,
                                        ClassLoader cl);
    public static Object        getTransactionalObjectId(Object obj);
    public static boolean       isDeleted(Object obj);
    public static boolean       isDirty(Object obj);
    public static boolean       isNew(Object obj);
    public static boolean       isPersistent(Object obj);
    public static boolean       isTransactional(Object obj);
    public static void          makeDirty(Object obj, String fieldName);
}
```

PersistenceManager

The PersistenceManager interface is the primary interface for JDO-aware software. It is the factory for Query and Transaction instances, and it contains methods to manage the lifecycle of instances.

```
public interface PersistenceManager {
    public void         close();
    public Transaction  currentTransaction();
    public void         deletePersistent(Object obj);
    public void         deletePersistentAll(Object[] objs);
```

```
public void              deletePersistentAll(Collection objs);
public void              evict(Object obj);
public void              evictAll(Object[] objs);
public void              evictAll(Collection objs);
public void              evictAll( );
public Extent            getExtent(Class persistenceCapableClass,
                                   boolean subclasses);
public boolean           getIgnoreCache( );
public boolean           getMultithreaded( );
public Object            getObjectById(Object oid, boolean validate);
public Object            getObjectId(Object obj);
public Class             getObjectIdClass(Class cls);
public PersistenceManagerFactory
                         getPersistenceManagerFactory( );
public Object            getTransactionalObjectId(Object obj);
public Object            getUserObject( );
public boolean           isClosed( );
public void              makeNontransactional(Object obj);
public void              makeNontransactionalAll(Object[] objs);
public void              makeNontransactionalAll(Collection objs);
public void              makePersistent(Object obj);
public void              makePersistentAll(Object[] objs);
public void              makePersistentAll(Collection objs);
public void              makeTransactional(Object obj);
public void              makeTransactionalAll(Object[] objs);
public void              makeTransactionalAll(Collection objs);
public void              makeTransient(Object obj);
public void              makeTransientAll(Object[] objs);
public void              makeTransientAll(Collection objs);
public Object            newObjectIdInstance(Class pcClass, String str);
public Query             newQuery( );
public Query             newQuery(Object compiled);
public Query             newQuery(String language, Object query);
public Query             newQuery(Class cls);
public Query             newQuery(Extent cln);
public Query             newQuery(Class cls, Collection cln);
public Query             newQuery(Class cls, String filter);
public Query             newQuery(Class cls, Collection cln, String filter);
public Query             newQuery(Extent cln, String filter);
public void              refresh(Object obj);
public void              refreshAll(Object[] objs);
public void              refreshAll(Collection objs);
public void              refreshAll( );
public void              retrieve(Object obj);
public void              retrieveAll(Collection objs);
public void              retrieveAll(Collection objs, boolean DFGonly);
public void              retrieveAll(Object[] objs);
public void              retrieveAll(Object[] objs, boolean DFGonly);
public void              setIgnoreCache(boolean flag);
public void              setMultithreaded(boolean flag);
public void              setUserObject(Object o);
}
```

Returned by: PersistenceManagerFactory.getPersistenceManager( ),
Extent.getPersistenceManager( ), Query.getPersistenceManager( ),
Transaction.getPersistenceManager( ),
JDOHelper.getPersistenceManager( )

PersistenceManagerFactory

The PersistenceManagerFactory is used to obtain PersistenceManager instances. All PersistenceManager instances obtained from the same PersistenceManagerFactory will have the same default properties.

PersistenceManagerFactory instances may be configured and serialized for later use. They may be stored via JNDI and looked up and used later. Any configured properties will be saved and restored.

If the ConnectionFactory property is set (non-null) then all the other connection properties (including ConnectionFactoryName) are ignored; otherwise, if ConnectionFactoryName is set (non-null) then all other connection properties are ignored. Similarly, if the Connection-Factory2 property is set (non-null), then ConnectionFactory2Name is ignored.

```
public interface PersistenceManagerFactory implements Serializable {
    public void              close( );
    public String            getConnectionDriverName( );
    public Object            getConnectionFactory( );
    public Object            getConnectionFactory2( );
    public String            getConnectionFactory2Name( );
    public String            getConnectionFactoryName( );
    public String            getConnectionURL( );
    public String            getConnectionUserName( );
    public boolean           getIgnoreCache( );
    public boolean           getMultithreaded( );
    public boolean           getNontransactionalRead( );
    public boolean           getNontransactionalWrite( );
    public boolean           getOptimistic( );
    public PersistenceManager getPersistenceManager( );
    public PersistenceManager getPersistenceManager(String userid, String password);
    public Properties        getProperties( );
    public boolean           getRestoreValues( );
    public boolean           getRetainValues( );
    public void              setConnectionDriverName(String driverName);
    public void              setConnectionFactory(Object connectionFactory);
    public void              setConnectionFactory2(Object connectionFactory);
    public void              setConnectionFactory2Name(
                                 String connectionFactoryName);
    public void              setConnectionFactoryName(
                                 String connectionFactoryName);
    public void              setConnectionPassword(String password);
    public void              setConnectionURL(String URL);
    public void              setConnectionUserName(String userName);
    public void              setIgnoreCache(boolean flag);
    public void              setMultithreaded(boolean flag);
    public void              setNontransactionalRead(boolean flag);
```

```
        public void            setNontransactionalWrite(boolean flag);
        public void            setOptimistic(boolean flag);
        public void            setRestoreValues(boolean restoreValues);
        public void            setRetainValues(boolean flag);
        public Collection       supportedOptions();
    }
```

Returned by   JDOHelper.getPersistenceManagerFactory(),
                    PersistenceManager.getPersistenceManagerFactory()

Query

The Query interface allows applications to obtain persistent instances from the datastore.
The PersistenceManager is the factory for Query instances. There may be many Query
instances associated with a PersistenceManager.

```
    public interface Query implements Serializable {
        public void                close(Object queryResult);
        public void                closeAll();
        public void                compile();
        public void                declareImports(String imports);
        public void                declareParameters(String parameters);
        public void                declareVariables(String variables);
        public Object              execute();
        public Object              execute(Object p1);
        public Object              execute(Object p1, Object p2);
        public Object              execute(Object p1, Object p2, Object p3);
        public Object              executeWithArray(Object[] parameters);
        public Object              executeWithMap(Map parameters);
        public boolean             getIgnoreCache();
        public PersistenceManager  getPersistenceManager();
        public void                setCandidates(Extent objs);
        public void                setCandidates(Collection objs);
        public void                setClass(Class cls);
        public void                setFilter(String filter);
        public void                setIgnoreCache(boolean ignoreCache);
        public void                setOrdering(String ordering);
    }
```

Returned by   PersistenceManager.newQuery()

Transaction

The Transaction interface provides for initiation and completion of transactions under user
control. It also provides methods for setting various options that control transaction
behavior during a transaction and cache behavior after the transaction completes.

```
    public interface Transaction {
        public void                begin();
        public void                commit();
        public boolean             getNontransactionalRead();
```

```
    public boolean          getNontransactionalWrite();
    public boolean          getOptimistic();
    public PersistenceManager getPersistenceManager();
    public boolean          getRestoreValues();
    public boolean          getRetainValues();
    public Synchronization  getSynchronization();
    public boolean          isActive();
    public void             rollback();
    public void             setNontransactionalRead(
                                boolean nontransactionalRead);
    public void             setNontransactionalWrite(
                                boolean nontransactionalWrite);
    public void             setOptimistic(boolean optimistic);
    public void             setRestoreValues(boolean restoreValues);
    public void             setRetainValues(boolean retainValues);
    public void             setSynchronization(Synchronization sync);
}
```

Returned by   `PersistenceManager.currentTransaction()`

Exceptions

JDO has an exception-class hierarchy used to represent the various kinds of exceptions that may occur. The JDOException class is at the root of the hierarchy and provides all of the methods that an application calls. All of its subclasses merely provide constructors called strictly by the JDO implementation to indicate that an error has occurred. Since an application never calls these constructors, we omit them from the class descriptions.

JDOCanRetryException

This is the base class for errors that can be retried.

```
public class JDOCanRetryException extends javax.jdo.JDOException {
}
```

Subclasses   `JDOUserException, JDODataStoreException`

JDODataStoreException

This class represents datastore exceptions that can be retried.

```
public class JDODataStoreException extends javax.jdo.JDOCanRetryException {
}
```

Subclasses   `JDOObjectNotFoundException`

JDOException

This is the base class for all JDO exceptions. It is a subclass of RuntimeException, and it does not need to be declared or caught. It includes a descriptive String, an optional nested Exception array, and an optional failed Object.

This class provides methods to retrieve the nested exception array and failed object. If there are multiple nested exceptions, then each might contain one failed object. This will be the case when an operation requires multiple instances (such as commit( ), makePersistentAll( ), etc.).

If the JDO PersistenceManager is internationalized, the descriptive string will also be internationalized.

```
public class JDOException extends java.lang.RuntimeException {
    public Object          getFailedObject( );
    public Throwable[]     getNestedExceptions( );
    public void            printStackTrace( );
    public void            printStackTrace(PrintStream s);
    public void            printStackTrace(PrintWriter s);
    public String          toString( );
}
```

Subclasses   JDOCanRetryException, JDOFatalException

JDOFatalDataStoreException

This is the base class for fatal datastore errors. It is derived from JDOFatalException. When this exception is thrown, the transaction has been rolled back without the user asking for it. The cause may be a connection timeout, an unrecoverable-media error, an unrecoverable-concurrency conflict, or other causes outside of the application's control.

```
public class JDOFatalDataStoreException extends javax.jdo.JDOFatalException {
}
```

Subclasses   JDOOptimisticVerificationException

JDOFatalException

This is the base class for errors that cannot be retried. It is derived from JDOException. This exception generally means that the transaction associated with the PersistenceManager has been rolled back, and the transaction should be abandoned.

```
public class JDOFatalException extends javax.jdo.JDOException {
}
```

Subclasses   JDOFatalDataStoreException, JDOFatalInternalException, JDOFatalUserException

JDOFatalInternalException

This is the base class for JDO implementation failures. It is a derived class of JDOFatalException. This exception should be reported to the vendor for corrective action. There is no user action to recover.

```
public class JDOFatalInternalException extends javax.jdo.JDOFatalException {
}
```

JDOFatalUserException

This is the base class for user errors that cannot be retried. It is derived from JDOFatalException. Reasons for this exception include:

- PersistenceManager was closed. This exception is thrown after close( ) was called, when any method except isClosed( ) is executed on the PersistenceManager instance, or when any method is called on the Transaction instance or any Query instance, Extent instance, or Iterator instance created by the PersistenceManager.

- Metadata is unavailable. This exception is thrown if the implementation cannot locate metadata for a class, which occurs when the class has not been registered.

```
public class JDOFatalUserException extends javax.jdo.JDOFatalException {
}
```

JDOObjectNotFoundException

This exception notifies the application that an object does not exist in the datastore. This exception is thrown when a hollow instance is used to fetch an object that does not exist in the datastore. This exception might result from a call to getObjectById( ) with the validate parameter set to true, or from navigating to an object that no longer exists in the datastore. You will never get this exception as a result of executing a query.

Throwing this exception does not change the status of any transaction in progress. The getFailedObject( ) method returns a reference to the failed instance. The failed instance is in the hollow state and has an identity that can be obtained by calling getObjectId( ) with the instance as a parameter. This can be used to determine the identity of the instance that could not be found.

```
public class JDOObjectNotFoundException extends javax.jdo.JDODataStoreException {
}
```

JDOOptimisticVerificationException

A verification step (described in Chapter 15) is performed on all instances that are new, modified, or deleted when you make a call to commit an optimistic transaction. If any instances fail this verification step, a JDOOptimisticVerificationException is thrown. It contains an array of nested exceptions; each nested exception contains an instance that failed verification.

```
public class JDOOptimisticVerificationException
            extends javax.jdo.JDOFatalDataStoreException {
}
```

JDOUnsupportedOptionException

This class is derived from JDOCanRetryException. This exception is thrown when an implementation does not implement an optional JDO feature.

```
public class JDOUnsupportedOptionException extends javax.jdo.JDOUserException {
}
```

JDOUserException

This is the base class for user errors that can be retried. It is derived from JDOCanRetryException. Reasons for this exception include:

Instance is not of a persistent class
> This exception is thrown when a method requires an instance of a persistent class and the instance passed to the method does not implement PersistenceCapable. This occurs if the class of the instance is not persistent and has not been enhanced. getFailedObject( ) returns the instance causing the exception.

Extent is not managed
> This exception is thrown when you call getExtent( ) with a class that does not have a managed extent.

Object exists
> For a class using application identity, the combined value of the primary key fields must be unique. This exception is thrown if the primary key fields are not unique. This can occur when a new instance, or an existing persistent instance that has had a primary key field changed, is flushed to the datastore. It might also be thrown during makePersistent( ) if an instance with the same primary key is already in the PersistenceManager cache. The failed Object has the failed instance.

Object is owned by another PersistenceManager
> This exception is thrown if you call makePersistent( ), makeTransactional( ), makeTransient( ), evict( ), refresh( ), or getObjectId( ) when the instance is already persistent or transactional in a different PersistenceManager. The failed Object has the failed instance.

Nonunique identity is not valid after transaction completion
> This exception is thrown if you call getObjectId( ) on an object after transaction completion and the identity is not managed by the application or datastore.

Unbound query parameter
> This exception is thrown during query compilation or execution if there is an unbound query parameter.

Query filter cannot be parsed
> This exception is thrown during query compilation or execution if the filter cannot be parsed.

Transaction is not active

This exception is thrown if the transaction is not active and you call makePersistent( ), deletePersistent( ), commit( ), or rollback( ).

Object deleted

This exception is thrown if you attempt to access any fields of a deleted instance (except to read a primary key field).

```
public class JDOUserException extends javax.jdo.JDOCanRetryException {
}
```

Subclasses   JDOUnsupportedOptionException

JDO Query Language BNF

The following set of grammars define the syntax of the JDO Query Language. Terminal symbols are shown in **bold**. Nonterminal symbols are shown in *italic*. The name of a nonterminal, followed by a colon, introduces the definition of the nonterminal. Subsequent lines specify one or more alternatives for the nonterminal with a level of indentation. A blank line indicates the end of the alternatives. An optional symbol in the syntax may occur with the nonterminals *DeclareParameters*, *DeclareVariables*, *DeclareImports*, and *SetOrdering*.

Parameter Declaration

The following grammar describes the syntax of the `Query.declareParameters()` argument:

```
DeclareParameters:
     Parameters ,
     Parameters

Parameters:
     Parameter
     Parameters , Parameter

Parameter:
     Type Identifier
```

Variable Declaration

The following grammar describes the syntax of the `Query.declareVariables()` argument:

```
DeclareVariables:
     Variables ;
     Variables
```

```
Variables:
    Variable
    Variables ; Variable

Variable:
    Type Identifier
```

Import Declaration

The following grammar describes the syntax of the Query.declareImports( ) argument:

```
DeclareImports:
    ImportDeclarations ;
    ImportDeclarations

ImportDeclarations:
    ImportDeclaration
    ImportDeclarations ; ImportDeclaration

ImportDeclaration:
    import Name
    import Name.*
```

Ordering Specification

The following grammar describes the syntax of the Query.setOrdering( ) argument:

```
SetOrdering:
    OrderSpecifications ,
    OrderSpecifications

OrderSpecifications:
    OrderSpecification
    OrderSpecifications , OrderSpecification

OrderSpecification:
    Expression ascending
    Expression descending
```

Type Specification

The following grammar describes a type specification used in the declaration of a parameter or variable and in a cast expression:

```
Type
    PrimitiveType
    Name

PrimitiveType:
    NumericType
    boolean
```

```
NumericType:
    IntegralType
    FloatingPointType

IntegralType:
    byte
    short
    int
    long
    char

FloatingPointType:
    float
    double
```

Names

A name is an identifier, which can be qualified by another name:

```
Name:
    Identifier
    QualifiedName

QualifiedName:
    Name . Identifier
```

Literal

A literal is the source-code representation of a value of a primitive, String, or null. The Java Language Specification defines the lexical structure used for *IntegerLiterals*, *FloatingPointLiterals*, *CharacterLiterals*, and *StringLiterals*:

```
IntegerLiteral:          see Java Language Specification...

FloatingPointLiteral:    see Java Language Specification...

CharacterLiteral:        see Java Language Specification...

StringLiteral:           see Java Language Specification...

BooleanLiteral:
    true
    false

NullLiteral:
    null
```

```
Literal:
    IntegerLiteral
    FloatingPointLiteral
    BooleanLiteral
    CharacterLiteral
    StringLiteral
    NullLiteral
```

Filter Expressions

The following grammar describes the syntax of a JDOQL filter:

```
Expression:
    ConditionalOrExpression

ConditionalOrExpression:
    ConditionalAndExpression
    ConditionalOrExpression || ConditionalAndExpression

ConditionalAndExpression:
    InclusiveOrExpression
    ConditionalAndExpression && InclusiveOrExpression

InclusiveOrExpression:
    AndExpression
    InclusiveOrExpression | AndExpression

AndExpression:
    EqualityExpression
    AndExpression & EqualityExpression

EqualityExpression:
    RelationalExpression
    EqualityExpression == RelationalExpression
    EqualityExpression != RelationalExpression

RelationalExpression:
    AdditiveExpression
    RelationalExpression <  AdditiveExpression
    RelationalExpression >  AdditiveExpression
    RelationalExpression <= AdditiveExpression
    RelationalExpression >= AdditiveExpression

AdditiveExpression:
    MultiplicativeExpression
    AdditiveExpression + MultiplicativeExpression
    AdditiveExpression - MultiplicativeExpression
```

```
MultiplicativeExpression:
    UnaryExpression
    MultiplicativeExpression * UnaryExpression
    MultiplicativeExpression / UnaryExpression

UnaryExpression:
    + UnaryExpression
    - UnaryExpression
    UnaryExpressionNotPlusMinus

UnaryExpressionNotPlusMinus:
    PostfixExpression
    ~ UnaryExpression
    ! UnaryExpression
    CastExpression

PostfixExpression:
    Primary
    Name


CastExpression:
    ( Type ) UnaryExpression

Primary:
    Literal
    this
    ( Expression )
    FieldAccess
    MethodInvocation

FieldAccess:
    Primary . Identifier

MethodInvocation:
    Primary . Identifier ( )
    Primary . Identifier ( ArgumentList )

ArgumentList:
    Expression
    ArgumentList , Expression
```

Source Code for Examples

This appendix contains the source code for many of the classes used in the examples of this book.

The com.mediamania.appserver package

This package includes classes that are described in Chapters 16 and 17 for using JDO in an application server environment.

com.mediamania.appserver.CashierBean

```
1   package com.mediamania.appserver;
2
3   import javax.ejb.*;
4
5   import javax.naming.InitialContext;
6   import javax.naming.Context;
7   import javax.naming.NamingException;
8
9   import java.util.Iterator;
10  import java.util.Date;
11
12  import com.mediamania.store.StoreQueries;
13  import com.mediamania.store.Customer;
14  import com.mediamania.store.Purchase;
15  import com.mediamania.store.Rental;
16  import com.mediamania.store.RentalItem;
17  import com.mediamania.store.MediaItem;
18
19  import javax.jdo.PersistenceManager;
20  import javax.jdo.PersistenceManagerFactory;
21
22  public class CashierBean implements javax.ejb.SessionBean {
23      private javax.ejb.SessionContext context;
24      private PersistenceManagerFactory pmf;
```

```
25      private PersistenceManager pm;
26      private String pmfName = "java:comp/env/jdo/MediaManiaPMF";
27
28      /**
29       * @see javax.ejb.SessionBean#setSessionContext(javax.ejb.SessionContext)
30       */
31      public void setSessionContext(javax.ejb.SessionContext aContext) {
32          context = aContext;
33          try {
34              Context ic = new InitialContext();
35              pmf = (PersistenceManagerFactory)ic.lookup(pmfName);
36          } catch (NamingException ex) {
37              throw new EJBException("setSessionContext", ex);
38          }
39      }
40
41      public void ejbActivate() {
42      }
43      public void ejbPassivate() {
44      }
45      public void ejbRemove() {
46      }
47      public void ejbCreate() {
48      }
49
50      public void checkout(
51          final java.lang.String lastName,
52          final java.lang.String firstName,
53          final java.util.Collection rentals,
54          final java.util.Collection purchases)
55              throws java.rmi.RemoteException {
56          PersistenceManager pm = pmf.getPersistenceManager();
57          Customer customer = StoreQueries.getCustomer(pm, firstName, lastName);
58          Iterator it = rentals.iterator();
59          while (it.hasNext()) {
60              RentalValueObject rvo = (RentalValueObject)it.next();
61              RentalItem ri = StoreQueries.getRentalItem
62                  (pm, rvo.serialNumber);
63              Rental rental = new Rental(customer, new Date(), ri);
64              customer.addTransaction(rental);
65              customer.addRental(rental);
66          }
67          it = purchases.iterator();
68          while (it.hasNext()) {
69              PurchaseValueObject pvo = (PurchaseValueObject)it.next();
70              MediaItem mediaItem = StoreQueries.getMediaItem(
71                  pm, pvo.title, pvo.format);
72              Purchase purchase = new Purchase(customer, new Date(), mediaItem);
73              customer.addTransaction(purchase);
74          }
75          pm.close();
76      }
77  }
```

com.mediamania.appserver.JDOPlugIn

```
1    package com.mediamania.appserver;
2
3    import javax.servlet.*;
4    import javax.servlet.http.*;
5
6    import javax.jdo.PersistenceManagerFactory;
7    import javax.jdo.PersistenceManager;
8    import javax.jdo.JDOHelper;
9    import javax.jdo.Extent;
10
11   import java.util.Properties;
12   import java.util.Iterator;
13
14   import java.io.InputStream;
15   import java.io.IOException;
16
17   import javax.naming.Context;
18   import javax.naming.InitialContext;
19   import javax.naming.NamingException;
20
21   import org.apache.struts.action.ActionServlet;
22   import org.apache.struts.action.PlugIn;
23   import org.apache.struts.config.ModuleConfig;
24
25   public class JDOPlugIn implements PlugIn {
26       private ServletContext ctx;
27       private String name;
28       private String path;
29       private String jndiName;
30       public JDOPlugIn( ) {
31       }
32
33       public void setName(String name) {
34           this.name = name;
35       }
36
37       public void setPath(String path) {
38           this.path = path;
39       }
40
41       public void setJndiName(String jndiName) {
42           this.jndiName = jndiName;
43       }
44
45       public void init(ActionServlet servlet, ModuleConfig config)
46               throws ServletException {
47           ctx = servlet.getServletContext();
48           if (name == null || name.length( ) == 0) {
49               throw new ServletException
50                   ("You must specify name.");
51           }
```

```
52          try {
53              PersistenceManagerFactory pmf;
54              if (path != null) {
55                  pmf = getPersistenceManagerFactoryFromPath(path);
56              } else if (jndiName != null) {
57                  pmf = getPersistenceManagerFactoryFromJndi(jndiName);
58              } else {
59                  throw new ServletException
60                      ("You must specify either path or jndiName.");
61              }
62              ctx.setAttribute(name, pmf);
63          } catch (Exception ex) {
64              throw new ServletException(
65                  "Unable to load PMF: name:" + name +
66                  ", path: " + path +
67                  ", jndiName: " + jndiName,
68                  ex);
69          }
70      }
71
72      private PersistenceManagerFactory
73              getPersistenceManagerFactoryFromPath(String path)
74                  throws IOException {
75          Properties props = new Properties();
76          InputStream in = ctx.getResourceAsStream(path);
77          props.load(in);
78          return JDOHelper.getPersistenceManagerFactory(props);
79      }
80
81      private PersistenceManagerFactory
82              getPersistenceManagerFactoryFromJndi(String jndiName)
83                  throws NamingException {
84          Context ic = new InitialContext();
85          return (PersistenceManagerFactory) ic.lookup(jndiName);
86      }
87
88      public void destroy() {}
89  }
```

com.mediamania.appserver.LookupMovieAction

```
1   package com.mediamania.appserver;
2
3   import javax.servlet.ServletContext;
4   import javax.servlet.http.HttpServletRequest;
5   import javax.servlet.http.HttpServletResponse;
6   import org.apache.struts.action.Action;
7   import org.apache.struts.action.ActionForm;
8   import org.apache.struts.action.ActionForward;
9   import org.apache.struts.action.ActionMapping;
10
```

```
11  import javax.jdo.PersistenceManagerFactory;
12  import javax.jdo.PersistenceManager;
13  import javax.jdo.JDOHelper;
14  import javax.jdo.Extent;
15  import javax.jdo.Transaction;
16  import javax.jdo.Query;
17  import javax.jdo.JDOException;
18
19  import java.util.Collection;
20  import java.util.Iterator;
21  import com.mediamania.content.Movie;
22
23  public class LookupMovieAction extends Action {
24      PersistenceManagerFactory pmf = null;
25      PersistenceManager pm = null;
26      public ActionForward execute(ActionMapping mapping,
27          ActionForm form,
28          HttpServletRequest request,
29          HttpServletResponse response)
30          throws Exception {
31          try {
32              ServletContext ctx = getServlet().getServletContext();
33              pmf = (PersistenceManagerFactory)ctx.getAttribute("jdo.Movies");
34              pm = pmf.getPersistenceManager();
35              Query q = pm.newQuery(Movie.class, "title == param1");
36              q.declareParameters ("String param1");
37              String movieName = request.getParameter("movieName");
38              Collection movies = (Collection)q.execute(movieName);
39              Movie movie = (Movie)movies.iterator().next();
40              String description = movie.getDescription();
41              ctx.setAttribute("movieDescription", description);
42          } catch (JDOException e) {
43          } finally {
44              if (pm != null) {
45                  pm.close();
46              }
47              pm = null;
48          }
49          return (mapping.findForward("success"));
50      }
51  }
```

com.mediamania.appserver.MediaValueObject

```
1  package com.mediamania.appserver;
2
3  import java.io.Serializable;
4
5  public class MediaValueObject implements Serializable {
6      public String title;
7  }
```

com.mediamania.appserver.MovieInfo

```
1   package com.mediamania.appserver;
2
3   import javax.servlet.*;
4   import javax.servlet.http.*;
5
6   import javax.jdo.PersistenceManagerFactory;
7   import javax.jdo.PersistenceManager;
8   import javax.jdo.JDOHelper;
9   import javax.jdo.Extent;
10  import javax.jdo.JDOException;
11
12  import java.util.Properties;
13  import java.util.Iterator;
14
15  import java.io.InputStream;
16  import java.io.IOException;
17
18  import javax.naming.Context;
19  import javax.naming.InitialContext;
20  import javax.naming.NamingException;
21
22  import com.mediamania.content.Movie;
23
24  public class MovieInfo extends HttpServlet {
25      PersistenceManagerFactory persistenceManagerFactory;
26      PersistenceManager pm;
27      public void init() throws ServletException {
28          try {
29              ServletContext ctx = getServletContext();
30              InputStream in = ctx.getResourceAsStream("WEB-INF/pmf.properties");
31              Properties props = new Properties();
32              props.load(in);
33              persistenceManagerFactory =
34                  JDOHelper.getPersistenceManagerFactory(props);
35          } catch (IOException ex) {
36              throw new ServletException("Unable to load PMF properties.", ex);
37          } catch (JDOException ex) {
38              throw new ServletException("Unable to create PMF resource.", ex);
39          } catch (Exception ex) {
40              throw new ServletException("Unable to initialize.", ex);
41          }
42
43      }
44
45      /**
46          Destroys the servlet.
47      */
48      public void destroy() {
49      }
50
```

```
51      /** Processes requests for both HTTP <code>GET</code>
52       * and <code>POST</code> methods.
53       * @param request servlet request
54       * @param response servlet response
55       */
56      protected void processRequest(HttpServletRequest request,
57          HttpServletResponse response)
58              throws ServletException, java.io.IOException {
59          pm = persistenceManagerFactory.getPersistenceManager();
60          response.setContentType("text/html");
61          java.io.PrintWriter out = response.getWriter();
62          out.println("<html>");
63          out.println("<head>");
64          out.println("<title>Servlet</title>");
65          out.println("</head>");
66          out.println("<body>");
67          out.print(formatMovieInfo());
68          out.println("</body>");
69          out.println("</html>");
70          out.close();
71          pm.close();
72      }
73
74      protected String formatMovieInfo() {
75          StringBuffer result = new StringBuffer();
76          Extent movies = pm.getExtent(Movie.class, true);
77          Iterator it = movies.iterator();
78          while (it.hasNext()) {
79              result.append("<P>");
80              Movie movie = (Movie)it.next();
81              result.append(movie.getDescription());
82          }
83          return result.toString();
84      }
85      /** Handles the HTTP <code>GET</code> method.
86       * @param request servlet request
87       * @param response servlet response
88       */
89      protected void doGet(HttpServletRequest request,
90          HttpServletResponse response)
91              throws ServletException, java.io.IOException {
92          processRequest(request, response);
93      }
94
95      /** Handles the HTTP <code>POST</code> method.
96       * @param request servlet request
97       * @param response servlet response
98       */
99      protected void doPost(HttpServletRequest request,
100         HttpServletResponse response)
101             throws ServletException, java.io.IOException {
102         processRequest(request, response);
103     }
104
```

```
105        /** Returns a short description of the servlet.
106         */
107        public String getServletInfo( ) {
108            return "Movie Information";
109        }
110
111    }
```

com.mediamania.appserver.PurchaseValueObject

```
1    package com.mediamania.appserver;
2
3    public class PurchaseValueObject extends MediaValueObject {
4        public String format;
5    }
```

com.mediamania.appserver.RentalValueObject

```
1    package com.mediamania.appserver;
2
3    public class RentalValueObject extends MediaValueObject {
4        public String serialNumber;
5    }
```

The com.mediamania.content package

This package includes classes that model information about the media content that is sold or rented at Media Mania stores.

com.mediamania.content.ContentQueries

```
1    package com.mediamania.content;
2
3    import java.util.Iterator;
4    import java.util.Collection;
5    import javax.jdo.*;
6
7    public class ContentQueries {
8        public static Studio getStudioByName(PersistenceManager pm,
9                                             String studioName) {
10           Extent studioExtent = pm.getExtent(com.mediamania.content.Studio.class,
11                                             false);
12           Query query = pm.newQuery(studioExtent, "name == studioName");
13           query.declareParameters("String studioName");
14           Collection result = (Collection) query.execute(studioName);
15           Iterator iter = result.iterator();
16           Studio studio = (Studio) (iter.hasNext() ? iter.next() : null);
17           query.close(result);
18           return studio;
19       }
```

```
20      public static MediaPerson getMediaPerson(PersistenceManager pm,
21                                      String person) {
22          Extent personExtent = pm.getExtent(
23                      com.mediamania.content.MediaPerson.class, false);
24          Query query = pm.newQuery(personExtent, "mediaName == person");
25          query.declareParameters("String person");
26          Collection result = (Collection) query.execute(person);
27          Iterator iter = result.iterator();
28          MediaPerson mediaPerson =
29              (MediaPerson) (iter.hasNext() ? iter.next() : null);
30          query.close(result);
31          return mediaPerson;
32      }
33  }
```

com.mediamania.content.Game

```
1   package com.mediamania.content;
2
3   import java.util.Date;
4
5   public class Game extends MediaContent {
6       private static  String[]    allRatings = {"EC","K-A","E","T","M","AO","RP"};
7
8       public Game() {
9       }
10      public Game(String title, Studio studio, Date releaseDate,
11              String rating, String reasons) {
12          super(title, studio, releaseDate, rating, reasons);
13      }
14
15      public boolean validRating(String rating) {
16          for (int i = 0; i < allRatings.length; ++i) {
17              if (rating.equals(allRatings[i])) return true;
18          }
19          return false;
20      }
21  }
```

com.mediamania.content.MediaContent

```
1   package com.mediamania.content;
2
3   import java.util.Date;
4   import java.util.Set;
5   import java.util.HashSet;
6   import java.util.Collections;
7   import java.text.SimpleDateFormat;
8   import java.lang.StringBuffer;
9
10  import com.mediamania.store.MediaItem;
11
12  public abstract class MediaContent {
```

```
13      private static SimpleDateFormat yearFmt = new SimpleDateFormat("yyyy");
14      private String      title;
15      private Studio      studio;
16      private Date        releaseDate;
17      private String      rating;
18      private String      ratingReasons;
19      private Set         mediaItems; // MediaItem
20
21      protected MediaContent()
22      { }
23      public MediaContent(String title, Studio studio, Date releaseDate,
24              String rating, String reasons) {
25          this.title = title;
26          this.studio = studio;
27          this.releaseDate = releaseDate;
28          this.rating = rating;
29          ratingReasons = reasons;
30          mediaItems = new HashSet();
31      }
32      public String getTitle() {
33          return title;
34      }
35      public Studio getStudio() {
36          return studio;
37      }
38      public Date getReleaseDate() {
39          return releaseDate;
40      }
41      public String getRating() {
42          return rating;
43      }
44      public String getRatingReasons() {
45          return ratingReasons;
46      }
47      public abstract boolean validRating(String rating);
48      public Set getMediaItems() {
49          return Collections.unmodifiableSet(mediaItems);
50      }
51      public void addMediaItem(MediaItem item) {
52          mediaItems.add(item);
53      }
54      public String getDescription() {
55          StringBuffer buffer = new StringBuffer();
56          buffer.append(title);
57          buffer.append(", ");
58          buffer.append(studio.getName());
59          buffer.append(", release date: ");
60          buffer.append(formatReleaseDate());
61          buffer.append(", rating: ");
62          buffer.append(rating);
63          buffer.append(", reasons for rating: ");
64          buffer.append(ratingReasons);
65          return buffer.toString();
66      }
```

```
67      public static Date parseReleaseDate(String val) {
68          Date date = null;
69          try {
70              date = yearFmt.parse(val);
71          } catch (java.text.ParseException exc) { }
72          return date;
73      }
74      public String formatReleaseDate() {
75          return yearFmt.format(releaseDate);
76      }
77  }
```

com.mediamania.content.MediaPerson

```
1   package com.mediamania.content;
2
3   import java.util.Date;
4   import java.util.Set;
5   import java.util.HashSet;
6   import java.util.Collections;
7
8   public class MediaPerson {
9       private String      mediaName;
10      private String      firstName;
11      private String      lastName;
12      private Date        birthDate;
13      private Set         actingRoles; // Role
14      private Set         moviesDirected; // Movie
15
16      private MediaPerson()
17      { }
18      public MediaPerson(String mediaName) {
19          this.mediaName = mediaName;
20          actingRoles = new HashSet();
21          moviesDirected = new HashSet();
22      }
23      public MediaPerson(String mediaName, String firstName, String lastName,
24                          Date birthDate) {
25          this.mediaName = mediaName;
26          this.firstName = firstName;
27          this.lastName  = lastName;
28          this.birthDate = birthDate;
29          actingRoles = new HashSet();
30          moviesDirected = new HashSet();
31      }
32      public String getName() {
33          return mediaName;
34      }
35      public String getFirstName() {
36          return firstName;
37      }
38      public String getLastName() {
39          return lastName;
40      }
```

```
41      public Date getBirthDate() {
42          return birthDate;
43      }
44      public void addRole(Role role) {
45          actingRoles.add(role);
46      }
47      public Set getRoles() {
48          return Collections.unmodifiableSet(actingRoles);
49      }
50      public void addMoviesDirected(Movie movie) {
51          moviesDirected.add(movie);
52      }
53      public Set getMoviesDirected() {
54          return Collections.unmodifiableSet(moviesDirected);
55      }
56  }
```

com.mediamania.content.Movie

```
1   package com.mediamania.content;
2
3   import java.util.Date;
4   import java.util.Set;
5   import java.util.HashSet;
6   import java.util.Collections;
7   import java.lang.StringBuffer;
8
9   public class Movie extends MediaContent {
10      private static  String[]    allRatings = {"G","PG","PG-13","R","NC-17"};
11      private         String      genres;
12      private         Set         cast; // Role
13      private         MediaPerson director;
14      private         int         runningTime;
15      private         String      webSite;
16
17      private Movie()
18      { }
19      public Movie(String title, Studio studio, Date releaseDate,
20              String rating, String reasons, String genres, int runningTime,
21              MediaPerson director) {
22          super(title, studio, releaseDate, rating, reasons);
23          this.runningTime = runningTime;
24          this.genres = genres;
25          cast = new HashSet();
26          this.director = director;
27          if (director != null) director.addMoviesDirected(this);
28      }
29      public boolean validRating(String rating) {
30          for (int i = 0; i < allRatings.length; ++i) {
31              if (rating.equals(allRatings[i])) return true;
32          }
33          return false;
34      }
35      public MediaPerson getDirector()
36      {
```

```
37          return director;
38      }
39      public Set getCast( ) {
40          return Collections.unmodifiableSet(cast);
41      }
42      public void addRole(Role r) {
43          cast.add(r);
44      }
45      public void removeRole(Role r) {
46          cast.remove(r);
47      }
48      public String getDescription( ) {
49          StringBuffer buffer = new StringBuffer( );
50          buffer.append("Movie: ");
51          buffer.append(super.getDescription( ));
52          buffer.append(", genre: ");
53          buffer.append(genres);
54          buffer.append(" running time: ");
55          buffer.append(runningTime);
56          return buffer.toString( );
57      }
58  }
```

com.mediamania.content.Role

```
1   package com.mediamania.content;
2
3   public class Role {
4       private String      name;
5       private MediaPerson actor;
6       private Movie       movie;
7
8       private Role( )
9       { }
10      public Role(String name, MediaPerson actor, Movie movie) {
11          this.name = name;
12          this.actor = actor;
13          this.movie = movie;
14          actor.addRole(this);
15          movie.addRole(this);
16      }
17      public String getName( ) {
18          return name;
19      }
20      public MediaPerson getActor( ) {
21          return actor;
22      }
23      public Movie getMovie( ) {
24          return movie;
25      }
26      public void setMovie(Movie theMovie) {
27          movie = theMovie;
28      }
29  }
```

com.mediamania.content.Studio.java

```
1   package com.mediamania.content;
2
3   import java.util.Set;
4   import java.util.HashSet;
5   import java.util.Collections;
6
7   public class Studio {
8       private String   name;
9       private Set      content; // MediaContent
10
11      private Studio()
12      { }
13      public Studio(String studioName) {
14          name = studioName;
15          content = new HashSet();
16      }
17      public String getName() {
18          return name;
19      }
20      public Set getContent() {
21          return Collections.unmodifiableSet(content);
22      }
23      public void addContent(MediaContent mc) {
24          content.add(mc);
25      }
26      public void removeContent(MediaContent mc) {
27          content.remove(mc);
28      }
29  }
```

The com.mediamania.hotcache package

This package contains the classes that can be used to support a hot cache, as presented in Chapter 14.

com.mediamania.hotcache.AbstractCache

```
1   package com.mediamania.hotcache;
2
3   import java.util.Map;
4   import java.util.HashMap;
5
6   import com.mediamania.prototype.PrototypeQueries;
7   import com.mediamania.MediaManiaApp;
8   import com.mediamania.prototype.Movie;
9
10  public abstract class AbstractCache extends MediaManiaApp
11      implements com.mediamania.hotcache.CacheAccess {
12
```

```
13      protected Map cache = new HashMap( );
14
15      /** Creates a new instance of AbstractCache.  The AbstractCache is the
16       * base class for MasterCache and SlaveCache.
17       */
18      protected AbstractCache( ) {
19      }
20
21      /** Get the Movie by title.  If the movie is not in the cache, put it in.
22       * @param title the title of the movie
23       * @return the movie instance
24       */
25      public Movie getMovieByTitle(String title) {
26          Movie movie = (Movie) cache.get(title);
27          if (movie == null) {
28              movie = PrototypeQueries.getMovie (pm, title);
29              if (movie != null) {
30                  cache.put (title, movie);
31              }
32          }
33          return movie;
34      }
35  }
```

com.mediamania.hotcache.AbstractDriver

```
1   package com.mediamania.hotcache;
2
3   import java.io.InputStream;
4   import java.io.InputStreamReader;
5   import java.io.IOException;
6   import java.io.Reader;
7   import java.io.BufferedReader;
8
9   import java.util.StringTokenizer;
10
11  import java.net.URL;
12  import java.net.MalformedURLException;
13
14  import com.mediamania.Utilities;
15
16  import com.mediamania.prototype.Movie;
17
18  public class AbstractDriver {
19      protected BufferedReader requestReader;
20      protected BufferedReader updateReader;
21      protected CacheAccess cache;
22      protected int timeoutMillis;
23      protected AbstractDriver(String updateURL, String requestURL,
24          String timeout) {
25          updateReader = openReader(updateURL);
26          requestReader = openReader(requestURL);
27          timeoutMillis = Integer.parseInt(timeout);
28      }
29
```

```
30      protected BufferedReader openReader (String urlName) {
31          try {
32              URL url = new URL(urlName);
33              InputStream is = url.openStream();
34              Reader r = new InputStreamReader(is);
35              return new BufferedReader(r);
36          } catch (Exception ex) {
37              return null;
38          }
39      }
40
41      protected void serviceReaders() {
42          boolean done = false;
43          boolean lastTime = false;
44          try {
45              while (!done) {
46                  if (updateReader.ready()) {
47                      handleUpdate();
48                      done = false;
49                      lastTime = false;
50                  } else if (requestReader.ready()) {
51                      handleRequest();
52                      done = false;
53                      lastTime = false;
54                  } else {
55                      try {
56                          Thread.sleep (timeoutMillis);
57                          if (lastTime) done = true;
58                          lastTime = true;
59                      } catch (InterruptedException ex) {
60                          done = true;
61                      }
62                  }
63              }
64          } catch (Exception ex) {
65              return;
66          }
67      }
68
69      protected void handleRequest() throws IOException {
70          String request = requestReader.readLine();
71          Movie movie = cache.getMovieByTitle(request);
72          System.out.println("Movie: " + movie.getTitle());
73      }
74
75      protected void handleUpdate() throws IOException {
76          String update = updateReader.readLine();
77          StringTokenizer tokenizer = new StringTokenizer(update, ";");
78          String movieName = tokenizer.nextToken();
79          String webSite = tokenizer.nextToken();
80          cache.updateWebSite (movieName, webSite);
81      }
82  }
```

com.mediamania.hotcache.CacheAccess

```
1    package com.mediamania.hotcache;
2
3    import com.mediamania.prototype.Movie;
4
5    /** Manage a cache of persistent Movie instances.
6     */
7    public interface CacheAccess {
8
9        /** Get the Movie by title.
10        * @param title the title of the movie
11        * @return the movie instance
12        */
13       Movie getMovieByTitle (String title);
14
15       /** Update the Movie website.
16        * @param title the title of the movie
17        * @param website the new website for the movie
18        */
19       void updateWebSite (String title, String website);
20   }
```

com.mediamania.hotcache.MasterCache

```
1    package com.mediamania.hotcache;
2
3    import java.util.Map;
4    import java.util.HashMap;
5
6    import com.mediamania.prototype.PrototypeQueries;
7    import com.mediamania.prototype.Movie;
8
9    public class MasterCache extends AbstractCache
10       implements com.mediamania.hotcache.CacheAccess {
11
12       /** Creates a new instance of MasterCache.  The MasterCache performs
13        * updates of the database and manages a cache of Movie.
14        */
15       public MasterCache() {
16       }
17
18       /** Update the Movie website.
19        * @param title the title of the movie
20        * @param website the new website for the movie
21        */
22       public void updateWebSite(String title, String website) {
23           Movie movie = getMovieByTitle (title);
24           if (movie != null) {
25               tx.begin();
26               movie.setWebSite (website);
27               tx.commit();
28           }
```

```
29      }
30
31      public void execute() {
32      }
33
34      protected static Map getPropertyOverrides()
35      {
36          Map overrides = new HashMap();
37          overrides.put ("javax.jdo.options.NontransactionalRead", "true");
38          overrides.put ("javax.jdo.options.RetainValues", "true");
39          return overrides;
40      }
41  }
```

com.mediamania.hotcache.MasterDriver

```
1   package com.mediamania.hotcache;
2
3   public class MasterDriver extends AbstractDriver {
4       protected MasterDriver(String updateURL, String requestURL,
5           String timeout) {
6               super(updateURL, requestURL, timeout);
7               cache = new MasterCache();
8       }
9
10      public static void main(String[] args) {
11          MasterDriver master = new MasterDriver(
12              args[0], args[1], args[2]);
13          master.serviceReaders();
14      }
15  }
```

com.mediamania.hotcache.SlaveCache

```
1   package com.mediamania.hotcache;
2
3   import java.util.Map;
4   import java.util.HashMap;
5
6   import com.mediamania.prototype.Movie;
7
8   public class SlaveCache extends AbstractCache
9       implements com.mediamania.hotcache.CacheAccess {
10
11      /** Creates a new instance of SlaveCache.  The SlaveCache performs
12       * lookups of the database and manages a cache of Movie.
13       */
14      public SlaveCache() {
15      }
16
17      /** Update the Movie website in the cache, only if it is already there.
18       * The datastore will be updated by the MasterCache.
19       * @param title the title of the movie
```

```
20        * @param website the new website for the movie
21        */
22       public void updateWebSite(String title, String website) {
23           Movie movie = (Movie)cache.get (title);
24           if (movie == null)
25               return;
26           movie.setWebSite (website);
27       }
28
29       public void execute( ) {
30       }
31
32       protected static Map getPropertyOverrides( )
33       {
34           Map overrides = new HashMap( );
35           overrides.put ("javax.jdo.options.NontransactionalRead", "true");
36           overrides.put ("javax.jdo.options.NontransactionalWrite", "true");
37           return overrides;
38       }
39   }
```

com.mediamania.hotcache.SlaveDriver

```
 1   package com.mediamania.hotcache;
 2
 3   public class SlaveDriver extends AbstractDriver {
 4       protected SlaveDriver(String updateURL, String requestURL,
 5           String timeout) {
 6               super(updateURL, requestURL, timeout);
 7               cache = new SlaveCache( );
 8       }
 9
10       public static void main(String[] args) {
11           SlaveDriver slave = new SlaveDriver(
12               args[0], args[1], args[2]);
13           slave.serviceReaders( );
14       }
15   }
```

The com.mediamania.store package

This package contains classes that model information that is specific to an individual store. It includes objects representing the media to be sold or rented, and information about the customers and the media items they have bought or rented.

com.mediamania.store.Address

```
 1   package com.mediamania.store;
 2
 3
 4   public class Address {
```

```
 5     private String    street;
 6     private String    city;
 7     private String    state;
 8     private String    zipcode;
 9
10     private Address()
11     { }
12
13     public Address(String street, String city, String state, String zipcode) {
14         this.street = street;
15         this.city = city;
16         this.state = state;
17         this.zipcode = zipcode;
18     }
19     public String getStreet() {
20         return street;
21     }
22     public String getCity() {
23         return city;
24     }
25     public String getState() {
26         return state;
27     }
28     public String getZipcode() {
29         return zipcode;
30     }
31 }
```

com.mediamania.store.Customer

```
 1  package com.mediamania.store;
 2
 3  import java.util.Set;
 4  import java.util.HashSet;
 5  import java.util.List;
 6  import java.util.ArrayList;
 7  import java.util.Collections;
 8
 9  public class Customer {
10      private String   firstName;
11      private String   lastName;
12      private Address  address;
13      private String   phone;
14      private String   email;
15      private Set      currentRentals; // Rental
16      private List     transactionHistory; // Transaction
17
18      private Customer()
19      { } public Customer(String firstName, String lastName, Address addr,
20      public Customer(String firstName, String lastName, Address addr,
21                      String phone, String email) {
22          this.firstName = firstName;
23          this.lastName = lastName;
24          address = addr;
```

```
25          this.phone = phone;
26          this.email = email;
27          currentRentals = new HashSet();
28          transactionHistory = new ArrayList();
29      }
30      public String getFirstName() {
31          return firstName;
32      }
33      public String getLastName() {
34          return lastName;
35      }
36      public Address getAddress() {
37          return address;
38      }
39      public String getPhone() {
40          return phone;
41      }
42      public String getEmail() {
43          return email;
44      }
45      public void addRental(Rental rental){
46          currentRentals.add(rental);
47      }
48      public Set getRentals() {
49          return Collections.unmodifiableSet(currentRentals);
50      }
51      public void addTransaction(Transaction trans) {
52          transactionHistory.add(trans);
53      }
54      public List getTransactionHistory() {
55          return Collections.unmodifiableList(transactionHistory);
56      }
57  }
```

com.mediamania.store.MediaItem

```
1   package com.mediamania.store;
2
3   import java.util.Set;
4   import java.util.HashSet;
5   import java.util.Collections;
6   import java.math.BigDecimal;
7   import com.mediamania.content.MediaContent;
8
9   public class MediaItem {
10      private MediaContent    content;
11      private String          format;
12      private BigDecimal      purchasePrice;
13      private RentalCode      rentalCode;
14      private Set             rentalItems; // RentalItem
15      private int             quantityInStockForPurchase;
16      private int             soldYTD;
17      private int             rentedYTD;
18
```

```
19      private MediaItem( )
20      { }
21
22      public MediaItem(MediaContent content, String format, BigDecimal price,
23                       RentalCode rentalCode, int number4sale) {
24          this.content = content;
25          content.addMediaItem(this);
26          this.format = format;
27          purchasePrice = price;
28          this.rentalCode = rentalCode;
29          rentalItems = new HashSet( );
30          quantityInStockForPurchase = number4sale;
31          soldYTD = 0;
32          rentedYTD = 0;
33      }
34      public MediaContent getMediaContent( ) {
35          return content;
36      }
37      public BigDecimal getPurchasePrice( ) {
38          return purchasePrice;
39      }
40      public String getFormat( ) {
41          return format;
42      }
43      public RentalCode getRentalCode( ) {
44          return rentalCode;
45      }
46      public void setRentalCode(RentalCode code) {
47          rentalCode = code;
48      }
49      public void addRentalItem(RentalItem rentalItem) {
50          rentalItems.add(rentalItem);
51      }
52      public Set getRentalItems( ) {
53          return Collections.unmodifiableSet(rentalItems);
54      }
55      public void sold(int qty) {
56          if (qty > quantityInStockForPurchase) {
57              // report error
58          }
59          quantityInStockForPurchase -= qty;
60          soldYTD += qty;
61      }
62  }
```

com.mediamania.store.Purchase

```
1   package com.mediamania.store;
2
3   import java.math.BigDecimal;
4   import java.util.Date;
5
6   public class Purchase extends Transaction {
```

```
 7        private MediaItem    mediaItem;
 8
 9        private Purchase( )
10        { }
11        public Purchase(Customer cust, Date date, BigDecimal price, MediaItem item){
12            super(cust, date);
13            setPrice(price);
14            mediaItem = item;
15            price = item.getPurchasePrice( );
16        }
17        public MediaItem getMediaItem( ) {
18            return mediaItem;
19        }
20    }
```

com.mediamania.store.Rental

```
 1    package com.mediamania.store;
 2
 3    import java.util.Date;
 4    import java.util.Calendar;
 5    import java.util.GregorianCalendar;
 6
 7    public class Rental extends Transaction {
 8        private RentalItem     rentalItem;
 9        private RentalCode     rentalCode;
10        private Date           returnDate;
11        private Date           actualReturnDate;
12
13        private Rental( )
14        { }
15
16        public Rental(Customer cust, Date date, RentalItem item) {
17            super(cust, date);
18            rentalItem = item;
19            item.setCurrentRental(this);
20            rentalCode = item.getMediaItem().getRentalCode( );
21            setPrice(rentalCode.getCost( ));
22            GregorianCalendar cal = new GregorianCalendar( );
23            cal.setTime(date);
24            cal.add(Calendar.DATE, rentalCode.getNumberOfDays( ));
25            returnDate = cal.getTime( );
26            actualReturnDate = null;
27        }
28        public RentalItem getRentalItem( ) {
29            return rentalItem;
30        }
31        public MediaItem getMediaItem( ) {
32            return rentalItem.getMediaItem( );
33        }
34        public void setDateReturned(Date d) {
35            actualReturnDate = d;
36        }
37    }
```

com.mediamania.store.RentalCode

```
1   package com.mediamania.store;
2
3   import java.math.BigDecimal;
4
5   public class RentalCode
6   {
7       private String      code;
8       private int         numberOfDays;
9       private BigDecimal  cost;
10      private BigDecimal  lateFeePerDay;
11
12      private RentalCode()
13      { }
14
15      public RentalCode(String code, int days,
16                      BigDecimal cost, BigDecimal lateFee) {
17          this.code = code;
18          numberOfDays = days;
19          this.cost = cost;
20          lateFeePerDay = lateFee;
21      }
22      public String getCode() {
23          return code;
24      }
25      public int getNumberOfDays() {
26          return numberOfDays;
27      }
28      public BigDecimal getCost() {
29          return cost;
30      }
31      public BigDecimal getLateFeePerDay() {
32          return lateFeePerDay;
33      }
34  }
```

com.mediamania.store.RentalItem

```
1   package com.mediamania.store;
2
3   public class RentalItem
4   {
5       private MediaItem       mediaItem;
6       private String          serialNumber;
7       private Rental          currentRental;
8
9       private RentalItem()
10      { }
11      public RentalItem(MediaItem item, String serialNum) {
12          mediaItem = item;
13          item.addRentalItem(this);
14          serialNumber = serialNum;
```

```
15          currentRental = null;
16      }
17      public MediaItem getMediaItem( ) {
18          return mediaItem;
19      }
20      public Rental getCurrentRental( ) {
21          return currentRental;
22      }
23      public void setCurrentRental(Rental rental) {
24          currentRental = rental;
25      }
26  }
```

com.mediamania.store.StoreQueries

```
1  package com.mediamania.store;
2
3  import java.util.Iterator;
4  import java.util.Collection;
5  import java.util.HashMap;
6  import java.util.Date;
7  import java.util.Properties;
8  import java.io.InputStream;
9  import java.io.IOException;
10 import java.math.BigDecimal;
11 import javax.jdo.*;
12 import com.mediamania.content.*;
13 import com.mediamania.store.*;
14
15 public class StoreQueries {
16
17     public static RentalCode getRentalCode(PersistenceManager pm,
18                                            String codeName) {
19         Extent codeExtent = pm.getExtent(RentalCode.class, false);
20         Query query = pm.newQuery(codeExtent, "code == codeName");
21         query.declareParameters("String codeName");
22         Collection result = (Collection) query.execute(codeName);
23         Iterator iter = result.iterator( );
24         RentalCode rentalCode =
25             (RentalCode) (iter.hasNext( ) ? iter.next( ) : null);
26         query.close(result);
27         return rentalCode;
28     }
29
30     public static Movie getMovieByTitle(PersistenceManager pm,
31                                         String movieTitle) {
32         Extent movieExtent = pm.getExtent(Movie.class, true);
33         Query query = pm.newQuery(movieExtent, "title == movieTitle");
34         query.declareParameters("String movieTitle");
35         Collection result = (Collection) query.execute(movieTitle);
36         Iterator iter = result.iterator( );
37         Movie movie = (Movie) (iter.hasNext( ) ? iter.next( ) : null);
38         query.close(result);
```

```
39          return movie;
40      }
41
42      public static Customer getCustomer(PersistenceManager pm,
43                                  String fname, String lname) {
44          Extent customerExtent = pm.getExtent(Customer.class, true);
45          String filter = "fname == firstName && lname == lastName";
46          Query query = pm.newQuery(customerExtent, filter);
47          query.declareParameters("String fname, String lname");
48          Collection result = (Collection) query.execute(fname, lname);
49          Iterator iter = result.iterator();
50          Customer customer = (Customer) (iter.hasNext() ? iter.next() : null);
51          query.close(result);
52          return customer;
53      }
54
55      public static void queryCustomers(PersistenceManager pm,
56                                  String city, String state) {
57          Extent customerExtent = pm.getExtent(Customer.class, true);
58          String filter = "address.city == city && address.state == state";
59          Query query = pm.newQuery(customerExtent, filter);
60          query.declareParameters("String city, String state");
61          query.setOrdering(
62          "address.zipcode ascending, lastName ascending, firstName ascending");
63          Collection result = (Collection) query.execute(city, state);
64          Iterator iter = result.iterator();
65          while (iter.hasNext()) {
66              Customer customer = (Customer) iter.next();
67              Address address = customer.getAddress();
68              System.out.print(address.getZipcode());      System.out.print(" ");
69              System.out.print(customer.getFirstName());   System.out.print(" ");
70              System.out.print(customer.getLastName());    System.out.print(" ");
71              System.out.println(address.getStreet());
72          }
73          query.close(result);
74      }
75
76      public static void queryMovie1(PersistenceManager pm,
77                                  String rating, int runtime, MediaPerson dir) {
78          Extent movieExtent = pm.getExtent(Movie.class, true);
79          String filter =
80          "rating == movieRating && runningTime <= runTime && director == dir";
81          Query query = pm.newQuery(movieExtent, filter);
82          query.declareParameters(
83                      "String movieRating, int runTime, MediaPerson dir");
84          Collection result = (Collection)
85                              query.execute(rating, new Integer(runtime), dir);
86          Iterator iter = result.iterator();
87          while (iter.hasNext()) {
88              Movie movie = (Movie) iter.next();
89              System.out.println(movie.getTitle());
90          }
91          query.close(result);
92      }
```

```
 93
 94    public static void queryMovie2(PersistenceManager pm,
 95                                 String rating, int runtime, MediaPerson dir,
 96                                 Date date) {
 97        Extent movieExtent = pm.getExtent(Movie.class, true);
 98        String filter = "rating == movieRating && runningTime <= runTime && " +
 99                        "director == dir && releaseDate >= date";
100        Query query = pm.newQuery(movieExtent, filter);
101        query.declareImports("import java.util.Date");
102        query.declareParameters(
103                "String movieRating, int runTime, MediaPerson dir, Date date");
104        HashMap parameters = new HashMap();
105        parameters.put("movieRating", rating);
106        parameters.put("runTime", new Integer(runtime));
107        parameters.put("dir", dir);
108        parameters.put("date", date);
109        Collection result = (Collection) query.executeWithMap(parameters);
110        Iterator iter = result.iterator();
111        while (iter.hasNext()) {
112            Movie movie = (Movie) iter.next();
113            System.out.println(movie.getTitle());
114        }
115        query.close(result);
116    }
117
118    public static void queryMovie3(PersistenceManager pm,
119                                 String rating, int runtime, MediaPerson dir,
120                                 Date date) {
121        Extent movieExtent = pm.getExtent(Movie.class, true);
122        String filter = "rating == movieRating && runningTime <= runTime && " +
123                        "director == dir && releaseDate >= date";
124        Query query = pm.newQuery(movieExtent, filter);
125        query.declareImports("import java.util.Date");
126        query.declareParameters(
127                "String movieRating, int runTime, MediaPerson dir, Date date");
128        Object[] parameters = { rating, new Integer(runtime), dir, date };
129        Collection result = (Collection) query.executeWithArray(parameters);
130        Iterator iter = result.iterator();
131        while (iter.hasNext()) {
132            Movie movie = (Movie) iter.next();
133            System.out.println(movie.getTitle());
134        }
135        query.close(result);
136    }
137
138    public static void queryMovie4(PersistenceManager pm) {
139        Extent movieExtent = pm.getExtent(Movie.class, true);
140        String filter = "!(rating == \"G\" || rating == \"PG\") && " +
141                        "(runningTime >= 60 && runningTime <= 105)";
142        Query query = pm.newQuery(movieExtent, filter);
143        Collection result = (Collection) query.execute();
144        Iterator iter = result.iterator();
145        while (iter.hasNext()) {
146            Movie movie = (Movie) iter.next();
```

```
147              System.out.println(movie.getTitle( ));
148          }
149          query.close(result);
150      }
151
152      public static void getDirectorAlsoActor(PersistenceManager pm) {
153          Extent movieExtent = pm.getExtent(Movie.class, true);
154          String filter = "cast.contains(role) && role.actor == director";
155          Query query = pm.newQuery(movieExtent, filter);
156          query.declareVariables("Role role");
157          Collection result = (Collection) query.execute( );
158          Iterator iter = result.iterator( );
159          while (iter.hasNext( )) {
160              Movie movie = (Movie) iter.next( );
161              System.out.print(movie.getTitle( ));
162              System.out.print(", ");
163              System.out.println(movie.getDirector().getName( ));
164          }
165      }
166
167      public static void queryTransactions(PersistenceManager pm, Customer cust) {
168          Query query = pm.newQuery(com.mediamania.store.Transaction.class,
169                                   cust.getTransactionHistory( ));
170          String filter =
171              "((Movie)(((Rental)this).rentalItem.mediaItem.content)).director." +
172              "mediaName == \"James Cameron\"";
173          query.declareImports("import com.mediamania.content.Movie");
174          query.setFilter(filter);
175          Collection result = (Collection) query.execute( );
176          Iterator iter = result.iterator( );
177          while (iter.hasNext( ) ){
178              Rental rental = (Rental) iter.next( );
179              MediaContent content =
180                      rental.getRentalItem().getMediaItem().getMediaContent( );
181              System.out.println(content.getTitle( ));
182          }
183          query.close(result);
184      }
185
186      public static void queryMoviesSeenInCity(PersistenceManager pm,
187                                              String city) {
188          String filter = "mediaItems.contains(item) &&" +
189                  "(item.rentalItems.contains(rentItem) && " +
190                  "(rentItem.currentRental.customer.address.city == city))";
191          Extent movieExtent = pm.getExtent(Movie.class, true);
192          Query query = pm.newQuery(movieExtent, filter);
193          query.declareImports("import com.mediamania.store.MediaItem; " +
194                      "import com.mediamania.store.RentalItem");
195          query.declareVariables("MediaItem item; RentalItem rentItem");
196          query.declareParameters("String city");
197          Collection result = (Collection) query.execute(city);
198          Iterator iter = result.iterator( );
199          while (iter.hasNext( )) {
200              Movie movie = (Movie) iter.next( );
```

```
201            System.out.println(movie.getTitle());
202        }
203        query.close(result);
204    }
205
206    public static void queryTransactionsInCity(PersistenceManager pm,
207                        String city, String state, Date acquired) {
208        Extent transactionExtent =
209                pm.getExtent(com.mediamania.store.Transaction.class, true);
210        Query query = pm.newQuery(transactionExtent);
211        query.declareParameters("String thecity, String thestate, Date date");
212        query.declareImports("import java.util.Date");
213        String filter = "customer.address.city == thecity && " +
214            "customer.address.state == thestate && acquisitionDate >= date";
215        query.setFilter(filter);
216        String order = "customer.address.zipcode descending, " +
217                "customer.lastName ascending, " +
218                "customer.firstName ascending, acquisitionDate ascending";
219        query.setOrdering(order);
220        Collection result = (Collection) query.execute(city, state, acquired);
221        Iterator iter = result.iterator();
222        while (iter.hasNext()) {
223            com.mediamania.store.Transaction tx =
224                    (com.mediamania.store.Transaction) iter.next();
225            Customer cust = tx.getCustomer();
226            Address addr = cust.getAddress();
227            System.out.print(addr.getZipcode());
228            System.out.print(cust.getLastName());  System.out.print(" ");
229            System.out.print(cust.getFirstName()); System.out.print(" ");
230            System.out.println(tx.getAcquisitionDate());
231        }
232        query.close(result);
233    }
234
235    public static void queryProfits(PersistenceManager pm, BigDecimal value,
236                        BigDecimal sellCost, BigDecimal rentCost) {
237        Query query = pm.newQuery(MediaItem.class);
238        query.declareImports("import java.math.BigDecimal");
239        query.declareParameters(
240            "BigDecimal value, BigDecimal sellCost, BigDecimal rentCost");
241        query.setFilter("soldYTD * (purchasePrice - sellCost) + " +
242                "rentedYTD * (rentalCode.cost - rentCost) > value");
243        Collection result = (Collection)query.execute(value, sellCost,rentCost);
244        Iterator iter = result.iterator();
245        while (iter.hasNext()) {
246            MediaItem item = (MediaItem) iter.next();
247            // process MediaItem
248        }
249        query.close(result);
250    }
251
252    public static RentalItem getRentalItem(
253                        PersistenceManager pm, String serialNumber) {
254        Query query = pm.newQuery(RentalItem.class);
```

```
255        query.declareParameters("String serialNumber");
256        query.setFilter("this.serialNumber == serialNumber");
257        Collection result = (Collection)query.execute(serialNumber);
258        Iterator iter = result.iterator();
259        RentalItem item = (RentalItem) (iter.hasNext() ? iter.next() : null);
260        query.close(result);
261        return item;
262    }
263
264    public static MediaItem getMediaItem(
265                      PersistenceManager pm, String title, String format) {
266        Query query = pm.newQuery(MediaItem.class);
267        query.declareParameters("String title, String format");
268        query.setFilter("this.format == format && content.title == title");
269        Collection result = (Collection)query.execute(title, format);
270        Iterator iter = result.iterator();
271        MediaItem item = (MediaItem) (iter.hasNext() ? iter.next() : null);
272        query.close(result);
273        return item;
274    }
275
276    public static Query newQuery(PersistenceManager pm, Class cl,InputStream is)
277                          throws IOException {
278        Properties props = new Properties();
279        props.load(is);
280        Query q = pm.newQuery(cl);
281        q.setFilter((String)props.get("filter"));
282        q.declareParameters((String)props.get("parameters"));
283        q.declareVariables((String)props.get("variables"));
284        q.setOrdering((String)props.get("ordering"));
285        q.declareImports((String)props.get("imports"));
286        q.setIgnoreCache(Boolean.getBoolean((String)props.get("ignoreCache")));
287        return q;
288    }
289 }
```

com.mediamania.store.Transaction

```
1   package com.mediamania.store;
2
3   import java.util.Date;
4   import java.math.BigDecimal;
5
6   public abstract class Transaction
7   {
8       protected  Customer    customer;
9       protected  Date        acquisitionDate;
10      protected  BigDecimal  price;
11
12      protected Transaction()
13      { }
```

```
14      protected Transaction(Customer cust, Date date) {
15          customer = cust;
16          acquisitionDate = date;
17      }
18      public abstract MediaItem getMediaItem( );
19
20      public Customer getCustomer( ) {
21          return customer;
22      }
23      public Date getAcquisitionDate( ) {
24          return acquisitionDate;
25      }
26      public BigDecimal getPrice( ) {
27          return price;
28      }
29      public void setPrice(BigDecimal price) {
30          this.price = price;
31      }
32  }
```

Index

Symbols

!, 163
!=, 161
&, 163
&&, 163
*, 165
+, 165
-, 165
., 166
/, 165
<, 163
<=, 163
==, 161, 180
>, 163
>=, 163
|, 163
||, 163
~, 165

A

abstract, 54
ACID transaction properties, 118
Action, 269
ActionServlet, 269
addition, 165
afterCompletion(), 124, 125, 126, 202
AND query operator, 163
antlr.jar, 9
Apache, 267
application assembly, 276
application identity, 79, 175, 179
    equals(), 181
    hashCode(), 181
    inner class, 181
    String constructor, 181
    toString(), 181
ApplicationIdentity, 36, 176
application-identity class, 79, 180–181
Array, 37, 66
array, 225, 297
array metadata attribute
    embedded-element, 297
array support, 37
ArrayList, 36, 65
    default to SCO, 223
ascending, 171
atomic, 118
atomic value, 83

B

bean-managed persistence, 287
before image, 208, 232, 233, 243, 244
beforeCompletion(), 124, 125
begin(), 13, 122, 302
BigDecimal
    default to SCO, 223
    mapping to SQL type, 77
    persistent field, 64
BIGINT SQL type, 77
BigInteger
    default to SCO, 223
    mapping to SQL type, 77
    persistent field, 64
binary addition, 165
binary compatibility, 97
binary large object (BLOB), 78
binary subtraction, 165

BIT SQL type, 77
bitwise complement, 165
BMP, 287
Boolean
    default to SCO, 223
    mapping to SQL type, 77
    persistent field, 64
boolean
    mapping to SQL type, 77
    persistent field, 64
    SCO, 223
bridge mapping, 72
btree.jar, 9
business delegates, 274
Byte
    default to SCO, 223
    mapping to SQL type, 77
    persistent field, 64
byte
    mapping to SQL type, 77
    persistent field, 64
    SCO, 223
BYTE SQL type, 77

C

cache, 40, 174
candidate class, 151
candidate set, 151
cascading delete, 143, 221
CashierBean, 275
cast expression, 167
cell, 72
CGI, 260
ChangeApplicationIdentity, 36, 202
char
    mapping to SQL type, 77
    persistent field, 64
    SCO, 223
CHAR SQL type, 77
Character
    default to SCO, 223
    mapping to SQL type, 77
    persistent field, 64
class, 57, 75, 296
class metadata, 58
class metadata attributes
    identity-type, 57, 176, 177, 186, 296
    name, 57, 296
    objectid-class, 57, 176, 177, 181, 186,
        190, 296

persistence-capable-superclass, 57, 59,
        296
    requires-extent, 57, 136, 296
ClassCastException, 64
client container, 49
CLOB, 77
clone, 230
close()
    Extent, 138, 298
    PersistenceManager, 116, 117, 122, 299
    PersistenceManagerFactory, 117, 301
    Query, 173, 302
closeAll(), 173
    Extent, 19, 138, 298
    Query, 302
closePersistenceManagerFactory, 35, 117
CMP, 287
coarse-grained objects, 290
Collection, 65
    default to SCO, 223
    persistent field, 64, 65
    size(), 159
collection, 65
collection, 65, 225, 297
collection metadata attributes
    element-type, 7, 65, 75, 86, 88, 194, 224,
        225, 297
    embedded-element, 225, 297
column, 72, 74
column datatypes, 73, 77
commit(), 13, 122, 123, 125, 142, 213, 302
Common Gateway Interface, 260
Common Object Request Broker
        Architecture (CORBA), 233
compile(), 160, 302
composite object, 144
composite-aggregation association, 144
connection management, 39
ConnectionDriverName, 106, 108
ConnectionFactory, 108, 109
connection-factory property
    DriverName, 109
    LoginTimeout, 109
    LogWriter, 109
    MaxPool, 109
    MinPool, 109
    MsWait, 109
    Password, 109
    PortNumber, 109
    ServerName, 109
    URL, 109
    UserName, 109

ConnectionFactory2, 110
ConnectionFactory2Name, 106, 110
ConnectionFactoryName, 106, 108, 109
ConnectionPassword, 106, 108, 109
ConnectionURL, 12, 106, 108, 109
ConnectionUserName, 106, 108, 109
connector, 282
consistent, 118
container-managed persistence, 50, 287
container-managed transaction, 278, 282
containment, 224
contains(), 148, 168, 169
controller servlet, 267
CRUD operations, 128
currentTransaction(), 11, 13, 29, 121, 123, 299
cursor stability, 119

D

data-access objects (DAO), 274
datastore identity, 175, 178
DatastoreIdentity, 36, 176
Date
    comparing in JDOQL, 163
    default to SCO, 223
    equality in JDOQL, 162
    mapping to SQL type, 77
    persistent field, 64
DATE SQL type, 77
DATETIME SQL type, 77
DECIMAL SQL type, 77
declareImports(), 152, 153, 155, 302
declareParameters(), 152, 154, 156, 302
declareVariables(), 151, 152, 169, 302
default constructor, 67
default fetch group, 217, 229
default-fetch-group attribute, 217, 297
delete propagation, 143
deletePersistent(), 26, 27, 142, 143, 210, 212, 224, 243, 257, 299
    jdoPreDelete(), 143, 221
deletePersistentAll(), 26, 27, 142, 299, 300
descending, 171
destroy(), 260
destroy( ), 260
different datastores, 43
dirty, 141, 210
dirty read, 119
distributed transaction, 39, 273, 281
division, 165
doGet(), 48, 260, 263

doPost(), 48, 260, 263
Double
    default to SCO, 223
    mapping to SQL type, 77
    persistent field, 64
double
    mapping to SQL type, 77
    persistent field, 64
    SCO, 223
DOUBLE SQL type, 77
DriverName connection-factory property, 109
durable, 118
dynamic content, 260

E

EIS, 38
EJB, 49, 272
    resource-ref element, 276
    res-ref-name attribute, 276
    res-type attribute, 276
EJB container, 50
EJB Server, 50
ejbActivate(), 279
ejbActivate( ), 281
ejbCreate(), 279
ejbFindByPrimaryKey(), 287
ejb-jar element
    assembly-descriptor element, 278
ejb-jar.xml file, 276
ejbLoad(), 287
ejbPassivate(), 279
ejbPassivate( ), 281, 283
EJBQL, 291
ejbRemove(), 279
ejbStore(), 287
element-type attribute, 7, 65, 75, 86, 88, 194, 224, 225, 297
embedded attribute, 224, 225, 297
embedded-element attribute, 225, 297
embedded-key attribute, 226, 297
embedded-value attribute, 226, 297
endsWith(), 166
Enterprise Information System, 38
Enterprise JavaBeans, 272, 273
entity beans, 286
equal (in queries), 161
equality, 174
equals(), 180, 182, 183, 186, 199, 204
    application identity, 181
evict(), 142, 230, 300
evictAll(), 131, 230, 300
eviction, 229

exceptions, 32
exclusive lock, 120
execute(), 156, 173, 302
executeWithArray(), 158, 302
executeWithMap(), 158
  Query, 302
existence-dependent components, 144
extension, 58, 297
extension metadata attributes
  key, 58, 297
  value, 58, 297
  vendor-name, 58, 75, 77, 85, 297
Extent, 29, 136, 298
  close(), 138, 298
  closeAll(), 19, 138, 298
  getCandidateClass(), 137, 298
  getPersistenceManager(), 137, 298
  hasSubclasses(), 137, 298
  interface declaration, 298
  iteration, 18, 137
  iterator(), 19, 137, 139, 298
  queries, 149

F

façade, 288
fetch group, 216
field, 63, 297
field mediation, 221
field metadata attributes
  default-fetch-group, 217, 297
  embedded, 224, 225, 297
  name, 63, 297
  null-value, 216, 297
  persistence-modifier, 68, 179, 215, 217,
    297
  primary-key, 179, 217, 297
File, 55
file I/O, 284
filter, 151
final field, 66, 67
final keyword, 54, 63
fine-grained objects, 290
firewall, 49
first normal form, 83
first-class objects, 222
Float
  default to SCO, 223
  mapping to SQL type, 77
  persistent field, 64
float
  mapping to SQL type, 77

persistent field, 64
SCO, 223
FLOAT SQL type, 77
flushing, 210
foreign key, 74, 82, 83
foreign-key constraint, 73
forward engineering, 71
FOStore, 12
Fostore, 12

G

getCandidateClass(), 137, 298
getConnectionDriverName(), 110, 301
getConnectionFactory(), 301
getConnectionFactory2(), 110, 301
getConnectionFactory2Name(), 110, 301
getConnectionFactoryName(), 110, 301
getConnectionURL(), 110, 301
getConnectionUserName(), 110, 301
getExtent(), 29, 137, 300
getFailedObject(), 33, 201, 304
getfield, 99, 102
getIgnoreCache()
  PersistenceManager, 139, 152, 300
  PersistenceManagerFactory, 301
  Query, 153, 302
getMetadata, 35
getMultithreaded()
  PersistenceManager, 127, 300
  PersistenceManagerFactory, 301
getNestedExceptions(), 33, 304
getNontransactionalRead()
  PersistenceManagerFactory, 111, 301
  Transaction, 302
getNontransactionalWrite()
  PersistenceManagerFactory, 111, 301
  Transaction, 303
getObjectById(), 196, 199–204, 209, 300
getObjectId()
  JDOHelper, 198, 299
  PersistenceManager, 196–205, 300
getObjectIdClass(), 197, 300
getOptimistic()
  PersistenceManagerFactory, 111, 112,
    122, 301
  Transaction, 112, 303
getPersistenceManager()
  Extent, 137, 298
  JDOHelper, 117, 128, 299
  PersistenceManagerFactory, 105,
    114–116, 126, 301

Query, 151, 302
Transaction, 122, 303
getPersistenceManagerFactory()
    JDOHelper, 12, 105–108, 115, 299
    PersistenceManager, 300
getProperties(), 115, 301
getRestoreValues()
    PersistenceManagerFactory, 301
    Transaction, 125, 303
getRetainValues()
    PersistenceManagerFactory, 111, 301
    Transaction, 303
getSynchronization(), 124, 303
getTransactionalObjectId()
    JDOHelper, 203, 299
    PersistenceManager, 199, 200, 203, 300
getUserObject(), 116, 300
getUserTransaction(), 282
greater-than, 163
greater-than or equal, 163

H

hashCode(), 180, 182, 183, 186, 204
    application identity, 181
HashMap, 36, 65
    default to SCO, 223
HashSet, 65
    default to SCO, 223
    persistent field, 64, 65
Hashtable, 36, 65
    default to SCO, 223
hasNext(), 138, 173
hasSubclasses(), 137, 298
hollow state, 206, 208
HTTP, 259
HTTPS, 259
HttpServlet, 260, 263
    service(), 263
Hypertext Transfer Protocol, 259

I

identity, 174
identity class, 177, 197
identity instance, 198
identity-type attribute, 57, 176, 177, 186, 296
IgnoreCache, 106, 111–114, 139, 152, 153
immutable class, 223
index, 73, 78
inheritance, 81, 288, 290
inheritance hierarchy, 58, 80

inherited fields, 67
init(), 260, 261
initial context, 262
instance callback, 220
instance of a transient class, 53
InstanceCallbacks, 30, 143, 220, 299
    interface declaration, 299
    jdoPostLoad(), 218, 220, 229, 299
    jdoPreClear(), 221, 230, 299
    jdoPreDelete(), 143, 221, 299
    jdoPreStore(), 221, 299
int
    mapping to SQL type, 77
    persistent field, 64
    SCO, 223
INT2 SQL type, 77
INT4 SQL type, 77
INT8 SQL type, 77
Integer
    default to SCO, 223
    mapping to SQL type, 77
    MAX_VALUE, 159
    persistent field, 64
INTEGER SQL type, 77
inverse member, 88
isActive(), 126, 303
isClosed(), 116, 300
isDeleted(), 211, 293, 299
isDirty(), 211, 293, 299
isEmpty(), 168
isNew(), 211, 293, 299
isolated, 118
isomorphic mapping, 84
isPersistent(), 211, 293, 299
isTransactional(), 211, 293, 299
Iterator
    hasNext(), 138, 173
    next(), 138, 173
    remove(), 138
iterator(), 19, 139, 298
    Extent, 137

J

J2EE, 104, 272
J2EE client container, 49
J2EE Java Connector Architecture, 39
Jakarta, 267
Java 2 Enterprise Edition, 272
Java Architecture for XML Binding
    (JAXB), 71
Java Database Connectivity (JDBC), 71
Java Message Service, 273

Java Naming and Directory Interface (JNDI), 104, 272
Java Native Interface (JNI), 54
Java security manager, 35
Java Transaction Service, 272
JavaMail, 273
JavaServer Page, 260
javax.jdo package, 28
javax.jdo.option, 35
javax.jdo.option.ApplicationIdentity, 36, 176
javax.jdo.option.Array, 37
javax.jdo.option.ArrayList, 36, 65
javax.jdo.option.ChangeApplicationIdentity, 36, 202
javax.jdo.option.ConnectionDriverName, 106
javax.jdo.option.ConnectionFactory2Name, 106
javax.jdo.option.ConnectionFactoryName, 106
javax.jdo.option.ConnectionPassword, 106
javax.jdo.option.ConnectionURL, 106
javax.jdo.option.ConnectionUserName, 106
javax.jdo.option.DatastoreIdentity, 36, 176
javax.jdo.option.HashMap, 36, 65
javax.jdo.option.Hashtable, 36, 65
javax.jdo.option.IgnoreCache, 106, 111–114
javax.jdo.option.LinkedList, 36, 65
javax.jdo.option.List, 37, 65
javax.jdo.option.Map, 36, 65
javax.jdo.option.Multithreaded, 106, 111, 127
javax.jdo.option.NonDurableIdentity, 36, 176
javax.jdo.option.NontransactionalRead, 37, 106, 111
javax.jdo.option.NontransactionalWrite, 37, 106, 111
javax.jdo.option.NullCollection, 37, 163
javax.jdo.option.Optimistic, 37, 106, 111
javax.jdo.option.RestoreValues, 106, 111
javax.jdo.option.RetainValues, 37, 106, 111
javax.jdo.option.TransientTransactional, 37, 231
javax.jdo.option.TreeMap, 36, 65
javax.jdo.option.TreeSet, 36, 65
javax.jdo.option.Vector, 36, 65
javax.jdo.PersistenceManagerFactoryClass, 106
javax.jdo.spi package, 34

javax.transaction.Status, 124
javax.transaction.Synchronization, 124
javax.transaction.UserTransaction, 118
JDBC, 46, 272, 282
JDBC driver, 48
jdo, 57, 296
JDO metadata, 55
JDO vendor, 38
JDOCanRetryException, 33, 303
    interface declaration, 303
JDOcentral.com, 9
JDODataStoreException, 33, 201, 303
    interface declaration, 303
JDOException, 32, 33, 304
    getFailedObject(), 33, 201, 304
    getNestedExceptions(), 33, 304
    interface declaration, 304
    printStackTrace(), 304
    toString(), 304
JDOFatalDataStoreException, 34, 304
    interface declaration, 304
JDOFatalException, 34, 304
    interface declaration, 304
JDOFatalInternalException, 34, 107, 305
    interface declaration, 305
JDOFatalUserException, 34, 107, 115, 116, 305
    interface declaration, 305
jdoFieldFlags, 102
jdoFlags, 100, 102, 208, 219
JDOHelper, 29, 299
    constructor, 299
    getObjectId(), 198, 299
    getPersistenceManager(), 117, 128, 299
    getPersistenceManagerFactory(), 12, 105–108, 115, 299
    getTransactionalObjectId(), 203, 299
    interface declaration, 299
    isDeleted(), 211, 293, 299
    isDirty(), 211, 293, 299
    isNew(), 211, 293, 299
    isPersistent(), 211, 293, 299
    isTransactional(), 211, 293, 299
    makeDirty(), 141, 246, 299
JDOImplHelper, 98
jdo.jar, 9, 98
JDOObjectNotFoundException, 33, 201, 305
    interface declaration, 305
JDOOptimisticVerificationException, 34, 305
JDOPermission, 35

JDOPermission("closePersistenceManager-
    Factory"), 35, 117
JDOPermission("getMetadata"), 35
JDOPermission("setStateManager"), 35
JDOPlugIn, 268
jdoPostLoad(), 218, 220, 229, 299
jdoPreClear(), 221, 230, 299
jdoPreDelete(), 143, 221, 299
jdoPreStore(), 221, 299
jdori-enhancer.jar, 9
jdori.jar, 9
jdoStateManager, 40, 100
JDOUnsupportedOptionException, 33, 111,
    112, 122, 202, 231, 236, 254, 306
    interface declaration, 306
JDOUserException, 33, 116, 117, 122, 124,
    125, 129, 130, 131, 137, 142, 144,
    150, 156, 157, 160, 177, 179, 196,
    200, 202, 210, 214, 216, 224, 232,
    234, 243, 253, 307
    interface declaration, 306
JMS, 273
JNDI, 49, 238, 261, 272, 280
join, 85
join condition, 73
join table, 83, 89
JSP, 48, 260
jta.jar, 9
JTS, 272

K

key attribute, 58, 297
key-type attribute, 65, 297
keyword in JDOQL, 154

L

less-than (in queries), 163
less-than or equal, 163
lifecycle state, 206
lifecycle-state interrogation, 232
LinkedList, 36, 65
    default to SCO, 223
List, 37, 65
    default to SCO, 223
local datastore, 46
local transaction, 273
Locale
    default to SCO, 223
    mapping to SQL type, 77
    persistent field, 64

location transparency, 50
lock instance, 120
lock table, 120
lock-compatibility matrix, 120
locking, 120
logical complement, 163
LoginTimeout connection-factory
    property, 109
LogWriter connection-factory property, 109
Long
    default to SCO, 223
    mapping to SQL type, 77
    persistent field, 64
long
    mapping to SQL type, 77
    persistent field, 64
    SCO, 223
LONGVARCHAR SQL type, 77

M

makeDirty(), 141, 246, 299
makeNontransactional(), 300
makeNontransactionalAll(), 131, 300
makePersistent(), 25, 125, 129, 143, 177,
    179, 207, 212, 233, 243, 244, 300
makePersistentAll(), 130, 300
makeTransactional(), 231, 232, 257, 300
makeTransactionalAll(), 131, 231, 300
makeTransient(), 234, 300
makeTransientAll(), 131, 234, 300
managed environment, 39
managed field, 67, 215
managed relationship, 88
many-to-many relationship, 88, 90
Map, 36, 65
    default to SCO, 223
map, 65, 226, 297
map class to a table, 75
map field to column, 76
map metadata attributes
    embedded-key, 226, 297
    embedded-value, 226, 297
    key-type, 65, 297
    value-type, 65, 297
mark field modified, 141
MaxPool connection-factory property, 109
mediation, 99, 100, 102, 207
MessageDrivenBean, 283
metadata element
    array, 225, 297
    class, 57, 296

metadata element (*continued*)
    collection, 65, 225, 297
    extension, 58, 297
    field, 297
    jdo, 57, 296
    map, 65, 226, 297
    package, 57, 296
metadata file name, 55
MinPool connection-factory property, 109
Model-View-Controller, 267
MsWait connection-factory property, 109
multiple PersistenceManagers, 41
multiplication, 165
Multithreaded, 106, 111, 127, 265
multithreading, 126
mutable class, 223
MVC2, 267

N

name attribute
    class element, 57, 296
    field element, 63, 297
    package element, 57, 296
name-mapping, 76
newObjectIdInstance(), 196, 203, 300
newQuery(), 149, 150, 161, 300
next(), 138, 173
no-arg constructor, 5, 6, 55, 66, 67, 178,
            181, 183, 196, 208, 212, 241, 278,
            292
nondurable identity, 175, 195, 196
NonDurableIdentity, 36, 176
nonmanaged environment, 39
non-static inner class, 54
NontransactionalRead, 37, 106, 111, 112,
            121, 214, 238, 240
NontransactionalWrite, 37, 106, 111, 112,
            121, 214, 245, 246, 258
normalized, 83
NoSuchElementException, 138, 152, 173
not equal (in queries), 161
NOT operator, 163
null collection, 171
null parameters, 129
NullCollection, 37, 163
NullPointerException, 129, 167
null-value attribute, 216, 297
Number
    default to SCO, 223
NUMBER SQL type, 77
numeric sign inversion, 165
NUMERIC SQL type, 77

O

Object
    persistent field, 64
object database, 70, 145
object identity, 174
objectid-class attribute, 57, 176, 177, 181,
            186, 190, 296
object-model evolution, 72
one-to-many relationship, 83
one-to-one relationship, 90
Optimistic, 37, 106, 111, 112, 122, 254, 256
OQL, 145
OR query operator, 163
ORDER BY, 147
ordering column, 92
ordering expression, 171
ordering specification, 149, 152, 171

P

package, 57, 296
package javax.jdo, 28
package javax.jdo.spi, 28, 34
package metadata attribute
    name, 57, 296
parallel transactions, 122
partial primary key, 195
Password connection-factory property, 109
persistence by reachability, 132, 143
persistence-aware class, 94
persistence-by-reachability, 25, 131, 227,
            234
PersistenceCapable, 34, 94, 95, 98, 99
persistence-capable, 129
persistence-capable-superclass
            attribute, 57, 58, 59, 296
PersistenceManager, 29, 299, 300
    close(), 116, 117, 122, 299
    currentTransaction(), 11, 13, 29, 121,
            123, 299
    deletePersistent(), 26, 27, 142, 143,
            210, 212, 224, 243, 257, 299
        jdoPreDelete(), 143, 221
    deletePersistentAll(), 26, 27, 142, 299,
            300
    evict(), 142, 230, 300
    evictAll(), 131, 230, 300
    getExtent(), 29, 137, 300
    getIgnoreCache(), 139, 152, 300
    getMultithreaded(), 127, 300
    getObjectById(), 196, 199–204, 209, 300
    getObjectId(), 196–205, 300

getObjectIdClass(), 197, 300
getPersistenceManagerFactory(), 300
getTransactionalObjectId(), 199, 200, 203, 300
getUserObject(), 116, 300
interface declaration, 299
isClosed(), 116, 300
makeNontransactional(), 300
makeNontransactionalAll(), 131, 300
makePersistent(), 25, 125, 129, 143, 177, 179, 207, 212, 233, 243, 244, 300
makePersistentAll(), 130, 300
makeTransactional(), 231, 232, 257, 300
makeTransactionalAll(), 131, 231, 300
makeTransient(), 234, 300
makeTransientAll(), 131, 234, 300
multiple, 126
newObjectIdInstance(), 196, 203, 300
newQuery(), 149, 150, 161, 300
refresh(), 229, 257, 300
refreshAll(), 131, 229, 257, 300
retrieve(), 218, 229, 230, 234, 300
retrieveAll(), 131, 218, 234, 300
setIgnoreCache(), 139, 152, 300
setMultithreaded(), 127, 300
setUserObject(), 116, 300
PersistenceManager per Application pattern, 264
PersistenceManager per Request pattern, 264, 265
PersistenceManager per Session, 265
PersistenceManager per Transactional Request pattern, 265
PersistenceManagerFactory, 29, 301
    close(), 117, 301
    getConnectionDriverName(), 110, 301
    getConnectionFactory(), 301
    getConnectionFactory2(), 110, 301
    getConnectionFactory2Name(), 110, 301
    getConnectionFactoryName(), 110, 301
    getConnectionURL(), 110, 301
    getConnectionUserName(), 110, 301
    getIgnoreCache(), 301
    getMultithreaded(), 301
    getNontransactionalRead(), 111, 301
    getNontransactionalWrite(), 111, 301
    getOptimistic(), 111, 112, 122, 301
    getPersistenceManager(), 105, 114–116, 126, 301
    getProperties(), 115, 301
    getRestoreValues(), 301
    getRetainValues(), 111, 301
    interface declaration, 301

setConnectionDriverName(), 110, 301
setConnectionFactory(), 108, 301
setConnectionFactory2(), 110, 301
setConnectionFactory2Name(), 110, 301
setConnectionFactoryName(), 110, 301
setConnectionPassword(), 110, 301
setConnectionURL(), 110, 301
setConnectionUserName(), 110, 301
setIgnoreCache(), 301
setMultithreaded(), 301
setNontransactionalRead(), 111, 301
setNontransactionalWrite(), 111, 302
setOptimistic(), 111, 122, 302
setRestoreValues(), 302
setRetainValues(), 111, 302
supportedOptions(), 112, 113, 176, 302
PersistenceManagerFactoryClass, 12, 106, 107
persistence-modifier attribute, 68, 179, 215, 217, 297
persistent class, 53
persistent instance, 54
persistent-clean state, 206, 210
persistent-deleted state, 207, 210
persistent-dirty state, 207, 210
persistent-new state, 206, 207
persistent-new-deleted state, 207, 210
persistent-nontransactional instance, 54, 207
persistent-nontransactional state, 207, 238, 239
PHP, 260
PlugIn, 267
polymorphism, 27, 64, 81, 82, 288
PortNumber connection-factory property, 109
preread policy, 219
primary key, 73, 74, 82, 83, 175, 179, 274
primary-key attribute, 179, 217, 297
primary-key field, 79, 179, 217
printStackTrace(), 304
private, 54, 63
processRequest(), 263
Properties, 12, 105, 106
protected, 54, 63
provisionally persistent, 133, 136, 207
public, 54, 63
putfield, 99, 102

Q

Query, 30, 158, 302
    close(), 173, 302
    closeAll(), 173, 302
    compile(), 160, 302

Query (*continued*)
   declareImports(), 152, 153, 155, 302
   declareParameters(), 152, 154, 156, 302
   declareVariables(), 151, 152, 169, 302
   execute(), 156, 173, 302
   executeWithArray(), 158, 302
   executeWithMap(), 302
   getIgnoreCache(), 153, 302
   getPersistenceManager(), 151, 302
   interface declaration, 302
   setCandidates(), 150, 302
   setClass(), 151, 302
   setFilter(), 151, 161, 302
   setIgnoreCache(), 153, 302
   setOrdering(), 152, 172, 302
query compilation, 159
query imports, 149
query namespaces, 153
query operator
   !, 163
   !=, 161
   &, 163
   &&, 163
   *, 165
   +, 165
   -, 165
   ., 166
   /, 165
   <, 163
   <=, 163
   ==, 161, 180
   >, 163
   >=, 163
   |, 163
   ||, 163
   ~, 165
   contains(), 148, 168, 169
   endsWith(), 166
   isEmpty(), 168
   startsWith(), 166
query parameter, 148
   declaration, 155
query variable, 148

R

reachability algorithm, 131–136, 208
read-committed isolation level, 119, 229
REAL SQL type, 77
reference enhancer, 10, 96, 97
referential integrity, 73
refresh(), 229, 257, 300
refreshAll(), 131, 229, 257, 300

registry service, 48
relational database, 1, 70
relational database server, 46
relational query language, 145
Remote Method Invocation (RMI), 233
remove(), 138
repeatable-read isolation level, 119, 229
requires-extent attribute, 57, 136, 296
resource adapter, 46
resource configuration, 276
resource manager, 273
resource reference, 261
resource-ref, 276
resource-ref servlet element, 261
RestoreValues, 106, 111, 112, 125, 208, 230, 242, 244, 258
RetainValues, 37, 106, 111, 112, 213, 230, 241, 258
retrieve(), 218, 229, 230, 234, 300
retrieveAll(), 131, 218, 234, 300
reverse-engineering, 72
rich client, 48, 49
rollback, 258
rollback(), 122, 123, 125, 213, 303
row, 72, 74
RuntimeException, 32, 33, 304

S

schema evolution, 72
second-class objects, 222
security, 273
SecurityException, 117
sequence, 79
Serializable, 178, 180
serializable isolation level, 119
serialization, 219, 284
ServerName connection-factory property, 109
service endpoint, 49
servlet, 260
session bean façade, 50
Set, 65
   default to SCO, 223
   persistent field, 64
set Session Context( ), 280
setCandidates(), 150, 302
setClass(), 151, 302
setConnectionDriverName(), 110, 301
setConnectionFactory(), 108, 301
setConnectionFactory2(), 110, 301
setConnectionFactory2Name(), 110, 301
setConnectionFactoryName(), 110, 301
setConnectionPassword(), 110, 301

setConnectionURL(), 110, 301
setConnectionUserName(), 110, 301
setFilter(), 151, 161, 302
setIgnoreCache(), 300
   PersistenceManager, 139, 152
   PersistenceManagerFactory, 301
   Query, 153, 302
setMessageDrivenContext(), 284
setMultithreaded()
   PersistenceManager, 127, 300
   PersistenceManagerFactory, 301
setNontransactionalRead()
   PersistenceManagerFactory, 111, 301
   Transaction, 303
setNontransactionalWrite()
   PersistenceManagerFactory, 111, 302
   Transaction, 303
setOptimistic()
   PersistenceManagerFactory, 111, 122,
     302
   Transaction, 303
setOrdering(), 152, 172, 302
setRestoreValues()
   PersistenceManagerFactory, 302
   Transaction, 125, 243, 303
setRetainValues()
   PersistenceManagerFactory, 111, 302
   Transaction, 303
setSessionContext(), 275, 280
setSessionContext( ), 275
setStateManager, 35
setSynchronization(), 124, 303
setUserObject(), 116, 300
shallow copy, 243
shared implementation cache, 44
shared lock, 120
sharing (FCO versus SCO), 226
Short
   default to SCO, 223
   mapping to SQL type, 77
   persistent field, 64
short
   mapping to SQL type, 77
   persistent field, 64
   SCO, 223
SingleThreadModel, 260
SingleThreadModel, 260
size()
   Collection, 159
SMALLINT SQL type, 77
SOAP, 49, 259
Socket, 55

SQL, 145
SQL 99, 73
SQL datastore, 46, 47
SQL functions
   GROUP BY, 285
   UNION, 285
SQL LIKE, 166
startsWith(), 166
state transitions, 206
stateful session beans, 280
stateless session bean façade, 288
stateless session beans, 274
StateManager, 35, 40, 98, 207
static, 54, 63
static content, 260
static field, 66
STATUS_COMMITTED, 124
STATUS_ROLLEDBACK, 124
StoreManager, 41
strict isolation, 119
String
   default to SCO, 223
   mapping to SQL type, 77
   persistent field, 64
strong reference, 209
Struts, 48, 267
struts-config.xml file, 269
struts-config.xml file, 268
subtable, 73
subtraction, 165
supportedOptions(), 112, 113, 176, 302
Synchronization, 9, 124
   afterCompletion(), 124, 125, 126, 202
   beforeCompletion(), 124, 125
synchronized, 54
System, 55

T

table, 72, 74
table inheritance, 73
tag library, 48, 267
this
   in queries, 154, 161
Thread, 55
thread safe, 126
TIMESTAMP SQL type, 77
TINYINT SQL type, 77
to-many relationship, 65
toString()
   application identity, 181
   identity, 203
   JDOException, 304

Transaction, 29, 302
    begin(), 13, 122, 302
    commit(), 13, 122, 123, 125, 142, 213,
        302
    getNontransactionalRead(), 302
    getNontransactionalWrite(), 303
    getOptimistic(), 112, 303
    getPersistenceManager(), 122, 303
    getRestoreValues(), 125, 303
    getRetainValues(), 303
    getSynchronization(), 124, 303
    interface declaration, 302
    isActive(), 126, 303
    rollback(), 122, 123, 125, 213, 303
    setNontransactionalRead(), 303
    setNontransactionalWrite(), 303
    setOptimistic(), 303
    setRestoreValues(), 125, 243, 303
    setRetainValues(), 303
    setSynchronization(), 124, 303
transaction demarcation, 122
transaction management, 39
transactional field, 215
transaction-isolation level, 119, 229
transaction-required, 278
transient, 54, 63
transient class, 53, 129
transient field, 66, 67
transient instance, 53, 54
transient lifecycle states, 232
transient state, 206, 207
transient transactional instance, 37, 54, 207,
        232
transient-clean state, 207, 232
transient-dirty state, 207, 232
TransientTransactional, 37, 231
transient-transactional instance, 231
transparency, 128
transparent data access, 128
transparent persistence, 128
TreeMap, 36, 65
    default to SCO, 223
TreeSet, 36, 65
    default to SCO, 223
type namespace, 153
type-discriminator column, 81, 82
type-mapping, 77

U

unary addition, 165
unary bitwise complement, 165
unbound variable, 148
UnsupportedOperationException, 138, 158
URL connection-factory property, 109
User-Defined Type (UDT), 73
UserName connection-factory property, 109
UserTransaction, 118, 266, 278, 281, 282
    begin( ), 266
    commit( ), 266
    rollback( ), 266

V

validate, 200
value attribute, 58, 297
value object, 277
value-type attribute, 65, 297
VARCHAR SQL type, 77
VARCHAR2 SQL type, 77
Vector, 36, 65
    default to SCO, 223
VendorName, 115
vendor-name attribute, 58, 75, 77, 85, 297
VersionNumber, 115
view servlet, 267
volatile, 54, 63

W

weak reference, 230, 265
web server, 48
web services, 48
web services endpoint, 48
web-app servlet element, 261
wild-card query, 166

X

xerces.jar, 9
XML, 55

About the Authors

David Jordan founded Object Identity, Inc. in 2001 to provide JDO consulting services. He became interested in the integration of object type systems and databases while earning his M.S. in Computer Science in the early 1980s. At Bell Labs in 1985, he initiated the development of the first C++ object database. He has developed a variety of applications using C++ object models on top of network, relational, and object database systems. Bell Labs appointed him a Distinguished Member of Technical Staff in 1990 for his contributions in object and database technologies.

The Object Data Management Group (ODMG) asked him to serve as their C++ editor in 1993. He served in that role until 2000 and was appointed their Java editor in 1998. He coedited four books published by the ODMG. David served as a *C++ Report* columnist describing the ODMG standard from 1994 to 1996, at which point he stopped to write his first book, *C++ Object Databases*.

David started using Java in late 1995. Upon his selection as ODMG's Java editor, he became a columnist for *Java Report*, initially covering ODMG and then JDO. David was part of the small group that initiated JSR-12, and he became one of the initial members of the JDO expert group. The JDO specification has a special acknowledgment of David's contributions to the JDO standard. When the JDOcentral.com community web site was formed, David was selected to serve as its moderator. David can be reached at *david.jordan@objectidentity.com*.

Craig Russell studied applied mathematics at Harvard University (B.A. '70–'71) and acquired practical experience working as a technician repairing mainframes with the computing power of a 1997 model laptop. His early experiences in distributed computing included building applications with CICS and DL/I and designing heterogeneous network server implementations for file, print, and communications sharing among personal computers. Craig later dealt with issues of persistent object interoperability among Smalltalk, C++, and Java and integrating object and relational databases using X/OPEN XA protocols and commercial transaction processing systems.

Craig served as the Java Chair of the Object Data Management Group and played a key role in the development of the ODMG 3.0 Java binding. For the next standard for database access from Java, the ODMG decided to support the Java Community Process as the delivery vehicle. With support from all major relational database and middleware vendors, Java Specification Request 12, Java Data Objects, was proposed in May 1999 and released in April 2002.

Concurrent with the development of the JDO standard, Craig's primary responsibility was to lead the implementation of the object-relational database engine for several Sun products, including Java Blend and Forte for Java Transparent Persistence. Craig currently is the architect for the Container Managed Persistence implementation of Sun ONE Application Server, where he deals with the reality of implementing the high-performance, specification-compliant version of the object-relational database component of the J2EE application server.

Colophon

Our look is the result of reader comments, our own experimentation, and feedback from distribution channels. Distinctive covers complement our distinctive approach to technical topics, breathing personality and life into potentially dry subjects.

The animal on the cover of *Java Data Objects* is a bilby (*Macrotis lagotis*), also known as a ninu, dalgyte, pinky, or rabbit-eared bandicoot. Bilbies are rabbit-sized marsupials with silky, blue-gray fur; long, pointed snouts; large, rabbit-like ears; and long, black tails with white tips. This strange combination of traits may appear awkward, but its delicate and cute features have actually made the bilby one of Australia's most attractive and celebrated mammals. For many Australians, the Easter Bilby has even replaced the rabbit as the popular Easter icon.

Bilbies have adapted well to the hot, arid climates they now habitate. Their long, slender tongues help them eat a diet of seeds, insects, bulbs, fruit, and fungi. Bilbies have well-developed forearms and long claws, which they use to dig the deep, spiralling burrows in which they live. Bilbies are strictly nocturnal, and during the day they plug the entrances to their holes with soil to protect them from extreme temperatures. Because bilbies are solitary animals, burrows usually have a single opening and a single occupant, though females often live with their young. Like other marsupials, females have a backward-opening pouch with eight teats, used to carry and protect their young for about 80 days. Bilbies usually have no more than two young at a time.

Once common throughout Australia, disease, agriculture clearing, spreading of the fox and feral cat, and the control campaign against the destructive rabbit (which was often unfairly grouped with the innocent bilby it resembles) have limited bilbies' habitats to isolated populations in Western Australia, the Northern Territory, and southwestern Queensland. Bilbies are now listed as endandered species by many Australian and international conservation groups.

Brian Sawyer was the production editor and copyeditor for *Java Data Objects*. Colleen Gorman was the proofreader. Genevieve d'Entremont and Claire Cloutier provided quality control. David Jordan and Craig Russell wrote the index, with the assistance of Reg Aubry.

Hanna Dyer designed the cover of this book, based on a series design by Edie Freedman. The cover image is a 19th-century engraving from *Animate Creation, Vol. II*. Emma Colby produced the cover layout with QuarkXPress 4.1 using Adobe's ITC Garamond font.

David Futato designed the interior layout. Andrew Savikas prepared this book in FrameMaker 5.5.6. The text font is Linotype Birka, and the heading font is Adobe Myriad Condensed. The code font is a modified version of LucasFont's TheSans Mono Condensed, designed by Luc(as) de Groot with modifications suggested by David Jordan. The illustrations that appear in the book were produced by Robert Romano and Jessamyn Read using Macromedia FreeHand 9 and Adobe Photoshop 6. This colophon was written by Brian Sawyer.

Other Titles Available from O'Reilly

Java

Java Performance Tuning, 2nd Edition

By Jack Shirazi
2nd Edition January 2003
588 pages, ISBN 0-596-00377-3

Significantly revised and expanded, this second edition not only covers Java 1.4, but adds new coverage of JDBC, NIO, Servlets, EJB and JavaServer Pages. The book remains a valuable resource for teaching developers how to create a tuning strategy, how to use profiling tools to understand a program's behavior, and how to avoid performance penalties from inefficient code, making them more efficient and effective. The result is code that's robust, maintainable and fast!

Java Security, 2nd Edition

By Scott Oaks
2nd Edition May 2001
618 pages, ISBN 0-596-00157-6

The second edition focuses on the platform features of Java that provide security—the class loader, bytecode verifier, and security manager—and recent additions to Java that enhance this security model: digital signatures, security providers, and the access controller. The book covers in depth the security model of Java 2, version 1.3, including the two new security APIs: JAAS and JSSE.

Java Database Best Practices

By George Reese
1st Edition June 2003 (est.)
304 pages (est.), ISBN 0-596-00522-9

Java Database Best Practices rescues developers from having to slog through books on each of the various APIs before they figure out which method to use! This guide introduces each of the dominant APIs, explores the methodology and design components that use those APIs, and then offers practices most appropriate for different types and makes of databases, and different types of applications.

Java RMI

By William Grosso
1st Edition November 2001
576 pages, ISBN 1-56592-452-5

Enterprise Java developers, especially those working with Enterprise JavaBeans, and Jini, need to understand RMI technology in order to write today's complex, distributed applications. O'Reilly's *Java RMI* thoroughly explores and explains this powerful but often overlooked technology. Included is a wealth of real-world examples that developers can implement and customize.

Java Swing, 2nd Edition

By Marc Loy, Robert Eckstein, David Wood, James Elliott & Brian Cole
2nd Edition November 2002
1278 pages, ISBN 0-596-00408-7

This second edition of *Java Swing* thoroughly covers all the features available in Java 2 SDK 1.3 and 1.4. More than simply a reference, this new edition takes a practical approach. It is a book by developers for developers, with hundreds of useful examples, from beginning level to advanced, covering every component available in Swing. Whether you're a seasoned Java developer or just trying to find out what Java can do, you'll find *Java Swing*, 2nd edition an indispensable guide.

Java Message Service

By Richard Monson-Haefel & David Chappell
1st Edition December 2000
238 pages, ISBN 0-596-00068-5

This book is a thorough introduction to Java Message Service (JMS) from Sun Microsystems. It shows how to build applications using the point-to-point and publish-and-subscribe models; use features like transactions and durable subscriptions to make applications reliable; and use messaging within Enterprise JavaBeans. It also introduces a new EJB type, the MessageDrivenBean, that is part of EJB 2.0, and discusses integration of messaging into J2EE.

O'REILLY®

To order: *800-998-9938* • *order@oreilly.com* • *www.oreilly.com*
Online editions of most O'Reilly titles are available by subscription at *safari.oreilly.com*
Also available at most retail and online bookstores.

Java

Java Extreme Programming Cookbook

By Eric M. Burke & Brian M. Coyner
1st Edition March 2003
288 pages, ISBN0-596-00387-0

Brimming with over 100 "recipes" for getting down to business and actually doing XP, the *Java Extreme Programming Cookbook* doesn't try to "sell" you on XP; it succinctly documents the most important features of popular open source tools for XP in Java—including Ant, Junit, HttpUnit, Cactus, Tomcat, XDoclet—and then digs right in, providing recipes for implementing the tools in real-world environments.

Java Enterprise Best Practices

By The O'Reilly Java Authors,
edited by Robert Eckstein
1st Edition December 2002
288 pages, ISBN 0-596-00384-6

This book is for intermediate and advanced Java developers, the ones who have been around the block enough times to understand just how complex—and unruly—an enterprise system can get. Each chapter in this collection contains several rules that provide insight into the "best practices" for creating and maintaining projects using the Java Enterprise APIs. Written by the world's leading Java experts, this book covers JDBC, RMI/CORBA, Servlets, JavaServer Pages and custom tag libraries, XML, Internationalization, JavaMail, Enterprise JavaBeans, and performance tuning.

Java Cookbook

By Ian Darwin
1st Edition June 2001
882 pages, ISBN 0-59600-170-3

This book offers Java developers short, focused pieces of code that are easy to incorporate into other programs. The idea is to focus on things that are useful, tricky, or both. The book's code segments cover all of the dominant APIs and many specialized APIs and should serve as a great "jumping-off place" for Java developers who want to get started in areas outside their specialization.

Learning Java, 2nd Edition

By Pat Niemeyer &
Jonathan Knudsen
2nd Edition June 2002
832 pages, ISBN 0-596-00285-8

This new edition of *Learning Java* comprehensively addresses important topics such as web applications, servlets, and XML. It provides full coverage of all Java 1.4 language features including assertions and exception chaining as well as new APIs such as regular expressions and NIO, the new I/O package. New Swing features and components are described along with updated coverage of the JavaBeans component architecture using the open source NetBeans IDE the latest information about Applets and the Java Plug-in for all major browsers.

Mac OS X for Java Geeks

By Will Iverson
1st Edition April 2003 (est.)
304 pages (est.), ISBN 0-596-00400-1

Mac OS X for Java Geeks delivers a complete and detailed look at the OS X platform for Java development. Based on the new 1.4 JDK and the 10.2 release of Mac OS X from Apple Computer, this is the most thorough guide available for both new and experienced Java developers who want to create cross-platform applications that take advantage of Mac OS X's unique functionality.

Java Management Extensions

By J. Steven Perry
1st Edition June 2002
312 pages, ISBN 0-596-00245-9

Java Management Extensions is a practical, hands-on guide to using the JMX APIs. This one-of-a kind book is a complete treatment of the JMX architecture (both the instrumentation level and the agent level), and it's loaded with real-world examples for implementing Management Extensions. It also contains useful information at the higher level about JMX (the "big picture") to help technical managers and architects who are evaluating various application management approaches and are considering JMX.

O'REILLY®

To order: *800-998-9938* • *order@oreilly.com* • *www.oreilly.com*
Online editions of most O'Reilly titles are available by subscription at *safari.oreilly.com*
Also available at most retail and online bookstores.

Java

Java Servlet Programming, 2nd Edition

By Jason Hunter with William Crawford
2nd Edition April 2001
780 pages, ISBN 0-596-00040-5

The second edition of this popular book has been completely updated to add the new features of the Java Servlet API Version 2.2, and new chapters on servlet security and advanced communication. In addition to complete coverage of the 2.2 specification, we have included bonus material on the new 2.3 version of the specification.

Java & XML, 2nd Edition

By Brett McLaughlin
2nd Edition September 2001
528 pages, ISBN 0-596-000197-5

New chapters on Advanced SAX, Advanced DOM, SOAP, and data binding, as well as new examples throughout, bring the second edition of *Java & XML* thoroughly up to date. Except for a concise introduction to XML basics, the book focuses entirely on using XML from Java applications. It's a worthy companion for Java developers working with XML or involved in messaging, web services, or the new peer-to-peer movement.

JavaServer Pages, 2nd Edition

By Hans Bergsten
2nd Edition August 2002
712 pages, ISBN 0-596-00317-X

Filled with useful examples and the depth, clarity, and attention to detail that made the first edition so popular with web developers, *JavaServer Pages*, 2nd Edition is completely revised and updated to cover the substantial changes in the 1.2 version of the JSP specifications, and includes coverage of the new JSTL Tag libraries—an eagerly anticipated standard set of JSP elements for the tasks needed in most JSP applications, as well as thorough coverage of Custom Tag Libraries.

J2EE Design Patterns

By William C.R. Crawford
& Jonathan Kaplan
1st Edition July 2003 (est.)
352 pages (est.), ISBN 0-596-00427-3

Crawford and Kaplan's *J2EE Design Patterns* takes a different approach than just simply presenting another catalog of design patterns. The authors broaden the scope by discussing ways to choose design patterns when building an enterprise application from scratch, looking closely at the real world tradeoffs that Java developers must weigh when architecting their applications. They also extend design patterns into areas not covered in other books, presenting original patterns for data modeling, transaction/process modeling, and interoperability. This design pattern book breaks the mold.

Enterprise JavaBeans, 3rd Edition

By Richard Monson-Haefel
3rd Edition September 2001
592 pages, ISBN 0-596-00226-2

Enterprise JavaBeans has been thoroughly updated for the new EJB Specification. Important changes in Version 2.0 include a completely new CMP (container-managed persistence) model that allows for much more complex business function modeling; local interfaces that will significantly improve performance of EJB applications; and the "message driven bean," an entirely new kind of Java bean based on asynchronous messaging and the Java Message Service.

O'REILLY®

To order: *800-998-9938* • *order@oreilly.com* • *www.oreilly.com*
Online editions of most O'Reilly titles are available by subscription at *safari.oreilly.com*
Also available at most retail and online bookstores.

How to stay in touch with O'Reilly

1. Visit our award-winning web site

http://www.oreilly.com/

★ "Top 100 Sites on the Web"—PC Magazine
★ CIO Magazine's Web Business 50 Awards

Our web site contains a library of comprehensive product information (including book excerpts and tables of contents), downloadable software, background articles, interviews with technology leaders, links to relevant sites, book cover art, and more. File us in your bookmarks or favorites!

2. Join our email mailing lists

Sign up to get email announcements of new books and conferences, special offers, and O'Reilly Network technology newsletters at:

http://elists.oreilly.com

It's easy to customize your free elists subscription so you'll get exactly the O'Reilly news you want.

3. Get examples from our books

To find example files for a book, go to:

http://www.oreilly.com/catalog

select the book, and follow the "Examples" link.

4. Work with us

Check out our web site for current employment opportunities:

http://jobs.oreilly.com/

5. Register your book

Register your book at:

http://register.oreilly.com

6. Contact us

O'Reilly & Associates, Inc.
1005 Gravenstein Hwy North
Sebastopol, CA 95472 USA
TEL: 707-827-7000 or 800-998-9938
　　　(6am to 5pm PST)
FAX: 707-829-0104

order@oreilly.com
For answers to problems regarding your order or our products. To place a book order online visit:

http://www.oreilly.com/order_new/

catalog@oreilly.com
To request a copy of our latest catalog.

booktech@oreilly.com
For book content technical questions or corrections.

corporate@oreilly.com
For educational, library, government, and corporate sales.

proposals@oreilly.com
To submit new book proposals to our editors and product managers.

international@oreilly.com
For information about our international distributors or translation queries. For a list of our distributors outside of North America check out:

http://international.oreilly.com/distributors.html

adoption@oreilly.com
For information about academic use of O'Reilly books, visit:

http://academic.oreilly.com

O'REILLY®

To order: 800-998-9938 • *order@oreilly.com* • *www.oreilly.com*
Online editions of most O'Reilly titles are available by subscription at *safari.oreilly.com*
Also available at most retail and online bookstores.